The Editor

Thomas Cooley is Professor of English at The Ohio State University. He is the author of *The Ivory Leg in the Ebony Cabinet: Madness, Race, and Gender in Victorian America*; *Educated Lives: The Rise of Modern Autobiography in America*; and *The Norton Guide to Writing*. He is the editor of *The Norton Sampler: Short Essays for Composition* and of an edition, in progress, of the letters of Sophia Hawthorne.

W. W. NORTON & COMPANY, INC.
Also Publishes

THE NORTON ANTHOLOGY OF AFRICAN AMERICAN LITERATURE
edited by Henry Louis Gates Jr. and Nellie Y. McKay et al.

THE NORTON ANTHOLOGY OF AMERICAN LITERATURE
edited by Nina Baym et al.

THE NORTON ANTHOLOGY OF CHILDREN'S LITERATURE
edited by Jack Zipes et al.

THE NORTON ANTHOLOGY OF CONTEMPORARY FICTION
edited by R. V. Cassill and Joyce Carol Oates

THE NORTON ANTHOLOGY OF ENGLISH LITERATURE
edited by M. H. Abrams and Stephen Greenblatt et al.

THE NORTON ANTHOLOGY OF LITERATURE BY WOMEN
edited by Sandra M. Gilbert and Susan Gubar

THE NORTON ANTHOLOGY OF MODERN AND CONTEMPORARY POETRY
edited by Jahan Ramazani, Richard Ellmann, and Robert O'Clair

THE NORTON ANTHOLOGY OF POETRY
edited by Margaret Ferguson, Mary Jo Salter, and Jon Stallworthy

THE NORTON ANTHOLOGY OF SHORT FICTION
edited by R. V. Cassill and Richard Bausch

THE NORTON ANTHOLOGY OF THEORY AND CRITICISM
edited by Vincent B. Leitch et al.

THE NORTON ANTHOLOGY OF WORLD LITERATURE
edited by Sarah Lawall et al.

THE NORTON FACSIMILE OF THE FIRST FOLIO OF SHAKESPEARE
prepared by Charlton Hinman

THE NORTON INTRODUCTION TO LITERATURE
edited by Alison Booth, J. Paul Hunter, and Kelly J. Mays

THE NORTON INTRODUCTION TO THE SHORT NOVEL
edited by Jerome Beaty

THE NORTON READER
edited by Linda H. Peterson and John C. Brereton

THE NORTON SAMPLER
edited by Thomas Cooley

THE NORTON SHAKESPEARE, BASED ON THE OXFORD EDITION
edited by Stephen Greenblatt et al.

For a complete list of Norton Critical Editions, visit
www.wwnorton.com/college/english/nce_home.htm

A NORTON CRITICAL EDITION

Mark Twain

ADVENTURES OF HUCKLEBERRY FINN

AN AUTHORITATIVE TEXT

CONTEXTS AND SOURCES

CRITICISM

THIRD EDITION

Edited by

THOMAS COOLEY

THE OHIO STATE UNIVERSITY

W · W · NORTON & COMPANY · *New York · London*

Copyright © 1999, 1990, 1977, 1962, 1961 by W. W. Norton & Company, Inc.

The text of ADVENTURES OF HUCKLEBERRY FINN, edited by Walter Blair and Victor Fischer, is © 1985 The Mark Twain Foundation. Published by arrrangement with the University of California Press.

The text of this book is composed in Fairfield Medium with the display set in Bernhard Modern.
Composition by Binghamton Valley Composition.
Manufacturing by Maple-Vail Book Group.

Library of Congress Cataloging-in-Publication Data
Twain, Mark, 1835–1910.
Adventures of Huckleberry Finn : an authoritative text, contexts and sources, criticism / Mark Twain ; edited by Thomas Cooley. — 3rd ed.
p.   cm. — (A Norton critical ed.)
Includes bibliographical references (p.).

ISBN 0-393-96640-2 (pbk.)

1. Finn, Huckleberry (Fictitious character)—Fiction.   2. Boys—Travel—Mississippi River—Fiction.   3. Boys—Missouri—Fiction.   4. Twain, Mark, 1835–1910. Adventures of Huckleberry Finn.   I. Cooley, Thomas, 1942–   .   II. Title. III. Series.
PS1305.T93 1998
813'.4—DC21   98-6901
                                                                      CIP

W. W. Norton & Company, Inc., 500 Fifth Avenue, New York, N.Y. 10110
www.wwnorton.com

W. W. Norton & Company Ltd., Castle House, 75/76 Wells Street, London W1T 3QT

6 7 8 9 0

Contents

Preface to the Third Edition   vii

A Note on the Text and Illustrations   xi

The Text of *Adventures of Huckleberry Finn*   1

Contexts and Sources

Mark Twain • [Letters about *Huckleberry Finn*]   299

• From the *Autobiography*   301

THE "POET LARIAT," THE "SWEET SINGER OF MICHIGAN," AND

     YOUNG SAM CLEMENS   303

Bloodgood H. Cutter • On the Death of His Beloved Wife   303

Julia A. Moore • Little Andrew   305

Sam Clemens • To Jennie *and* To Mollie   306

Publishing Circular • Confidential Terms to Agents   307

A BANNED BOOK: ONE HUNDRED YEARS OF "TROUBLE" FOR

     HUCK'S BOOK   308

Boston *Transcript*, March 1885   308

Springfield *Republican*, March 1885   308

Mark Twain • Replies to the Newspapers   308

John H. Wallace • The Case against *Huck Finn*   309

Earl F. Briden • Kemble's "Specialty" and the Pictorial

     Countertext of *Huckleberry Finn*   310

David Carkeet • The Dialects in *Huckleberry Finn*   319

Mark Twain • A True Story, Repeated Word for Word as I

     Heard It   320

• Sociable Jimmy   324

Criticism

EARLY RESPONSES 329

[William Ernest Henley] • [Review] *The Adventures
of Huckleberry Finn* 329

Brander Matthews • [Review: *Adventures of
Huckleberry Finn*] 330

[Robert Bridges] • Mark Twain's Blood-Curdling Humor 334

Thomas Sergeant Perry • [The First Major American
Review] 334

MODERN VIEWS 337

Victor A. Doyno • *From* Writing *Huck Finn*: Mark Twain's
Creative Process 337

T. S. Eliot • [Introduction to *Adventures of Huckleberry
Finn*] 348

Jane Smiley • Say It Ain't So, Huck: Second Thoughts
on Mark Twain's "Masterpiece" 354

David L. Smith • Huck, Jim, and American Racial
Discourse 362

Shelley Fisher Fishkin • Jimmy [from *Was Huck Black?*] 375

James R. Kincaid • Voices on the Mississippi [Review of
Was Huck Black?] 383

Toni Morrison • [This Amazing, Troubling Book] 385

Mark Twain: A Chronology 393
Selected Bibliography 397

Preface to the Third Edition

The youthful hero of Mark Twain's masterpiece is well over a hundred years old now, but he and his troublesome book—"if I'd knowed what trouble it was to make a book I wouldn't a tackled it"—are in more hot water than ever. Originally, Huck and his *Adventures* were banned from public libraries and schools for being crude and using bad grammar. Now the issue is racism.

Is *Adventures of Huckleberry Finn* a racist book? Huck himself likes comfort—the comfort of fishing naked from the raft, the comfort of sleeping while Jim takes his watch—but reading Huck's opus even in private, much less as part of a class, is a profoundly uncomfortable experience for many people, and not just because Mark Twain uses a single demeaning racial epithet more than 200 times in the book. Does this mean that we shouldn't read it? Or that the book shouldn't be taught in the public schools? (At what level is another question.)

"Fear and alarm," says Toni Morrison, "are what I remember most about my first encounter with Mark Twain's *Adventures of Huckleberry Finn.*" When Morrison read the book a second time "under the supervision of an English teacher in junior high school," she felt no less uncomfortable—rather more." Her discomfort did not reside just in Huck's (or Mark Twain's) name-calling, however. Removing the book from required reading lists, she says, is "a narrow notion of how to handle the offense Mark Twain's use of the term 'nigger' would occasion for black students and the corrosive effect it would have on white ones." Banning the book because its *language* is uncomfortable or offensive, says Morrison, constitutes "a purist yet elementary kind of censorship designed to appease adults rather than educate children. Amputate the problem, band-aid the solution."

If there is a single aspect of *Huck Finn* that most readers agree on, in fact, it is the power of Huck's language—when he is being free with the syntax and vocabulary of social and racial convention implied by "standard" or "white" or "King's" English. Surely, the racism in *Huck Finn* lies not in the author's language, however offensive at times, but in the social and racial conventions imbedded in that language, the prevailing moral grammar of nineteenth-century America, toward which Mark Twain was profoundly ambivalent—Morrison would say silent—and in which Huck himself professes firmly to believe. The "all right, then, I'll go to hell" scene works only if we, as readers, really believe that Huck really believes he is committing an immoral (and socially unacceptable) act when he vows to free Jim.

So Morrison is right: the "brilliance of *Huckleberry Finn* is that it *is* the argument it raises." (To discover the true source, or sources, of her "alarm" when reading *Huck Finn*, see Morrison's remarkable Introduction to the book, pp. 385–92.

Some readers will find a different sort of license to read Huck Finn's troublesome book in Shelley Fisher Fishkin's *Was Huck Black?*, a study that advances the seemingly implausible argument that Huck, in his capacity as first-person narrator of Mark Twain's narrative, actually speaks in a black "voice." By this, Fishkin does not mean that Huck is a black youth in whiteface or that he is not, as Clemens claimed, actually based on Tom Blankenship. She argues, rather, that Huck's liberating vernacular has much in common with the speech patterns of African Americans in the nineteenth century, particularly a "sociable" youth Mark Twain met on a lecture tour in the 1870s as he was writing *Tom Sawyer*. (See Fishkin's "Jimmy," pp. 375–83, and Mark Twain's "Sociable Jimmy," pp. 324–26.

Whether Huck Finn's voice is "black" or "white," it is his speaking voice that, along with Mark Twain's evocation of the great river, gives Huck's narrative its distinctive place in American literature. Here, for example, is a passage describing Huck's separation from Jim in a dense, white (no less) fog:

> I throwed the paddle down. I heard the whoop again; it was behind me yet, but in a different place; it kept coming, and kept changing its place, and I kept answering, till by and by it was in front of me again and I knowed the current had swung the canoe's head down stream and I was all right, if that was Jim and not some other rafts-man hollering. I couldn't tell nothing about voices in a fog, for nothing don't look natural nor sound natural in a fog.

This is the language of speech, and it is very different from the language in which most American literature was written before 1885. The language of Irving, Emerson, Thoreau, Hawthorne, and even Melville was a formal, "literary" language; at its worst, it was sometimes inflated into what Mark Twain called "the showiest kind of book-talk." Mark Twain's greatest achievement in *Huck Finn*, perhaps, was to make a spoken language do everything a literary language alone could do before him. Nothing is lost when Huck describes his panic in the fog, or the coming of a storm, or Pap's malice, or Jim's kindness—all in the vocabulary and syntax of the uneducated son of the town drunk, whose special way of seeing beyond conventional prejudices required an unconventional way of speaking. Nothing was lost, and a great deal was gained for a literature that is so often *told* in the first person by narrators whose innocence is the highest knowledge.

In this third Norton Critical Edition of *Huck Finn*, the only essay in criticism retained from earlier editions is T. S. Eliot's Introduction, which praises his fellow Missourian for his poetic evocation of the Mississippi River. Paired with it is a recent dissenting opinion by Jane Smiley, who thinks *Uncle Tom's Cabin* is "by far" a better book than *Huck Finn*. Other new contributions, besides those already mentioned, include essays by David Carkeet on the dialects, Earl F. Briden on the illustrations, Victor A. Doyno on the composition of the text, and John H. Wallace and David L. Smith on the racism issue; also included are James R. Kincaid's cautionary review of *Was Huck Black?*; samples of young Sam Clemens's bad poetry and Mark Twain's first extended attempt ("A True Story") to reproduce African American speech; more early reviews and responses, including the first *negative* review; and, most important of all, an authoritative text of *Huck Finn*, with original illustrations, produced as part of The Mark Twain Project by the University of California, Berkeley, in cooperation with the University of Iowa.

For their expert help with preparing this third Norton Critical Edition of *Adventures of Huckleberry Finn*, I wish especially to thank Victor A. Doyno, Barbara Joy Cooley, and Carol Bemis.

A Note on the Text and Illustrations

Adventures of *Huckleberry Finn* was first published in England in December 1884 and in America in February 1885. The text of this third Norton Critical Edition is that of the authoritative Iowa-California edition (Berkeley: University of California Press, 1988), edited by Walter Blair and Victor Fischer with the assistance of Dahlia Armon and Harriet Elinor Smith. The result of decades of work by scores of Mark Twain scholars, this meticulously reconstructed text is based upon all surviving sources—except the newly recovered first half of the manuscript—over which Mark Twain exercised authorial control, including the American first edition, the second half of the manuscript, the Charles L. Webster company's proofsheets and prospectus, pre-publication excerpts from the *Century Magazine*, and for the raft episode, the first American edition of *Life on the Mississippi* (Boston: James R. Osgood and Company, 1883). The illustrations are the originals by Edward Winsor Kemble; the illustrations for the raft episode are by John Harley from *Life on the Mississippi*.

The Text of
ADVENTURES OF
HUCKLEBERRY FINN

E.W. Kemble
·1884·

HUCKLEBERRY FINN

ADVENTURES OF

HUCKLEBERRY FINN

(TOM SAWYER'S COMRADE)

SCENE: THE MISSISSIPPI VALLEY
TIME: FORTY TO FIFTY YEARS AGO

BY

MARK TWAIN

NOTICE

EXPLANATORY

IN this book a number of dialects are used, to wit: the Missouri negro dialect; the extremest form of the backwoods South-Western dialect; the ordinary "Pike-County" dialect; and four modified varieties of this last. The shadings have not been done in a hap-hazard fashion, or by guess-work; but pains-takingly, and with the trustworthy guidance and support of personal familiarity with these several forms of speech.

I make this explanation for the reason that without it many readers would suppose that all these characters were trying to talk alike and not succeeding.

THE AUTHOR.

Contents

CHAPTER I.
Civilizing Huck.—Miss Watson.—Tom Sawyer Waits 13

CHAPTER II.
The Boys Escape Jim.—Tom Sawyer's Gang.—Deep-laid Plans . 18

CHAPTER III.
A Good Going-over.—Grace Triumphant.—"One of Tom Sawyer's Lies" 23

CHAPTER IV.
Huck and the Judge.—Superstition. 27

CHAPTER V.
Huck's Father.— The Fond Parent.—Reform 31

CHAPTER VI.
He Went for Judge Thatcher.—Huck Decides to Leave.—Political Economy.—Thrashing Around 36

CHAPTER VII.
Laying for Him.—Locked in the Cabin.—Sinking the Body.— Resting 43

CHAPTER VIII.
Sleeping in the Woods.—Raising the Dead.—Exploring the Island.—Finding Jim.—Jim's Escape.—Signs.—"Balum" 49

CHAPTER IX.
The Cave.—The Floating House 59

CHAPTER X.
The Find.—Old Hank Bunker.—In Disguise. 63

CHAPTER XI.
Huck and the Woman.—The Search.—Prevarication.—Going to Goshen 67

CHAPTER XII.
Slow Navigation.—Borrowing Things.—Boarding the Wreck.— The Plotters.—Hunting for the Boat 74

CHAPTER XIII.
Escaping from the Wreck.—The Watchman.—Sinking 81

CHAPTER XIV.
A General Good Time.—The Harem.—French 86

CHAPTER XV.
Huck Loses the Raft.—In the Fog.—Huck Finds the Raft.—
Trash.. 91

CHAPTER XVI.
"Give Us a Rest."—The Corpse-Maker Crows.—"The Child of
Calamity."—They Both Weaken.—Little Davy Steps In.—
After the Battle.—Ed's Adventures.—Something Queer.—A
Haunted Barrel.—It Brings a Storm.—The Barrel Pursues.—
Killed by Lightning.—Allbright Atones.—Ed Gets Mad.—
Snake or Boy?—"Snake Him Out."—Some Lively Lying.—Off
and Overboard.—Expectations.—A White Lie.—Floating
Currency.—Running by Cairo.—Swimming Ashore 96

CHAPTER XVII.
An Evening Call.—The Farm in Arkansaw.—Interior Decora-
tions.—Stephen Dowling Bots.—Poetical Effusions 117

CHAPTER XVIII.
Col. Grangerford.—Aristocracy.—Feuds.—The Testament.—Re-
covering the Raft.—The Wood-pile.—Pork and Cabbage..... 125

CHAPTER XIX.
Tying Up Day-times.—An Astronomical Theory.—Running a Temperance Revival.—The Duke of Bridgewater.—The Troubles
of Royalty 135

CHAPTER XX.
Huck Explains.—Laying Out a Campaign.—Working the Camp-
meeting.—A Pirate at the Camp-meeting.—The Duke as a
Printer 143

CHAPTER XXI.
Sword Exercise.—Hamlet's Soliloquy.—They Loafed Around
Town.—A Lazy Town.—Old Boggs.—Dead 151

CHAPTER XXII.
Sherburn.—Attending the Circus.—Intoxication in the Ring.—
The Thrilling Tragedy 161

CHAPTER XXIII.
"Sold!"—Royal Comparisons.—Jim Gets Homesick 166

CHAPTER XXIV.
Jim in Royal Robes.—They Take a Passenger.—Getting Information.—Family Grief 171

CHAPTER XXV.
"Is It *Them?*"—Singing the "Doxologer."—Awful Square.—Funeral Orgies.—A Bad Investment 177

CHAPTER XXVI.
A Pious King.—The King's Clergy.—She Asked His Pardon.—
Hiding in the Room.—Huck Takes the Money 184

CHAPTER XXVII.

The Funeral.—Satisfying Curiosity.—Suspicious of Huck.—
Quick Sales and Small Profits   192

CHAPTER XXVIII.

The Trip to England.—"The Brute!"—Mary Jane Decides to
Leave.—Huck Parting with Mary Jane.—Mumps.—The Oppo-
sition Line   198

CHAPTER XXIX.

Contested Relationship.—The King Explains the Loss.—A
Question of Handwriting.—Digging up the Corpse.—Huck
Escapes   207

CHAPTER XXX.

The King Went for Him.—A Royal Row.—Powerful Mellow . . .   216

CHAPTER XXXI.

Ominous Plans.—News from Jim.—Old Recollections.—A
Sheep Story.—Valuable Information   219

CHAPTER XXXII.

Still and Sunday-like.—Mistaken Identity.—Up a Stump.—In a
Dilemma   228

CHAPTER XXXIII.

A Nigger Stealer.—Southern Hospitality.—A Pretty Long Bless-
ing.—Tar and Feathers   234

CHAPTER XXXIV.

The Hut by the Ash-Hopper.—Outrageous.—Climbing the Lightning Rod.—Troubled with Witches   241

CHAPTER XXXV.

Escaping Properly.—Dark Schemes.—Discrimination in Steal-
ing.—A Deep Hole   246

CHAPTER XXXVI.

The Lightning Rod.—His Level Best.—A Bequest to Posterity.—
A High Figure   253

CHAPTER XXXVII.

The Last Shirt.—Mooning Around.—Sailing Orders.—The
Witch Pie   258

CHAPTER XXXVIII.

The Coat of Arms.—A Skilled Superintendent.—Unpleasant
Glory.—A Tearful Subject   264

CHAPTER XXXIX.

Rats.—Lively Bed-fellows.—The Straw Dummy   270

CHAPTER XL.

Fishing.—The Vigilance Committee.—A Lively Run.—Jim Ad-
vises a Doctor   275

CHAPTER XLI.

The Doctor.—Uncle Silas.—Sister Hotchkiss.—Aunt Sally in
Trouble   281

CHAPTER XLII.

Tom Sawyer Wounded.—The Doctor's Story.—Tom Con-
fesses.—Aunt Polly Arrives.—"Hand Out Them Letters". . . .   287

CHAPTER THE LAST.

Out of Bondage.—Paying the Captive.—Yours Truly, Huck
Finn   294

Illustrations

Huckleberry Finn. *Frontispiece*	2
The Widow's	13
Learning about Moses and the "Bulrushers"	14
Miss Watson	15
Huck Stealing Away	17
They Tip-toed Along	18
Jim	19
Tom Sawyer's Band of Robbers	20
Huck Creeps into his Window	22
Miss Watson's Lecture	23
The Robbers Dispersed	25
Rubbing the Lamp	26
! ! ! ! !	27
Judge Thatcher surprised	28
Jim Listening	29
"Pap"	31
Huck and his Father	32
Reforming the Drunkard	34
Falling from Grace	35
Getting out of the Way	36
Solid Comfort	37
Thinking it Over	38
Raising a Howl	40
"Git Up!"	43
The Shanty	44
Shooting the Pig	46
Taking a Rest	47
In the Woods	49
Watching the Boat	50
Discovering the Camp Fire	52
Jim and the Ghost	54
Misto Bradish's Nigger	58
Exploring the Cave	59
In the Cave	60
Jim sees a Dead Man	61
They Found Eight Dollars	63
Jim and the Snake	64
Old Hank Bunker	65
"A Fair Fit"	66
"Come In"	67
"Him and another Man"	69
She puts up a Snack	71
"Hump Yourself!"	73
On the Raft	74
He sometimes Lifted a Chicken	76
"Please don't, Bill"	78
"It ain't Good Morals"	79
"O my Lordy, Lordy!"	80
In a Fix	81
"Hello, What's Up?"	83
The Wreck	84
We turned in and Slept	85
Turning over the Truck	86
Solomon and his Million Wives	87
The story of "Sollermun"	88
"We Would Sell the Raft"	91
Among the Snags	92
Asleep on the Raft	94
"It *Amounted* to Something being a Raftsman"	96
"I Swum down along the Raft"	97
"He Jumped up in the Air"	98
"Went around in a Little Circle"	99
"He Knocked them Sprawling"	100
An Old-fashioned Break-down	102
The Mysterious Barrel	103
"Soon there was a Regular Storm"	104
"The Lightning Killed Two Men"	105
"Grabbed the Little Child"	106
"Ed got up Mad"	107
"Who are you?"	108
"Charles William Allbright, Sir"	109
Overboard	110
"Boy, that's a Lie"	112
"Here I is, Huck"	113
Climbing up the Bank	116
"Who's There?"	117
"Buck"	118
"It made Her look too Spidery"	122
"They got him out and emptied Him "	123
The House	124
Col. Grangerford	125
Young Harney Shepherdson	127
Miss Charlotte	128
"And asked me if I Liked Her"	130
"Behind the Wood-rank"	133

Hiding Day-times	135	"Gentlemen—Gentle*men*!"	212
"And Dogs a-Coming"	138	"Jim Lit Out"	214
"By rights I am a Duke!"	140	The King shakes Huck	216
"I am the Late Dauphin!"	141	The Duke went for Him	217
Tail Piece	142	Spanish Moss	219
On the Raft	143	"Who Nailed Him?"	221
The King as Juliet	146	Thinking	223
"Courting on the Sly"	147	He gave him Ten Cents	225
"A Pirate for Thirty Years"	148	Striking for the Back Country	226
Another little Job	150	Still and Sunday-like	228
Practicing	151	She hugged him tight	230
Hamlet's Soliloquy	153	"Who do you reckon 't is?"	232
"Gimme a Chaw"	155	"It was Tom Sawyer"	234
A Little Monthly Drunk	157	"Mr. Archibald Nichols, I	
The Death of Boggs	158	presume?"	236
Sherburn steps out	161	A pretty long Blessing	238
A Dead Head	163	Traveling By Rail	239
He shed Seventeen Suits	164	Vittles	241
Tragedy	166	A Simple Job	243
Their Pockets Bulged	167	Witches	245
Henry the Eighth in Boston		Getting Wood	246
Harbor	169	One of the Best Authorities	248
Harmless	171	The Breakfast Horn	249
Adolphus	173	Smouching the Knives	251
He fairly emptied that Young		Going down the Lightning	
Fellow	174	Rod	253
"Alas, our Poor Brother"	176	Stealing spoons	255
"You Bet it is"	177	Tom advises a Witch Pie	257
Leaking	178	The Rubbage Pile	258
Making up the "Deffisit"	180	"Missus, dey's a Sheet Gone"	259
Going for him	181	In a Tearing Way	261
The Doctor	182	One of his Ancestors	263
The Bag of Money	183	Jim's Coat of Arms	264
The Cubby	184	A Tough Job	266
Supper with the Hare-Lip	185	Buttons on their Tails	268
"Honest Injun"	187	Irrigation	269
The Duke looks under the		Keeping off Dull Times	270
Bed	189	Sawdust Diet	272
Huck takes the Money	191	Trouble is Brewing	273
A Crack in the Dining Room		Fishing	275
Door	192	Every one had a Gun	276
The Undertaker	193	Tom caught on a Splinter	278
"He had a Rat!"	194	Jim advises a Doctor	280
"Was you in my Room?"	196	The Doctor	281
Jawing	197	Uncle Silas in Danger	282
In Trouble	198	Old Mrs. Hotchkiss	283
Indignation	199	Aunt Sally talks to Huck	286
How to Find Them	200	Tom Sawyer wounded	287
He Wrote	202	The Doctor speaks for Jim	288
Hanner with the Mumps	203	Tom rose square up in Bed	291
The Auction	205	"Hand out them Letters"	293
The True Brothers	207	Out of Bondage	294
The Doctor leads Huck	209	Tom's Liberality	295
The Duke Wrote	210	Yours Truly	296

The Adventures of Huckleberry Finn

Chapter I.

YOU don't know about me, without you have read a book by the name of "The Adventures of Tom Sawyer,"[1] but that ain't no matter. That book was made by Mr. Mark Twain, and he told the truth, mainly. There was things which he stretched, but mainly he told the truth. That is nothing. I never seen anybody but lied, one time or another, without it was aunt Polly, or the widow, or maybe Mary. Aunt Polly—Tom's aunt Polly, she is—and Mary, and the widow Douglas, is all told about in that book—which is mostly a true book; with some stretchers, as I said before.

THE WIDOW'S.

Now the way that the book winds up, is this: Tom and me found the money that the robbers hid in the cave, and it made us rich. We got six thousand dollars apiece—all gold. It was an awful sight of money when it was piled up. Well, Judge Thatcher, he took it and put it out at interest, and it fetched us a dollar a day apiece, all the year round—more than a body could tell what to do with. The widow Douglas, she took me for her son, and allowed she would sivilize me; but it was rough living in the house all the time, considering how dismal regular and decent the widow was in all her ways; and so when I couldn't stand it no longer, I lit out. I got into my old rags, and my sugar-hogshead[2] again, and was free and satisfied. But Tom Sawyer, he

---

1. Published in 1876. When Mark Twain began *Huckleberry Finn*, the stories of Tom and Huck were still closely linked in his mind. In 1876 he thought he was halfway through "another boy's book," but it was to take eight more years of labor, by fits and starts, before Mark Twain finished "Huck Finn's Autobiography." Except, perhaps, for the controversial ending, the new book carried its hero and the American novel far beyond *Tom Sawyer* and the boy-book tradition.
2. A large barrel.

hunted me up and said he was going to start a band of robbers, and I might join if I would go back to the widow and be respectable. So I went back.

The widow she cried over me, and called me a poor lost lamb, and she called me a lot of other names, too, but she never meant no harm by it. She put me in them new clothes again, and I couldn't do nothing but sweat and sweat, and feel all cramped up. Well, then, the old thing commenced again. The widow rung a bell for supper, and you had to come

LEARNING ABOUT MOSES AND THE "BULRUSHERS."

to time. When you got to the table you couldn't go right to eating, but you had to wait for the widow to tuck down her head and grumble a little over the victuals, though there warn't really anything the matter with them. That is, nothing only everything was cooked by itself. In a barrel of odds and ends it is different; things get mixed up, and the juice kind of swaps around, and the things go better.

After supper she got out her book and learned me about Moses and the Bulrushers;[3] and I was in a sweat to find out all about him; but by and by she let it out that Moses had been dead a considerable long time;

3. The widow wants to be compared with the Pharaoh's daughter (Exodus 2.1–10) who discovered the baby Moses floating on the Nile in a basket made of bulrushes and adopted him as the widow has adopted Huck. Having no piety to be proud of, Huck claims no kinship with the deliverer of the Hebrews and the archetypal deliverer of African American folklore; but he soon leads a slave from bondage, escaping over water past a point of no return named Cairo and missing the promised land at journey's end.

so then I didn't care no more about him; because I don't take no stock in dead people.

Pretty soon I wanted to smoke, and asked the widow to let me. But she wouldn't. She said it was a mean practice and wasn't clean, and I must try to not do it any more. That is just the way with some people. They get down on a thing when they don't know nothing about it. Here she was a bothering about Moses, which was no kin to her, and no use to anybody, being gone, you see, yet finding a power of fault with me for doing a thing that had some good in it. And she took snuff too; of course that was all right, because she done it herself.

Her sister, Miss Watson, a tolerable slim old maid, with goggles on, had just come to live with her, and took a set at me now, with a spelling-book. She worked me middling hard for about an hour, and

Miss Watson

then the widow made her ease up. I couldn't stood it much longer. Then for an hour it was deadly dull, and I was fidgety. Miss Watson would say, "Don't put your feet up there, Huckleberry;" and "don't scrunch up like that, Huckleberry—set up straight;" and pretty soon she would say, "Don't gap and stretch like that, Huckleberry—why don't you try to behave?" Then she told me all about the bad place, and I said I wished I was there. She got mad, then, but I didn't mean no harm. All I wanted was to go somewheres; all I wanted was a change, I warn't particular. She said it was wicked to say what I said; said she wouldn't say it for the whole world; *she* was going to live so as to go to the good place. Well, I couldn't see no advantage in going where she was going, so I made up my mind I wouldn't try for it. But I never said so, because it would only make trouble, and wouldn't do no good.

Now she had got a start, and she went on and told me all about the good place. She said all a body would have to do there was to go around all day long with a harp and sing, forever and ever. So I didn't think much of it. But I never said so. I asked her if she reckoned Tom Sawyer would go there, and she said, not by a considerable sight. I was glad about that, because I wanted him and me to be together.

Miss Watson she kept pecking at me, and it got tiresome and lonesome. By and by they fetched the niggers in and had prayers, and then everybody was off to bed. I went up to my room with a piece of candle and put it on the table. Then I set down in a chair by the window and tried to think of something cheerful but it warn't no use. I felt so lonesome I most wished I was dead.[4] The stars was shining, and the leaves rustled in the woods ever so mournful; and I heard an owl, away off, who-whooing about somebody that was dead, and a whippowill and a dog crying about somebody that was going to die; and the wind was trying to whisper something to me and I couldn't make out what it was, and so it made the cold shivers run over me. Then away out in the woods I heard that kind of a sound that a ghost makes when it wants to tell about something that's on its mind and can't make itself understood, and so can't rest easy in its grave and has to go about that way every night grieving. I got so down-hearted and scared, I did wish I had some company. Pretty soon a spider went crawling up my shoulder, and I flipped it off and it lit in the candle; and before I could budge it was all shriveled up. I didn't need anybody to tell me that that was an awful bad sign and would fetch me some bad luck, so I was scared and most shook the clothes off of me. I got up and turned around in my tracks three times and crossed my breast every time; and then I tied up a little lock of my hair with a thread to keep witches away. But I hadn't no confidence. You do that when you've lost a horse-shoe that you've found, instead of nailing it up over the door, but I hadn't ever heard anybody say it was any way to keep off bad luck when you'd killed a spider.

I set down again, a shaking all over, and got out my pipe for a smoke; for the house was all as still as death, now, and so the widow wouldn't know. Well, after a long time I heard the clock away off in the town go boom—boom—boom—twelve licks—and all still again—stiller than ever. Pretty soon I heard a twig snap, down in the dark amongst the trees—something was a stirring. I set still and listened. Directly I could just barely hear a *"me-yow! me-yow!"* down there. That was good! Says I, *"me-yow! me-yow!"* as soft as I could, and then I put out the light and

---

4. Samuel Clemens's boyhood in Hannibal, Missouri, was almost as violent as Huck's, and his fiction depicts the world of boyhood as both idyll and nightmare. This is the first hint of Huck's preoccupation with death throughout the novel.

scrambled out of the window onto the shed. Then I slipped down to the ground and crawled in amongst the trees, and sure enough there was Tom Sawyer waiting for me.

HUCK STEALING AWAY.

Chapter II.

We went tip-toeing along a path amongst the trees back towards the end of the widow's garden, stooping down so as the branches wouldn't scrape our heads. When we was passing by the kitchen I fell over a root and made a noise. We scrouched down and laid still. Miss Watson's big nigger, named Jim, was setting in the kitchen door; we could see him pretty clear, because there was a light behind him. He got up and stretched his neck out about a minute, listening. Then he says.

"Who dah?"

He listened some more; then he come tip-toeing down and stood right between us; we could a touched him, nearly. Well, likely it was minutes and minutes that there warn't a sound, and we all there so close together. There was a place on my ankle that got to itching; but I

THEY TIP-TOED ALONG.

dasn't scratch it; and then my ear begun to itch; and next my back, right between my shoulders. Seemed like I'd die if I couldn't scratch. Well, I've noticed that thing plenty of times since. If you are with the quality, or at a funeral, or trying to go to sleep when you ain't sleepy—if you are anywheres where it won't do for you to scratch, why you will itch all over in upwards of a thousand places. Pretty soon Jim says:

"Say—who is you? Whar is you? Dog my cats ef I didn' hear sumf'n. Well, I knows what I's gwyne to do. I's gwyne to set down here and listen tell I hears it agin."

So he set down on the ground betwixt me and Tom. He leaned his back up against a tree, and stretched his legs out till one of them most touched one of mine. My nose begun to itch. It itched till the tears come into my eyes. But I dasn't scratch. Then it begun to itch on the inside. Next I got to itching underneath. I didn't know how I was going to set still. This miserableness went on as much as six or seven minutes; but it seemed a sight longer than that. I was itching in eleven different places now. I reckoned I couldn't stand it more'n a minute longer, but I set my teeth hard and got ready to try. Just then Jim begun to breathe heavy; next he begun to snore—and then I was pretty soon comfortable again.

Tom he made a sign to me—kind of a little noise with his mouth—and we went creeping away on our hands and knees. When we was ten foot off, Tom whispered to me and wanted to tie Jim to the tree for fun; but I said no; he might wake and make a disturbance, and then they'd find out I warn't in. Then Tom said he hadn't got candles enough, and he would slip in the kitchen and get some more. I didn't want him to try. I said Jim might wake up and come. But Tom wanted to resk it; so we slid in there and got three candles, and Tom laid five cents on the table for pay. Then we got out, and I was in a sweat to get away; but nothing would do Tom but he must crawl to where Jim was, on his hands and knees, and play something on him. I waited, and it seemed a good while, everything was so still and lonesome.

As soon as Tom was back, we cut along the path, around the garden fence, and by and by fetched up on the steep top of the hill the other side of the house. Tom said he slipped Jim's hat off of his head and hung it on a limb right over him, and Jim stirred a little, but he didn't wake. Afterwards Jim said the witches bewitched him and put him in a trance, and

JIM.

rode him all over the State, and then set him under the trees again and hung his hat on a limb to show who done it. And next time Jim told it he said they rode him down to New Orleans; and after that, every time he told it he spread it more and more, till by and by he said they rode him all over the world, and tired him most to death, and his back was all over sad-dle-boils. Jim was monstrous proud about it, and he got so he wouldn't hardly notice the other niggers. Nig-gers would come miles to hear Jim tell about it, and he was more looked up to than any nigger in that country. Strange niggers would stand with their mouths open and look him all over, same as if he was a wonder. Niggers is always talking about witches in the dark by the kitchen fire; but whenever one was talking and letting on to know all about such things, Jim would hap-pen in and say, "Hm! What you know 'bout witches?" and that nigger was corked up and had to take a back seat. Jim always kept that five-center piece around his neck with a string and said it was a charm the devil give to him with his own hands and told him he could cure anybody with it and fetch witches whenever he wanted to, just by saying something to it; but he never told what it was he said to it. Niggers would come from all around there and give Jim anything they had, just for a sight of that five-center piece; but they wouldn't touch it, because the devil had had his hands on it. Jim was most ruined, for a servant, because he got so stuck up on account of having seen the devil and been rode by witches.

Well, when Tom and me got to the edge of the hill-top, we looked away down into the village[1] and could see three or four lights twinkling, where there was sick folks, may be; and the stars over us was sparkling ever so fine; and down by the village was the river, a whole mile broad, and awful still and grand. We went down the hill and found Jo Harper, and Ben Rogers, and two or three more of the boys, hid in the old tan-yard. So we unhitched a skiff[2] and pulled down the river two mile and a half, to the big scar on the hillside, and went ashore.

We went to a clump of bushes, and Tom made everybody swear to keep the secret, and then showed them a hole in the hill, right in the thickest part of the bushes. Then we lit the candles and crawled in on our hands and knees. We went about two hundred yards, and then the cave opened up. Tom poked about amongst the passages and pretty soon ducked under a wall where you wouldn't a noticed that there was a hole. We went along a narrow place and got into a kind of room, all damp and sweaty and cold, and there we stopped. Tom says:

"Now we'll start this band of robbers and call it Tom Sawyer's Gang. Everybody that wants to join has got to take an oath, and write his name in blood."

Everybody was willing. So Tom got out a sheet of paper that he had wrote the oath on, and read it. It swore every boy to stick to the band, and never tell any of the secrets; and if anybody done anything to any boy in the band, whichever boy was ordered to kill that person and his

TOM SAWYER'S BAND OF ROBBERS.

family must do it, and he mustn't eat and he mustn't sleep till he had killed them and hacked a cross in their breasts,[3] which was the sign of the band. And nobody that didn't belong to the band could use that mark, and if he did he must be sued; and if he done it again he must be

---

1. St. Petersburg, a fictionalized version of Hannibal, Missouri, where Sam Clemens lived from age three to age seventeen.
2. A flat-bottomed open boat.
3. As in Robert Montgomery Bird's romance *Nick of the Woods; or, The Jibbenainosay* (1837).

killed. And if anybody that belonged to the band told the secrets, he must have his throat cut, and then have his carcass burnt up and the ashes scattered all around, and his name blotted off of the list with blood and never mentioned again by the gang, but have a curse put on it and be forgot, forever.

Everybody said it was a real beautiful oath, and asked Tom if he got it out of his own head. He said, some of it, but the rest was out of pirate books, and robber books, and every gang that was high-toned had it.

Some thought it would be good to kill the *families* of boys that told the secrets. Tom said it was a good idea, so he took a pencil and wrote it in. Then Ben Rogers says:

"Here's Huck Finn, he hain't got no family—what you going to do 'bout him?"

"Well, hain't he got a father?" says Tom Sawyer.

"Yes, he's got a father, but you can't never find him, these days. He used to lay drunk with the hogs in the tanyard, but he hain't been seen in these parts for a year or more."

They talked it over, and they was going to rule me out, because they said every boy must have a family or somebody to kill, or else it wouldn't be fair and square for the others. Well, nobody could think of anything to do—everybody was stumped, and set still. I was most ready to cry; but all at once I thought of a way, and so I offered them Miss Watson—they could kill her. Everybody said:

"Oh, she'll do, she'll do. That's all right. Huck can come in."

Then they all stuck a pin in their fingers to get blood to sign with, and I made my mark on the paper.

"Now," says Ben Rogers, "what's the line of business of this Gang?"

"Nothing only robbery and murder," Tom said.

"But who are we going to rob? houses—or cattle—or—"

"Stuff! stealing cattle and such things ain't robbery, it's burglary," says Tom Sawyer. "We ain't burglars. That ain't no sort of style. We are highwaymen. We stop stages and carriages on the road, with masks on, and kill the people and take their watches and money."

"Must we always kill the people?"

"Oh, certainly. It's best. Some authorities think different, but mostly it's considered best to kill them. Except some that you bring to the cave here and keep them till they're ransomed."

"Ransomed? What's that?"

"I don't know. But that's what they do. I've seen it in books; and so of course that's what we've got to do."

"But how can we do it if we don't know what it is?"

"Why blame it all, we've *got* to do it. Don't I tell you it's in the books? Do you want to go to doing different from what's in the books, and get things all muddled up?"

"Oh, that's all very fine to *say*, Tom Sawyer, but how in the nation[4] are these fellows going to be ransomed if we don't know how to do it to them? that's the thing I want to get at. Now what do you *reckon* it is?"

"Well I don't know. But per'aps if we keep them till they're ransomed, it means that we keep them till they're dead."

---

4. Euphemism for "damnation."

"Now, that's something *like*. That'll answer. Why couldn't you said that before? We'll keep them till they're ransomed to death—and a bothersome lot they'll be, too, eating up everything and always trying to get loose."

"How you talk, Ben Rogers. How can they get loose when there's a guard over them, ready to shoot them down if they move a peg?"

"A guard. Well, that *is* good. So somebody's got to set up all night and never get any sleep, just so as to watch them. I think that's foolishness. Why can't a body take a club and ransom them as soon as they get here?"

"Because it ain't in the books so—that's why. Now Ben Rogers, do you want to do things regular, or don't you?—that's the idea. Don't you reckon that the people that made the books knows what's the correct thing to do? Do you reckon *you* can learn 'em anything? Not by a good deal. No, sir, we'll just go on and ransom them in the regular way."

"All right. I don't mind; but I say it's a fool way, anyhow. Say—do we kill the women, too?"

"Well, Ben Rogers, if I was as ignorant as you I wouldn't let on. Kill the women? No—nobody ever saw anything in the books like that. You fetch them to the cave, and you're always as polite as pie to them; and by and by they fall in love with you and never want to go home any more."

"Well, if that's the way, I'm agreed, but I don't take no stock in it. Mighty soon we'll have the cave so cluttered up with women, and fellows waiting to be ransomed, that there won't be no place for the robbers. But go ahead, I ain't got nothing to say."

Little Tommy Barnes was asleep, now, and when they waked him up he was scared, and cried, and said he wanted to go home to his ma, and didn't want to be a robber any more.

So they all made fun of him, and called him cry-baby, and that made him mad, and he said he would go straight and tell all the secrets. But Tom give him five cents to keep quiet, and said we would all go home and meet next week and rob somebody and kill some people.

Ben Rogers said he couldn't get out much, only Sundays, and so he wanted to begin next Sunday; but all the boys said it would be wicked to do it on Sunday, and that settled the thing. They agreed to get together and fix a day as soon as they could, and then we elected Tom Sawyer first captain and Jo Harper second captain of the Gang, and so started home.

I clumb up the shed and crept into my window just before day was breaking. My new clothes was all greased up and clayey, and I was dog-tired.

HUCK CREEPS INTO HIS WINDOW.

Chapter III.

MISS WATSON'S LECTURE.

WELL I got a good going-over in the morning, from old Miss Watson, on account of my clothes; but the widow she didn't scold, but only cleaned off the grease and clay and looked so sorry that I thought I would behave a while if I could. Then Miss Watson she took me in the closet and prayed,[1] but nothing come of it. She told me to pray every day, and whatever I asked for I would get it. But it warn't so. I tried it. Once I got a fish-line, but no hooks. It warn't any good to me without hooks. I tried for the hooks three or four times, but somehow I couldn't make it work. By and by, one day, I asked Miss Watson to try for me, but she said I was a fool. She never told me why, and I couldn't make it out no way.

I set down, one time, back in the woods, and had a long think about it. I says to myself, if a body can get anything they pray for, why don't Deacon Winn get back the money he lost on pork? Why can't the widow get back her silver snuff-box that was stole? Why can't Miss Watson fat up? No, says I to myself, there ain't nothing in it. I went and told the widow about it, and she said the thing a body could get by praying for it was "spiritual gifts." This was too many for me, but she told me what she meant—I must help other people, and do everything I could for other people, and look out for them all the time, and never think about myself. This was including Miss Watson, as I took it. I went out in the woods and turned it over in my mind a long time, but I couldn't see no advantage about it—except for the other people—so at last I reckoned I wouldn't worry about it any more, but just let it go. Sometimes the widow would take me one side and talk about Providence in a way to make a body's mouth water; but maybe next day Miss Watson would take hold and knock it all down again. I judged I could see that there was two Providences, and a poor chap would stand considerable show with the widow's Providence, but if Miss Watson's got him there warn't no help for him any more. I thought it all out, and reckoned I would belong to the widow's, if he wanted me, though I couldn't make out how

---

1. Miss Watson has interpreted Matthew 6.6 literally: "But thou, when thou prayest, enter into thy closet."

23

he was agoing to be any better off then than what he was before, seeing I was so ignorant and so kind of low-down and ornery.

Pap he hadn't been seen for more than a year, and that was comfortable for me; I didn't want to see him no more. He used to always whale me when he was sober and could get his hands on me; though I used to take to the woods most of the time when he was around. Well, about this time he was found in the river drowned, about twelve mile above town, so people said. They judged it was him, anyway; said this drowned man was just his size, and was ragged, and had uncommon long hair—which was all like pap—but they couldn't make nothing out of the face, because it had been in the water so long it warn't much like a face at all. They said he was floating on his back in the water. They took him and buried him on the bank. But I warn't comfortable long, because I happened to think of something. I knowed mighty well that a drowned man don't float on his back, but on his face. So I knowed, then, that this warn't pap, but a woman dressed up in a man's clothes. So I was uncomfortable again. I judged the old man would turn up again by and by, though I wished he wouldn't.

We played robber now and then about a month, and then I resigned. All the boys did. We hadn't robbed nobody, we hadn't killed any people, but only just pretended. We used to hop out of the woods and go charging down on hog-drovers and women in carts taking garden stuff to market, but we never hived any of them. Tom Sawyer called the hogs "ingots," and he called the turnips and stuff "julery" and we would go to the cave and pow-wow over what we had done and how many people we had killed and marked. But I couldn't see no profit in it. One time Tom sent a boy to run about town with a blazing stick, which he called a slogan (which was the sign for the Gang to get together), and then he said he had got secret news by his spies that next day a whole parcel of Spanish merchants and rich A-rabs was going to camp in Cave Hollow with two hundred elephants, and six hundred camels, and over a thousand "sumter"[2] mules, all loaded down with di'monds, and they didn't have only a guard of four hundred soldiers, and so we would lay in ambuscade, as he called it, and kill the lot and scoop the things. He said we must slick up our swords and guns, and get ready. He never could go after even a turnip-cart but he must have the swords and guns all scoured up for it; though they was only lath and broom-sticks, and you might scour at them till you rotted and then they warn't worth a mouthful of ashes more than what they was before. I didn't believe we could lick such a crowd of Spaniards and A-rabs, but I wanted to see the camels and elephants, so I was on hand next day, Saturday, in the ambuscade; and when we got the word, we rushed out of the woods and down the hill. But there warn't no Spaniards and A-rabs, and there warn't no camels nor no elephants. It warn't anything but a Sunday-school picnic, and only a primer-class at that. We busted it up, and chased the children up the hollow; but we never got anything but some doughnuts and jam, though Ben Rogers got a rag doll, and Jo Harper got a hymn-book and a tract; and then the teacher charged in and made us drop everything and cut. I didn't see no

---

2. "Sumpter," fancy name for a pack animal.

THE ROBBERS DISPERSED.

di'monds, and I told Tom Sawyer so. He said there was loads of them there, anyway; and he said there was A-rabs there, too, and elephants and things. I said, why couldn't we see them, then? He said if I warn't so ignorant, but had read a book called "Don Quixote,"[3] I would know without asking. He said it was all done by enchantment. He said there was hundreds of soldiers there, and elephants and treasure, and so on, but we had enemies which he called magicians, and they had turned the whole thing into an infant Sunday school, just out of spite. I said, all right, then the thing for us to do was to go for the magicians. Tom Sawyer said I was a numskull.

"Why," says he, "a magician could call up a lot of genies, and they would hash you up like nothing before you could say Jack Robinson. They are as tall as a tree and as big around as a church."

"Well," I says, "s'pose we got some genies to help *us*—can't we lick the other crowd then?"

"How you going to get them?"

"I don't know. How do *they* get them?"

"Why they rub an old tin lamp or an iron ring, and then the genies come tearing in, with the thunder and lightning a-ripping around and the smoke a-rolling, and everything they're told to do they up and do it. They don't think nothing of pulling a shot tower[4] up by the roots, and belting a Sunday-school superintendent over the head with it—or any other man."

"Who makes them tear around so?"

"Why, whoever rubs the lamp or the ring. They belong to whoever rubs the lamp or the ring, and they've got to do whatever he says. If he tells them to build a palace forty miles long, out of di'monds, and fill it full of chewing gum, or whatever you want, and fetch an emperor's daughter from China for you to marry, they've got to do it—and they've got to do it before sun-up next morning, too. And more—they've got to waltz that palace around over the country wherever you want it, you understand."

"Well," says I, "I think they are a pack of flatheads for not keeping the palace themselves 'stead of fooling them away like that. And what's

3. The ancient *Arabian Nights' Entertainments* (first English translation 1838–41) and the "hero" of Cervantes' picaresque narrative (1605) are the chief romance authorities Tom garbles here. The one most often satirized by Clemens was Sir Walter Scott.
4. Where gunshot was made by dropping molten lead into water.

more—if I was one of them I would see a man in Jericho before I would drop my business and come to him for the rubbing of an old tin lamp."

"How you talk, Huck Finn. Why, you'd *have* to come when he rubbed it, whether you wanted to or not."

"What, and I as high as a tree and as big as a church? All right, then; I *would* come; but I lay I'd make that man climb the highest tree there was in the country."

"Shucks, it ain't no use to talk to you, Huck Finn. You don't seem to know anything, somehow—perfect sap-head."

I thought all this over for two or three days, and then I reckoned I would see if there was anything in it. I got an old tin lamp and an iron ring and went out in the woods and rubbed and rubbed till I sweat like an Injun, calculating to build a palace and sell it; but it warn't no use, none of the genies come. So then I judged that all that stuff was only just one of Tom Sawyer's lies. I reckoned he believed in the A-rabs and the elephants, but as for me I think different. It had all the marks of a Sunday school.

RUBBING THE LAMP.

Chapter IV.

!!!!!

WELL, three or four months run along, and it was well into the winter, now. I had been to school most all the time, and could spell, and read, and write just a little, and could say the multiplication table up to six times seven is thirty-five, and I don't reckon I could ever get any further than that if I was to live forever. I don't take no stock in mathematics, anyway.

At first I hated the school, but by and by I got so I could stand it. Whenever I got uncommon tired I played hookey, and the hiding I got next day done me good and cheered me up. So the longer I went to school the easier it got to be. I was getting sort of used to the widow's ways, too, and they warn't so raspy on me. Living in a house, and sleeping in a bed, pulled on me pretty tight, mostly, but before the cold weather I used to slide out and sleep in the woods, sometimes, and so that was a rest to me. I liked the old ways best, but I was getting so I liked the new ones, too, a little bit. The widow said I was coming along slow but sure, and doing very satisfactory. She said she warn't ashamed of me.

One morning I happened to turn over the salt-cellar at breakfast. I reached for some of it as quick as I could, to throw over my left shoulder and keep off the bad luck, but Miss Watson was in ahead of me, and crossed me off. She says, "Take your hands away, Huckleberry—what a mess you are always making." The widow put in a good word for me, but that warn't going to keep off the bad luck, I knowed that well enough. I started out, after breakfast, feeling worried and shaky, and wondering where it was going to fall on me, and what it was going to be. There is ways to keep off some kinds of bad luck, but this wasn't one of them kind; so I never tried to do anything, but just poked along low-spirited and on the watch-out.

I went down the front garden and clumb over the stile,[1] where you go through the high board fence. There was an inch of new snow on the

1. Double sets of steps straddling a fence.

ground, and I seen somebody's tracks. They had come up from the quarry and stood around the stile a while, and then went on around the garden fence. It was funny they hadn't come in, after standing around so. I couldn't make it out. It was very curious, somehow. I was going to follow around, but I stooped down to look at the tracks first. I didn't notice anything at first, but next I did. There was a cross in the left boot-heel made with big nails, to keep off the devil.

I was up in a second and shinning down the hill. I looked over my shoulder every now and then, but I didn't see nobody. I was at Judge Thatcher's as quick as I could get there. He said:

"Why, my boy, you are all out of breath. Did you come for your interest?"

"No sir," I says; "is there some for me?"

"Oh, yes, a half-yearly is in, last night. Over a hundred and fifty dollars. Quite a fortune for you. You better let me invest it along with your six thousand, because if you take it you'll spend it."

"No sir," I says, "I don't want to spend it. I don't want it at all—nor the six thousand, nuther. I want you to take it; I want to give it to you—the six thousand and all."

He looked surprised. He couldn't seem to make it out. He says:

"Why, what can you mean, my boy?"

I says, "Don't you ask me no questions about it, please. You'll take it—won't you?"

He says:

"Well I'm puzzled. Is something the matter?"

"Please take it," says I, "and don't ask me nothing—then I won't have to tell no lies."

JUDGE THATCHER SURPRISED.

He studied a while, and then he says:

"Oho-o. I think I see. You want to *sell* all your property to me—not give it. That's the correct idea."

Then he wrote something on a paper and read it over, and says:

"There—you see it says 'for a consideration.' That means I have bought it of you and paid you for it. Here's a dollar for you. Now, you sign it."

So I signed it, and left.

Miss Watson's nigger, Jim, had a hair-ball as big as your fist, which had been took out of the fourth stomach of an ox, and he used to do magic with it.[2] He said there was a spirit inside of it, and it knowed everything. So I went to him that night and told him pap was here again, for I found his tracks in the snow. What I wanted to know, was, what he was going to do, and was he going to stay? Jim got out his hair-ball, and said something over it, and then he held it up and dropped it on the floor. It fell pretty solid, and only rolled about an inch. Jim tried it again, and then another time, and it acted just the same. Jim got down on his knees and put his ear against it and listened: But it warn't no use; he said it wouldn't talk. He said sometimes it wouldn't talk without money. I told him I had an old slick counterfeit quarter that warn't no good because the brass showed through the silver a little, and it wouldn't pass nohow, even if the brass didn't show, because it was so slick it felt greasy, and so that would tell on it every time. (I reckoned I wouldn't say nothing about the dollar I got from the judge.) I said it was pretty bad money, but maybe the hair-ball would take it, because maybe it wouldn't know the difference. Jim smelt it, and bit it, and rubbed it, and said he would manage so the hair-ball would think it was good. He said he would split open a raw Irish potato and stick the quarter in between and keep it there all night, and next morning you couldn't see

JIM LISTENING

2. Most of Jim's superstitions have European origins, but the hair-ball is from African voodoo.

no brass, and it wouldn't feel greasy no more, and so anybody in town would take it in a minute, let alone a hair-ball. Well, I knowed a potato would do that, before, but I had forgot it.

Jim put the quarter under the hair-ball and got down and listened again. This time he said the hair-ball was all right. He said it would tell my whole fortune if I wanted it to. I says, go on. So the hair-ball talked to Jim, and Jim told it to me. He says:

"Yo' ole father doan' know, yit, what he's a-gwyne to do. Sometimes he spec he'll go 'way, en den agin he spec he'll stay. De bes' way is to res' easy en let de ole man take his own way. Dey's two angels hoverin' roun' 'bout him. One uv 'em is white en shiny, en t'other one is black. De white one gits him to go right, a little while, den de black one sail in en bust it all up. A body can't tell, yit, which one gwyne to fetch him at de las'. But you is all right. You gwyne to have considable trouble in yo' life, en considable joy. Sometimes you gwyne to git hurt, en sometimes you gwyne to git sick; but every time you's gwyne to git well again. Dey's two gals flyin' 'bout you in yo' life. One uv 'em's light en t'other one is dark. One is rich en t'other is po'. You's gwyne to marry de po' one fust en de rich one by en by. You wants to keep 'way fum de water as much as you kin, en don't run no resk, 'kase it's down in de bills dat you's gwyne to git hung."

When I lit my candle and went up to my room that night, there set pap, his own self!

Chapter V.

I HAD SHUT the door to. Then I turned around, and there he was. I used to be scared of him all the time, he tanned me so much. I reckoned I was scared now, too; but in a minute I see I was mistaken. That is, after the first jolt, as you may say, when my breath sort of hitched—he being so unexpected; but right away after, I see I warn't scared of him worth bothering about.

He was most fifty, and he looked it. His hair was long and tangled and greasy, and hung down, and you could see his eyes shining through like he was behind vines. It was all black, no gray; so was his long, mixed-up whiskers. There warn't no color in his face, where his face showed; it was white; not like another man's white, but a white to make a body sick, a white to make a body's flesh crawl—a tree-toad white, a fish-belly white. As for his clothes—just rags, that was all. He had one ankle resting on t'other knee; the boot on that foot was busted, and two of his toes stuck through, and he worked them now and then. His hat was laying on the floor; an old black slouch with the top caved in, like a lid.

"PAP."

I stood a-looking at him; he set there a-looking at me, with his chair tilted back a little. I set the candle down. I noticed the window was up; so he had clumb in by the shed. He kept a-looking me all over. By and by he says:

"Starchy clothes—very. You think you're a good deal of a big bug, *don't* you?"

"Maybe I am, maybe I ain't," I says.

"Don't you give me none o' your lip," says he. "You've put on considerble many frills since I been away. I'll take you down a peg before I get done with you. You're educated, too, they say; can read and write. You think you're better'n your father, now, don't you, because he can't? *I'll* take it out of you. Who told you you might meddle with such hifalut'n foolishness, hey?—who told you you could?"

"The widow. She told me."

31

"The widow, hey?—and who told the widow she could put in her shovel about a thing that ain't none of her business?"

"Nobody never told her."

"Well, I'll learn her how to meddle. And looky here—you drop that school, you hear? I'll learn people to bring up a boy to put on airs over his own father and let on to be better'n what *he* is. You lemme catch you fooling around that school again, you hear? Your mother couldn't read, and she couldn't write, nuther, before she died. None of the family couldn't, before *they* died. *I* can't; and here you're a-swelling yourself up like this. I ain't the man to stand it—you hear? Say—lemme hear you read."

I took up a book and begun something about General Washington and the wars. When I'd read about a half a minute, he fetched the book a whack with his hand and knocked it across the house. He says:

"It's so. You can do it. I had my doubts when you told me. Now looky here; you stop that putting on frills. I won't have it. I'll lay for you, my smarty; and if I catch you about that school I'll tan you good. First you know you'll get religion, too. I never see such a son."

He took up a little blue and yaller picture of some cows and a boy, and says:

"What's this?"

"It's something they give me for learning my lessons good."

He tore it up, and says—

"I'll give you something better—I'll give you a cowhide."

He set there a-mumbling and a-growling a minute, and then he says—

"*Ain't* you a sweet-scented dandy, though? A bed; and bed-clothes; and a look'n-glass; and a piece of carpet on the floor—and your own

HUCK AND HIS FATHER.

father got to sleep with the hogs in the tanyard. I never see such a son. I bet I'll take some o' these frills out o' you before I'm done with you. Why there ain't no end to your airs—they say you're rich. Hey?—how's that?"

"They lie—that's how."

"Looky here—mind how you talk to me; I'm a-standing about all I can stand, now—so don't gimme no sass. I've been in town two days, and I hain't heard nothing but about you bein' rich. I heard about it away down the river, too. That's why I come. You git me that money tomorrow—I want it."

"I hain't got no money."

"It's a lie. Judge Thatcher's got it. You git it. I want it."

"I hain't got no money, I tell you. You ask Judge Thatcher; he'll tell you the same."

"All right. I'll ask him; and I'll make him pungle,[1] too, or I'll know the reason why. Say—how much you got in your pocket? I want it."

"I hain't got only a dollar, and I want that to—"

"It don't make no difference what you want it for—you just shell it out."

He took it and bit it to see if it was good, and then he said he was going down town to get some whisky; said he hadn't had a drink all day. When he had got out on the shed, he put his head in again, and cussed me for putting on frills and trying to be better than him; and when I reckoned he was gone, he come back and put his head in again, and told me to mind about that school, because he was going to lay for me and lick me if I didn't drop that.

Next day he was drunk, and he went to Judge Thatcher's and bully-ragged him and tried to make him give up the money, but he couldn't, and then he swore he'd make the law force him.

The judge and the widow went to law to get the court to take me away from him and let one of them be my guardian; but it was a new judge that had just come, and he didn't know the old man; so he said courts mustn't interfere and separate families if they could help it; said he'd druther not take a child away from its father. So Judge Thatcher and the widow had to quit on the business.

That pleased the old man till he couldn't rest. He said he'd cowhide me till I was black and blue if I didn't raise some money for him. I borrowed three dollars from Judge Thatcher, and pap took it and got drunk and went a-blowing around and cussing and whooping and carrying on; and he kept it up all over town, with a tin pan, till most midnight; then they jailed him, and next day they had him before court, and jailed him again for a week. But he said *he* was satisfied; said he was boss of his son, and he'd make it warm for *him*.

When he got out the new judge said he was agoing to make a man of him. So he took him to his own house, and dressed him up clean and nice, and had him to breakfast and dinner and supper with the family, and was just old pie to him, so to speak. And after supper he talked to

1. Pay up, hand over.

him about temperance and such things till the old man cried, and said he'd been a fool, and fooled away his life; but now he was agoing to turn over a new leaf and be a man nobody wouldn't be ashamed of, and he hoped the judge would help him and not look down on him. The judge said he could hug him for them words; so *he* cried, and his wife she cried again; pap said he'd been a man that had always been misunderstood before, and the judge said he believed it. The old man said that what a man wanted that was down, was sympathy; and the judge said it was so; so they cried again. And when it was bedtime, the old man rose up and held out his hand, and says:

"Look at it gentlemen, and ladies all; take ahold of it; shake it. There's a hand that was the hand of a hog; but it ain't so no more; it's the hand of a man that's started in on a new life, and'll die before he'll go back. You mark them words—don't forget I said them. It's a clean hand now; shake it—don't be afeard."

So they shook it, one after the other, all around, and cried. The

REFORMING THE DRUNKARD.

judge's wife she kissed it. Then the old man he signed a pledge—made his mark. The judge said it was the holiest time on record, or something like that. Then they tucked the old man into a beautiful room, which was the spare room, and in the night sometime he got powerful thirsty and clumb out onto the porch-roof and slid down a stanchion and traded his new coat for a jug of forty-rod,[2] and clumb back again and had a good old time; and towards daylight he crawled out again, drunk as a fiddler, and rolled off the porch and broke his left arm in two places and was most froze to death when somebody found him after sun-up. And when they come to look at that spare room, they had to take soundings before they could navigate it.

2. Whiskey strong enough to knock a man forty rods or kill him at that distance.

The judge he felt kind of sore. He said he reckoned a body could reform the ole man with a shot-gun, maybe, but he didn't know no other way.

FALLING FROM GRACE.

Chapter VI

GETTING OUT OF THE WAY.

WELL pretty soon the old man was up and around again, and then he went for Judge Thatcher in the courts to make him give up that money, and he went for me, too, for not stopping school. He catched me a couple of times and thrashed me, but I went to school just the same, and dodged him or out-run him most of the time. I didn't want to go to school much, before, but I reckoned I'd go now to spite pap. That law trial was a slow business; appeared like they warn't ever going to get started on it; so every now and then I'd borrow two or three dollars off of the judge for him, to keep from getting a cowhiding. Every time he got money he got drunk; and every time he got drunk he raised Cain around town; and every time he raised Cain he got jailed. He was just suited— this kind of thing was right in his line.

He got to hanging around the widow's too much, and so she told him at last, that if he didn't quit using around there she would make trouble for him. Well, *wasn't* he mad? He said he would show who was Huck Finn's boss. So he watched out for me one day in the spring, and catched me, and took me up the river about three mile, in a skiff, and crossed over to the Illinois shore where it was woody and there warn't no houses but an old log hut in a place where the timber was so thick you couldn't find it if you didn't know where it was.

He kept me with him all the time, and I never got a chance to run off. We lived in that old cabin, and he always locked the door and put the key under his head, nights. He had a gun which he had stole, I reckon, and we fished and hunted, and that was what we lived on. Every little while he locked me in and went down to the store, three miles, to the ferry, and traded fish and game for whisky and fetched it home and got drunk and had a good time, and licked me. The widow she found out where I was, by and by, and she sent a man over to try to get hold of me, but pap drove him off with the gun, and it warn't long after that till I was used to being where I was, and liked it, all but the cowhide part.

It was kind of lazy and jolly, laying off comfortable all day, smoking and fishing, and no books nor study. Two months or more run along, and my

SOLID COMFORT.

clothes got to be all rags and dirt, and I didn't see how I'd ever got to like
it so well at the widow's, where you had to wash, and eat on a plate, and
comb up, and go to bed and get up regular, and be forever bothering over
a book and have old Miss Watson pecking at you all the time. I didn't
want to go back no more. I had stopped cussing, because the widow
didn't like it; but now I took to it again because pap hadn't no objections.
It was pretty good times up in the woods there, take it all around.

But by and by pap got too handy with his hick'ry, and I couldn't stand
it. I was all over welts. He got to going away so much, too, and locking
me in. Once he locked me in and was gone three days. It was dreadful
lonesome. I judged he had got drowned and I wasn't ever going to get
out any more. I was scared. I made up my mind I would fix up some way
to leave there. I had tried to get out of that cabin many a time, but I
couldn't find no way. There warn't a window to it big enought for a dog
to get through. I couldn't get up the chimbly, it was too narrow. The
door was thick solid oak slabs. Pap was pretty careful not to leave a
knife or anything in the cabin when he was away; I reckon I had hunted
the place over as much as a hundred times; well, I was 'most all the time
at it, because it was about the only way to put in the time. But this time
I found something at last; I found an old rusty wood-saw without any
handle; it was laid in between a rafter and the clapboards of the roof. I
greased it up and went to work. There was an old horse-blanket nailed
against the logs at the far end of the cabin behind the table, to keep the
wind from blowing through the chinks and putting the candle out. I got
under the table and raised the blanket and went to work to saw a section of the big bottom log out, big enough to let me through. Well, it
was a good long job, but I was getting towards the end of it when I heard
pap's gun in the woods. I got rid of the signs of my work, and dropped
the blanket and hid my saw, and pretty soon pap come in.

Pap warn't in a good humor—so he was his natural self. He said he
was down to town, and everything was going wrong. His lawyer said he

reckoned he would win his lawsuit and get the money, if they ever got started on the trial; but then there was ways to put it off a long time, and Judge Thatcher knowed how to do it. And he said people allowed there'd be another trial to get me away from him and give me to the widow for my guardian, and they guessed it would win, this time. This shook me up considerable, because I didn't want to go back to the widow's any more and be so cramped up and sivilized, as they called it. Then the old man got to cussing, and cussed everything and everybody he could think of, and then cussed them all over again to make sure he hadn't skipped any, and after that he polished off with a kind of a general cuss all round, including a considerable parcel of people which he didn't know the names of, and so called them what's-his-name, when he got to them, and went right along with his cussing.

He said he would like to see the widow get me. He said he would watch out, and if they tried to come any such game on him he knowed of a place six or seven mile off, to stow me in, where they might hunt till they dropped and they couldn't find me. That made me pretty uneasy again, but only for a minute; I reckoned I wouldn't stay on hand till he got that chance.

The old man made me go to the skiff and fetch the things he had got. There was a fifty-pound sack of corn meal, and a side of bacon, ammunition, and a four-gallon jug of whisky, and an old book and two

THINKING IT OVER.

newspapers for wadding,[1] besides some tow.[2] I toted up a load, and went back and set down on the bow of the skiff to rest. I thought it all over, and I reckoned I would walk off with the gun and some lines,

1. To hold the powder in Pap's gun.
2. Flax or hemp fibers.

and take to the woods when I run away. I guessed I wouldn't stay in one place, but just tramp right across the country, mostly night times, and hunt and fish to keep alive, and so get so far away that the old man nor the widow couldn't ever find me any more. I judged I would saw out and leave that night if pap got drunk enough, and I reckoned he would. I got so full of it I didn't notice how long I was staying, till the old man hollered and asked me whether I was asleep or drownded.

I got the things all up to the cabin, and then it was about dark. While I was cooking supper the old man took a swig or two and got sort of warmed up, and went to ripping again. He had been drunk over in town, and laid in the gutter all night, and he was a sight to look at. A body would a thought he was Adam, he was just all mud.[3] Whenever his liquor begun to work, he most always went for the govment. This time he says:

"Call this a govment! why, just look at it and see what it's like. Here's the law a-standing ready to take a man's son away from him—a man's own son, which he has had all the trouble and all the anxiety and all the expense of raising. Yes, just as that man has got that son raised at last, and ready to go to work and begin to do suthin' for *him* and give him a rest, the law up and goes for him. And they call *that* govment! That ain't all, nuther. The law backs that old Judge Thatcher up and helps him to keep me out o' my property. Here's what the law does. The law takes a man worth six thousand dollars and upards, and jams him into an old trap of a cabin like this, and lets him go round in clothes that ain't fitten for a hog. They call that govment! A man can't get his rights in a govment like this. Sometimes I've a mighty notion to just leave the country for good and all. Yes, and I *told* 'em so; I told old Thatcher so to his face. Lots of 'em heard me, and can tell what I said. Says I, for two cents I'd leave the blamed country and never come anear it agin. Them's the very words. I says, look at my hat—if you call it a hat—but the lid raises up and the rest of it goes down till it's below my chin, and then it ain't rightly a hat at all, but more like my head was shoved up through a jint o' stove-pipe. Look at it, says I—such a hat for me to wear—one of the wealthiest men in this town, if I could git my rights.

"Oh, yes, this is a wonderful govment, wonderful. Why, looky here. There was a free nigger there, from Ohio; a mulatter, most as white as a white man. He had the whitest shirt on you ever see, too, and the shiniest hat; and there ain't a man in that town that's got as fine clothes as what he had; and he had a gold watch and chain, and a silver-headed cane—the awfulest old gray-headed nabob in the State. And what do you think? they said he was a p'fessor in a college, and could talk all kinds of languages, and knowed everything.[4] And that ain't the wust. They said he could *vote*, when he was at home. Well, that let me out. Thinks I, what is the country a-coming to? It was 'lection day, and I was just about to go and vote, myself, if I warn't too drunk to get there; but when they told me there was a State in this country where they'd let that nigger vote, I drawed out. I says I'll never vote agin. Them's the very

3. Adam is created "of the dust of the ground" in Genesis 2.7.
4. In the 1860s, such a learned professor, Dr. John C. Mitchell (1827–1900), taught Greek, Latin, and mathematics at what was then Wilberforce College in Ohio.

words I said; they all heard me; and the country may rot for all me—I'll never vote again as long as I live. And to see the cool way of that nigger—why, he wouldn't a give me the road if I hadn't shoved him out o' the way. I says to the people, why ain't this nigger put up at auction and sold?—that's what I want to know. And what do you reckon they said? Why, they said he couldn't be sold till he'd been in the State six months, and he hadn't been there that long yet. There, now—that's a specimen. They call that a govment that can't sell a free nigger till he's been in the State six months. Here's a govment that calls itself a govment, and lets on to be a govment, and thinks it is a govment, and yet's got to set stock-still for six whole months before it can take ahold of a prowling, thieving, infernal, white-shirted free nigger, and—"[5]

Pap was agoing on so, he never noticed where his old limber legs was taking him to, so he went head over heels over the tub of salt pork, and barked both shins, and the rest of his speech was all the hottest kind of language—mostly hove at the nigger and the govment, though he give the tub some, too, all along, here and there. He hopped around the cabin considerable, first on one leg and then on the other, holding first one shin and then the other one, and at last he let out with his left foot all of a sudden and fetched the tub a rattling kick. But it warn't good judgment, because that was the boot that had a couple of his toes leaking out of the front end of it; so now he raised a howl that fairly made a

RAISING A HOWL.

5. The original constitution of Missouri prohibited freed slaves and people of multiracial ancestry from entering the state. This provision was stricken out in the "second Missouri compromise" of 1820; however, increasingly strict laws were passed in the 1830s and 1840s. By 1850, a sworn statement by a white "proved" ownership of a black "fugitive" who lacked freedom papers. Roxy's case in *Pudd'nhead Wilson* shows how easily a free black could be sold down the river.

body's hair raise, and down he went in the dirt, and rolled there, and held his toes; and the cussing he done then laid over anything he had ever done previous. He said so his own self, afterwards. He had heard old Sowberry Hagan in his best days, and he said it laid over him, too; but I reckon that was sort of piling it on, maybe.

After supper pap took the jug, and said he had enough whisky there for two drunks and one delirium tremens. That was always his word. I judged he would be blind drunk in about an hour, and then I would steal the key, or saw myself out, one or t'other. He drank, and drank, and tumbled down on his blankets, by and by; but luck didn't run my way. He didn't go sound asleep, but was uneasy. He groaned, and moaned, and thrashed around this way and that, for a long time. At last I got so sleepy I couldn't keep my eyes open, all I could do, and so before I knowed what I was about I was sound asleep, and the candle burning.

I don't know how long I was asleep, but all of a sudden there was an awful scream and I was up. There was pap, looking wild and skipping around every which way and yelling about snakes. He said they was crawling up his legs; and then he would give a jump and scream, and say one had bit him on the cheek—but I couldn't see no snakes. He started and run round and round the cabin, hollering "take him off! take him off! he's biting me on the neck!" I never see a man look so wild in the eyes. Pretty soon he was all fagged out, and fell down panting; then he rolled over and over, wonderful fast, kicking things every which way, and striking and grabbing at the air with his hands, and screaming, and saying there was devils ahold of him. He wore out, by and by, and laid still a while, moaning. Then he laid stiller, and didn't make a sound. I could hear the owls and the wolves, away off in the woods, and it seemed terrible still. He was laying over by the corner. By and by he raised up, part way, and listened, with his head to one side. He says very low:

"Tramp—tramp—tramp; that's the dead; tramp—tramp—tramp; they're coming after me; but I won't go—Oh, they're here! don't touch me—don't! hands off—they're cold; let go—Oh, let a poor devil alone!"

Then he went down on all fours and crawled off begging them to let him alone, and he rolled himself up in his blanket and wallowed in under the old pine table, still a-begging; and then he went to crying. I could hear him through the blanket.

By and by he rolled out and jumped up on his feet looking wild, and he see me and went for me. He chased me round and round the place, with a clasp-knife, calling me the Angel of Death and saying he would kill me and then I couldn't come for him no more. I begged, and told him I was only Huck, but he laughed *such* a screechy laugh, and roared and cussed, and kept on chasing me up. Once when I turned short and dodged under his arm he made a grab and got me by the jacket between my shoulders, and I thought I was gone; but I slid out of the jacket quick as lightning, and saved myself. Pretty soon he was all tired out, and dropped down with his back against the door, and said he would rest a minute and then kill me. He put his knife under him, and said he would sleep and get strong, and then he would see who was who.

So he dozed off, pretty soon. By and by I got the old split-bottom[6] chair and clumb up, as easy as I could, not to make any noise, and got down the gun. I slipped the ramrod down it to make sure it was loaded, and then I laid it across the turnip barrel, pointing towards pap, and set down behind it to wait for him to stir. And how slow and still the time did drag along.

---

6. Splint-bottom.

CHAPTER VII.

"GIT UP!"

up! what you 'bout!"

I opened my eyes and looked around, trying to make out where I was. It was after sun-up, and I had been sound asleep. Pap was standing over me, looking sour—and sick, too. He says—

"What you doin' with this gun?"

I judged he didn't know nothing about what he had been doing, so I says:

"Somebody tried to get in, so I was laying for him."

"Why didn't you roust me out?"

"Well I tried to, but I couldn't; I couldn't budge you."

"Well, all right. Don't stand there palavering all day, but out with you and see if there's a fish on the lines for breakfast. I'll be along in a minute."

He unlocked the door and I cleared out, up the river bank. I noticed some pieces of limbs and such things floating down, and a sprinkling of bark; so I knowed the river had begun to rise. I reckoned I would have great times, now, if I was over at the town. The June rise used to be always luck for me; because as soon as that rise begins, here comes cord-wood floating down, and pieces of log rafts—sometimes a dozen logs together; so all you have to do is to catch them and sell them to the wood yards and the sawmill.

I went along up the bank with one eye out for pap and t'other one out for what the rise might fetch along. Well, all at once, here comes a canoe; just a beauty, too, about thirteen or fourteen foot long, riding high like a duck. I shot head first off of the bank, like a frog, clothes and all on, and struck out for the canoe. I just expected there'd be somebody laying down in it, because people often done that to fool folks, and when a chap had pulled a skiff out most to it they'd raise up and laugh at him. But it warn't so this time. It was a drift-canoe, sure enough, and I clumb in and paddled her ashore. Thinks I, the old man will be glad when he sees this—she's worth ten dollars. But when I got to shore pap wasn't in sight yet, and as I was running her into a little creek like a gully, all hung over with vines and willows, I struck another idea; I judged I'd hide her good, and then, stead of taking to the woods when I run off, I'd go down the river about fifty mile and camp in one place for good, and not have such a rough time tramping on foot.

43

It was pretty close to the shanty, and I thought I heard the old man coming, all the time; but I got her hid; and then I out and looked around a bunch of willows, and there was the old man down the path apiece just drawing a bead on a bird with his gun. So he hadn't seen anything.

When he got along, I was hard at it taking up a "trot" line.[1] He abused me a little for being so slow, but I told him I fell in the river and that was what made me so long. I knowed he would see I was wet, and then he would be asking questions. We got five cat-fish off of the lines and went home.

THE SHANTY.

While we laid off, after breakfast, to sleep up, both of us being about wore out, I got to thinking that if I could fix up some way to keep pap and the widow from trying to follow me, it would be a certainer thing than trusting to luck to get far enough off before they missed me; you see, all kinds of things might happen. Well, I didn't see no way for a while, but by and by pap raised up a minute, to drink another barrel of water, and he says:

"Another time a man comes a-prowling round here, you roust me out, you hear? That man warn't here for no good. I'd a shot him. Next time, you roust me out, you hear?"

Then he dropped down and went to sleep again—but what he had been saying give me the very idea I wanted. I says to myself, I can fix it now so nobody won't think of following me.

About twelve o'clock we turned out and went along up the bank. The river was coming up pretty fast, and lots of drift-wood going by on the rise. By and by, along comes part of a log raft—nine logs fast together. We went out with the skiff and towed it ashore. Then we had dinner.

---

1. Fishing line strung out over the water to hold shorter lines with baited hooks.

Anybody but pap would a waited and seen the day through, so as to catch more stuff; but that warn't pap's style. Nine logs was enough for one time; he must shove right over to town and sell. So he locked me in and took the skiff and started off towing the raft about half-past three. I judged he wouldn't come back that night. I waited till I reckoned he had got a good start, then I out with my saw and went to work on that log again. Before he was t'other side of the river I was out of the hole; him and his raft was just a speck on the water away off yonder.

I took the sack of corn meal and took it to where the canoe was hid, and shoved the vines and branches apart and put it in; then I done the same with the side of bacon; then the whisky jug; I took all the coffee and sugar there was, and all the ammunition; I took the wadding; I took the bucket and gourd, I took a dipper and a tin cup, and my old saw and two blankets, and the skillet and the coffee-pot. I took fish-lines and matches and other things—everything that was worth a cent. I cleaned out the place. I wanted an axe, but there wasn't any, only the one out at the wood pile, and I knowed why I was going to leave that. I fetched out the gun, and now I was done.

I had wore the ground a good deal, crawling out of the hole and dragging out so many things. So I fixed that as good as I could from the outside by scattering dust on the place, which covered up the smoothness and the sawdust. Then I fixed the piece of log back into its place, and put two rocks under it and one against it to hold it there,—for it was bent up at that place, and didn't quite touch ground. If you stood four or five foot away and didn't know it was sawed, you wouldn't ever notice it; and besides, this was the back of the cabin and it warn't likely anybody would go fooling around there.

It was all grass clear to the canoe; so I hadn't left a track. I followed around to see. I stood on the bank and looked out over the river. All safe. So I took the gun and went up a piece into the woods and was hunting around for some birds, when I see a wild pig; hogs soon went wild in them bottoms after they had got away from the prairie farms. I shot this fellow and took him into camp.

I took the axe and smashed in the door—I beat it and hacked it considerable, a-doing it. I fetched the pig in and took him back nearly to the table and hacked into his throat with the axe, and laid him down on the ground to bleed—I say ground, because it *was* ground—hard packed, and no boards. Well, next I took an old sack and put a lot of big rocks in it,—all I could drag—and I started it from the pig and dragged it to the door and through the woods down to the river and dumped it in, and down it sunk, out of sight. You could easy see that something had been dragged over the ground. I did wish Tom Sawyer was there, I knowed he would take an interest in this kind of business, and throw in the fancy touches. Nobody could spread himself like Tom Sawyer in such a thing as that.

Well, last I pulled out some of my hair, and bloodied the axe good, and stuck it on the back side, and slung the axe in the corner. Then I took up the pig and held him to my breast with my jacket (so he couldn't drip) till I got a good piece below the house and then dumped him into the river. Now I thought of something else. So I went and got the bag of meal and my old saw out of the canoe and fetched them to the

SHOOTING THE PIG.

house. I took the bag to where it used to stand, and ripped a hole in the bottom of it with the saw, for there warn't no knives and forks on the place—pap done everything with his clasp-knife, about the cooking. Then I carried the sack about a hundred yards across the grass and through the willows east of the house, to a shallow lake that was five mile wide and full of rushes—and ducks too, you might say, in the season. There was a slough or a creek leading out of it on the other side, that went miles away, I don't know where, but it didn't go to the river. The meal sifted out and made a little track all the way to the lake. I dropped pap's whetstone there too, so as to look like it had been done by accident. Then I tied up the rip in the meal sack with a string, so it wouldn't leak no more, and took it and my saw to the canoe again.

It was about dark, now; so I dropped the canoe down the river under some willows that hung over the bank, and waited for the moon to rise. I made fast to a willow; then I took a bite to eat, and by and by laid down in the canoe to smoke a pipe and lay out a plan. I says to myself, they'll follow the track of that sackful of rocks to the shore and then drag the river for me. And they'll follow that meal track to the lake and go browsing down the creek that leads out of it to find the robbers that killed me and took the things. They won't ever hunt the river for anything but my dead carcass. They'll soon get tired of that, and won't bother no more about me. All right; I can stop anywhere I want to. Jackson's Island[2] is good enough for me; I know that island pretty well, and nobody ever comes there. And then I can paddle over to town, nights, and slink around and pick up things I want. Jackson's Island's the place.

I was pretty tired, and the first thing I knowed, I was asleep. When I woke up I didn't know where I was, for a minute. I set up and looked around, a little scared. Then I remembered. The river looked miles and

2. The island described in *Tom Sawyer*, actually Glasscock's Island, now eroded away by the Mississippi.

miles across. The moon was so bright I could a counted the drift logs
that went a slipping along, black and still, hundreds of yards out from
shore. Everything was dead quiet, and it looked late, and *smelt* late. You
know what I mean—I don't know the words to put it in.

I took a good gap and a stretch, and was just going to unhitch and
start, when I heard a sound away over the water. I listened. Pretty soon
I made it out. It was that dull kind of a regular sound that comes from
oars working in rowlocks when it's a still night. I peeped out through
the willow branches, and there it was—a skiff, away across the water. I
couldn't tell how many was in it. It kept a-coming, and when it was
abreast of me I see there warn't but one man in it. Thinks I, maybe it's
pap, though I warn't expecting him. He dropped below me, with the
current, and by and by he come a-swinging up shore in the easy water,
and he went by so close I could a reached out the gun and touched him.
Well, it *was* pap, sure enough—and sober, too, by the way he laid to his
oars.

I didn't lose no time. The next minute I was a-spinning down stream
soft but quick in the shade of the bank. I made two mile and a half, and
then struck out a quarter of a mile or more towards the middle of the
river, because pretty soon I would be passing the ferry landing and people might see me and hail me. I got out amongst the drift-wood and
then laid down in the bottom of the canoe and let her float. I laid there
and had a good rest and a smoke out of my pipe, looking away into the
sky, not a cloud in it. The sky looks ever so deep when you lay down on
your back in the moonshine; I never knowed it before. And how far a
body can hear on the water such nights! I heard people talking at the
ferry landing. I heard what they said, too, every word of it. One man
said it was getting towards the long days and the short nights, now.
T'other one said *this* warn't one of the short ones, he reckoned—and
then they laughed, and he said it over again and they laughed again;

TAKING A REST.

then they waked up another fellow and told him, and laughed, but he didn't laugh; he ripped out something brisk and said let him alone. The first fellow said he 'lowed to tell it to his old woman—she would think it was pretty good; but he said that warn't nothing to some things he had said in his time. I heard one man say it was nearly three o'clock, and he hoped daylight wouldn't wait more than about a week longer. After that, the talk got further and further away, and I couldn't make out the words any more, but I could hear the mumble; and now and then a laugh, too, but it seemed a long ways off.

I was away below the ferry now. I rose up and there was Jackson's Island, about two mile and a half down stream, heavy-timbered and standing up out of the middle of the river, big and dark and solid, like a steamboat without any lights. There warn't any signs of the bar at the head—it was all under water, now.

It didn't take me long to get there. I shot past the head at a ripping rate, the current was so swift, and then I got into the dead water and landed on the side towards the Illinois shore. I run the canoe into a deep dent in the bank that I knowed about; I had to part the willow branches to get in; and when I made fast nobody could a seen the canoe from the outside.

I went up and set down on a log at the head of the island and looked out on the big river and the black driftwood, and away over to the town, three mile away, where there was three or four lights twinkling. A monstrous big lumber raft was about a mile up stream, coming along down, with a lantern in the middle of it. I watched it come creeping down, and when it was most abreast of where I stood I heard a man say, "Stern oars, there! heave her head to stabboard!"[3] I heard that just as plain as if the man was by my side.

There was a little gray in the sky, now; so I stepped into the woods and laid down for a nap before breakfast.

---

3. Starboard, the right-hand side facing forward; "labbord" or "larboard" instead of "port" was Mark Twain's usual term for the left-hand side.

Chapter VIII.

IN THE WOODS.

The sun was up so high when I waked, that I judged it was after eight o'clock. I laid there in the grass and the cool shade, thinking about things and feeling rested and ruther comfortable and satisfied. I could see the sun out at one or two holes, but mostly it was big trees all about, and gloomy in there amongst them. There was freckled places on the ground where the light sifted down through the leaves, and the freckled places swapped about a little, showing there was a little breeze up there. A couple of squirrels set on a limb and jabbered at me very friendly.

I was powerful lazy and comfortable—didn't want to get up and cook breakfast. Well, I was dozing off again, when I thinks I hears a deep sound of "boom!" away up the river. I rouses up and rests on my elbow and listens; pretty soon I hears it again. I hopped up and went and looked out at a hole in the leaves, and I see a bunch of smoke laying on the water a long ways up—about abreast the ferry. And there was the ferry-boat full of people, floating along down. I knowed what was the matter, now. "Boom!" I see the white smoke squirt out of the ferry-boat's side. You see, they was firing cannon over the water, trying to make my carcass come to the top.

I was pretty hungry, but it warn't going to do for me to start a fire, because they might see the smoke. So I set there and watched the cannon-smoke and listened to the boom. The river was a mile wide, there, and it always looks pretty on a summer morning—so I was having a good enough time seeing them hunt for my remainders, if I only had a bite to eat. Well, then I happened to think how they always put quicksilver in loaves of bread and float them off because they always go right to the drownded carcass and stop there. So says I, I'll keep a lookout, and if any of them's floating around after me, I'll give them a show. I changed to the Illinois edge of the island to see what luck I could have, and I warn't disappointed. A big double loaf come along, and I most got it, with a long stick, but my foot slipped and she floated

WATCHING THE BOAT.

out further. Of course I was where the current set in the closest to the shore—I knowed enough for that. But by and by along comes another one, and this time I won. I took out the plug and shook out the little dab of quicksilver, and set my teeth in. It was "baker's bread"—what the quality[1] eat—none of your low-down corn-pone.[2]

I got a good place amongst the leaves, and set there on a log, munching the bread and watching the ferry-boat, and very well satisfied. And then something struck me. I says, now I reckon the widow or the parson or somebody prayed that this bread would find me, and here it has gone and done it. So there ain't no doubt but there is something in that thing. That is, there's something in it when a body like the widow or the parson prays, but it don't work for me, and I reckon it don't work for only just the right kind.

I lit a pipe and had a good long smoke and went on watching. The ferry-boat was floating with the current, and I allowed I'd have a chance to see who was aboard when she come along, because she would come in close, where the bread did. When she'd got pretty well along down towards me, I put out my pipe and went to where I fished out the bread, and laid down behind a log on the bank in a little open place. Where the log forked I could peep through.

By and by she come along, and she drifted in so close that they could a run out a plank and walked ashore. Most everybody was on the boat.

1. People of high social status.
2. Cheaper because made with coarse cornmeal and usually without milk or eggs.

Pap, and Judge Thatcher, and Becky Thatcher, and Jo Harper, and Tom Sawyer, and his old aunt Polly, and Sid and Mary, and plenty more. Everybody was talking about the murder, but the captain broke in and says:

"Look sharp, now; the current sets in the closest here, and maybe he's washed ashore and got tangled amongst the brush at the water's edge. I hope so, anyway."

I didn't hope so. They all crowded up and leaned over the rails, nearly in my face, and kept still, watching with all their might. I could see them first-rate, but they couldn't see me. Then the captain sung out:

"Stand away!" and the cannon let off such a blast right before me that it made me deef with the noise and pretty near blind with the smoke, and I judged I was gone. If they'd a had some bullets in, I reckon they'd a got the corpse they was after. Well, I see I warn't hurt, thanks to goodness. The boat floated on and went out of sight around the shoulder of the island. I could hear the booming, now and then, further and further off, and by and by after an hour, I didn't hear it no more. The island was three mile long. I judged they had got to the foot, and was giving it up. But they didn't yet a while. They turned around the foot of the island and started up the channel on the Missouri side, under steam, and booming once in a while as they went. I crossed over to that side and watched them. When they got abreast the head of the island they quit shooting and dropped over to the Missouri shore and went home to the town.

I knowed I was all right now. Nobody else would come a-hunting after me. I got my traps out of the canoe and made me a nice camp in the thick woods. I made a kind of a tent out of my blankets to put my things under so the rain couldn't get at them. I catched a cat-fish and haggled him open with my saw, and towards sundown I started my camp fire and had supper. Then I set out a line to catch some fish for breakfast.

When it was dark I set by my camp fire smoking, and feeling pretty satisfied; but by and by it got sort of lonesome, and so I went and set on the bank and listened to the currents washing along, and counted the stars and drift-logs and rafts that come down, and then went to bed; there ain't no better way to put in time when you are lonesome; you can't stay so, you soon get over it.

And so for three days and nights. No difference—just the same thing. But the next day I went exploring around down through the island. I was boss of it; it all belonged to me, so to say, and I wanted to know all about it; but mainly I wanted to put in the time. I found plenty strawberries, ripe and prime; and green summer-grapes, and green razberries; and the green blackberries was just beginning to show. They would all come handy by and by, I judged.

Well, I went fooling along in the deep woods till I judged I warn't far from the foot of the island. I had my gun along, but I hadn't shot nothing; it was for protection; thought I would kill some game nigh home. About this time I mighty near stepped on a good sized snake, and it went sliding off through the grass and flowers, and I after it, trying to get a shot at it. I clipped along, and all of a sudden I bounded right on to the ashes of a camp fire that was still smoking.

DISCOVERING THE CAMP FIRE.

My heart jumped up amongst my lungs. I never waited for to look further, but uncocked my gun and went sneaking back on my tip-toes as fast as ever I could. Every now and then I stopped a second, amongst the thick leaves, and listened; but my breath come so hard I couldn't hear nothing else. I slunk along another piece further, then listened again; and so on, and so on; if I see a stump, I took it for a man; if I trod on a stick and broke it, it made me feel like a person had cut one of my breaths in two and I only got half, and the short half, too.

When I got to camp I warn't feeling very brash, there warn't much sand in my craw; but I says, this ain't no time to be fooling around. So I got all my traps into my canoe again so as to have them out of sight, and I put out the fire and scattered the ashes around to look like an old last year's camp, and then clumb a tree.

I reckon I was up in the tree two hours; but I didn't see nothing, I didn't hear nothing—I only *thought* I heard and seen as much as a thousand things. Well, I couldn't stay up there forever; so at last I got down, but I kept in the thick woods and on the lookout all the time. All I could get to eat was berries and what was left over from breakfast.

By the time it was night I was pretty hungry. So when it was good and dark, I slid out from shore before moonrise and paddled over to the Illinois bank—about a quarter of a mile. I went out in the woods and cooked a supper, and I had about made up my mind I would stay there all night, when I hear a *plunkety-plunk, plunkety-plunk*, and says to myself, horses coming; and next I hear people's voices. I got everything into the canoe as quick as I could, and then went creeping through the woods to see what I could find out. I hadn't got far when I hear a man say:

"We better camp here, if we can find a good place; the horses is about beat out. Let's look around."

I didn't wait, but shoved out and paddled away easy. I tied up in the old place, and reckoned I would sleep in the canoe.

I didn't sleep much. I couldn't, somehow, for thinking. And every time I waked up I thought somebody had me by the neck. So the sleep didn't do me no good. By and by I says to myself, I can't live this way; I'm agoing to find out who it is that's here on the island with me; I'll find it out or bust. Well, I felt better, right off.

So I took my paddle and slid out from shore just a step or two, and then let the canoe drop along down amongst the shadows. The moon was shining, and outside of the shadows it made it most as light as day. I poked along well onto an hour, everything still as rocks and sound asleep. Well by this time I was most down to the foot of the island. A little ripply, cool breeze begun to blow, and that was as good as saying the night was about done. I give her a turn with the paddle and brung her nose to shore; then I got my gun and slipped out and into the edge of the woods. I set down there on a log and looked out through the leaves. I see the moon go off watch and the darkness begin to blanket the river. But in a little while I see a pale streak over the tree-tops, and knowed the day was coming. So I took my gun and slipped off towards where I had run across that camp fire, stopping every minute or two to listen. But I hadn't no luck, somehow; I couldn't seem to find the place. But by and by, sure enough, I catched a glimpse of fire, away through the trees. I went for it, cautious and slow. By and by I was close enough to have a look, and there laid a man on the ground. It most give me the fan-tods.[3] He had a blanket around his head, and his head was nearly in the fire. I set there behind a clump of bushes, in about six foot of him, and kept my eyes on him steady. It was getting gray daylight, now. Pretty soon he gapped, and stretched himself, and hove off the blanket, and it was Miss Watson's Jim! I bet I was glad to see him. I says:

"Hello, Jim!" and skipped out.

He bounced up and stared at me wild. Then he drops down on his knees, and puts his hands together and says:

"Doan' hurt me—don't! I hain't ever done no harm to a ghos'. I awluz liked dead people, en done all I could for 'em. You go en git in de river agin, whah you b'longs, en doan' do nuffn to Ole Jim, 'at 'uz awluz yo' fren'."

Well, I warn't long making him understand I warn't dead. I was ever so glad to see Jim. I warn't lonesome, now. I told him I warn't afraid of *him* telling the people where I was. I talked along, but he only set there and looked at me; never said nothing. Then I says:

"It's good daylight. Le's get breakfast. Make up your camp fire good."

"What's de use er makin' up de camp fire to cook strawbries en sich truck? But you got a gun, hain't you? Den we kin git sumfn better den strawbries."

"Strawberries and such truck," I says. "Is that what you live on?"

---

3. The shakes, the willies; slang variant of "fantasy."

JIM AND THE GHOST.

"I couldn' git nuffn else," he says.

"Why, how long you been on the island, Jim?"

"I come heah de night arter you's killed."

"What, all that time?"

"Yes-indeedy."

"And ain't you had nothing but that kind of rubbage to eat?"

"No, sah—nuffn else."

"Well, you must be most starved, ain't you?"

"I reck'n I could eat a hoss. I think I could. How long you ben on de islan'?"

"Since the night I got killed."

"No! W'y, what has you lived on? But you got a gun. Oh, yes, you got a gun. Dat's good. Now you kill sumfn en I'll make up de fire."

So we went over to where the canoe was, and while he built a fire in a grassy open place amongst the trees, I fetched meal and bacon and coffee, and coffee-pot and frying-pan, and sugar and tin cups, and the nigger was set back considerable, because he reckoned it was all done with witchcraft. I catched a good big cat-fish, too, and Jim cleaned him with his knife, and fried him.

When breakfast was ready, we lolled on the grass and eat it smoking hot. Jim laid it in with all his might, for he was most about starved. Then when we had got pretty well stuffed, we laid off and lazied.

By and by Jim says:

"But looky here, Huck, who wuz it dat 'uz killed in dat shanty, ef it warn't you?"

Then I told him the whole thing, and he said it was smart. He said Tom Sawyer couldn't get up no better plan than what I had. Then I says:

"How do you come to be here, Jim, and how'd you get here?"

He looked pretty uneasy, and didn't say nothing for a minute. Then he says:

"Maybe I better not tell."

"Why, Jim?"

"Well, dey's reasons. But you wouldn' tell on me ef I 'uz to tell you, would you, Huck?"

"Blamed if I would, Jim."

"Well, I b'lieve you, Huck. I—I *run off.*"

"Jim!"

"But mind, you said you wouldn't tell—you know you said you wouldn't tell, Huck."

"Well, I did. I said I wouldn't, and I'll stick to it. Honest *injun* I will. People would call me a low down Ablitionist and despise me for keeping mum—but that don't make no difference. I ain't agoing to tell, and I ain't agoing back there anyways. So now, le's know all about it."

"Well, you see, it 'uz dis way. Ole Missus—dat's Miss Watson—she pecks on me all de time, en treats me pooty rough, but she awluz said she wouldn' sell me down to Orleans. But I noticed dey wuz a nigger trader roun' de place considable, lately, en I begin to git oneasy. Well, one night I creeps to de do', pooty late, en de do' warn't quite shet, en I hear ole missus tell de widder she gwyne to sell me down to Orleans, but she didn' want to, but she could git eight hund'd dollars for me, en it 'uz sich a big stack o' money she couldn' resis'. De widder she try to git her to say she wouldn' do it, but I never waited to hear de res'. I lit out mighty quick, I tell you.

"I tuck out en shin down de hill en 'spec to steal a skift 'long de sho' som'ers 'bove de town, but dey wuz people a-stirrin' yit, so I hid in de ole tumble-down cooper[4] shop on de bank to wait for everybody to go 'way. Well, I wuz dah all night. Dey wuz somebody roun' all de time. 'Long 'bout six in de mawnin', skifts begin to go by, en 'bout eight er nine every skift dat went 'long wuz talkin' 'bout how yo' pap come over to de town en say you's killed. Dese las' skifts wuz full o' ladies en genlmen agoin' over for to see de place. Sometimes dey'd pull up at de sho' en take a res' b'fo' dey started acrost, so by de talk I got to know all 'bout de killin'. I 'uz powerful sorry you's killed, Huck, but I ain't no mo', now.

"I laid dah under de shavins all day. I 'uz hungry, but I warn't afeared; bekase I knowed ole missus en de widder wuz goin' to start to de camp-meetn' right arter breakfas' en be gone all day, en dey knows I goes off wid de cattle 'bout daylight, so dey wouldn' 'spec to see me roun' de place, en so dey wouldn' miss me tell arter dark in de evenin'. De yuther servants wouldn' miss me, kase dey'd shin out en take holiday, soon as de ole folks 'uz out'n de way.

"Well, when it come dark I tuck out up de river road, en went 'bout two mile er more to whah dey warn't no houses. I'd made up my mine 'bout what I's agwyne to do. You see ef I kep' on tryin' to git away afoot, de dogs 'ud track me; ef I stole a skift to cross over, dey'd miss dat skift, you see, en dey'd know 'bout whah I'd lan' on de yuther side en whah to pick up my track. So I says, a raff is what I's arter; it doan' *make* no track.

"I see a light a-comin' roun' de p'int, bymeby, so I wade' in en shove' a log ahead o' me, en swum more'n half-way acrost de river, en got in 'mongst de drift-wood, en kep' my head down low, en kinder swum agin de

4. Barrelmaker.

current tell de raff come along. Den I swum to de stern uv it, en tuck
aholt. It clouded up en 'uz pooty dark for a little while. So I clumb up en
laid down on de planks. De men 'uz all 'way yonder in de middle, whah de
lantern wuz. De river wuz arisin' en dey wuz a good current; so I reck'n'd
'at by fo' in de mawnin' I'd be twenty-five mile down de river, en den I'd slip
in, jis' b'fo' daylight, en swim asho' en take to de woods on de Illinoi side.

"But I didn' have no luck. When we 'uz mos' down to de head er de
islan', a man begin to come aft wid de lantern. I see it warn't no use fer
to wait, so I slid overboad, en struck out fer de islan'.[5] Well, I had a
notion I could lan' mos' anywhers, but I couldn't—bank too bluff. I 'uz
mos' to de foot er de islan' b'fo' I foun' a good place. I went into de
woods en jedged I wouldn' fool wid raffs no mo', long as dey move de
lantern roun' so. I had my pipe en a plug er dog-leg, en some matches
in my cap, en dey warn't wet, so I 'uz all right."

"And so you ain't had no meat nor bread to eat all this time? Why
didn't you get mud-turkles?"

"How you gwyne to git'm? You can't slip up on um en grab um; en
how's a body gwyne to hit um wid a rock? How could a body do it in de
night? en I warn't gwyne to show mysef on de bank in de daytime."

"Well, that's so. You've had to keep in the woods all the time, of
course. Did you hear 'em shooting the cannon?"

"Oh, yes. I knowed dey was arter you. I see um go by heah; watched
um thoo de bushes."

Some young birds come along, flying a yard or two at a time and lighting. Jim said it was a sign it was going to rain. He said it was a sign when
young chickens flew that way, and so he reckoned it was the same way
when young birds done it. I was going to catch some of them, but Jim
wouldn't let me. He said it was death. He said his father laid mighty sick
once, and some of them catched a bird, and his old granny said his
father would die, and he did.

And Jim said you mustn't count the things you are going to cook for
dinner, because that would bring bad luck. The same if you shook the
table-cloth after sundown. And he said if a man owned a bee-hive, and
that man died, the bees must be told about it before sun-up next morning, or else the bees would all weaken down and quit work and die. Jim
said bees wouldn't sting idiots; but I didn't believe that, because I had
tried them lots of times myself, and they wouldn't sting me.

I had heard about some of these things before, but not all of them.
Jim knowed all kinds of signs. He said he knowed most everything. I
said it looked to me like all the signs was about bad luck, and so I asked
him if there warn't any good-luck signs. He says:

"Mighty few—an' *dey* ain' no use to a body. What you want to know
when good luck's a-comin' for? want to keep it off?" And he said: "Ef

5. Huck earlier locates Jackson's Island only a quarter of a mile from the Illinois shore. What is to
prevent Jim from crossing that short space to free soil? Illinois, and especially southern Illinois,
where kidnapping and slave-catching were a thriving business, enforced the Fugitive Slave Act of
1793; thus Jim, without freedom papers, would be subject to arrest and indentured labor until
claimed by his "owner." By going downriver to Cairo and then northeast up the Ohio, Jim might
also have been safer because Ohio had a far more extensive Underground Railroad than any
other state. This plan, however, would take Huck and Jim into territory that Mark Twain did not
know as well as the Mississippi, which may help account for why he stalled so often and so long
in the composing process.

you's got hairy arms en a hairy breas', it's a sign dat you's agwyne to be rich. Well, dey's some use in a sign like dat, 'kase it's so fur ahead. You see, maybe you's got to be po' a long time fust, en so you might git discourage' en kill yo'sef 'f you didn' know by de sign dat you gwyne to be rich bymeby."

"Have you got hairy arms and a hairy breast, Jim?"

"What's de use to ax dat question? don' you see I has?"

"Well, are you rich?"

"No, but I ben rich wunst, and gwyne to be rich agin. Wunst I had foteen dollars, but I tuck to specalat'n', en got busted out."

"What did you speculate in, Jim?"

"Well, fust I tackled stock."

"What kind of stock?"

"Why, live stock. Cattle, you know. I put ten dollars in a cow. But I ain' gwyne to resk no mo' money in stock. De cow up 'n' died on my han's."

"So you lost the ten dollars."

"No, I didn' lose it all. I on'y los' 'bout nine of it. I sole de hide en taller for a dollar en ten cents."

"You had five dollars and ten cents left. Did you speculate any more?"

"Yes. You know dat one-laigged nigger dat b'longs to ole Misto Bradish? well, he sot up a bank, en say anybody dat put in a dollar would git fo' dollars mo' at de en' er de year. Well, all de niggers went in, but dey didn' have much. I wuz de on'y one dat had much. So I stuck out for mo' dan fo' dollars, en I said 'f I didn' git it I'd start a bank mysef. Well o' course dat nigger want' to keep me out er de business, bekase he say dey warn't business 'nough for two banks, so he say I could put in my five dollars en he pay me thirty-five at de en' er de year.

"So I done it. Den I reck'n'd I'd inves' de thirty-five dollars right off en keep things a-movin'. Dey wuz a nigger name' Bob, dat had ketched a wood-flat,[6] en his marster didn' know it; en I bought it off'n him en told him to take de thirty-five dollars when de en' er de year come; but somebody stole de wood-flat dat night, en nex' day de one-laigged nigger say de bank 's busted. So dey didn' none uv us git no money."

"What did you do with the ten cents, Jim?"

"Well, I 'uz gwyne to spen' it, but I had a dream, en de dream tole me to give it to a nigger name' Balum—Balum's Ass[7] dey call him for short, he's one er dem chuckle-heads, you know. But he's lucky, dey say, en I see I warn't lucky. De dream say let Balum inves' de ten cents en he'd make a raise for me. Well, Balum he tuck de money, en when he wuz in church he hear de preacher say dat whoever give to de po' len' to de Lord, en boun' to git his money back a hund'd times. So Balum he tuck en give de ten cents to de po', en laid low to see what wuz gwyne to come of it."

"Well, what did come of it, Jim?"

"Nuffn' never come of it. I couldn' manage to k'leck dat money no way; en Balum he couldn'. I ain' gwyne to len' no mo' money 'dout I see

6. A flat-bottomed boat for transporting lumber.
7. Sent to curse the Israelites (Numbers 22.21–34), Balaam was blind to the presence of God's avenging angel, and the ass was the true seer. Mark Twain burlesques the prophet's role here, but in Chapter X Jim accurately foretells serious danger.

MISTO BRADISH'S NIGGER.

de security. Boun' to git yo' money back a hund'd times, de preacher says! Ef I could git de ten *cents* back, I'd call it squah, en be glad er de chanst."

"Well, it's all right, anyway, Jim, long as you're going to be rich again some time or other."

"Yes—en I's rich now, come to look at it. I owns mysef, en I's wuth eight hund'd dollars. I wisht I had de money, I wouldn' want no mo'."

Chapter IX.

EXPLORING THE CAVE.

I wanted to go and look at a place right about the middle of the island, that I'd found when I was exploring; so we started, and soon got to it, because the island was only three miles long and a quarter of a mile wide.

This place was a tolerable long steep hill or ridge, about forty foot high. We had a rough time getting to the top, the sides was so steep and the bushes so thick. We tramped and clumb around all over it, and by and by found a good big cavern in the rock, most up to the top on the side towards Illinois. The cavern was as big as two or three rooms bunched together, and Jim could stand up straight in it. It was cool in there. Jim was for putting our traps in there, right away, but I said we didn't want to be climbing up and down there all the time.

Jim said if we had the canoe hid in a good place, and had all the traps in the cavern, we could rush there if anybody was to come to the island, and they would never find us without dogs. And besides, he said them little birds had said it was going to rain, and did I want the things to get wet?

So we went back and got the canoe and paddled up abreast the cavern, and lugged all the traps up there. Then we hunted up a place close by to hide the canoe in, amongst the thick willows. We took some fish off of the lines and set them again, and begun to get ready for dinner.

The door of the cavern was big enough to roll a hogshead in, and on one side of the door the floor stuck out a little bit and was flat and a good place to build a fire on. So we built it there and cooked dinner.

We spread the blankets inside for a carpet, and eat our dinner in there. We put all the other things handy at the back of the cavern. Pretty soon it darkened up and begun to thunder and lighten; so the birds was right about it. Directly it begun to rain, and it rained like all fury, too, and I never see the wind blow so. It was one of these regular summer storms. It would get so dark that it looked all blue-black out-

IN THE CAVE.

side, and lovely; and the rain would thrash along by so thick that the trees off a little ways looked dim and spider-webby; and here would come a blast of wind that would bend the trees down and turn up the pale underside of the leaves; and then a perfect ripper of a gust would follow along and set the branches to tossing their arms as if they was just wild; and next, when it was just about the bluest and blackest—*fst!* it was as bright as glory and you'd have a little glimpse of tree-tops a-plunging about, away off yonder in the storm, hundreds of yards further than you could see before; dark as sin again in a second, and now you'd hear the thunder let go with an awful crash and then go rumbling, grumbling, tumbling down the sky towards the under side of the world, like rolling empty barrels down stairs, where it's long stairs and they bounce a good deal, you know.

"Jim, this is nice," I says. "I wouldn't want to be nowhere else but here. Pass me along another hunk of fish and some hot cornbread."

"Well, you wouldn't a ben here, 'f it hadn't a ben for Jim. You'd a ben down dah in de woods widout any dinner, en gittn' mos' drownded, too, dat you would, honey. Chickens knows when it's gwyne to rain, en so do de birds, chile."[1]

The river went on raising and raising for ten or twelve days, till at last it was over the banks. The water was three or four foot deep on the island in the low places and on the Illinois bottom. On that side it was a good many miles wide; but on the Missouri side it was the same old distance across—a half a mile—because the Missouri shore was just a wall of high bluffs.

---

1. When the missing half of Mark Twain's manuscript turned up more than a hundred years after it was composed, a buried treasure came to light at this point in the narrative. Originally, Jim here told Huck a comic ghost story about encountering a cadaver in a medical college. Though it ascribes to Jim a personal history that is found nowhere else in the book, Mark Twain excised the passage from the published version.

Daytimes we paddled all over the island in the canoe. It was mighty cool and shady in the deep woods even if the sun was blazing outside. We went winding in and out amongst the trees; and sometimes the vines hung so thick we had to back away and go some other way. Well, on every old broken-down tree, you could see rabbits, and snakes, and such things; and when the island had been overflowed a day or two, they got so tame, on account of being hungry, that you could paddle right up and put your hand on them if you wanted to; but not the snakes and turtles—they would slide off in the water. The ridge our cavern was in, was full of them. We could a had pets enough if we'd wanted them.

One night we catched a little section of a lumber raft—nice pine planks. It was twelve foot wide and about fifteen or sixteen foot long, and the top stood above water six or seven inches, a solid level floor. We could see saw-logs go by in the daylight, sometimes, but we let them go; we didn't show ourselves in daylight.

Another night, when we was up at the head of the island, just before daylight, here comes a frame house down, on the west side. She was a two-story, and tilted over, considerable. We paddled out and got aboard—clumb in at an up-stairs window. But it was too dark to see yet, so we made the canoe fast and set in her to wait for daylight.

The light begun to come before we got to the foot of the island. Then we looked in at the window. We could make out a bed, and a table, and two old chairs, and lots of things around about on the floor; and there was clothes hanging against the wall. There was something laying on the floor in the far corner that looked like a man. So Jim says:

"Hello, you!"

But it didn't budge. So I hollered again, and then Jim says:

"De man ain't asleep—he's dead. You hold still—I'll go en see."

He went and bent down and looked, and says:

"It's a dead man. Yes, indeedy; naked, too. He's ben shot in de back. I

JIM SEES A DEAD MAN.

reck'n he's ben dead two er three days. Come in, Huck, but doan' look at his face—it's too gashly."

I didn't look at him at all. Jim throwed some old rags over him, but he needn't done it; I didn't want to see him. There was heaps of old greasy cards scattered around over the floor, and old whisky bottles, and a couple of masks made out of black cloth; and all over the walls was the ignorantest kind of words and pictures, made with charcoal. There was two old dirty calico dresses, and a sun-bonnet, and some women's under-clothes, hanging against the wall, and some men's clothing, too. We put the lot into the canoe; it might come good. There was a boy's old speckled straw hat on the floor; I took that too. And there was a bottle that had had milk in it; and it had a rag stopper for a baby to suck. We would a took the bottle, but it was broke. There was a seedy old chest, and an old hair trunk with the hinges broke. They stood open, but there warn't nothing left in them that was any account. The way things was scattered about, we reckoned the people left in a hurry and warn't fixed so as to carry off most of their stuff.

We got an old tin lantern, and a butcher knife without any handle, and a bran-new Barlow knife[2] worth two bits in any store, and a lot of tallow candles, and a tin candlestick, and a gourd, and a tin cup, and a ratty old bed-quilt off the bed, and a reticule with needles and pins and beeswax and buttons and thread and all such truck in it, and a hatchet and some nails, and a fish-line as thick as my little finger, with some monstrous hooks on it, and a roll of buckskin, and a leather dog-collar, and a horse-shoe, and some vials of medicine that didn't have no label on them; and just as we was leaving I found a tolerable good curry-comb, and Jim he found a ratty old fiddle-bow, and a wooden leg. The straps was broke off of it, but barring that, it was a good enough leg, though it was too long for me and not long enough for Jim, and we couldn't find the other one, though we hunted all around.

And so, take it all around, we made a good haul. When we was ready to shove off, we was a quarter of a mile below the island, and it was pretty broad day; so I made Jim lay down in the canoe and cover up with the quilt, because if he set up, people could tell he was a nigger a good ways off. I paddled over to the Illinois shore, and drifted down most a half a mile doing it. I crept up the dead water under the bank, and hadn't no accidents and didn't see nobody. We got home all safe.

2. A one-bladed jackknife, named for the inventor.

Chapter X.

THEY FOUND EIGHT DOLLARS.

After breakfast I wanted to talk about the dead man and guess out how he come to be killed, but Jim didn't want to. He said it would fetch bad luck; and besides, he said, he might come and ha'nt us; he said a man that warn't buried was more likely to go a-ha'nting around than one that was planted and comfortable. That sounded pretty reasonable, so I didn't say no more; but I couldn't keep from studying over it and wishing I knowed who shot the man, and what they done it for.

We rummaged the clothes we'd got, and found eight dollars in silver sewed up in the lining of an old blanket overcoat. Jim said he reckoned the people in that house stole the coat, because if they'd a knowed the money was there they wouldn't a left it. I said I reckoned they killed him, too; but Jim didn't want to talk about that. I says:

"Now you think it's bad luck; but what did you say when I fetched in the snake-skin that I found on the top of the ridge day before yesterday? You said it was the worst bad luck in the world to touch a snake-skin with my hands. Well, here's your bad luck! We've raked in all this truck and eight dollars besides. I wish we could have some bad luck like this every day, Jim."

"Never you mind, honey, never you mind. Don't you git too peart. It's a-comin'. Mind I tell you, it's a-comin'."

It did come, too. It was a Tuesday that we had that talk. Well, after dinner Friday, we was laying around in the grass at the upper end of the ridge, and got out of tobacco. I went to the cavern to get some, and found a rattlesnake in there. I killed him, and curled him up on the foot of Jim's blanket, ever so natural, thinking there'd be some fun when Jim found him there. Well, by night I forgot all about the snake, and when Jim flung himself down on the blanket while I struck a light, the snake's mate was there, and bit him.

He jumped up yelling, and the first thing the light showed was the varmint curled up and ready for another spring. I laid him out in a

63

JIM AND THE SNAKE.

second with a stick, and Jim grabbed pap's whisky jug and begun to pour it down.

He was barefooted, and the snake bit him right on the heel. That all comes of my being such a fool as to not remember that wherever you leave a dead snake its mate always comes there and curls around it. Jim told me to chop off the snake's head and throw it away, and then skin the body and roast a piece of it. I done it, and he eat it and said it would help cure him. He made me take off the rattles and tie them around his wrist, too. He said that that would help. Then I slid out quiet and throwed the snakes clear away amongst the bushes; for I warn't going to let Jim find out it was all my fault, not if I could help it.

Jim sucked and sucked at the jug, and now and then he got out of his head and pitched around and yelled; but every time he come to himself he went to sucking at the jug again. His foot swelled up pretty big, and so did his leg; but by and by the drunk begun to come, and so I judged he was all right; but I'd druther been bit with a snake than pap's whisky.

Jim was laid up for four days and nights. Then the swelling was all gone and he was around again. I made up my mind I wouldn't ever take aholt of a snake-skin again with my hands, now that I see what had come of it. Jim said he reckoned I would believe him next time. And he said that handling a snake-skin was such awful bad luck that maybe we hadn't got to the end of it yet. He said he druther see the new moon over his left shoulder as much as a thousand times than take up a snake-skin in his hand. Well, I was getting to feel that way myself, though I've always reckoned that looking at the new moon over your left shoulder is one of the carelessest and foolishest things a body can do. Old Hank Bunker done it once, and bragged about it; and in less than two years he got drunk and fell off of the shot tower and spread himself out so that he was just a kind of a layer, as you may say; and they slid him edgeways between two barn doors for a coffin, and buried him so, so they say, but I didn't see it. Pap told me. But anyway, it all come of looking at the moon that way, like a fool.

OLD HANK BUNKER.

Well, the days went along, and the river went down between its banks again; and about the first thing we done was to bait one of the big hooks with a skinned rabbit and set it and catch a cat-fish that was as big as a man, being six foot two inches long, and weighed over two hundred pounds. We couldn't handle him, of course; he would a flung us into Illinois. We just set there and watched him rip and tear around till he drownded. We found a brass button in his stomach, and a round ball, and lots of rubbage. We split the ball open with the hatchet, and there was a spool in it. Jim said he'd had it there a long time, to coat it over so and make a ball of it. It was as big as fish as was ever catched in the Mississippi, I reckon. Jim said he hadn't ever seen a bigger one. He would a been worth a good deal over at the village. They peddle out such a fish as that by the pound in the market house there; everybody buys some of him; his meat's as white as snow and makes a good fry.

Next morning I said it was getting slow and dull, and I wanted to get a stirring up, some way. I said I reckoned I would slip over the river and find out what was going on. Jim liked that notion; but he said I must go in the dark and look sharp. Then he studied it over and said, couldn't I put on some of them old things and dress up like a girl? That was a good notion, too. So we shortened up one of the calico gowns and I turned up my trowser-legs to my knees and got into it. Jim hitched it behind with the hooks, and it was a fair fit. I put on the sun-bonnet and tied it under my chin, and then for a body to look in and see my face was like looking down a joint of stove-pipe. Jim said nobody would know me, even in the daytime, hardly. I practiced around all day to get the hang of the things, and by and by I could do pretty well in them, only Jim said I didn't walk like a girl; and he said I must quit pulling up my gown to get at my britches pocket. I took notice, and done better.

"A FAIR FIT."

I started up the Illinois shore in the canoe just after dark.

I started across to the town from a little below the ferry landing, and the drift of the current fetched me in at the bottom of the town. I tied up and started along the bank. There was a light burning in a little shanty that hadn't been lived in for a long time, and I wondered who had took up quarters there. I slipped up and peeped in at the window. There was a woman about forty year old in there, knitting by a candle that was on a pine table. I didn't know her face; she was a stranger, for you couldn't start a face in that town that I didn't know. Now this was lucky, because I was weakening; I was getting afraid I had come; people might know my voice and find me out. But if this woman had been in such a little town two days she could tell me all I wanted to know; so I knocked at the door, and made up my mind I wouldn't forget I was a girl.

Chapter XI.

"COME IN."

"COME IN," says the woman, and I did. She says:

"Take a cheer."

I done it. She looked me all over with her little shiny eyes, and says:

"What might your name be?"

"Sarah Williams."

"Where 'bouts do you live? In this neighborhood?"

"No'm. In Hookerville, seven mile below. I've walked all the way and I'm all tired out."

"Hungry, too, I reckon. I'll find you something."

"No'm, I ain't hungry. I was so hungry I had to stop two mile below here at a farm; so I ain't hungry no more. It's what makes me so late. My mother's down sick, and out of money and everything, and I come to tell my uncle Abner Moore. He lives at the upper end of the town, she says. I hain't ever been here before. Do you know him?"

"No; but I don't know everybody yet. I haven't lived here quite two weeks. It's a considerable ways to the upper end of the town. You better stay here all night. Take off your bonnet."

"No," I says, "I'll rest a while, I reckon, and go on. I ain't afeard of the dark."

She said she wouldn't let me go by myself, but her husband would be in by and by, maybe in a hour and a half, and she'd send him along with me. Then she got to talking about her husband, and about her relations up the river, and her relations down the river, and about how much better off they used to was, and how they didn't know but they'd made a mistake coming to our town, instead of letting well alone—and so on and so on, till I was afeard I had made a mistake coming to her to find out what was going on in the town; but by and by she dropped onto pap and the murder, and then I was pretty willing to let her clatter right along. She told about me and Tom Sawyer finding the six thousand dollars (only she got it ten) and all about pap and what a hard lot he was, and what a hard lot I was, and at last she got down to where I was murdered. I says:

"Who done it? We've heard considerable about these goings on, down in Hookerville, but we don't know who 'twas that killed Huck Finn."

67

"Well, I reckon there's a right smart chance of people *here* that'd like to know who killed him. Some thinks old Finn done it himself."

"No—is that so?"

"Most everybody thought it at first. He'll never know how nigh he come to getting lynched. But before night they changed around and judged it was done by a runaway nigger named Jim."

"Why *he*—"

I stopped. I reckoned I better keep still. She run on, and never noticed I had put in at all.

"The nigger run off the very night Huck Finn was killed. So there's a reward out for him—three hundred dollars. And there's a reward out for old Finn too—two hundred dollars. You see, he come to town the morning after the murder, and told about it, and was out with 'em on the ferry-boat hunt, and right away after he up and left. Before night they wanted to lynch him, but he was gone, you see. Well, next day they found out the nigger was gone; they found out he hadn't ben seen sence ten o'clock the night the murder was done. So then they put it on him, you see, and while they was full of it, next day back comes old Finn and went boo-hooing to Judge Thatcher to get money to hunt for the nigger all over Illinois with. The judge give him some, and that evening he got drunk and was around till after midnight with a couple of mighty hard looking strangers, and then went off with them. Well, he hain't come back sence, and they ain't looking for him back till this thing blows over a little, for people thinks now that he killed his boy and fixed things so folks would think robbers done it, and then he'd get Huck's money without having to bother a long time with a lawsuit. People do say he warn't any too good to do it. Oh, he's sly, I reckon. If he don't come back for a year, he'll be all right. You can't prove anything on him, you know; everything will be quieted down then, and he'll walk into Huck's money as easy as nothing."

"Yes, I reckon so, 'm. I don't see nothing in the way of it. Has everybody quit thinking the nigger done it?"

"Oh, no, not everybody. A good many thinks he done it. But they'll get the nigger pretty soon, now, and maybe they can scare it out of him."

"Why, are they after him yet?"

"Well, you're innocent, ain't you! Does three hundred dollars lay round every day for people to pick up? Some folks thinks the nigger ain't far from here. I'm one of them—but I hain't talked it around. A few days ago I was talking with an old couple that lives next door in the log shanty, and they happened to say hardly anybody ever goes to that island over yonder that they call Jackson's Island. Don't anybody live there? says I. No, nobody, says they. I didn't say any more, but I done some thinking. I was pretty near certain I'd seen smoke over there, about the head of the island, a day or two before that, so I says to myself, like as not that nigger's hiding over there; anyway, says I, it's worth the trouble to give the place a hunt. I hain't seen any smoke sence, so I reckon maybe he's gone, if it was him; but husband's going over to see—him and another man. He was gone up the river; but he got back to-day and I told him as soon as he got here two hours ago."

I had got so uneasy I couldn't set still. I had to do something with my hands; so I took up a needle off of the table and went to threading it.

My hands shook, and I was making a bad job of it. When the woman stopped talking, I looked up, and she was looking at me pretty curious, and smiling a little. I put down the needle and thread and let on to be interested—and I was, too—and says:

"Three hundred dollars is a power of money. I wish my mother could get it. Is your husband going over there to-night?"

"Oh, yes. He went up town with the man I was telling you of, to get a boat and see if they could borrow another gun. They'll go over after midnight."

"Couldn't they see better if they was to wait till daytime?"

"Yes. And couldn't the nigger see better, too? After midnight he'll likely be asleep, and they can slip around through the woods and hunt up his camp fire all the better for the dark, if he's got one."

"I didn't think of that."

"HIM AND ANOTHER MAN."

The woman kept looking at me pretty curious, and I didn't feel a bit comfortable. Pretty soon she says:

"What did you say your name was, honey?"

"M—Mary Williams."

Somehow it didn't seem to me that I said it was Mary before, so I didn't look up; seemed to me I said it was Sarah; so I felt sort of cornered, and was afeared maybe I was looking it, too. I wished the woman would say something more; the longer she set still, the uneasier I was. But now she says:

"Honey, I thought you said it was Sarah when you first come in?"

"Oh, yes'm, I did. Sarah Mary Williams. Sarah's my first name. Some calls me Sarah, some calls me Mary."

"Oh, that's the way of it?"

"Yes'm."

I was feeling better, then, but I wished I was out of there, anyway. I couldn't look up yet.

Well, the woman fell to talking about how hard times was, and how poor they had to live, and how the rats was as free as if they owned the place, and so forth, and so on, and then I got easy again. She was right about the rats. You'd see one stick his nose out of a hole in the corner every little while. She said she had to have things handy to throw at them when she was alone, or they wouldn't give her no peace. She showed me a bar of lead, twisted up into a knot, and said she was a good shot with it generly, but she'd wrenched her arm a day or two ago, and didn't know whether she could throw true, now. But she watched for a chance, and directly she banged away at a rat, but she missed him wide, and said "Ouch!" it hurt her arm so. Then she told me to try for the next one. I wanted to be getting away before the old man got back, but of course I didn't let on. I got the thing, and the first rat that showed his nose I let drive, and if he'd a stayed where he was he'd a been a tolerable sick rat. She said that that was first-rate, and she reckoned I would hive the next one. She went and got the lump of lead and fetched it back and brought along a hank of yarn, which she wanted me to help her with. I held up my two hands and she put the hank over them and went on talking about her and her husband's matters. But she broke off to say:

"Keep your eye on the rats. You better have the lead in your lap, handy."

So she dropped the lump into my lap, just at that moment, and I clapped my legs together on it and she went on talking. But only about a minute. Then she took off the hank and looked me straight in the face, but very pleasant, and says:

"Come, now—what's your real name?"

"Wh-what, mum?"

"What's your real name? Is it Bill, or Tom, or Bob?—or what is it?"

I reckon I shook like a leaf, and I didn't know hardly what to do. But I says:

"Please to don't poke fun at a poor girl like me, mum. If I'm in the way, here, I'll—"

"No, you won't. Set down and stay where you are. I ain't going to hurt you, and I ain't going to tell on you, nuther. You just tell me your secret, and trust me. I'll keep it; and what's more, I'll help you. So'll my old man, if you want him to. You see, you're a runaway 'prentice—that's all. It ain't anything. There ain't any harm in it. You've been treated bad, and you made up your mind to cut. Bless you, child, I wouldn't tell on you. Tell me all about it, now—that's a good boy."

So I said it wouldn't be no use to try to play it any longer, and I would just make a clean breast and tell her everything, but she mustn't go back on her promise. Then I told her my father and mother was dead, and the law had bound me out to a mean old farmer in the country thirty mile back from the river, and he treated me so bad I couldn't stand it no longer; he went away to be gone a couple of days, and so I took my chance and stole some of his daughter's old clothes, and cleared out, and I had been three nights coming the thirty miles; I traveled nights, and hid day-times and slept, and the bag of bread and meat I carried from home lasted me all the way and I had a plenty. I said I believed my uncle Abner Moore would take care of me, and so that was why I struck out for this town of Goshen.

"Goshen, child? This ain't Goshen. This is St. Petersburg. Goshen's ten mile further up the river. Who told you this was Goshen?"

"Why, a man I met at day-break this morning, just as I was going to turn into the woods for my regular sleep. He told me when the roads forked I must take the right hand, and five mile would fetch me to Goshen."

"He was drunk I reckon. He told you just exactly wrong."

"Well, he did act like he was drunk, but it ain't no matter now. I got to be moving along. I'll fetch Goshen before day-light."

"Hold on a minute. I'll put you up a snack to eat. You might want it."

So she put me up a snack, and says:

"Say—when a cow's laying down, which end of her gets up first? Answer up prompt, now—don't stop to study over it. Which end gets up first?"

"The hind end, mum."

"Well, then, a horse?"

"The for'rard end, mum."

"Which side of a tree does the most moss grow on?"

"North side."

SHE PUTS UP A SNACK.

"If fifteen cows is browsing on a hillside, how many of them eats with their heads pointed the same direction?"

"The whole fifteen, mum."

"Well, I reckon you *have* lived in the country. I thought maybe you was trying to hocus me again. What's your real name, now?"

"George Peters, mum."

"Well, try to remember it, George. Don't forget and tell me it's Elexander before you go, and then get out by saying it's George-Elexander when I catch you. And don't go about women in that old calico. You do a girl tolerable poor, but you might fool men, maybe. Bless you, child, when you set out to thread a needle, don't hold the thread still and fetch the needle up to it; hold the needle still and poke the thread at it—that's the way a woman most always does; but a man always does t'other way. And when you throw at a rat or anything, hitch yourself up a tip-toe, and fetch your hand up over your head as awkard as you can, and miss your rat about six or seven foot. Throw stiff-armed from the shoulder, like there was a pivot there for it to turn on—like a girl; not from the wrist and elbow, with your arm out to one side, like a boy. And mind you, when a girl tries to catch anything in her lap, she throws her knees apart; she don't clap them together, the way you did when you catched the lump of lead. Why, I spotted you for a boy when you was threading the needle; and I contrived the other things just to make certain. Now trot along to your uncle, Sarah Mary Williams George Elexander Peters, and if you get into trouble you send word to Mrs. Judith Loftus, which is me, and I'll do what I can to get you out of it. Keep the river road, all the way, and next time you tramp, take shoes and socks with you. The river road's a rocky one, and your feet'll be in a condition when you get to Goshen, I reckon."

I went up the bank about fifty yards, and then I doubled on my tracks and slipped back to where my canoe was, a good piece below the house. I jumped in and was off in a hurry. I went up stream far enough to make the head of the island, and then started across. I took off the sun-bonnet, for I didn't want no blinders on, then. When I was about the middle, I hear the clock begin to strike; so I stops and listens; the sound come faint over the water, but clear—eleven. When I struck the head of the island I never waited to blow, though I was most winded, but I shoved right into the timber where my old camp used to be, and started a good fire there on a high-and-dry spot.

Then I jumped in the canoe and dug out for our place a mile and a half below, as hard as I could go. I landed, and slopped through the timber and up the ridge and into the cavern. There Jim laid, sound asleep on the ground. I roused him out and says:

"Git up and hump yourself, Jim! There ain't a minute to lose. They're after us!"

Jim never asked no questions, he never said a word; but the way he worked for the next half an hour showed about how he was scared. By that time everything we had in the world was on our raft and she was ready to be shoved out from the willow cove where she was hid. We put out the camp fire at the cavern the first thing, and didn't show a candle outside after that.

I took the canoe out from shore a little piece and took a look, but if there was a boat around I couldn't see it, for stars and shadows ain't good to see by. Then we got out the raft and slipped along down in the shade, past the foot of the island dead still, never saying a word.

"HUMP YOURSELF!"

Chapter XII.

ON THE RAFT.

MUST a been close onto one o'clock when we got below the island at last, and the raft did seem to go mighty slow. If a boat was to come along, we was going to take to the canoe and break for the Illinois shore; and it was well a boat didn't come, for we hadn't ever thought to put the gun into the canoe, or a fishing-line or anything to eat. We was in ruther too much of a sweat to think of so many things. It warn't good judgment to put *everything* on the raft.

If the men went to the island, I just expect they found the camp fire I built, and watched it all night for Jim to come. Anyways, they stayed away from us, and if my building the fire never fooled them it warn't no fault of mine. I played it as low-down on them as I could.

When the first streak of day begun to show, we tied up to a tow-head in a big bend on the Illinois side, and hacked off cotton-wood branches with the hatchet and covered up the raft with them so she looked like there had been a cave-in in the bank there. A tow-head is a sand-bar that has cotton-woods on it as thick as harrow-teeth.

We had mountains on the Missouri shore and heavy timber on the Illinois side, and the channel was down the Missouri shore at that place, so we warn't afraid of anybody running across us. We laid there all day and watched the rafts and steamboats spin down the Missouri shore, and up-bound steamboats fight the big river in the middle. I told Jim all about the time I had jabbering with that woman; and Jim said she was a smart one, and if she was to start after us herself *she* wouldn't set down and watch a camp fire—no, sir, she'd fetch a dog. Well, then, I said, why couldn't she tell her husband to fetch a dog? Jim said he bet she did think of it by the time the men was ready to start, and he believed they must a gone up town to get a dog and so they lost all that time, or else we would-n't be here on a tow-head sixteen or seventeen mile below the vil-lage—no, indeedy, we would be in that same old town again. So I said I didn't care what was the reason they didn't get us, as long as they didn't.

When it was beginning to come on dark, we poked our heads out of the cottonwood thicket and looked up, and down, and across; nothing in sight; so Jim took up some of the top planks of the raft and built a snug wigwam to get under in blazing weather and rainy, and to keep the things dry. Jim made a floor for the wigwam, and raised it a foot or more above the level of the raft, so now the blankets and all the traps was out of the reach of steamboat waves. Right in the middle of the wigwam we made a layer of dirt about five or six inches deep with a frame around it for to hold it to its place; this was to build a fire on in sloppy weather or chilly; the wigwam would keep it from being seen. We made an extra steering oar, too, because one of the others might get broke, on a snag or something. We fixed up a short forked stick to hang the old lantern on; because we must always light the lantern whenever we see a steamboat coming down stream, to keep from getting run over; but we wouldn't have to light it for up-stream boats unless we see we was in what they call a "crossing;" for the river was pretty high yet, very low banks being still a little under water; so up-bound boats didn't always run the channel, but hunted easy water.

This second night we run between seven and eight hours, with a current that was making over four mile an hour. We catched fish, and talked, and we took a swim now and then to keep off sleepiness. It was kind of solemn, drifting down the big still river, laying on our backs looking up at the stars, and we didn't ever feel like talking loud, and it warn't often that we laughed, only a little kind of a low chuckle. We had mighty good weather, as a general thing, and nothing ever happened to us at all, that night, nor the next, nor the next.

Every night we passed towns, some of them away up on black hillsides, nothing but just a shiny bed of lights, not a house could you see. The fifth night we passed St. Louis, and it was like the whole world lit up. In St. Petersburg they used to say there was twenty or thirty thousand people in St. Louis, but I never believed it till I see that wonderful spread of lights at two o'clock that still night. There warn't a sound there; everybody was asleep.

Every night, now, I used to slip ashore, towards ten o'clock, at some little village, and buy ten or fifteen cents' worth of meal or bacon or other stuff to eat; and sometimes I lifted a chicken that warn't roosting comfortable, and took him along. Pap always said, take a chicken when you get a chance, because if you don't want him yourself you can easy find somebody that does, and a good deed ain't ever forgot. I never see pap when he didn't want the chicken himself, but that is what he used to say, anyway.

Mornings, before daylight, I slipped into corn fields and borrowed a watermelon, or a mushmelon, or a punkin, or some new corn, or things of that kind. Pap always said it warn't no harm to borrow things, if you was meaning to pay them back, sometime; but the widow said it warn't anything but a soft name for stealing, and no decent body would do it. Jim said he reckoned the widow was partly right and pap was partly right; so the best way would be for us to pick out two or three things from the list and say we wouldn't borrow them any more—then he reckoned it wouldn't be no harm to borrow the others. So we talked it over all one night, drifting along down the river, trying to make up our minds

HE SOMETIMES LIFTED A CHICKEN.

whether to drop the watermelons, or the cantelopes, or the mushmelons, or what. But towards daylight we got it all settled satisfactory, and concluded to drop crabapples and p'simmons. We warn't feeling just right, before that, but it was all comfortable now. I was glad the way it come out, too, because crabapples ain't ever good, and the p'simmons wouldn't be ripe for two or three months yet.

We shot a water-fowl, now and then, that got up too early in the morning or didn't go to bed early enough in the evening. Take it all around, we lived pretty high.[1]

The fifth night below St. Louis we had a big storm after midnight, with a power of thunder and lightning, and the rain poured down in a solid sheet. We stayed in the wigwam and let the raft take care of itself. When the lightning glared out we could see a big straight river ahead, and high rocky bluffs on both sides. By and by says I, "He1-*lo*, Jim, looky yonder!" It was a steamboat that had killed herself on a rock. We was drifting straight down for her. The lightning showed her very distinct. She was leaning over, with part of her upper deck above water, and you could see every little chimbly-guy[2] clean and clear, and a chair by the big bell, with an old slouch hat hanging on the back of it when the flashes come.

Well, it being away in the night, and stormy, and all so mysterious-like, I felt just the way any other boy would a felt, when I see that wreck laying there so mournful and lonesome in the middle of the river: I

1. Inserted retrospectively in the manuscript, the second half of this chapter and the next two chapters were not written until the summer of 1883, the period in which Mark Twain finally completed his narrative, including the controversial ending.
2. Wires bracing the chimneys.

wanted to get aboard of her and slink around a little, and see what there was there. So I says:

"Le's land on her, Jim."

But Jim was dead against it, at first. He says:

"I doan want to go fool'n 'long er no wrack. We's doin' blame' well, en we better let blame' well alone, as de good book says. Like as not dey's a watchman on dat wrack."

"Watchman your grandmother," I says; "there ain't nothing to watch but the texas[3] and the pilot house; and do you reckon anybody's going to resk his life for a texas and a pilot house such a night as this, when it's likely to break up and wash off down the river any minute?" Jim couldn't say nothing to that, so he didn't try. "And besides," I says, "we might borrow something worth having, out of the captain's stateroom. Seegars, *I* bet you—and cost five cents apiece, solid cash. Steamboat captains is always rich, and get sixty dollars a month, and *they* don't care a cent what a thing costs, you know, long as they want it. Stick a candle in your pocket; I can't rest, Jim, till we give her a rummaging. Do you reckon Tom Sawyer would ever go by this thing? Not for pie, he wouldn't. He'd call it an adventure—that's what he'd call it; and he'd land on that wreck if it was his last act. And wouldn't he throw style into it?—wouldn't he spread himself, nor nothing? Why, you'd think it was Christopher C'lumbus discovering Kingdom-Come. I wish Tom Sawyer *was* here."

Jim he grumbled a little, but give in. He said we mustn't talk any more than we could help, and then talk mighty low. The lightning showed us the wreck again, just in time, and we fetched the starboard derrick, and made fast there.

The deck was high out, here. We went sneaking down the slope of it to labboard, in the dark, towards the texas, feeling our way slow with our feet, and spreading our hands out to fend off the guys, for it was so dark we couldn't see no sign of them. Pretty soon we struck the forward end of the skylight, and clumb onto it; and the next step fetched us in front of the captain's door, which was open; and by jimminy, away down through the texas hall we see a light! and all in the same second we seem to hear low voices in yonder!

Jim whispered and said he was feeling powerful sick; and told me to come along. I says, all right; and was going to start for the raft; but just then I heard a voice wail out and say:

"O, please don't, boys; I swear I won't ever tell!"

Another voice said, pretty loud:

"It's a lie, Jim Turner. You've acted this way before. You always want more'n your share of the truck, and you've always got it, too, because you've swore't if you didn't you'd tell. But this time you've said it jist one time too many. You're the meanest, treacherousest hound in this country."

By this time Jim was gone for the raft. I was just a-biling with curiosity; and I says to myself, Tom Sawyer wouldn't back out now, and so I won't either; I'm agoing to see what's going on here. So I dropped on my hands and knees, in the little passage, and crept aft in the dark, till there warn't but about one stateroom betwixt me and the cross-hall of

---

3. Officer's cabin on the upper deck of the steamboat. The pilot house on a Mississippi steamboat was usually on top of the texas; the "skylight," which Huck and Jim reach first, was part of the "texas deck."

the texas. Then, in there I see a man stretched on the floor and tied hand and foot, and two men standing over him, and one of them had a dim lantern in his hand, and the other one had a pistol. This one kept pointing the pistol at the man's head on the floor and saying,—

"I'd *like* to! And I orter, too, a mean skunk!"

The man on the floor would shrivel up and say, "O, please don't, Bill—I hain't ever goin' to tell."

And every time he said that, the man with the lantern would laugh, and say:

" 'Deed you *ain't!* You never said no truer thing 'n that, you bet you." And once he said: "Hear him beg! and yit if we hadn't got the best of him and tied him, he'd a killed us both. And what *for?* Jist for noth'n'. Jist because we stood on our *rights*—that's what for. But I lay you ain't agoin' to threaten nobody any more, Jim Turner. Put *up* that pistol, Bill."

"PLEASE DON'T, BILL."

Bill says:

"I don't want to, Jake Packard. I'm for killin' him—and didn't he kill old Hatfield jist the same way—and don't he deserve it?"

"But I don't *want* him killed, and I've got my reasons for it."

"Bless yo' heart for them words, Jake Packard!—I'll never forgit you, long's I live!" says the man on the floor, sort of blubbering.

Packard didn't take no notice of that, but hung up his lantern on a nail, and started towards where I was, there in the dark, and motioned Bill to come. I crawfished as fast as I could, about two yards, but the boat slanted so that I couldn't make very good time; so, to keep from getting run over and catched, I crawled into a stateroom on the upper side. The men come a-pawing along in the dark, and when Packard got to my stateroom, he says:

"Here—come in here."

And in he come, and Bill after him. But before they got in, I was up in the upper berth, cornered, and sorry I come. Then they stood there, with their hands on the ledge of the berth, and talked. I couldn't see them, but I could tell where they was, and how close they was, by the whisky they'd been having. I was glad I didn't drink whisky; but it wouldn't made much difference, anyway, because most of the time they couldn't a treed me, because I didn't breathe. I was too scared. And besides, a body *couldn't* breathe, and hear such talk. They talked low and earnest. Bill wanted to kill Turner. He says:

"He's said he'll tell, and he will. If we was to give both our shares to him, *now*, it wouldn't make no difference, after the row, and the way we've served him. Shore's you're born, he'll turn State's evidence, now you hear *me*. I'm for putting him out of his troubles."

"So'm I," says Packard, very quiet.

"Blame it, I'd sorter begun to think you wasn't. Well, then, that's all right. Le's go and do it."

"Hold on, a minute; I hain't had my say, yit. You listen to me. Shooting's good, but there's quieter ways, if the thing's *got* to be done. But what *I* say, is this: it ain't good sense to go court'n around after a halter, if you can git at what you're up to in some way that's jist as good and at the same time don't bring you into no resks. Ain't that so?"

"You bet it is. But how you goin' to manage it this time?"

"Well, my idea is this: we'll rustle around and gether up whatever pickins we've overlooked in the staterooms, and shove for shore and hide the truck. Then we'll wait. Now I say it ain't agoin' to be more'n two hours befo' this wrack breaks up and washes off down the river.

"IT AIN'T GOOD MORALS."

See? He'll be drownded, and won't have nobody to blame for it but his own self. I reckon that's a considerable sight better'n killin' of him. I'm unfavorable to killin' a man as long as you can git around it; it ain't good sense, it ain't good morals. Ain't I right?"

"Yes—I reck'n you are. But s'pose she *don't* break up and wash off?"

"Well, we can wait the two hours, anyway, and see, can't we?"

"All right, then; come along."

So they started, and I lit out, all in a cold sweat, and scrambled forward. It was dark as pitch there; but I said, in a kind of a coarse whisper, "Jim!" and he answered up, right at my elbow, with a sort of a moan, and I says:

"Quick, Jim, it ain't no time for fooling around and moaning; there's a gang of murderers in yonder, and if we don't hunt up their boat and set her drifting down the river so these fellows can't get away from the wreck, there's one of 'em going to be in a bad fix. But if we find their boat we can put *all* of 'em in a bad fix—for the Sheriff 'll get 'em. Quick—hurry! I'll hunt the labboard side, you hunt the stabboard. You start at the raft, and—"

"O my lordy, lordy! *Raf'*? Dey ain' no raf' no mo', she done broke loose en gone!—en here we is!"

"O MY LORDY, LORDY!"

Chapter XIII

IN A FIX.

WELL, I catched my breath, and most fainted. Shut up on a wreck with such a gang as that! But it warn't no time to be sentimentering. We'd *got* to find that boat, now—had to have it for ourselves. So we went a-quaking and shaking down the stabboard side, and slow work it was, too—seemed a week before we got to the stern. No sign of a boat. Jim said he didn't believe he could go any further—so scared he hadn't hardly any strength left, he said. But I said come on, if we get left on this wreck, we are in a fix, sure. So on we prowled, again. We struck for the stern of the texas, and found it, and then scrabbled along forwards on the skylight, hanging on from shutter to shutter, for the edge of the skylight was in the water. When we got pretty close to the cross-hall door, there was the skiff, sure enough!—I could just barely see her. I felt ever so thankful. In another second I would a been aboard of her; but just then the door opened. One of the men stuck his head out, only about a couple of foot from me, and I thought I was gone; but he jerked it in again, and says:

"Heave that blame lantern out o' sight, Bill!"

He flung a bag of something into the boat, and then got in, himself, and set down. It was Packard. Then Bill *he* come out and got in. Packard says, in a low voice:

"All ready—shove off!"

I couldn't hardly hang on to the shutters, I was so weak. But Bill says:

"Hold on—'d you go through him?"

"No. Didn't you?"

"No. So he's got his share o' the cash, yet."

"Well, then, come along—no use to take truck and leave money."

"Say—won't he suspicion what we're up to?"

"Maybe he won't. But we got to have it anyway. Come along."

So they got out and went in.

The door slammed to, because it was on the careened side; and in a half second I was in the boat, and Jim come a-tumbling after me. I out with my knife and cut the rope, and away we went!

81

We didn't touch an oar, and we didn't speak nor whisper, nor hardly even breathe. We went gliding swift along, dead silent, past the tip of the paddle-box, and past the stern; then in a second or two more we was a hundred yards below the wreck, and the darkness soaked her up, every last sign of her, and we was safe, and knowed it.

When we was three or four hundred yards down stream, we see the lantern show like a little spark at the texas door, for a second, and we knowed by that that the rascals had missed their boat, and was beginning to understand that they was in just as much trouble, now, as Jim Turner was.

Then Jim manned the oars, and we took out after our raft. Now was the first time that I begun to worry about the men—I reckon I hadn't had time to, before. I begun to think how dreadful it was, even for murderers, to be in such a fix. I says to myself, there ain't no telling but I might come to be a murderer myself, yet, and then how would *I* like it? So says I to Jim:

"The first light we see, we'll land a hundred yards below it or above it, in a place where it's a good hiding place for you and the skiff, and then I'll go and fix up some kind of a yarn, and get somebody to go for that gang and get them out of their scrape, so they can be hung when their time comes."

But that idea was a failure; for pretty soon it begun to storm again, and this time worse than ever. The rain poured down, and never a light showed; everybody in bed, I reckon. We boomed along down the river, watching for lights and watching for our raft. After a long time the rain let up, but the clouds staid, and the lightning kept whimpering, and by and by a flash showed us a black thing ahead, floating, and we made for it.

It was the raft, and mighty glad was we to get aboard of it again. We seen a light, now, away down to the right, on shore. So I said I would go for it. The skiff was half full of plunder which that gang had stole, there on the wreck. We hustled it onto the raft in a pile, and I told Jim to float along down, and show a light when he judged he had gone about two mile, and keep it burning till I come; then I manned my oars and shoved for the light. As I got down towards it, three or four more showed—up on a hillside. It was a village. I closed in above the shore-light, and laid on my oars and floated. As I went by, I see it was a lantern hanging on the jack-staff of a double-hull ferry boat. Everything was dead still, nobody stirring. I floated in under the stern, made fast, and clumb aboard. I skimmed around for the watchman, a-wondering whereabouts he slept; and by and by I found him roosting on the bitts,[1] forward, with his head down between his knees. I give his shoulder two or three little shoves, and begun to cry.

He stirred up, in a kind of a startlish way; but when he see it was only me, he took a good gap and stretch, and then he says:

"Hello, what's up? Don't cry, bub. What's the trouble?"

I says:

"Pap, and mam, and sis, and—"

Then I broke down. He says:

"O, dang it, now, *don't* take on so, we all has to have our troubles, and this'n'll come out all right. What's the matter with 'em?"

"They're—they're—are you the watchman of the boat?"

---

1. Pairs of short posts with a crosspiece for securing cables.

"Yes," he says, kind of pretty-well-satisfied like, "I'm the captain, and the owner, and the mate, and the pilot, and watchman, and head deck-hand; and sometimes I'm the freight and passengers. I ain't as rich as old Jim Hornback, and I can't be so blame' generous and good to Tom, Dick and Harry as what he is, and slam around money the way he does, but I've told him a many a time 't I wouldn't trade places with him; for, says I, a sailor's life's the life for me, and I'm derned if I'd live two mile out o'town, where there ain't nothing ever goin' on, not for all his spon-dulicks[2] and as much more on top of it. Says I—"

I broke in and says:

"They're in an awful peck of trouble, and—"

"*Who* is?"

"Why, pap, and mam, and sis, and Miss Hooker; and if you'd take your ferry boat and go up there—"

"Up where? Where are they?"

"On the wreck."

"What wreck?"

"Why, there ain't but one."

"HELLO, WHAT'S UP?"

"What, you don't mean the *Walter Scott?*"[3]

"Yes."

"Good land! what are they doin' *there*, for gracious sakes?"

"Well, they didn't go there a-purpose."

"I bet they didn't! Why, great goodness, there ain't no chance for 'em if they don't git off mighty quick! Why, how in the nation did they ever git into such a scrape?"

---

2. Money, cash.

3. In Chapter XLVI of *Life on the Mississippi* (1883), Mark Twain charged that *Ivanhoe* and "the Sir Walter Scott disease" helped incite the American Civil War by infesting the South with the "sham grandeurs, sham gauds, and sham chivalries of a brainless and worthless long-vanished society."

"Easy enough. Miss Hooker was a-visiting, up there to the town—"

"Yes, Booth's Landing—go on."

"She was a visiting, there at Booth's Landing, and just in the edge of the evening she started over with her nigger woman in the horse—ferry, to stay all night at her friend's house, Miss What-you-may-call-her, I disremember her name, and they lost their steering-oar, and swung around and went a-floating down, stern-first, about two mile, and saddle-baggsed on the wreck, and the ferry man and the nigger woman and the horses was all lost, but Miss Hooker she made a grab and got aboard the wreck. Well, about an hour after dark, we come along down in our trading-scow, and it was so dark we didn't notice the wreck till we was right on it; and so *we* saddle-baggsed; but all of us was saved but Bill Whipple—and oh, he *was* the best cretur!—I most wish't it had been me, I do."

"My George! it's the beatenest thing I ever struck. And *then* what did you all do?"

"Well, we hollered and took on, but it's so wide, there, we couldn't make nobody hear. So pap said somebody got to get ashore and get help, somehow. I was the only one that could swim; so I made a dash for it, and Miss Hooker she said if I didn't strike help sooner, come here and hunt up her uncle, and he'd fix the thing. I made the land about a mile below, and been fooling along ever since, trying to get people to do something, but they said, 'What, in such a night and such a current? there ain't no sense in it; go for the steam-ferry.' Now if you'll go, and—"

"By Jackson, I'd *like* to, and blame it I don't know but I will; but who in the dingnation's agoin' to *pay* for it? Do you reckon your pap—"

"Why *that's* all right. Miss Hooker she told me, *particular*, that her uncle Hornback—"

"Great guns! is *he* her uncle? Looky here, you break for that light over yonder-way, and turn out west when you git there, and about a quarter of a mile out you'll come to the tavern; tell 'em to dart you out to Jim Hornback's, and he'll foot the bill. And don't you fool around any, because he'll want to know the news. Tell him I'll have his niece all safe

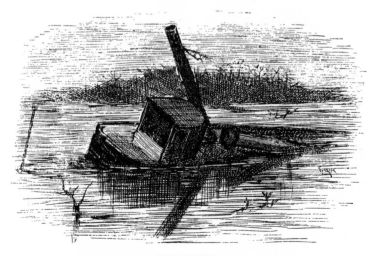

THE WRECK.

before he can get to town. Hump yourself, now; I'm agoing up around the corner, here, to roust out my engineer."

I struck for the light, but as soon as he turned the corner I went back and got into my skiff and bailed her out and then pulled up shore in the easy water about six hundred yards, and tucked myself in among some woodboats; for I couldn't rest easy till I could see the ferryboat start. But take it all around, I was feeling ruther comfortable, on accounts of taking all this trouble for that gang, for not many would a done it. I wished the widow knowed about it. I judged she would be proud of me for helping these rapscallions, because rapscallions and dead beats is the kind the widow and good people takes the most interest in.

Well, before long, here comes the wreck, dim and dusky, sliding along down! A kind of cold shiver went through me, and then I struck out for her. She was very deep, and I see in a minute there warn't much chance for anybody being alive in her. I pulled all around her, and hollered a little, but there wasn't any answer; all dead still. I felt a little bit heavy-hearted about the gang, but not much, for I reckoned if they could stand it, I could.

Then here comes the ferryboat; so I shoved for the middle of the river on a long down-stream slant; and when I judged I was out of eye-reach, I laid on my oars, and looked back and see her go and smell around the wreck for Miss Hooker's remainders, because the captain would know her uncle Hornback would want them; and then pretty soon the ferryboat give it up and went for shore, and I laid into my work and went a-booming down the river.

It did seem a powerful long time before Jim's light showed up; and when it did show, it looked like it was a thousand mile off. By the time I got there the sky was beginning to get a little gray in the east; so we struck for an island, and hid the raft, and sunk the skiff, and turned in and slept like dead people.

WE TURNED IN AND SLEPT.

Chapter XIV.

B Y AND BY, when we got up, we turned over the truck the gang had stole off of the wreck, and found boots, and blankets, and clothes, and all sorts of other things, and a lot of books, and a spyglass and three boxes of seegars. We hadn't ever been this rich before, in neither of our lives. The seegars was prime. We laid off all the afternoon in the woods, talking, and me reading the books, and having a general good time. I told Jim all about what happened inside the wreck, and at the ferryboat; and I said these kinds of things was adventures; but he said he didn't want no more adventures. He said that when I went in the texas and he crawled back to get on the raft

TURNING OVER THE TRUCK.

and found her gone, he nearly died; because he judged it was all up with *him*, anyway it could be fixed; for if he didn't get saved he would get drownded; and if he did get saved, whoever saved him would send him back home so as to get the reward, and then Miss Watson would sell him south, sure. Well, he was right; he was most always right; he had an uncommon level head, for a nigger.

I read considerable to Jim about kings, and dukes, and earls and such, and how gaudy they dressed and how much style they put on, and called each other your majesty, and your grace, and your lordship, and so on, 'stead of mister; and Jim's eyes bugged out, and he was interested. He says:

"I didn' know dey was so many un um. I hain't hearn 'bout none un um, skasely, but ole king Sollermun, onless you counts dem kings dat's in a pack er k'yards. How much do a king git?"

"Get?" I says; "why, they get a thousand dollars a month if they want it; they can have just as much as they want; everything belongs to them."

"*Ain'* dat gay? En what dey got to do, Huck?"

"*They* don't do nothing! Why, how you talk. They just set around."

"No—is dat so?"

"Of course it is. They just set around. Except maybe when there's a war; then they go to the war. But other times they just lazy around; or go hawking—just hawking and sp—Sh!—d' you hear a noise?"

We skipped out and looked; but it warn't nothing but the flutter of a steamboat's wheel away down coming around the point; so we come back.

"Yes," says I, "and other times, when things is dull, they fuss with the parlyment; and if everybody don't go just so, he whacks their heads off. But mostly they hang round the harem."

"Roun'de which?"

"Harem."

"What's de harem?"

"The place where he keeps his wives. Don't you know about the harem? Solomon had one; he had about a million wives."

"Why, yes, dat's so; I—I'd done forgot it. A harem's a bo'd'n house, I reck'n. Mos' likely dey has rackety times in de nussery. En I reck'n de wives quarrels considable; en dat 'crease de racket. Yit dey say Soller-mun de wises' man dat ever live'. I doan' take no stock in dat. Bekase

SOLOMON AND HIS MILLION WIVES.

why: would a wise man want to live in de mids' er sich a blimblammin' all de time? No—'deed he wouldn't. A wise man 'ud take en buil' a biler-factry; en den he could shet *down* de biler-factry when he want to res'."

"Well, but he *was* the wisest man, anyway; because the widow she told me so, her own self."

"I doan k'yer what de widder say, he *warn't* no wise man, nuther. He had some er de dad-fetchedes' ways I ever see. Does you know 'bout dat chile dat he 'uz gwyne to chop in two?"[1]

"Yes; the widow told me all about it."

1. I Kings 3.16–27. When two women claimed the same newborn son, King Solomon threatened to divide him with a sword, whereupon the true mother identified herself by begging him to give the child to the other woman.

"*Well*, den! Warn' dat de beatenes' notion in de worl'? You jis' take en look at it a minute. Dah's de stump, dah—dat's one er de women; heah's you—dat's de yuther one; I's Sollermun; en dishyer dollar bill's de chile. Bofe un you claims it. What does I do? Does I shin aroun' mongs' de neighbors en fine out which un you de bill *do* b'long to, en han' it over to de right one, all safe en soun', de way dat anybody dat had any gump-tion would? No—I take en whack de bill in *two*, en give half un it to you, en de yuther half to de yuther woman. Dat's de way Sollermun was gwyne to do wid de chile. Now I want to ast you: what's de use er dat half a bill?—can't buy noth'n wid it. En what use is a half a chile? I would'n give a dern for a million un um."

"But hang it, Jim; you've clean missed the point—blame it, you've missed it a thousand mile."

"Who? Me? Go 'long. Doan talk to *me* 'bout yo' pints. I reck'n I knows sense when I sees it; en dey ain' no sense in sich doin's as dat. De 'spute warn' 'bout a half a chile, de 'spute was 'bout a whole chile; en de man dat think he kin settle a 'spute 'bout a whole chile wid a half a chile, doan know enough to come in out'n de rain. Doan talk to me 'bout Sollermun, Huck, I knows him by de back."

"But I tell you you don't get the point."

"Blame de pint! I reck'n I knows what I knows. En mine you, de *real* pint is down furder—it's down deeper. It lays in de way Sollermun was

THE STORY OF "SOLLERMUN."

raised. You take a man dat's got on'y one er two chillen: is dat man gwyne to be waseful o' chillen? No, he ain't; he can't 'ford it. *He* know how to value 'em. But you take a man dat's got 'bout five million chillen runnin' roun' de house, en it's diffunt. *He* as soon chop a chile in two as a cat. Dey's plenty mo'. A chile er two, mo' er less, warn't no consekens to Sollermun, dad fetch him!"

I never see such a nigger. If he got a notion in his head once, there warn't no getting it out again. He was the most down on Solomon of any nigger I ever see. So I went to talking about other kings, and let Solomon slide. I told about Louis Sixteenth that got his head cut off in France long time ago; and about his little boy the dolphin,[2] that would a been a king, but they took and shut him up in jail, and some say he died there.

"Po' little chap."

"But some says he got out and got away, and come to America."

"Dat's good! But he'll be pooty lonesome—dey ain' no kings here, is dey, Huck?"

"No."

"Den he cain't git no situation. What he gwyne to do?"

"Well, I don't know. Some of them gets on the police, and some of them learns people how to talk French."

"Why, Huck, doan de French people talk de same way we does?"

"*No*, Jim; you couldn't understand a word they said—not a single word."

"Well, now, I be ding-busted! How do dat come?"

"*I* don't know; but it's so. I got some of their jabber out of a book. Spose a man was to come to you and say *Polly-voo-franzy*—what would you think?"

"I wouldn' think nuff'n; I'd take en bust him over de head. Dat is, ef he warn't white. I wouldn't 'low no nigger to call me dat."

"Shucks, it ain't calling you anything. It's only saying, do you know how to talk French."

"Well, den, why couldn't he *say* it?"

"Why, he *is* a-saying it. That's a Frenchman's *way* of saying it."

"Well, it's a blame' ridicklous way, en I doan want to hear no mo' 'bout it. Dey ain' no sense in it."

"Looky here, Jim, does a cat talk like we do?"

"No, a cat don't."

"Well, does a cow?"

"No, a cow don't, nuther."

"Does a cat talk like a cow, or a cow talk like a cat?"

"No, dey don't."

"It's natural and right for 'em to talk different from each other, ain't it?"

" 'Course."

"And ain't it natural and right for a cat and a cow to talk different from *us*?"

"Why, mos' sholy it is."

"Well, then, why ain't it natural and right for a *Frenchman* to talk different from us?—you answer me that."

"Is a cat a man, Huck?"

2. The dauphin, Louis Charles (1785–1795?), survived the execution of his guillotined father, Louis XVI, in 1793 but almost certainly died in prison. Rumors of his escape and survival persisted, however, and imposters claiming to be the lost dauphin turned up even in frontier America. One "Aminidab Fitz-Louis Dolphin Borebon," for example, is mentioned as the "Dolphin" in the Hannibal, Mo., *Journal* of 1853.

"No."

"Well, den, dey ain't no sense in a cat talkin' like a man. Is a cow a man?—er is a cow a cat?"

"No, she ain't either of them."

"Well, den, she ain' got no business to talk like either one er the yuther of 'em. Is a Frenchman a man?"

"Yes."

"*Well*, den! Dad blame it, why doan he *talk* like a man?—you answer me *dat!*"

I see it warn't no use wasting words—you can't learn a nigger to argue. So I quit.

Chapter XV.

"WE WOULD SELL THE RAFT."

WE JUDGED that three nights more would fetch us to Cairo,[1] at the bottom of Illinois, where the Ohio River comes in, and that was what we was after. We would sell the raft and get on a steamboat and go way up the Ohio amongst the free States, and then be out of trouble.

Well, the second night a fog begun to come on, and we made for a tow-head to tie to, for it wouldn't do to try to run in fog; but when I paddled ahead in the canoe, with the line, to make fast, there wasn't anything but little saplings to tie to. I passed the line around one of them right on the edge of the cut bank, but there was a stiff current, and the raft come booming down so lively she tore it out by the roots and away she went. I see the fog closing down, and it made me so sick and scared I couldn't budge for most a half a minute it seemed to me— and then there wasn't no raft in sight; you couldn't see twenty yards. I jumped into the canoe and run back to the stern and grabbed the paddle and set her back a stroke. But she didn't come. I was in such a hurry I hadn't untied her. I got up and tried to untie her, but I was so excited my hands shook so I couldn't hardly do anything with them.

As soon as I got started I took out after the raft, hot and heavy, right down the tow-head. That was all right as far as it went, but the tow-head warn't sixty yards long, and the minute I flew by the foot of it I shot out into the solid white fog, and hadn't no more idea which way I was going than a dead man.

Thinks I, it won't do to paddle; first I know I'll run into the bank or a tow-head or something; I got to set still and float, and yet it's mighty fidgety business to have to hold your hands still at such a time. I whooped and listened. Away down there, somewheres, I hears a small whoop, and up comes my spirits. I went tearing after it, listening sharp to hear it again. The next time it come, I see I warn't heading for it but heading away to the right of it. And the next time, I was heading away to the left of it—and not gaining on it much, either, for I was flying

1. Pronounced "Kay-row."

91

around, this way and that and t' other, but it was going straight ahead all the time.

I did wish the fool would think to beat a tin pan, and beat it all the time, but he never did, and it was the still places between the whoops that was making the trouble for me. Well, I fought along, and directly I hears the whoop *behind* me. I was tangled good, now. That was somebody else's whoop, or else I was turned around.

I throwed the paddle down. I heard the whoop again; it was behind me yet, but in a different place; it kept coming, and kept changing its place, and I kept answering, till by and by it was in front of me again and I knowed the current had swung the canoe's head down stream and I was all right, if that was Jim and not some other raftsman hollering. I couldn't tell nothing about voices in a fog, for nothing don't look natural nor sound natural in a fog.

The whooping went on, and in about a minute I come a booming down on a cut bank with smoky ghosts of big trees on it, and the current threw me off to the left and shot by, amongst a lot of snags that fairly roared, the current was tearing by them so swift.

In another second or two it was solid white and still again. I set perfectly still, then, listening to my heart thump, and I reckon I didn't draw a breath while it thumped a hundred.

I just give up, then. I knowed what the matter was. That cut bank was an island, and Jim had gone down t'other side of it. It wasn't no towhead, that you could float by in ten minutes. It had the big timber of a regular island; it might be five or six mile long and more than a half a mile wide.

I kept quiet, with my ears cocked, about fifteen minutes, I reckon. I was floating along, of course, four or five mile an hour; but you don't ever think of that. No, you *feel* like you are laying dead still on the water; and if a little glimpse of a snag slips by, you don't think to yourself how fast *you're* going, but you catch your breath and think, my! how

AMONG THE SNAGS.

that snag's tearing along. If you think it ain't dismal and lonesome out in a fog that way, by yourself, in the night, you try it once—you'll see.

Next, for about a half an hour, I whoops now and then; at last I hears the answer a long ways off, and tries to follow it, but I couldn't do it, and directly I judged I'd got into a nest of tow-heads, for I had little dim glimpses of them on both sides of me, sometimes just a narrow channel between; and some that I couldn't see, I knowed was there, because I'd hear the wash of the current against the old dead brush and trash that hung over the banks. Well, I warn't long losing the whoops, down amongst the tow-heads; and I only tried to chase them a little while, anyway, because it was worse than chasing a Jack-o-lantern. You never knowed a sound dodge around so, and swap places so quick and so much.

I had to claw away from the bank pretty lively, four or five times, to keep from knocking the islands out of the river; and so I judged the raft must be butting into the bank every now and then, or else it would get further ahead and clear out of hearing—it was floating a little faster than what I was.

Well, I seemed to be in the open river again, by and by, but I couldn't hear no sign of a whoop nowheres. I reckoned Jim had fetched up on a snag, maybe, and it was all up with him. I was good and tired, so I laid down in the canoe and said I wouldn't bother no more. I didn't want to go to sleep, of course; but I was so sleepy I couldn't help it; so I thought I would take just one little cat-nap.

But I reckon it was more than a cat-nap, for when I waked up the stars was shining bright, the fog was all gone, and I was spinning down a big bend stern first. First I didn't know where I was; I thought I was dreaming; and when things begun to come back to me, they seemed to come up dim out of last week.

It was a monstrous big river here, with the tallest and the thickest kind of timber on both banks; just a solid wall, as well as I could see, by the stars. I looked away down stream, and seen a black speck on the water. I took out after it; but when I got to it it warn't nothing but a couple of saw-logs made fast together. Then I see another speck, and chased that; then another, and this time I was right. It was the raft.

When I got to it Jim was setting there with his head down between his knees, asleep, with his right arm hanging over the steering oar. The other oar was smashed off, and the raft was littered up with leaves and branches and dirt. So she'd had a rough time.

I made fast and laid down under Jim's nose on the raft, and begun to gap, and stretch my fists out against Jim, and says:

"Hello, Jim, have I been asleep? Why didn't you stir me up?"

"Goodness gracious, is dat you, Huck? En you ain' dead—you ain' drownded—you's back agin? It's too good for true, honey, it's too good for true. Lemme look at you, chile, lemme feel o'you. No, you ain' dead! you's back agin, live en soun', jis de same ole Huck—de same ole Huck, thanks to goodness!"

"What's the matter with you, Jim? You been a drinking?"

"Drinkin'? Has I ben a drinkin'? Has I had a chance to be a drinkin'?"

"Well, then, what makes you talk so wild?"

"How does I talk wild?"

ASLEEP ON THE RAFT.

"*How?* why, hain't you been talking about my coming back, and all that stuff, as if I'd been gone away?"

"Huck—Huck Finn, you look me in de eye; look me in de eye. *Hain't* you ben gone away?"

"Gone away? Why, what in the nation do you mean? *I* hain't been gone anywheres. Where would I go to?"

"Well, looky here, boss, dey's sumf'n wrong, dey is. Is I *me*, or who *is* I? Is I heah, or whah *is* I? Now dat's what I wants to know."

"Well, I think you're here, plain enough, but I think you're a tangle-headed old fool, Jim."

"I is, is I? Well you answer me dis. Didn't you tote out de line in de canoe, fer to make fas' to de tow-head?"

"No, I didn't. What tow-head? I hain't seen no tow-head."

"You hadn't seen no tow-head? Looky here—didn't de line pull loose en de raf' go a hummin' down de river, en leave you en de canoe behine in de fog?"

"What fog?"

"Why *de* fog. De fog dat's ben aroun' all night. En didn't you whoop, en didn't I whoop, tell we got mix' up in de islands en one un us got los' en t'other one was jis' as good as los', 'kase he didn' know whah he wuz? En didn't I bust up agin a lot er dem islands en have a turrible time en mos' git drownded? Now ain' dat so, boss—ain' it so? You answer me dat."

"Well, this is too many for me, Jim. I hain't seen no fog, nor no islands, nor no troubles, nor nothing. I been setting here talking with you all night till you went to sleep about ten minutes ago, and I reckon I done the same. You couldn't a got drunk in that time, so of course you've been dreaming."

"Dad fetch it, how is I gwyne to dream all dat in ten minutes?"

"Well, hang it all, you did dream it, because there didn't any of it happen."

"But Huck, it's all jis' as plain to me as—"

"It don't make no difference how plain it is, there ain't nothing in it. I know, because I've been here all the time."

Jim didn't say nothing for about five minutes, but set there studying over it. Then he says:

"Well, den, I reck'n I did dream it, Huck; but dog my cats ef it ain't de powerfullest dream I ever see. En I hain't ever had no dream b'fo' dat's tired me like dis one."

"Oh, well, that's all right, because a dream does tire a body like everything, sometimes. But this one was a staving dream—tell me all about it, Jim."

So Jim went to work and told me the whole thing right through, just as it happened, only he painted it up considerable. Then he said he must start in and " 'terpret" it, because it was sent for a warning. He said the first tow-head stood for a man that would try to do us some good, but the current was another man that would get us away from him. The whoops was warnings that would come to us every now and then, and if we didn't try hard to make out to understand them they'd just take us into bad luck, 'stead of keeping us out of it. The lot of tow-heads was troubles we was going to get into with quarrelsome people and all kinds of mean folks, but if we minded our business and didn't talk back and aggravate them, we would pull through and get out of the fog and into the big clear river, which was the free States, and wouldn't have no more trouble.

It had clouded up pretty dark just after I got onto the raft, but it was clearing up again, now.

"Oh, well, that's all interpreted well enough, as far as it goes, Jim," I says; "but what does *these* things stand for?"

It was the leaves and rubbish on the raft, and the smashed oar. You could see them first rate, now.

Jim looked at the trash, and then looked at me, and back at the trash again. He had got the dream fixed so strong in his head that he couldn't seem to shake it loose and get the facts back into its place again, right away. But when he did get the thing straightened around, he looked at me steady, without ever smiling, and says:

"What do dey stan' for? I's gwyne to tell you. When I got all wore out wid work, en wid de callin' for you, en went to sleep, my heart wuz mos' broke bekase you wuz los', en I didn' k'yer no mo' what become er me en de raf'. En when I wake up en fine you back agin, all safe en soun', de tears come en I could a got down on my knees en kiss' yo' foot I's so thankful. En all you wuz thinkin 'bout wuz how you could make a fool uv ole Jim wid a lie. Dat truck dah is *trash*; en trash is what people is dat puts dirt on de head er dey fren's en makes 'em ashamed."

Then he got up slow, and walked to the wigwam, and went in there, without saying anything but that. But that was enough. It made me feel so mean I could almost kissed *his* foot to get him to take it back.

It was fifteen minutes before I could work myself up to go and humble myself to a nigger—but I done it, and I warn't ever sorry for it afterwards, neither. I didn't do him no more mean tricks, and I wouldn't done that one if I'd a knowed it would make him feel that way.

Chapter XVI

"IT *AMOUNTED* TO SOMETHING
BEING A RAFTSMAN."

W E SLEPT most all day, and started out at night, a little ways behind a monstrous long raft that was as long going by as a procession. She had four long sweeps[1] at each end, so we judged she carried as many as thirty men, likely. She had five big wigwams aboard, wide apart, and an open camp fire in the middle, and a tall flag-pole at each end. There was a power of style about her. It *amounted* to something being a raftsman on such a craft as that.

We went drifting down into a big bend, and the night clouded up and got hot. The river was very wide, and was walled with solid timber on both sides; you couldn't see a break in it hardly ever, or a light. We talked about Cairo, and wondered whether we would know it when we got to it. I said likely we wouldn't, because I had heard say there warn't but about a dozen houses there, and if they didn't happen to have them lit up, how was we going to know we was passing a town? Jim said if the two big rivers joined together there, that would show. But I said maybe we might think we was passing the foot of an island and coming into the same old river again. That disturbed Jim—and me too. So the question was, what to do? I said, paddle ashore the first time a light showed, and tell them pap was behind, coming along with a trading-scow, and was a green hand at the business, and wanted to know how far it was to Cairo. Jim thought it was a good idea, so we took a smoke on it and waited.

But you know a young person can't wait very well when he is impatient to find a thing out.[2] We talked it over, and by and by Jim said it

---

1. Oars.
2. Here begins the "Raftsman's Passage" or "raft episode," which Mark Twain published in 1883 in *Life on the Mississippi* as "a chapter from a book which I have been working at." In the first edition of *Huck Finn*, however, Mark Twain omitted the passage because his publisher wanted to shorten the book to match *Tom Sawyer*, so the two could be sold as a set for $4.75. Well beyond the author's lifetime, therefore, millions of readers knew *Huck Finn* only with the passage excised. Because the omission was just the result of a marketing scheme (later abandoned) and because it did not represent Mark Twain's original intent, the passage has been restored here along with the illustrations by John Harley from *Life on the Mississippi*. As the Mark Twain scholar Tom Quirk has observed, "the inclusion of the raft episode ought not be too disturbing. We may, if we choose, teach the episode out of the book, just as, before, some of us taught it into the book."

was such a black night, now, that it wouldn't be no risk to swim down to the big raft and crawl aboard and listen,—they would talk about Cairo, because they would be calculating to go ashore there for a spree, maybe, or anyway they would send boats ashore to buy whisky or fresh meat or something. Jim had a wonderful level head, for a nigger: he could most always start a good plan when you wanted one.

I stood up and shook my rags off and jumped into the river, and struck out for the raft's light. By and by, when I got down nearly to her, I eased up and went slow and cautious. But everything was all right—nobody at the sweeps. So I swum down along the raft till I was most

"I SWUM DOWN ALONG
THE RAFT."

abreast the camp fire in the middle, then I crawled aboard and inched along and got in amongst some bundles of shingles on the weather side of the fire. There was thirteen men there—they was the watch on deck of course. And a mighty rough-looking lot, too. They had a jug, and tin cups, and they kept the jug moving. One man was singing—roaring, you may say; and it wasn't a nice song—for a parlor anyway. He roared through his nose, and strung out the last word of every line very long. When he was done they all fetched a kind of Injun war-whoop, and then another was sung. It begun:

> "There was a woman in our towdn,
>   In our towdn did dwed'l,
> She loved her husband dear-i-lee,
>   But another man twyste as wed'l.
>
> Singing too, riloo, riloo, riloo,
>   Ri-too, riloo, rilay - - - e,
> She loved her husband dear-i-lee,
>   But another man twyste as wed'l."

And so on—fourteen verses. It was kind of poor, and when he was going to start on the next verse one of them said it was the tune the old cow died on; and another one said, "Oh, give us a rest." And another one told him to take a walk. They made fun of him till he got mad and jumped up and begun to cuss the crowd, and said he could lam any thief in the lot.

They was all about to make a break for him, but the biggest man there jumped up and says:

"Set whar you are, gentlemen. Leave him to me; he's my meat."

Then he jumped up in the air three times and cracked his heels together every time. He flung off a buckskin coat that was all hung with fringes, and says, "You lay thar tell the chawin-up's done;" and flung his hat down, which was all over ribbons, and says, "You lay thar tell his sufferins is over."

"HE JUMPED UP IN THE AIR."

Then he jumped up in the air and cracked his heels together again and shouted out:

"Whoo-oop! I'm the old original iron-jawed, brass-mounted, copper-bellied corpse-maker from the wilds of Arkansaw!—Look at me! I'm the man they call Sudden Death and General Desolation! Sired by a hurricane, dam'd by an earthquake, half-brother to the cholera, nearly related to the small-pox on the mother's side! Look at me! I take nineteen alligators and a bar'l of whisky for breakfast when I'm in robust health, and a bushel of rattlesnakes and a dead body when I'm ailing! I split the everlasting rocks with my glance, and I squench the thunder when I speak! Whoo-oop! Stand back and give me room according to my strength! Blood's my natural drink, and the wails of the dying is music to my ear! Cast your eye on me, gentlemen!—and lay low and hold your breath, for I'm 'bout to turn myself loose!"

All the time he was getting this off, he was shaking his head and looking fierce, and kind of swelling around in a little circle, tucking up his wrist-bands, and now and then straightening up and beating his breast with his fist, saying, "Look at me, gentlemen!" When he got through, he jumped up and cracked his heels together three times, and let off a roaring "whoo-oop! I'm the bloodiest son of a wildcat that lives!"

Then the man that had started the row tilted his old slouch hat down over his right eye; then he bent stooping forward, with his back sagged and his south end sticking out far, and his fists a-shoving out and drawing in in front of him, and so went around in a little circle about three times, swelling himself up and breathing hard. Then he straightened, and jumped up and cracked his heels together three times before he lit again (that made them cheer), and he begun to shout like this:

"Whoo-oop! bow your neck and spread, for the kingdom of sorrow's a-coming! Hold me down to the earth, for I feel my powers a-working! whoo-oop! I'm a child of sin, *don't* let me get a start! Smoked glass, here, for all! Don't attempt to look at me with the naked eye, gentlemen! When I'm playful I use the meridians of longitude and parallels of latitude for a seine, and drag the Atlantic Ocean for whales! I scratch my head with the lightning and purr myself to sleep with the thunder! When I'm cold, I bile the Gulf of Mexico and bathe in it; when I'm hot I fan myself with an equinoctial storm; when I'm thirsty I reach up and suck a cloud dry like a sponge; when I range the earth hungry, famine follows in my tracks! Whoo-oop! Bow your neck and spread! I put my hand on the sun's face and make it night in the earth; I bite a piece out of the moon and hurry the seasons; I shake myself and crumble the mountains! Contemplate me through leather—*don't* use the naked eye! I'm the man with a petrified heart and biler-iron bowels! The massacre of isolated communities is the pastime of my idle moments, the destruction of nationalities the serious business of my life! The boundless vastness of the great American desert is my enclosed property, and I bury my dead on my own premises!" He jumped up and cracked his heels together three times before he lit (they cheered him again), and as he come down he shouted out: "Whoo-oop! bow your neck and spread, for the pet child of calamity's a-coming!"

"WENT AROUND
IN A LITTLE CIRCLE."

Then the other one went to swelling around and blowing again—the first one—the one they called Bob; next, the Child of Calamity chipped in again, bigger than ever; then they both got at it at the same time, swelling round and round each other and punching their fists most into each other's faces, and whooping and jawing like Injuns; then Bob called the Child names, and the Child called him names back again: next, Bob called him a heap rougher names and the Child come back at him with the very worst kind of language; next, Bob knocked the Child's hat off, and the Child picked it up and kicked Bob's ribbony hat about six foot; Bob went and got it and said never mind, this warn't going to be the last of this thing, because he was a man that never forgot and never forgive, and so the Child better look out, for there was a time a-coming, just as sure as he was a living man, that he would have to answer to him with the best blood in his body. The Child said no man was willinger than he was for that time to come, and he would give Bob fair warning, *now*, never to cross his path again, for he could never rest till he had waded in his blood, for such was his nature, though he was sparing him now on account of his family, if he had one.

Both of them was edging away in different directions, growling and shaking their heads and going on about what they was going to do; but a little black-whiskered chap skipped up and says:

"Come back here, you couple of chicken-livered cowards, and I'll thrash the two of ye!"

And he done it, too. He snatched them, he jerked them this way and that, he booted them around, he knocked them sprawling faster than

"HE KNOCKED THEM SPRAWLING."

they could get up. Why, it warn't two minutes till they begged like dogs—and how the other lot did yell and laugh and clap their hands all the way through, and shout "Sail in, Corpse-Maker!" "Hi! at him again, Child of Calamity!" "Bully for you, little Davy!" Well, it was a perfect pow-wow for a while. Bob and the Child had red noses and black eyes when they got through. Little Davy made them own up that they was sneaks and cowards and not fit to eat with a dog or drink with a nigger; then Bob and the Child shook hands with each other, very solemn, and said they had always respected each other and was willing to let bygones be bygones. So then they washed their faces in the river; and just then there was a loud order to stand by for a crossing, and some of them went forward to man the sweeps there, and the rest went aft to handle the after-sweeps.

I laid still and waited for fifteen minutes, and had a smoke out of a pipe that one of them left in reach; then the crossing was finished, and they stumped back and had a drink around and went to talking and singing again. Next they got out an old fiddle, and one played, and another patted juba,[3] and the rest turned themselves loose on a regular old-fashioned keel-boat break-down. They couldn't keep that up very long without getting winded, so by and by they settled around the jug again.

They sung "jolly, jolly raftsman's the life for me,"[4] with a rousing chorus, and then they got to talking about differences betwixt hogs, and their different kind of habits; and next about women and their different ways; and next about the best ways to put out houses that was afire; and next about what ought to be done with the Injuns; and next about what a king had to do, and how much he got; and next about how to make cats fight; and next about what to do when a man has fits; and next about differences betwixt clear-water rivers and muddy-water ones. The man they called Ed said the muddy Mississippi water was wholesomer to drink than the clear water of the Ohio; he said if you let a pint of this yaller Mississippi water settle, you would have about a half to three quarters of an inch of mud in the bottom, according to the stage of the river, and then it warn't no better than Ohio water—what you wanted to do was to keep it stirred up—and when the river was low, keep mud on hand to put in and thicken the water up the way it ought to be.

The Child of Calamity said that was so; he said there was nutritiousness in the mud, and a man that drunk Mississippi water could grow corn in his stomach if he wanted to. He says:

"You look at the graveyards; that tells the tale. Trees won't grow worth shucks in a Cincinnati graveyard, but in a Sent Louis graveyard they grow upwards of eight hundred foot high. It's all on account of the water the people drunk before they laid up. A Cincinnati corpse don't richen a soil any."

And they talked about how Ohio water didn't like to mix with Mississippi water. Ed said if you take the Mississippi on a rise when the Ohio is low, you'll find a wide band of clear water all the way down the east

3. Patting knees, hands, right shoulder, left shoulder—or a similar sequence—in time to the music.
4. A minstrel song of 1844 attributed to Daniel Emmett, with lyrics by Andrew Evans.

AN OLD-FASHIONED BREAK-DOWN.

side of the Mississippi for a hundred mile or more, and the minute you get out a quarter of a mile from shore and pass the line, it is all thick and yaller the rest of the way across. Then they talked about how to keep tobacco from getting mouldy, and from that they went into ghosts and told about a lot that other folks had seen; but Ed says:

"Why don't you tell something that you've seen yourselves? Now let me have a say. Five years ago I was on a raft as big as this, and right along here it was a bright moonshiny night, and I was on watch and boss of the stabboard oar forrard, and one of my pards was a man named Dick Allbright, and he come along to where I was sitting, forrard—gaping and stretching, he was—and stooped down on the edge of the raft and washed his face in the river, and come and set down by me and got out his pipe, and had just got it filled, when he looks up and says,—

" 'Why looky-here,' he says, 'ain't that Buck Miller's place, over yander in the bend?'

" 'Yes,' says I, 'it is—why?' He laid his pipe down and leant his head on his hand, and says,—

" 'I thought we'd be furder down.' I says,—

" 'I thought it too, when I went off watch'—we was standing six hours on and six off—'but the boys told me,' I says, 'that the raft didn't seem to hardly move, for the last hour,'—says I, 'though she's a slipping along all right, now,' says I. He give a kind of a groan, and says,—

" 'I've seed a raft act so before, along here,' he says, ' 'pears to me the current has most quit above the head of this bend durin' the last two years,' he says.

"Well, he raised up two or three times, and looked away off and around on the water. That started me at it, too. A body is always doing what he sees somebody else doing, though there mayn't be no sense in

it. Pretty soon I see a black something floating on the water away off to
stabboard and quartering behind us. I see he was looking at it, too. I
says,—

" 'What's that?' He says, sort of pettish,—

" 'Tain't nothing but an old empty bar'l.'

" 'An empty bar'l!' says I, 'why,' says I, 'a spy-glass is a fool to *your* eyes.
How can you tell it's an empty bar'l?' He says,—

" 'I don't know; I reckon it ain't a bar'l, but I thought it might be,' says
he.

" 'Yes,' I says, 'so it might be, and it might be anything else, too; a body
can't tell nothing about it, such a distance as that,' I says.

"We hadn't nothing else to do, so we kept on watching it. By and by I
says,—

" 'Why looky-here, Dick Allbright, that thing's a-gaining on us, I
believe.'

"He never said nothing. The thing gained and gained, and I judged it
must be a dog that was about tired out. Well, we swung down into the
crossing, and the thing floated across the bright streak of the moonshine, and, by George, it *was* a bar'l. Says I,—

" 'Dick Allbright, what made you think that thing was a bar'l, when it
was a half a mile off,' says I. Says he,—

" 'I don't know.' Says I,—

" 'You tell me, Dick All-
bright.' He says,—

" 'Well, I knowed it was a
bar'l; I've seen it before; lots
has seen it; they says it's a
ha'nted bar'l.'

"I called the rest of the
watch, and they come and
stood there, and I told them
what Dick said. It floated
right along abreast, now, and
didn't gain any more. It was
about twenty foot off. Some
was for having it aboard, but
the rest didn't want to. Dick
Allbright said rafts that had
fooled with it had got bad
luck by it. The captain of the
watch said he didn't believe
in it. He said he reckoned the
bar'l gained on us because it

THE MYSTERIOUS BARREL.

was in a little better current than what we was. He said it would leave
by and by.

"So then we went to talking about other things, and we had a song,
and then a breakdown; and after that the captain of the watch called for
another song; but it was clouding up, now, and the bar'l stuck right thar
in the same place, and the song didn't seem to have much warm-up to
it, somehow, and so they didn't finish it, and there warn't any cheers,

but it sort of dropped flat, and nobody said anything for a minute. Then everybody tried to talk at once, and one chap got off a joke, but it warn't no use, they didn't laugh, and even the chap that made the joke didn't laugh at it, which ain't usual. We all just settled down glum, and watched the bar'l, and was oneasy and oncomfortable. Well, sir, it shut down black and still, and then the wind begin to moan around, and next the lightning begin to play and the thunder to grumble. And pretty soon there was a regular storm, and in the middle of it a man that was running aft stumbled and fell and sprained his ankle so that he had to lay up. This made the boys shake their heads. And every time the lightning

"SOON THERE WAS A REGULAR STORM."

come, there was that bar'l with the blue lights winking around it. We was always on the look-out for it. But by and by, towards dawn, she was gone. When the day come we couldn't see her anywhere, and we warn't sorry, neither.

"But next night about half-past nine, when there was songs and high jinks going on, here she comes again, and took her old roost on the stabboard side. There warn't no more high jinks. Everybody got solemn; nobody talked; you couldn't get anybody to do anything but set around moody and look at the bar'l. It begun to cloud up again. When the watch changed, the off watch stayed up, 'stead of turning in. The storm ripped and roared around all night, and in the middle of it another man tripped and sprained his ankle, and had to knock off. The bar'l left towards day, and nobody see it go.

"Everybody was sober and down in the mouth all day. I don't mean the kind of sober that comes of leaving liquor alone,—not that. They was quiet, but they all drunk more than usual,—not together,—but each man sidled off and took it private, by himself.

"After dark the off watch didn't turn in; nobody sung, nobody talked; the boys didn't scatter around, neither; they sort of huddled together, forrard; and for two hours they set there, perfectly still, looking steady in the one direction, and heaving a sigh once in a while. And then, here comes the bar'l again. She took up her old place. She staid there all night; nobody turned in. The storm come on again, after midnight. It got awful dark; the rain poured down; hail, too; the thunder boomed and roared and bellowed; the wind blowed a hurricane; and the lightning spread over everything in big sheets of glare, and showed the whole raft as plain as day; and the river lashed up white as milk as far as you could see for miles, and there was that bar'l jiggering along, same as ever. The captain ordered the watch to man the after sweeps for a crossing, and nobody would go,—no more sprained ankles for them, they said. They wouldn't even *walk* aft. Well then, just then the sky split wide open, with a crash, and the lightning killed two men of the after watch, and crippled two more. Crippled them how, says you? Why, *sprained their ankles!*

"The bar'l left in the dark betwixt lightnings, towards dawn. Well, not a body eat a bite at breakfast that morning. After that the men loafed around, in twos and threes, and talked low together. But none of them herded with Dick Allbright. They all give him the cold shake. If he come around where any of the men was, they split up and sidled away. They wouldn't man the sweeps with him. The captain had all the skiffs hauled up on the raft, along-side of his wigwam, and wouldn't let the dead men be took ashore to be planted; he didn't believe a man that got ashore would come back; and he was right.

"After night come, you could see pretty plain that there was going to be trouble if that bar'l come again; there was such a muttering going on. A good many wanted to kill Dick All-bright, because he'd seen the bar'l on other trips, and that had an ugly look. Some wanted to put him ashore. Some said, let's all go ashore in a pile, if the bar'l comes again.

"THE LIGHTNING
KILLED TWO MEN."

"This kind of whispers was still going on, the men being bunched together forrard watching for the bar'l, when, lo and behold you, here she comes again. Down she comes, slow and steady, and settles into her old tracks. You could a heard a pin drop. Then up comes the captain, and says:

" 'Boys, don't be a pack of children and fools; I don't want this bar'l to be dogging us all the way to Orleans, and *you* don't; well, then, how's the best way to stop it? Burn it up,—that's the way. I'm going to fetch it aboard,' he says. And before anybody could say a word, in he went.

"He swum to it, and as he come pushing it to the raft, the men spread to one side. But the old man got it aboard and busted in the head, and there was a baby in it! Yes sir, a stark naked baby. It was Dick Allbright's baby; he owned up and said so.

" 'Yes,' he says, a-leaning over it, 'yes, it is my own lamented darling, my poor lost Charles William Allbright deceased,' says he,—for he could curl his tongue around the bulliest words in the language when he was a mind to, and lay them before you without a jint started, anywhere. Yes, he said he used to live up at the head of this bend, and one night he choked his child, which was crying, not intending to kill it,—which was prob'ly a lie,—and then he was scared, and buried it in a bar'l, before his wife got home, and off he went, and struck the northern trail and went to rafting; and this was the third year that the bar'l had chased him. He said the bad luck always begun light, and lasted till four men was killed, and then the bar'l didn't come any more after that. He said if the men would stand it one more night,—and was agoing on like that,—but the men had got enough. They started to get out a boat to take him ashore and lynch him, but he grabbed the little child all of a sudden and jumped overboard with it hugged up to his breast and shed-

ding tears, and we never see him again in this life, poor old suffer-ing soul, nor Charles William neither."

"*Who* was shedding tears?" says Bob; "was it Allbright or the baby?"

"Why, Allbright, of course; didn't I tell you the baby was dead? Been dead three years—how could it cry?"

"Well, never mind how it could cry—how could it *keep* all that time?" says Davy. "You an-swer me that."

"I don't know how it done it," says Ed. "It done it though—that's all I know about it."

"Say—what did they do with the bar'l?" says the Child of Calamity.

"Why, they hove it overboard, and it sunk like a chunk of lead."

"Edward, did the child look like it was choked?" says one.

"GRABBED THE LITTLE CHILD."

"Did it have its hair parted?" says another.

"What was the brand on that bar'l, Eddy?" says a fellow they called Bill.

"Have you got the papers for them statistics, Edmund?" says Jimmy.

"Say, Edwin, was you one of the men that was killed by the lightning?" says Davy.

"Him? O, no, he was both of 'em," says Bob. Then they all hawhawed.

"Say, Edward, don't you reckon you'd better take a pill? You look bad—don't you feel pale?" says the Child of Calamity.

"O, come, now, Eddy," says Jimmy, "show up; you must a kept part of that bar'l to prove the thing by. Show us the bunghole—*do*—and we'll all believe you."

"Say, boys," says Bill, "less divide it up. Thar's thirteen of us. I can swaller a thirteenth of the yarn, if you can worry down the rest."

Ed got up mad and said they could all go to some place which he ripped out pretty savage, and then walked off aft cussing to himself, and they yelling and jeering at him, and roaring and laughing so you could hear them a mile.

"ED GOT UP MAD."

"Boys, we'll split a watermelon on that," says the Child of Calamity; and he come rummaging around in the dark amongst the shingle bundles where I was, and put his hand on me. I was warm and soft and naked; so he says "Ouch!" and jumped back.

"Fetch a lantern or a chunk of fire here, boys—there's a snake here as big as a cow!"

So they run there with a lantern and crowded up and looked in on me.

"Come out of that, you beggar!" says one.

"Who are you?" says another.

"What are you after here? Speak up prompt, or overboard you go."

"Snake him out, boys. Snatch him out by the heels."

I began to beg, and crept out amongst them trembling. They looked me over, wondering, and the Child of Calamity says:

"A cussed thief! Lend a hand and less heave him overboard!"

"No," says Big Bob, "less get out the paint-pot and paint him a sky blue all over from head to heel, and *then* heave him over!"

"Good! that's it. Go for the paint, Jimmy."

When the paint come, and Bob took the brush and was just going to begin, the others laughing and rubbing their hands, I begun

"WHO ARE YOU?"

to cry, and that sort of worked on Davy, and he says:

" 'Vast there! He's nothing but a cub. I'll paint the man that tetches him!"

So I looked around on them, and some of them grumbled and growled, and Bob put down the paint, and the others didn't take it up.

"Come here to the fire, and less see what you're up to here," says Davy. "Now set down there and give an account of yourself. How long have you been aboard here?"

"Not over a quarter of a minute, sir," says I.

"How did you get dry so quick?"

"I don't know, sir. I'm always that way, mostly."

"Oh, you are, are you? What's your name?"

I warn't going to tell my name. I didn't know what to say, so I just says: "Charles William Allbright, sir."

Then they roared—the whole crowd; and I was mighty glad I said that, because maybe laughing would get them in a better humor.

When they got done laughing, Davy says:

"It won't hardly do, Charles William. You couldn't have growed this much in five year, and you was a baby when you come out of the bar'l, you know, and dead at that. Come, now, tell a straight story, and nobody'll hurt you, if you ain't up to anything wrong. What *is* your name?"

"Aleck Hopkins, sir. Aleck James Hopkins."

"Well, Aleck, where did you come from, here?"

"CHARLES WILLIAM ALLBRIGHT, SIR."

"From a trading scow. She lays up the bend yonder. I was born on her. Pap has traded up and down here all his life; and he told me to swim off here, because when you went by he said he would like to get some of you to speak to a Mr. Jonas Turner, in Cairo, and tell him—"

"Oh, come!"

"Yes, sir, it's as true as the world; Pap he says—"

"Oh, your grandmother!"

They all laughed, and I tried again to talk, but they broke in on me and stopped me.

"Now, looky-here," says Davy; "you're scared, and so you talk wild. Honest, now, do you live in a scow, or is it a lie?"

"Yes, sir, in a trading scow. She lays up at the head of the bend. But I warn't born in her. It's our first trip."

"Now you're talking! What did you come aboard here, for? To steal?"

"No, sir, I didn't. It was only to get a ride on the raft. All boys does that."

"Well, I know that. But what did you hide for?"

"Sometimes they drive the boys off."

"So they do. They might steal. Looky-here; if we let you off this time, will you keep out of these kind of scrapes hereafter?"

" 'Deed I will, boss. You try me."

"All right, then. You ain't but little ways from shore. Overboard with you, and don't you make a fool of yourself another time this way. Blast it, boy, some raftsmen would rawhide you till you were black and blue!"

I didn't wait to kiss good-bye, but went overboard and broke for shore. When Jim come along by and by, the big raft was away out of sight around the point. I swum out and got aboard, and was mighty glad to see home again.

There warn't nothing to do, now, but to look out sharp for the town, and not pass it without seeing it. He said he'd be mighty sure to see it, because he'd be a free man the minute he seen it, but if he missed it he'd be in the slave country again and no more show for freedom. Every little while he jumps up and says:

"Dah she is!"

But it warn't. It was Jack-o-lanterns, or lightning-bugs; so he set down again, and went to watching, same as before. Jim said it made him all over trembly and feverish to be so close to freedom. Well, I can tell you it made me all over trembly and feverish, too, to hear him, because I begun to get it through my head that he *was* most free—and who was to blame for it? Why, *me*. I couldn't get that out of my conscience, no how nor no way. It got to troubling me so I couldn't rest; I couldn't stay still in one place. It hadn't ever come home to me before, what this thing was that I was doing. But now it did; and it staid with me, and scorched me more and more. I tried to make out to myself that *I* warn't to blame, because *I* didn't run Jim off from his rightful owner; but it warn't no use, conscience up and says, every time, "But you knowed he was running for his freedom, and you could a paddled ashore and told somebody." That was so—I couldn't get around that, noway. That was where it pinched. Conscience says to me, "What had poor Miss Watson done to you, that you could see her nigger go off right under your eyes and never say one single word? What did that poor old woman do to you, that you could treat her so mean? Why, she tried to learn you your book, she tried to learn you your manners, she tried to be good to you every way she knowed how. *That's* what she done."

I got to feeling so mean and so miserable I most wished I was dead. I fidgeted up and down the raft, abusing myself to myself, and Jim was fidgeting up and down past me. We neither of us could keep still. Every time he danced around and says, "Dah's Cairo!" it went through me like a shot, and I thought if it *was* Cairo I reckoned I would die of miserableness.

Jim talked out loud all the time while I was talking to myself. He was saying how the first thing he would do when he got to a free State he would go to saving up money and never spend a single cent, and when he got enough he would buy his wife, which was owned on a farm close to where Miss Watson lived; and then they would both work to buy the two children, and if their master wouldn't sell them, they'd get an Ab'litionist to go and steal them.

It most froze me to hear such talk. He wouldn't ever dared to talk such talk in his life before. Just see what a difference it made in him the minute he judged he was about free. It was according to the old saying, "give a nigger an inch and he'll take an ell."[5] Thinks I, this is what comes

---

5. An Old English ell was the distance from the elbow to the tip of the middle finger, or approximately forty-five inches. Huck is accusing Jim of taking advantage of a small concession.

of my not thinking. Here was this nigger which I had as good as helped
to run away, coming right out flat-footed and saying he would steal his
children—children that belonged to a man I didn't even know; a man
that hadn't ever done me no harm.

I was sorry to hear Jim say that, it was such a lowering of him. My
conscience got to stirring me up hotter than ever, until at last I says
to it, "Let up on me—it ain't too late, yet—I'll paddle ashore at the
first light, and tell." I felt easy, and happy, and light as a feather,
right off. All my troubles was gone. I went to looking out sharp for a
light, and sort of singing to myself. By and by one showed. Jim sings
out:

"We's safe, Huck, we's safe! Jump up and crack yo' heels, dat's de
good ole Cairo at las', I jis knows it!"

I says:

"I'll take the canoe and go see, Jim. It mightn't be, you know."

He jumped and got the canoe ready, and put his old coat in the bottom for me to set on, and give me the paddle; and as I shoved off, he
says:

"Pooty soon I'll be a-shout'n for joy, en I'll say, it's all on accounts
o'Huck; I's a free man, en I couldn't ever ben free ef it hadn' ben for
Huck; Huck done it. Jim won't ever forgit you, Huck; you's de bes' fren'
Jim's ever had; en you's de *only* fren' ole Jim's got now."

I was paddling off, all in a sweat to tell on him; but when he says this,
it seemed to kind of take the tuck all out of me. I went along slow then,
and I warn't right down certain whether I was glad I started or whether
I warn't. When I was fifty yards off, Jim says:

"Dah you goes, de ole true Huck; de on'y white genlman dat ever kep'
his promise to ole Jim."

Well, I just felt sick. But I says, I *got* to do it—I can't get *out* of it.
Right then, along comes a skiff with two men in it, with guns, and they
stopped and I stopped. One of them says:

"What's that, yonder?"

"A piece of a raft," I says.

"Do you belong on it?"

"Yes, sir."

"Any men on it?"

"Only one, sir."

"Well, there's five niggers run off to-night, up yonder above the head
of the bend. Is your man white or black?"

I didn't answer up prompt. I tried to, but the words wouldn't come. I
tried, for a second or two, to brace up and out with it, but I warn't man
enough—hadn't the spunk of a rabbit. I see I was weakening; so I just
give up trying, and up and says—

"He's white."

"I reckon we'll go and see for ourselves."

"I wish you would," says I, "because it's pap that's there, and maybe
you'd help me tow the raft ashore where the light is. He's sick—and so
is mam and Mary Ann."

"Oh, the devil! we're in a hurry, boy. But I s'pose we've got to. Come—
buckle to your paddle, and let's get along."

I buckled to my paddle and they laid to their oars. When we had made a stroke or two, I says:

"Pap'll be mighty much obleeged to you, I can tell you. Everybody goes away when I want them to help me tow the raft ashore, and I can't do it by myself."

"Well, that's infernal mean. Odd, too. Say, boy, what's the matter with your father?"

"It's the—a—the—well, it ain't anything, much."

They stopped pulling. It warn't but a mighty little ways to the raft, now. One says:

"Boy, that's a lie. What *is* the matter with your pap? Answer up square, now, and it'll be the better for you."

"I will, sir, I will, honest—but don't leave us, please. It's the—the— gentlemen, if you'll only pull ahead, and let me heave you the head-line, you won't have to come a-near the raft—please do."

"Set her back, John, set her back!" says one. They backed water. "Keep away, boy—keep to looard.[6] Confound it, I just expect the wind has blowed

"BOY, THAT'S A LIE."

it to us. Your pap's got the small-pox, and you know it precious well. Why didn't you come out and say so? Do you want to spread it all over?"

"Well," says I, a-blubbering, "I've told everybody before, and then they just went away and left us."

"Poor devil, there's something in that. We are right down sorry for you, but we—well, hang it, we don't want the small-pox, you see. Look here, I'll tell you what to do. Don't you try to land by yourself, or you'll smash everything to pieces. You float along down about twenty miles and you'll come to a town on the left-hand side of the river. It will be long after sun-up, then, and when you ask for help, you tell them your folks are all down with chills and fever. Don't be a fool again, and let

6. Leeward, the side away from the wind.

people guess what is the matter. Now we're trying to do you a kindness; so you just put twenty miles between us, that's a good boy. It wouldn't do any good to land yonder where the light is—it's only a wood-yard. Say—reckon your father's poor, and I'm bound to say he's in pretty hard luck. Here—I'll put a twenty dollar gold piece on this board, and you get it when it floats by. I feel mighty mean to leave you, but my kingdom! it won't do to fool with small-pox, don't you see?"

"Hold on, Parker," says the other man, "here's a twenty to put on the board for me. Good-bye, boy, you do as Mr. Parker told you, and you'll be all right."

"That's so, my boy—good-bye, good-bye. If you see any runaway niggers, you get help and nab them, and you can make some money by it."

"Good-bye, sir," says I, "I won't let no runaway niggers get by me if I can help it."

They went off, and I got aboard the raft, feeling bad and low, because I knowed very well I had done wrong, and I see it warn't no use for me to try to learn to do right; a body that don't get *started* right when he's little, ain't got no show—when the pinch comes there ain't nothing to back him up and keep him to his work, and so he gets beat. Then I thought a minute, and says to myself, hold on,—s'pose you'd a done right and give Jim up; would you felt better than what you do now? No, says I, I'd feel bad—I'd feel just the same way I do now. Well, then, says I, what's the use you learning to do right, when it's troublesome to do right and ain't no trouble to do wrong, and the wages is just the same? I was stuck. I couldn't answer that. So I reckoned I wouldn't bother no more about it, but after this always do whichever come handiest at the time.

I went into the wigwam; Jim warn't there. I looked all around; he warn't anywhere. I says:

"HERE I IS, HUCK."

"Jim!"

"Here I is, Huck. Is dey out o' sight yit? Don't talk loud."

He was in the river, under the stern oar, with just his nose out. I told him they was out of sight, so he come aboard. He says:

"I was a-listenin' to all de talk, en I slips into de river en was gwyne to shove for sho' if dey come aboard. Den I was gwyne to swim to de raf' agin when dey was gone. But lawsy, how you did fool 'em, Huck! Dat *wuz* de smartes' dodge! I tell you, chile, I 'speck it save' ole Jim—ole Jim ain't gwyne to forgit you for dat, honey."

Then we talked about the money. It was a pretty good raise, twenty dollars apiece. Jim said we could take deck passage on a steamboat now, and the money would last us as far as we wanted to go in the free States. He said twenty mile more warn't far for the raft to go, but he wished we was already there.

Towards daybreak we tied up, and Jim was mighty particular about hiding the raft good. Then he worked all day fixing things in bundles, and getting all ready to quit rafting.

That night about ten we hove in sight of the lights of a town away down in a left-hand bend.

I went off in the canoe, to ask about it. Pretty soon I found a man out in the river with a skiff, setting a trot-line. I ranged up and says:

"Mister, is that town Cairo?"

"Cairo? no. You must be a blame' fool."

"What town is it, mister?"

"If you want to know, go and find out. If you stay here botherin' around me for about a half a minute longer, you'll get something you won't want."

I paddled to the raft. Jim was awful disappointed, but I said never mind, Cairo would be the next place, I reckoned.

We passed another town before daylight, and I was going out again; but it was high ground, so I didn't go. No high ground about Cairo, Jim said. I had forgot it. We laid up for the day, on a tow-head tolerable close to the left-hand bank. I begun to suspicion something. So did Jim. I says:

"Maybe we went by Cairo in the fog that night."

He says:

"Doan' less talk about it, Huck. Po' niggers can't have no luck. I awluz 'spected dat rattle-snake skin warn't done wid its work."

"I wish I'd never seen that snake-skin, Jim—I do wish I'd never laid eyes on it."

"It ain't yo' fault, Huck; you didn' know. Don't you blame yo'self 'bout it."

When it was daylight, here was the clear Ohio water in shore, sure enough, and outside was the old regular Muddy! So it was all up with Cairo.[7]

We talked it all over. It wouldn't do to take to the shore; we couldn't take the raft up the stream, of course. There warn't no way but to wait

7. Cairo lies at the point where the relatively clear Ohio flows into the muddy Mississippi. Since they now see water from both rivers, Huck and Jim realize they have gone too far. As Peter Beidler has pointed out, however, it is unclear, without the "raftsman's passage," how Huck and Jim all of a sudden know what they didn't know a few pages before.

for dark, and start back in the canoe and take the chances. So we slept all day amongst the cotton-wood thicket, so as to be fresh for the work, and when we went back to the raft about dark the canoe was gone!

We didn't say a word for a good while. There warn't anything to say. We both knowed well enough it was some more work of the rattle-snake skin; so what was the use to talk about it? It would only look like we was finding fault, and that would be bound to fetch more bad luck—and keep on fetching it, too, till we knowed enough to keep still.

By and by we talked about what we better do, and found there warn't no way but just to go along down with the raft till we got a chance to buy a canoe to go back in. We warn't going to borrow it when there warn't anybody around, the way pap would do, for that might set people after us.

So we shoved out, after dark, on the raft.

Anybody that don't believe yet, that it's foolishness to handle a snake-skin, after all that that snake-skin done for us, will believe it now, if they read on and see what more it done for us.

The place to buy canoes is off of rafts laying up at shore. But we didn't see no rafts laying up; so we went along during three hours and more. Well, the night got gray, and ruther thick, which is the next meanest thing to fog. You can't tell the shape of the river, and you can't see no distance. It got to be very late and still, and then along comes a steamboat up the river. We lit the lantern, and judged she would see it. Up-stream boats didn't generly come close to us; they go out and follow the bars and hunt for easy water under the reefs; but nights like this they bull right up the channel against the whole river.

We could hear her pounding along, but we didn't see her good till she was close. She aimed right for us. Often they do that and try to see how close they can come without touching; sometimes the wheel bites off a sweep, and then the pilot sticks his head out and laughs, and thinks he's mighty smart. Well, here she comes, and we said she was going to try to shave us; but she didn't seem to be sheering off a bit. She was a big one, and she was coming in a hurry, too, looking like a black cloud with rows of glow-worms around it; but all of a sudden she bulged out, big and scary, with a long row of wide-open furnace doors shining like red-hot teeth, and her monstrous bows and guards hanging right over us. There was a yell at us, and a jingling of bells to stop the engines, a pow-wow of cussing, and whistling of steam—and as Jim went overboard on one side and I on the other, she come smashing straight through the raft.[8]

I dived—and I aimed to find the bottom, too, for a thirty-foot wheel had got to go over me, and I wanted it to have plenty of room. I could always stay under water a minute; this time I reckon I staid under water a minute and a half. Then I bounced for the top in a hurry, for I was nearly busting. I popped out to my arm-pits and blowed the water out of my nose, and puffed a bit. Of course there was a booming current; and of course that boat started her engines again ten seconds after she

---

8. Until the discovery in 1991 of the missing half of the manuscript, it was believed that Mark Twain broke off here in the summer of 1876 and did not resume composition of *Huck Finn* until three years later. Actually, the manuscript reveals that he wrote on into the next chapter to the point where Huck asks Buck what a feud is. Only there, says Victor A. Doyno, did the author "set his 446-page manuscript aside."

stopped them, for they never cared much for raftsmen; so now she was churning along up the river, out of sight in the thick weather, though I could hear her.

I sung out for Jim about a dozen times, but I didn't get any answer; so I grabbed a plank that touched me while I was "treading water," and struck out for shore, shoving it ahead of me. But I made out to see that the drift of the current was towards the left-hand shore, which meant that I was in a crossing; so I changed off and went that way.[9]

It was one of these long, slanting, two-mile crossings; so I was a good long time in getting over. I made a safe landing, and clum up the bank.

CLIMBING UP THE BANK.

I couldn't see but a little ways, but I went poking along over rough ground for a quarter of a mile or more, and then I run across a big old-fashioned double log house before I noticed it. I was going to rush by and get away, but a lot of dogs jumped out and went to howling and barking at me, and I knowed better than to move another peg.

9. The current carries Huck toward the Kentucky shore "but finally lands him just over the line in Tennessee, near Darnell's Point, about two miles below Compromise Landing, Kentucky" [Iowa-California *Huck Finn*, 398].

Chapter XVII.

"WHO'S THERE?"

IN ABOUT half a minute somebody spoke out of a window, without putting his head out, and says:

"Be done, boys! Who's there?"

I says:

"It's me."

"Who's me?"

"George Jackson, sir."

"What do you want?"

"I don't want nothing, sir. I only want to go along by, but the dogs won't let me."

"What are you prowling around here this time of night, for—hey?"

"I warn't prowling around, sir; I fell overboard off of the steamboat."

"Oh, you did, did you? Strike a light there, somebody. What did you say your name was?"

"George Jackson, sir. I'm only a boy."

"Look here; if you're telling the truth, you needn't be afraid—nobody'll hurt you. But don't try to budge; stand right where you are. Rouse out Bob and Tom, some of you, and fetch the guns. George Jackson, is there anybody with you?"

"No, sir, nobody."

I heard the people stirring around in the house, now, and see a light. The man sung out:

"Snatch that light away, Betsy, you old fool—ain't you got any sense? Put it on the floor behind the front door. Bob, if you and Tom are ready, take your places."

"All ready."

"Now, George Jackson, do you know the Shepherdsons?"

"No, sir—I never heard of them."

"Well, that may be so, and it mayn't. Now, all ready. Step forward, George Jackson. And mind, don't you hurry—come mighty slow. If there's anybody with you, let him keep back—if he shows himself he'll be shot. Come along, now. Come slow; push the door open, yourself— just enough to squeeze in, d'you hear?"

I didn't hurry, I couldn't if I'd a wanted to. I took one slow step at a time, and there warn't a sound, only I thought I could hear my heart. The dogs were as still as the humans, but they followed a little behind me. When I got to the three log door-steps, I heard them unlocking and unbarring and unbolting. I put my hand on the door and pushed it a little and a little more, till somebody said, "There, that's enough—put your head in." I done it, but I judged they would take it off.

The candle was on the floor, and there they all was, looking at me, and me at them, for about a quarter of a minute. Three big men with guns pointed at me, which made me wince, I tell you; the oldest, gray and about sixty, the other two thirty or more—all of them fine and handsome—and the sweetest old gray-headed lady, and back of her two young women which I couldn't see right well. The old gentleman says:

"There—I reckon it's all right. Come in."

As soon as I was in, the old gentleman he locked the door and barred it and bolted it, and told the young men to come in with their guns, and they all went in a big parlor that had a new rag carpet on the floor, and got together in a corner that was out of range of the front windows—there warn't none on the side. They held the candle, and took a good look at me, and all said, "Why *he* ain't a Shepherdson—no, there ain't any Shepherdson about him." Then the old man said he hoped I wouldn't mind being searched for arms, because he didn't mean no harm by it—it

"BUCK."

was only to make sure. So he didn't pry into my pockets, but only felt outside with his hands, and said it was all right. He told me to make myself easy and at home, and tell all about myself; but the old lady says:

"Why bless you, Saul, the poor thing's as wet as he can be; and don't you reckon it may be he's hungry?"

"True for you, Rachel—I forgot."

So the old lady says:

"Betsy" (this was a nigger woman), "you fly around and get him something to eat, as quick as you can, poor thing; and one of you girls go and wake up Buck and tell him— Oh, here he is himself. Buck, take this little stranger and get the wet clothes off from him and dress him up in some of yours that's dry."

Buck looked about as old as me—thirteen or fourteen or along there,[1] though he was a little bigger than me. He hadn't on anything but a shirt, and he was very frowsy-

---

1. In a notebook entry for 1895, Mark Twain identifies Huck as "a boy of 14."

headed. He come in gaping and digging one fist into his eyes, and he was dragging a gun along with the other one. He says:

"Ain't they no Shepherdsons around?"

They said, no, 'twas a false alarm.

"Well," he says, "if they'd a ben some, I reckon I'd a got one."

They all laughed, and Bob says:

"Why, Buck, they might have scalped us all, you've been so slow in coming."

"Well, nobody come after me, and it ain't right. I'm always kep' down; I don't get no show."

"Never mind, Buck, my boy," says the old man, "you'll have show enough, all in good time, don't you fret about that. Go 'long with you now, and do as your mother told you."

When we got up stairs to his room, he got me a coarse shirt and a roundabout² and pants of his, and I put them on. While I was at it he asked me what my name was, but before I could tell him, he started to telling me about a blue jay and a young rabbit he had catched in the woods day before yesterday, and he asked me where Moses was when the candle went out. I said I didn't know; I hadn't heard about it before, no way.

"Well, guess," he says.

"How'm I going to guess," says I, "when I never heard tell about it before?"

"But you can guess, can't you? It's just as easy."

"*Which* candle?" I says.

"Why, any candle," he says.

"I don't know where he was," says I; "where was he?"

"Why he was in the *dark!* That's where he was!"

"Well, if you knowed where he was, what did you ask me for?"

"Why, blame it, it's a riddle, don't you see? Say, how long are you going to stay here? You got to stay always. We can just have booming times—they don't have no school now. Do you own a dog? I've got a dog—and he'll go in the river and bring out chips that you throw in. Do you like to comb up, Sundays, and all that kind of foolishness? You bet I don't, but ma she makes me. Confound these ole britches, I reckon I'd better put 'em on, but I'd ruther not, it's so warm. Are you all ready? All right—come along, old hoss."

Cold corn-pone, cold corn-beef, butter and butter-milk—that is what they had for me down there, and there ain't nothing better that ever I've come across yet. Buck and his ma and all of them smoked cob pipes, except the nigger woman, which was gone, and the two young women. They all smoked and talked, and I eat and talked. The young women had quilts around them, and their hair down their backs. They all asked me questions, and I told them how pap and me and all the family was living on a little farm down at the bottom of Arkansaw, and my sister Mary Ann run off and got married and never was heard of no more, and Bill went to hunt them and he warn't heard of no more, and Tom and Mort died, and then there warn't nobody but just me and

2. A short, close jacket.

pap left, and he was just trimmed down to nothing, on account of his troubles; so when he died I took what there was left, because the farm didn't belong to us, and started up the river, deck passage, and fell overboard; and that was how I come to be here. So they said I could have a home there as long as I wanted it. Then it was most daylight, and everybody went to bed, and I went to bed with Buck, and when I waked up in the morning, drat it all, I had forgot what my name was. So I laid there about an hour trying to think, and when Buck waked up, I says:

"Can you spell, Buck?"

"Yes," he says.

"I bet you can't spell my name," says I.

"I bet you what you dare I can," says he.

"All right," says I, "go ahead."

"G-o-r-g-e J-a-x-o-n—there now," he says.

"Well," says I, "you done it, but I didn't think you could. It ain't no slouch of a name to spell—right off without studying."

I set it down, private, because somebody might want *me* to spell it, next, and so I wanted to be handy with it and rattle it off like I was used to it.

It was a mighty nice family, and a mighty nice house, too. I hadn't seen no house out in the country before that was so nice and had so much style. It didn't have an iron latch on the front door, nor a wooden one with a buckskin string, but a brass knob to turn, the same as houses in a town. There warn't no bed in the parlor, not a sign of a bed; but heaps of parlors in towns has beds in them. There was a big fireplace that was bricked on the bottom, and the bricks was kept clean and red by pouring water on them and scrubbing them with another brick; sometimes they washed them over with red water-paint that they call Spanish-brown, same as they do in town. They had big brass dog-irons that could hold up a saw-log. There was a clock on the middle of the mantel-piece, with a picture of a town painted on the bottom half of the glass front, and a round place in the middle of it for the sun, and you could see the pendulum swing behind it. It was beautiful to hear that clock tick; and sometimes when one of these peddlers had been along and scoured her up and got her in good shape, she would start in and strike a hundred and fifty before she got tuckered out. They wouldn't took any money for her.

Well, there was a big outlandish parrot on each side of the clock, made out of something like chalk, and painted up gaudy. By one of the parrots was a cat made of crockery, and a crockery dog by the other; and when you pressed down on them they squeaked, but didn't open their mouths nor look different nor interested. They squeaked through underneath. There was a couple of big wild-turkey-wing fans spread out behind those things. On a table in the middle of the room was a kind of a lovely crockery basket that had apples and oranges and peaches and grapes piled up in it which was much redder and yellower and prettier than real ones is, but they warn't real because you could see where pieces had got chipped off and showed the white chalk or whatever it was, underneath.

This table had a cover made out of beautiful oil-cloth, with a red and blue spread-eagle painted on it, and a painted border all around. It come all the way from Philadelphia, they said. There was some books too, piled up perfectly exact, on each corner of the table. One was a big family Bible, full of pictures. One was "Pilgrim's Progress,"[3] about a man that left his family it didn't say why. I read considerable in it now and then. The statements was interesting, but tough. Another was "Friendship's Offering," full of beautiful stuff and poetry; but I didn't read the poetry. Another was Henry Clay's Speeches,[4] and another was Dr. Gunn's Family Medicine,[5] which told you all about what to do if a body was sick or dead. There was a Hymn Book, and a lot of other books. And there was nice split-bottom chairs, and perfectly sound, too—not bagged down in the middle and busted, like an old basket.

They had pictures hung on the walls—mainly Washingtons and Lafayettes, and battles, and Highland Marys,[6] and one called "Signing the Declaration." There was some that they called crayons, which one of the daughters which was dead made her own self when she was only fifteen years old. They was different from any pictures I ever see before; blacker, mostly, than is common. One was a woman in a slim black dress, belted small under the arm-pits, with bulges like a cabbage in the middle of the sleeves, and a large black scoop-shovel bonnet with a black veil, and white slim ankles crossed about with black tape, and very wee black slippers, like a chisel, and she was leaning pensive on a tombstone on her right elbow, under a weeping willow, and her other hand hanging down her side holding a white handkerchief and a reticule, and underneath the picture it said "Shall I Never See Thee More Alas." Another one was a young lady with her hair all combed up straight to the top of her head, and knotted there in front of a comb like a chair-back, and she was crying into a handkerchief and had a dead bird laying on its back in her other hand with its heels up, and underneath the picture it said "I Shall Never Hear Thy Sweet Chirrup More Alas." There was one where a young lady was at a window looking up at the moon, and tears running down her cheeks; and she had an open letter in one hand with black sealing-wax showing on one edge of it, and she was mashing a locket with a chain to it against her mouth, and underneath the picture it said "And Art Thou Gone Yes Thou Art Gone Alas." These was all nice pictures, I reckon, but I didn't somehow seem to take to them, because if ever I was down a little, they always give me the fan-tods. Everybody was sorry she died, because she had laid out a lot more of these pictures to do, and a body could see by what she had done what they had lost. But I reckoned, that with her disposition, she was having a better time in the graveyard. She was at work on what they said was her greatest picture when she took sick, and every day and every

---

3. *The Pilgrim's Progress from This World, to That Which Is to Come* (1678), a religious allegory by John Bunyan, one of the few books routinely found in rural American households before the Civil War. Mark Twain himself owned several copies.
4. A U.S. congressman, senator, and secretary of state, the sometimes irascible Clay (1777–1852) was closely identified with Kentucky.
5. A popular household medical encyclopedia, first published in 1830 under the title *Domestic Medicine or Poor Man's Friend, in the House of Affliction, Pain, and Sickness.*
6. Mary Campbell, the sweetheart of Scottish poet Robert Burns, was a fitting subject of pathetic painting and verse because she died soon after they met. "Signing the Declaration" is probably an engraving of the famous painting on that subject, completed in 1820, by John Trumbull (1756–1843).

"IT MADE HER LOOK TOO SPIDERY."

night it was her prayer to be allowed to live till she got it done, but she never got the chance. It was a picture of a young woman in a long white gown, standing on the rail of a bridge all ready to jump off, with her hair all down her back, and looking up to the moon, with the tears running down her face, and she had two arms folded across her breast, and two arms stretched out in front, and two more reaching up towards the moon—and the idea was, to see which pair would look best and then scratch out all the other arms; but, as I was saying, she died before she got her mind made up, and now they kept this picture over the head of the bed in her room, and every time her birthday come they hung flowers on it. Other times it was hid with a little curtain. The young woman in the picture had a kind of a nice sweet face, but there was so many arms it made her look too spidery, seemed to me.

This young girl kept a scrap-book when she was alive, and used to paste obituaries and accidents and cases of patient suffering in it out of the *Presbyterian Observer*, and write poetry after them out of her own head. It was very good poetry. This is what she wrote about a boy by the name of Stephen Dowling Bots that fell down a well and was drownded:

ODE TO STEPHEN DOWLING BOTS, DEC'D.[7]

And did young Stephen sicken,
 And did young Stephen die?
And did the sad hearts thicken,
 And did the mourners cry?

No; such was not the fate of
 Young Stephen Dowling Bots;
Though sad hearts round him thickened,
 'Twas not from sickness' shots.

No whooping-cough did rack his frame,
 Nor measles drear, with spots;

---

7. Deceased. Emmeline's tin ear is inherited from such poetasters as Julia A. Moore, the "Sweet Singer of Michigan" (1847–1920), and Bloodgood Cutter, the "poet lariat" of *Innocents Abroad* (1819–1906). Examples of their (and young Sam Clemens's own) stricken verse appear on pp. 303–06.

Not these impaired the sacred name
    Of Stephen Dowling Bots.

Despised love struck not with woe
    That head of curly knots,
Nor stomach troubles laid him low,
    Young Stephen Dowling Bots.

O no. Then list with tearful eye,
    Whilst I his fate do tell.
His soul did from this cold world fly,
    By falling down a well.

They got him out and emptied him;
    Alas it was too late;
His spirit was gone for to sport aloft
    In the realms of the good and great.

If Emmeline Grangerford could make poetry like that before she was
fourteen, there ain't no telling what she could a done by and by. Buck
said she could rattle off poetry like nothing. She didn't ever have to stop
to think. He said she would slap down a line, and if she couldn't find
anything to rhyme with it she would just scratch it out and slap down
another one, and go ahead. She warn't particular, she could write about
anything you choose to give her to write about, just so it was sadful.

"THEY GOT HIM OUT AND EMPTIED HIM."

Every time a man died, or a woman died, or a child died, she would be on hand with her "tribute" before he was cold. She called them tributes. The neighbors said it was the doctor first, then Emmeline, then the undertaker—the undertaker never got in ahead of Emmeline but once, and then she hung fire on a rhyme for the dead person's name, which was Whistler. She warn't ever the same, after that; she never complained, but she kind of pined away and did not live long. Poor thing, many's the time I made myself go up to the little room that used to be hers and get out her poor old scrap-book and read in it when her pictures had been aggravating me and I had soured on her a little. I liked all that family, dead ones and all, and warn't going to let anything come between us. Poor Emmeline made poetry about all the dead people when she was alive, and it didn't seem right that there warn't nobody to make some about her, now she was gone; so I tried to sweat out a verse or two myself, but I couldn't seem to make it go, somehow. They kept Emmeline's room trim and nice and all the things fixed in it just the way she liked to have them when she was alive, and nobody ever slept there. The old lady took care of the room herself, though there was plenty of niggers, and she sewed there a good deal and read her Bible there, mostly.

Well, as I was saying about the parlor, there was beautiful curtains on the windows: white, with pictures painted on them, of castles with vines all down the walls, and cattle coming down to drink. There was a little old piano, too, that had tin pans in it, I reckon, and nothing was ever so lovely as to hear the young ladies sing, "The Last Link is Broken" and play "The Battle of Prague" on it.[8] The walls of all the rooms was plastered, and most had carpets on the floors, and the whole house was whitewashed on the outside.

THE HOUSE.

It was a double house, and the big open place betwixt them was roofed and floored, and sometimes the table was set there in the middle of the day, and it was a cool, comfortable place. Nothing couldn't be better. And warn't the cooking good, and just bushels of it too!

8. The first, published about 1840 by William Clifton, is the lament ("The last link is broken that bound me to thee") of a resigned lover who gives up a "misleading" and "unheeding" partner. The second is a jarring program piece for piano by Franz Kotswara (1730–1791) of Bohemia.

Chapter XVIII.

COL. GRANGERFORD.

Col Grangerford was a gentleman, you see. He was a gentleman all over; and so was his family. He was well born, as the saying is, and that's worth as much in a man as it is in a horse, so the widow Douglas said, and nobody ever denied that she was of the first aristocracy in our town; and pap he always said it, too, though he warn't no more quality than a mud-cat,[1] himself. Col. Grangerford was very tall and very slim, and had a darkish-paly complexion, not a sign of red in it anywheres; he was clean-shaved every morning, all over his thin face, and he had the thinnest kind of lips, and the thinnest kind of nostrils, and a high nose, and heavy eyebrows, and the blackest kind of eyes, sunk so deep back that they seemed like they was looking out of caverns at you, as you may say. His forehead was high, and his hair was black and straight, and hung to his shoulders. His hands was long and thin, and every day of his life he put on a clean shirt and a full suit from head to foot made out of linen so white it hurt your eyes to look at it; and on Sundays he wore a blue tail-coat with brass buttons on it. He carried a mahogany cane with a silver head to it. There warn't no frivolishness about him, not a bit, and he warn't ever loud. He was as kind as he could be—you could feel that, you know, and so you had confidence. Sometimes he smiled, and it was good to see; but when he straightened himself up like a liberty-pole, and the lightning begun to flicker out from under his eyebrows you wanted to climb a tree first, and find out what the matter was afterwards. He didn't ever have to tell anybody to mind their manners—everybody was always good mannered where he was. Everybody loved to have him around, too; he was sunshine most always—I mean he made it seem like good weather. When he turned into a cloud-bank it was awful dark for a half a minute and that was enough; there wouldn't nothing go wrong again for a week.

1. A variety of catfish.

When him and the old lady come down in the morning, all the family got up out of their chairs and give them good-day, and didn't set down again till they had set down. Then Tom and Bob went to the sideboard where the decanters was, and mixed a glass of bitters and handed it to him, and he held it in his hand and waited till Tom's and Bob's was mixed, and then they bowed and said "Our duty to you, sir, and madam;" and *they* bowed the least bit in the world and said thank you, and so they drank, all three, and Bob and Tom poured a spoonful of water on the sugar and the mite of whisky or apple brandy in the bottom of their tumblers, and give it to me and Buck, and we drank to the old people too.

Bob was the oldest, and Tom next. Tall, beautiful men with very broad shoulders and brown faces, and long black hair and black eyes. They dressed in white linen from head to foot, like the old gentleman, and wore broad Panama hats.

Then there was Miss Charlotte, she was twenty-five, and tall and proud and grand, but as good as she could be, when she warn't stirred up; but when she was, she had a look that would make you wilt in your tracks, like her father. She was beautiful.

So was her sister, Miss Sophia, but it was a different kind. She was gentle and sweet, like a dove, and she was only twenty.

Each person had their own nigger to wait on them—Buck, too. My nigger had a monstrous easy time, because I warn't used to having anybody do anything for me, but Buck's was on the jump most of the time.

This was all there was of the family, now; but there used to be more—three sons; they got killed; and Emmeline that died.

The old gentleman owned a lot of farms, and over a hundred niggers. Sometimes a stack of people would come there, horseback, from ten or fifteen mile around, and stay five or six days, and have such junketings round about and on the river, and dances and picnics in the woods, daytimes, and balls at the house, nights. These people was mostly kin-folks of the family. The men brought their guns with them. It was a handsome lot of quality, I tell you.

There was another clan of aristocracy around there—five or six families—mostly of the name of Shepherdson. They was as high-toned, and well born, and rich and grand, as the tribe of Grangerfords. The Shepherdsons and the Grangerfords used the same steamboat landing, which was about two mile above our house; so sometimes when I went up there with a lot of our folks I used to see a lot of the Shepherdsons there, on their fine horses.

One day Buck and me was away out in the woods, hunting, and heard a horse coming. We was crossing the road. Buck says:

"Quick! Jump for the woods!"

We done it, and then peeped down the woods through the leaves. Pretty soon a splendid young man come galloping down the road, setting his horse easy and looking like a soldier. He had his gun across his pommel. I had seen him before. It was young Harney Shepherdson. I heard Buck's gun go off at my ear, and Harney's hat tumbled off from his head. He grabbed his gun and rode straight to the place where we was hid. But we didn't wait. We started through the woods on a run.

YOUNG HARNEY SHEPHERDSON.

The woods warn't thick, so I looked over my shoulder, to dodge the bullet, and twice I seen Harney cover Buck with his gun; and then he rode away the way he come—to get his hat, I reckon, but I couldn't see. We never stopped running till we got home. The old gentleman's eyes blazed a minute—'twas pleasure, mainly, I judged—then his face sort of smoothed down, and he says, kind of gentle:

"I don't like that shooting from behind a bush. Why didn't you step into the road, my boy?"

"The Shepherdsons don't, father. They always take advantage."

Miss Charlotte she held her head up like a queen while Buck was telling his tale, and her nostrils spread and her eyes snapped. The two young men looked dark, but never said nothing. Miss Sophia she turned pale, but the color come back when she found the man warn't hurt.

Soon as I could get Buck down by the corn-cribs under the trees by ourselves, I says:

"Did you want to kill him, Buck?"

"Well, I bet I did."

"What did he do to you?"

"Him? He never done nothing to me."

"Well, then, what did you want to kill him for?"

"Why nothing—only it's on account of the feud."[2]

2. In *Life on the Mississippi* (chapter 26), Mark Twain said that the real-life feud—between the Darnells (or Darnalls) and the Watsons—on which this fictional one is closely based was maybe "about a horse or a cow"; by changing the names, he further alludes to the traditionary enmity between farmer ("granger") and rancher ("shepherd").

MISS CHARLOTTE

"What's a feud?"

"Why, where was you raised? Don't you know what a feud is?"

"Never heard of it before—tell me about it."

"Well," says Buck, "a feud is this way. A man has a quarrel with another man, and kills him; then that other man's brother kills *him*; then the other brothers, on both sides, goes for one another; then the *cousins* chip in—and by and by everybody's killed off, and there ain't no more feud. But it's kind of slow, and takes a long time."

"Has this one been going on long, Buck?"

"Well I should *reckon!* it started thirty year ago, or som'ers along there. There was trouble 'bout something and then a lawsuit to settle it; and the suit went agin one of the men, and so he up and shot the man that won the suit—which he would naturally do, of course. Anybody would."

"What was the trouble about, Buck?—land?"

"I reckon maybe—I don't know."

"Well, who done the shooting?—was it a Grangerford or a Shepherdson?"

"Laws, how do *I* know? it was so long ago."

"Don't anybody know?"

"Oh, yes, pa knows, I reckon, and some of the other old folks; but they don't know, now, what the row was about in the first place."

"Has there been many killed, Buck?"

"Yes—right smart chance of funerals. But they don't always kill. Pa's got a few buck-shot in him; but he don't mind it 'cuz he don't weigh much anyway. Bob's been carved up some with a bowie, and Tom's been hurt once or twice."

"Has anybody been killed this year, Buck?"

"Yes, we got one and they got one. 'Bout three months ago, my cousin Bud, fourteen year old, was riding through the woods, on t'other side of the river, and didn't have no weapon with him, which was blame' foolishness, and in a lonesome place he hears a horse a-coming behind him, and sees old Baldy Shepherdson a-linkin' after him with his gun in his hand and his white hair a-flying in the wind; and 'stead of jumping off and taking to the brush, Bud 'lowed he could outrun him; so they had it, nip and tuck, for five mile or more, the old man a-gaining all the time; so at last Bud seen it warn't any use, so he stopped and faced around so as to have the bullet holes in front, you know, and the old man he rode up and shot him down. But he didn't git much chance to enjoy his luck, for inside of a week our folks laid *him* out."

"I reckon that old man was a coward, Buck."

"I reckon he *warn't* a coward. Not by a blame' sight. There ain't a coward amongst them Shepherdsons—not a one. And there ain't no cowards amongst the Grangerfords, either. Why, that old man kep' up his end in a fight one day, for a half an hour, against three Grangerfords, and come out winner. They was all a-horseback; he lit off of his horse and got behind a little wood-pile, and kep' his horse before him to stop the bullets; but the Grangerfords staid on their horses and capered around the old man, and peppered away at him, and he peppered away at them. Him and his horse both went home pretty leaky and crippled, but the Grangerfords had to be *fetched* home—and one of 'em was dead, and another died the next day. No, sir; if a body's out hunting for cowards, he don't want to fool away any time amongst them Shepherdsons, becuz they don't breed any of that *kind*."

Next Sunday we all went to church, about three mile, everybody a-horseback. The men took their guns along, so did Buck, and kept them between their knees or stood them handy against the wall. The Shepherdsons done the same. It was pretty ornery preaching—all about brotherly love, and such-like tiresomeness; but everybody said it was a good sermon, and they all talked it over going home, and had such a powerful lot to say about faith, and good works, and free grace, and preforeordestination,[3] and I don't know what all, that it did seem to me to be one of the roughest Sundays I had run across yet.

About an hour after dinner everybody was dozing around, some in their chairs and some in their rooms, and it got to be pretty dull. Buck and a dog was stretched out on the grass in the sun, sound asleep. I went up to our room, and judged I would take a nap myself. I found that sweet Miss Sophia standing in her door, which was next to ours, and she took me in her room and shut the door very soft, and asked me if I liked her, and I said I did; and she asked me if I would do something for her and not tell anybody, and I said I would. Then she said she'd forgot her Testament, and left it in the seat at church, between two other books and would I slip out quiet and go there and fetch it to her, and not say nothing to nobody. I said I would. So I slid out and slipped off up the road, and there warn't anybody at the church, except maybe a

---

3. Huck mixes together two cardinal doctrines of Presbyterianism: predestination and foreordination.

hog or two, for there warn't any lock on the door, and hogs likes a pun-
cheon floor[4] in summertime because it's cool. If you notice, most folks
don't go to church only when they've got to; but a hog is different.

"AND ASKED ME IF I LIKED HER."

Says I to myself something's up—it ain't natural for a girl to be in
such a sweat about a Testament; so I give it a shake, and out drops a little piece of paper with *"Half-past-two"* wrote on it with a pencil. I ransacked it, but couldn't find anything else. I couldn't make anything out
of that, so I put the paper in the book again, and when I got home and
up stairs, there was Miss Sophia in her door waiting for me. She pulled
me in and shut the door; then she looked in the Testament till she
found the paper, and as soon as she read it she looked glad; and before
a body could think, she grabbed me and give me a squeeze, and said I
was the best boy in the world, and not to tell anybody. She was mighty
red in the face, for a minute, and her eyes lighted up and it made her
powerful pretty. I was a good deal astonished, but when I got my breath
I asked her what the paper was about, and she asked me if I had read it,
and I said no, and she asked me if I could read writing, and I told her
"no, only coarse-hand,"[5] and then she said the paper warn't anything
but a book-mark to keep her place, and I might go and play now.

I went off down to the river, studying over this thing, and pretty soon
I noticed that my nigger was following along behind. When we was out
of sight of the house, he looked back and around a second, and then
comes a-running, and says:

4. Made of log slabs with the rounded sides downward.
5. Printing.

"Mars Jawge, if you'll come down into de swamp, I'll show you a whole stack o' water-moccasins."

Thinks I, that's mighty curious; he said that yesterday. He oughter know a body don't love water-moccasins enough to go around hunting for them. What is he up to anyway? So I says—

"All right, trot ahead."

I followed a half a mile, then he struck out over the swamp and waded ankle deep as much as another half mile. We come to a little flat piece of land which was dry and very thick with trees and bushes and vines, and he says—

"You shove right in dah, jist a few steps, mars Jawge, dah's whah dey is. I's seed 'm befo', I don't k'yer to see 'em no mo'."

Then he slopped right along and went away, and pretty soon the trees hid him. I poked into the place a-ways, and come to a little open patch as big as a bedroom, all hung around with vines, and found a man laying there asleep—and by jings it was my old Jim!

I waked him up, and I reckoned it was going to be a grand surprise to him to see me again, but it warn't. He nearly cried, he was so glad, but he warn't surprised. Said he swum along behind me, that night, and heard me yell every time, but dasn't answer, because he didn't want nobody to pick *him* up, and take him into slavery again. Says he—

"I got hurt a little, en couldn't swim fas', so I wuz a considable ways behine you, towards de las'; when you landed I reck'ned I could ketch up wid you on de lan' 'dout havin' to shout at you, but when I see dat house I begin to go slow. I 'uz off too fur to hear what dey say to you—I wuz 'fraid o' de dogs—but when it 'uz all quiet agin, I knowed you's in de house, so I struck out for de woods to wait for day. Early in de mawnin' some er de niggers come along, gwyne to de fields, en dey tuck me en showed me dis place, whah de dogs can't track me on accounts o' de water, en dey brings me truck to eat every night, en tells me how you's a gitt'n along."

"Why didn't you tell my Jack to fetch me here sooner, Jim?"

"Well, 'twarn't no use to 'sturb you, Huck, tell we could do sumfn—but we's all right, now. I ben a-buyin' pots en pans en vittles, as I got a chanst, en a patchin' up de raf', nights, when—"

"*What* raft, Jim?"

"Our ole raf'."

"You mean to say our old raft warn't smashed all to flinders?"

"No, she warn't. She was tore up a good deal—one en' of her was—but dey warn't no great harm done, on'y our traps was mos' all los'. Ef we hadn' dive' so deep en swum so fur under water, en de night hadn' ben so dark, en we warn't so sk'yerd, en ben sich punkin-heads, as de sayin' is, we'd a seed de raf'. But it's jis' as well we didn't, 'kase now she's all fixed up agin mos' as good as new, en we's got a new lot o' stuff, too, in de place o' what 'uz los'."

"Why, how did you get hold of the raft again, Jim—did you catch her?"

"How I gwyne to ketch her, en I out in de woods? No, some er de niggers foun' her ketched on a snag, along heah in de ben', en dey hid her in a crick, 'mongst de willows, en dey wuz so much jawin' 'bout which un 'um she b'long to de mos', dat I come to heah 'bout it pooty soon, so

I ups en settles de trouble by tellin' 'um she don't b'long to none uv um, but to you en me; en I ast 'm if dey gwyne to grab a young white genl-man's propaty, en git a hid'n for it? Den I gin 'm ten cents apiece, en dey 'uz mighty well satisfied, en wisht some mo' raf's 'ud come along en make 'm rich agin. Dey's mighty good to me, dese niggers is, en what-ever I wants 'm to do fur me, I doan' have to ast 'm twice, honey. Dat Jack's a good nigger, en pooty smart."

"Yes, he is. He ain't ever told me you was here; told me to come, and he'd show me a lot of water-moccasins. If anything happens, *he* ain't mixed up in it. He can say he never seen us together, and it'll be the truth."

I don't want to talk much about the next day. I reckon I'll cut it pretty short. I waked up about dawn, and was agoing to turn over and go to sleep again, when I noticed how still it was—didn't seem to be anybody stirring. That warn't usual. Next I noticed that Buck was up and gone. Well, I gets up, a-wondering, and goes down stairs—nobody around; everything as still as a mouse. Just the same outside; thinks I, what does it mean? Down by the wood-pile I comes across my Jack, and says:

"What's it all about?"

Says he:

"Don't you know, mars Jawge?"

"No," says I, "I don't."

"Well, den, Miss Sophia's run off! 'deed she has. She run off in de night, sometime—nobody don't know jis' when—run off to git married to dat young Harney Shepherdson, you know—leastways, so dey 'spec. De fambly foun' it out, 'bout half an hour ago—maybe a little mo'—en I *tell* you dey warn't no time los'. Sich another hurryin' up guns en hosses *you* never see! De women folks has gone for to stir up de relations, en ole mars Saul en de boys tuck dey guns en rode up de river road for to try to ketch dat young man en kill him 'fo' he kin git across de river wid Miss Sophia. I reck'n dey's gwyne to be mighty rough times."

"Buck went off 'thout waking me up."

"Well I reck'n he *did!* Dey warn't gwyne to mix you up in it. Mars Buck he loaded up his gun en 'lowed he's gwyne to fetch home a Shep-herdson or bust. Well, dey'll be plenty un 'm dah, I reck'n, en you bet you he'll fetch one ef he gits a chanst."

I took up the river road as hard as I could put. By and by I begin to hear guns a good ways off. When I come in sight of the log store and the wood-pile where the steamboats lands, I worked along under the trees and brush till I got to a good place, and then I clumb up into the forks of a cotton-wood that was out of reach, and watched. There was a wood-rank four foot high, a little ways in front of the tree, and first I was going to hide behind that; but maybe it was luckier I didn't.

There was four or five men cavorting around on their horses in the open place before the log store, cussing and yelling, and trying to get at a couple of young chaps that was behind the wood-rank alongside of the steamboat landing—but they couldn't come it. Every time one of them showed himself on the river side of the wood-pile he got shot at. The two boys was squatting back to back behind the pile, so they could watch both ways.

"BEHIND THE WOOD-RANK."

By and by the men stopped cavorting around and yelling. They started riding towards the store; then up gets one of the boys, draws a steady bead over the wood-rank, and drops one of them out of his saddle. All the men jumped off of their horses and grabbed the hurt one and started to carry him to the store; and that minute the two boys started on the run. They got half-way to the tree I was in before the men noticed. Then the men see them, and jumped on their horses and took out after them. They gained on the boys, but it didn't do no good, the boys had too good a start; they got to the wood-pile that was in front of my tree, and slipped in behind it, and so they had the bulge on the men again. One of the boys was Buck, and the other was a slim young chap about nineteen years old.

The men ripped around awhile, and then rode away. As soon as they was out of sight, I sung out to Buck and told him. He didn't know what to make of my voice coming out of the tree, at first. He was awful surprised. He told me to watch out sharp and let him know when the men come in sight again; said they was up to some devilment or other— wouldn't be gone long. I wished I was out of that tree, but I dasn't come down. Buck begun to cry and rip, and 'lowed that him and his cousin Joe (that was the other young chap) would make up for this day, yet. He said his father and his two brothers was killed, and two or three of the enemy. Said the Shepherdsons laid for them, in ambush. Buck said his father and brothers ought to waited for their relations—the Shepherdsons was too strong for them. I asked him what was become of young Harney and Miss Sophia. He said they'd got across the river and was safe. I was glad of that; but the way Buck did take on because he didn't manage to kill Harney that day he shot at him—I hain't ever heard anything like it.

All of a sudden, bang! bang! bang! goes three or four guns—the men had slipped around through the woods and come in from behind without their horses! The boys jumped for the river—both of them hurt— and as they swum down the current the men run along the bank shooting at them and singing out, "Kill them, kill them!" It made me so sick

I most fell out of the tree. I ain't agoing to tell *all* that happened—it would make me sick again if I was to do that. I wished I hadn't ever come ashore that night, to see such things. I ain't ever going to get shut of them—lots of times I dream about them.

I staid in the tree till it begun to get dark, afraid to come down. Sometimes I heard guns away off in the woods; and twice I seen little gangs of men gallop past the log store with guns; so I reckoned the trouble was still agoing on. I was mighty down-hearted; so I made up my mind I wouldn't ever go anear that house again, because I reckoned I was to blame, somehow. I judged that that piece of paper meant that Miss Sophia was to meet Harney somewheres at half-past two and run off; and I judged I ought to told her father about that paper and the curious way she acted, and then maybe he would a locked her up and this awful mess wouldn't ever happened.

When I got down out of the tree, I crept along down the river bank a piece, and found the two bodies laying in the edge of the water, and tugged at them till I got them ashore; then I covered up their faces, and got away as quick as I could. I cried a little when I was covering up Buck's face, for he was mighty good to me.

It was just dark, now. I never went near the house, but struck through the woods and made for the swamp. Jim warn't on his island, so I tramped off in a hurry for the crick, and crowded through the willows, red-hot to jump aboard and get out of that awful country—the raft was gone! My souls, but I was scared! I couldn't get my breath for most a minute. Then I raised a yell. A voice not twenty-five foot from me, says—

"Good lan'! is dat you, honey? Doan' make no noise."

It was Jim's voice—nothing ever sounded so good before. I run along the bank a piece and got aboard, and Jim he grabbed me and hugged me, he was so glad to see me. He says—

"Laws bless you, chile, I 'uz right down sho' you's dead agin. Jack's been heah, he say he reck'n you's ben shot, kase you didn' come home no mo'; so I's jes' dis minute a startin' de raf' down towards de mouf er de crick, so's to be all ready for to shove out en leave soon as Jack comes agin en tells me for certain you *is* dead. Lawsy, I's mighty glad to git you back agin, honey."

I says—

"All right—that's mighty good; they won't find me, and they'll think I've been killed, and floated down the river—there's something up there that'll help them to think so—so don't you lose no time, Jim, but just shove off for the big water as fast as ever you can."

I never felt easy till the raft was two mile below there and out in the middle of the Mississippi. Then we hung up our signal lantern, and judged that we was free and safe once more. I hadn't had a bite to eat since yesterday; so Jim he got out some corn-dodgers and buttermilk, and pork and cabbage, and greens—there ain't nothing in the world so good, when it's cooked right—and whilst I eat my supper we talked, and had a good time. I was powerful glad to get away from the feuds, and so was Jim to get away from the swamp. We said there warn't no home like a raft, after all. Other places do seem so cramped up and smothery, but a raft don't. You feel mighty free and easy and comfortable on a raft.

Chapter XIX

Two or three days and nights went by; I reckon I might say they swum by, they slid along so quiet and smooth and lovely. Here is the way we put in the time. It was a monstrous big river down there—sometimes a mile and a half wide; we run nights, and laid up and hid day-times; soon as night was most gone, we stopped navigating and tied up—nearly always in the dead water under a towhead; and then cut young cotton-woods and willows and hid the raft with them. Then we set out the lines. Next we slid into the river and had a swim, so as to freshen up and cool off; then we set down

HIDING DAY-TIMES

on the sandy bottom where the water was about knee deep, and watched the daylight come. Not a sound, anywheres—perfectly still—just like the whole world was asleep, only sometimes the bull-frogs a-cluttering, maybe. The first thing to see, looking away over the water, was a kind of dull line—that was the woods on t'other side—you couldn't make nothing else out; then a pale place in the sky; then more paleness, spreading around; then the river softened up, away off, and warn't black any more, but gray; you could see little dark spots drifting along, ever so far away—trading scows, and such things; and long black streaks—rafts; sometimes you could hear a sweep screaking; or jumbled up voices, it was so still, and sounds come so far; and by and by you could see a streak on the water which you know by the look of the streak that there's a snag there in a swift current which breaks on it and makes that streak look that way; and you see the mist curl up off of the water, and the east reddens up, and the river, and you make out a log cabin in the edge of the woods, away on the bank on t'other side of the river, being a wood-yard, likely, and piled by them cheats so you can throw a dog through it anywheres;[1] then the nice breeze springs up, and comes fanning you from over there, so cool and fresh, and sweet to smell, on account of the woods and the flowers; but sometimes not that

1. The yard's customers were cheated because stacks of wood were sold by volume, gaps included.

135

way, because they've left dead fish laying around, gars, and such, and they do get pretty rank; and next you've got the full day, and everything smiling in the sun, and the songbirds just going it!

A little smoke couldn't be noticed, now, so we would take some fish off of the lines, and cook up a hot breakfast. And afterwards we would watch the lonesomeness of the river, and kind of lazy along, and by and by lazy off to sleep. Wake up, by and by, and look to see what done it, and maybe see a steamboat, coughing along up stream, so far off towards the other side you couldn't tell nothing about her only whether she was stern-wheel or side-wheel; then for about an hour there wouldn't be nothing to hear nor nothing to see—just solid lonesomeness. Next you'd see a raft sliding by, away off yonder, and maybe a galoot on it chopping, because they're most always doing it on a raft; you'd see the axe flash, and come down—you don't hear nothing; you see that axe go up again, and by the time it's above the man's head, then you hear the *k'chunk!*— it had took all that time to come over the water. So we would put in the day, lazying around, listening to the stillness. Once there was a thick fog, and the rafts and things that went by was beating tin pans so the steamboats wouldn't run over them. A scow or a raft went by so close we could hear them talking and cussing and laughing—heard them plain; but we couldn't see no sign of them; it made you feel crawly, it was like spirits carrying on that way in the air. Jim said he believed it was spirits; but I says:

"No, spirits wouldn't say, 'dern the dern fog.'"

Soon as it was night, out we shoved; when we got her out to about the middle, we let her alone, and let her float wherever the current wanted her to; then we lit the pipes, and dangled our legs in the water and talked about all kinds of things—we was always naked, day and night, whenever the mosquitoes would let us—the new clothes Buck's folks made for me was too good to be comfortable, and besides I didn't go much on clothes, nohow.

Sometimes we'd have that whole river all to ourselves for the longest time. Yonder was the banks and the islands, across the water; and maybe a spark—which was a candle in a cabin window—and sometimes on the water you could see a spark or two—on a raft or a scow, you know; and maybe you could hear a fiddle or a song coming over from one of them crafts. It's lovely to live on a raft. We had the sky, up there, all speckled with stars, and we used to lay on our backs and look up at them, and discuss about whether they was made, or only just happened—Jim he allowed they was made, but I allowed they happened; I judged it would have took too long to *make* so many. Jim said the moon could a *laid* them; well, that looked kind of reasonable, so I didn't say nothing against it, because I've seen a frog lay most as many, so of course it could be done. We used to watch the stars that fell, too, and see them streak down. Jim allowed they'd got spoiled and was hove out of the nest.

Once or twice of a night we would see a steamboat slipping along in the dark, and now and then she would belch a whole world of sparks up out of her chimbleys, and they would rain down in the river and look awful pretty; then she would turn a corner and her lights would wink

out and her pow-wow[2] shut off and leave the river still again; and by and
by her waves would get to us, a long time after she was gone, and joggle
the raft a bit, and after that you wouldn't hear nothing for you couldn't
tell how long, except maybe frogs or something.

After midnight the people on shore went to bed, and then for two or
three hours the shores was black—no more sparks in the cabin windows. These sparks was our clock—the first one that showed again
meant morning was coming, so we hunted a place to hide and tie up,
right away.

One morning about day-break, I found a canoe[3] and crossed over a
chute to the main shore—it was only two hundred yards—and paddled
about a mile up a crick amongst the cypress woods, to see if I couldn't
get some berries. Just as I was passing a place where a kind of a cow-
path crossed the crick, here comes a couple of men tearing up the path
as tight as they could foot it. I thought I was a goner, for whenever anybody was after anybody I judged it was *me*—or maybe Jim. I was about
to dig out from there in a hurry, but they was pretty close to me then,
and sung out and begged me to save their lives—said they hadn't been
doing nothing, and was being chased for it—said there was men and
dogs a-coming. They wanted to jump right in, but I says—

"Don't you do it. I don't hear the dogs and horses yet; you've got time
to crowd through the brush and get up the crick a little ways; then you
take to the water and wade down to me and get in—that'll throw the
dogs off the scent."

They done it, and soon as they was aboard I lit out for our tow-head,
and in about five or ten minutes we heard the dogs and the men away
off, shouting. We heard them come along towards the crick, but could-
n't see them; they seemed to stop and fool around a while; then, as we
got further and further away all the time, we couldn't hardly hear them
at all; by the time we had left a mile of woods behind us and struck the
river, everything was quiet, and we paddled over to the tow-head and
hid in the cotton-woods and was safe.

One of these fellows was about seventy, or upwards, and had a bald
head and very gray whiskers. He had an old battered-up slouch hat on,
and a greasy blue woolen shirt, and ragged old blue jeans britches
stuffed into his boot tops, and home-knit galluses[4]—no, he only had
one. He had an old long-tailed blue jeans coat with slick brass buttons,
flung over his arm, and both of them had big fat ratty-looking carpet-
bags.

The other fellow was about thirty and dressed about as ornery. After
breakfast we all laid off and talked, and the first thing that come out was
that these chaps didn't know one another.

---

2. Racket, commotion.
3. During the three years he set the manuscript aside, Mark Twain apparently forgot that the canoe
   had been lost in chapter 16, for when he started writing again, Huck simply "took the canoe," an
   inconsistency the author did not correct to "found a canoe" until the book was in page-proofs.
   Earlier the canoe had to be "lost" because it would have afforded Huck and Jim the means of
   heading north. Evidently, Mark Twain wanted to keep his narrative in familiar territory, even
   though it meant sending an escaping slave south. By 1879, the author no longer had to worry
   about such minor logical obstacles as canoes because he had thought up the duke and the king,
   who take control of the raft and direct it downriver along the shore.
4. Suspenders.

"AND DOGS A-COMING."

"What got you into trouble?" says the baldhead to t'other chap.

"Well, I'd been selling an article to take the tartar off the teeth—and it does take it off, too, and generly the enamel along with it—but I staid about one night longer than I ought to, and was just in the act of sliding out when I ran across you on the trail this side of town, and you told me they were coming, and begged me to help you to get off. So I told you I was expecting trouble myself and would scatter out *with* you. That's the whole yarn—what's yourn?"

"Well, I'd ben a-runnin' a little temperance revival thar, 'bout a week, and was the pet of the women-folks, big and little, for I was makin' it mighty warm for the rummies, I *tell* you, and takin' as much as five or six dollars a night—ten cents a head, children and niggers free—and business a growin' all the time; when somehow or another a little report got around, last night, that I had a way of puttin' in my time with a private jug, on the sly. A nigger rousted me out this mornin', and told me the people was getherin' on the quiet, with their dogs and horses, and they'd be along pretty soon and give me 'bout half an hour's start, and then run me down, if they could; and if they got me they'd tar and feather me and ride me on a rail, sure.[5] I didn't wait for no breakfast—I warn't hungry."

"Old man," says the young one, "I reckon we might double-team it together; what do you think?"

"I ain't undisposed. What's your line—mainly?"

5. For Kemble's illustration of this cruel practice, see "Traveling by Rail" on p. 239.

"Jour printer,[6] by trade; do a little in patent medicines; theatre-actor—tragedy, you know; take a turn at mesmerism and phrenology[7] when there's a chance; teach singing-geography school for a change; sling a lecture, sometimes—oh, I do lots of things—most anything that comes handy, so it ain't work. What's your lay?"

"I've done considerble in the doctoring way in my time. Layin' on o' hands is my best holt—for cancer, and paralysis, and sich things; and I k'n tell a fortune pretty good, when I've got somebody along to find out the facts for me. Preachin's my line, too; and workin' camp-meetin's; and missionaryin' around."

Nobody never said anything for a while; then the young man hove a sigh and says—

"Alas!"

"What're you alassin' about?" says the baldhead.

"To think I should have lived to be leading such a life, and be degraded down into such company." And he begun to wipe the corner of his eye with a rag.

"Dern your skin, ain't the company good enough for you?" says the baldhead, pretty pert and uppish.

"Yes, it *is* good enough for me; it's as good as I deserve; for who fetched me so low, when I was so high? *I* did myself. I don't blame *you*, gentlemen—far from it; I don't blame anybody. I deserve it all. Let the cold world do its worst; one thing I know—there's a grave somewhere for me. The world may go on just as it's always done, and take everything from me—loved ones, property, everything—but it can't take that. Some day I'll lie down in it and forget it all, and my poor broken heart will be at rest." He went on a-wiping.

"Drot your pore broken heart," says the baldhead; "what are you heaving your pore broken heart at *us* f'r? *We* hain't done nothing."

"No, I know you haven't. I ain't blaming you, gentlemen. I brought myself down—yes, I did it myself. It's right I should suffer—perfectly right—I don't make any moan."

"Brought you down from whar? Whar was you brought down from?"

"Ah, you would not believe me; the world never believes—let it pass—'tis no matter. The secret of my birth—"

"The secret of your birth? Do you mean to say—"

"Gentlemen," says the young man, very solemn, "I will reveal it to you, for I feel I may have confidence in you. By rights I am a duke!"

Jim's eyes bugged out when he heard that; and I reckon mine did, too. Then the baldhead says: "No! you can't mean it?"

"Yes. My great-grandfather, eldest son of the Duke of Bridgewater, fled to this country about the end of the last century, to breathe the pure air of freedom; married here, and died, leaving a son, his own father dying about the same time. The second son of the late duke seized the title and estates—the infant real duke was ignored. I am the lineal descendant of that infant—I am the rightful Duke of Bridgewa-

6. Journeyman printer, one who worked by the day.
7. Hyponotism and the pseudoscience of reading character from the natural bumps and valleys of the head.

"BY RIGHTS I AM A DUKE!"

ter; and here am I, forlorn, torn from my high estate, hunted of men, despised by the cold world, ragged, worn, heart-broken, and degraded to the companionship of felons on a raft!"

Jim pitied him ever so much, and so did I. We tried to comfort him, but said it warn't much use, he couldn't be much comforted; said if we was a mind to acknowledge him, that would do him more good than most anything else; so we said we would, if he would tell us how. He said we ought to bow, when we spoke to him, and say "Your Grace," or "My Lord," or "Your Lordship"—and he wouldn't mind it if we called him plain "Bridgewater," which he said was a title, anyway, and not a name; and one of us ought to wait on him at dinner, and do any little thing for him he wanted done.

Well, that was all easy, so we done it. All through dinner Jim stood around and waited on him, and says, "Will yo' Grace have some o' dis, or some o' dat?" and so on, and a body could see it was mighty pleasing to him.

But the old man got pretty silent, by and by—didn't have much to say, and didn't look pretty comfortable over all that petting that was going on around that duke. He seemed to have something on his mind. So, along in the afternoon, he says:

"Looky here, Bilgewater," he says, "I'm nation sorry for you, but you ain't the only person that's had troubles like that."

"No?"

"No, you ain't. You ain't the only person that's ben snaked down wrongfully out'n a high place."

"Alas!"

"No, you ain't the only person that's had a secret of his birth." And by jings, *he* begins to cry.

"Hold! What do you mean?"

"Bilgewater, kin I trust you?" says the old man, still sort of sobbing.

"To the bitter death!" He took the old man by the hand and squeezed it, and says, "The secret of your being: speak!"

"Bilgewater, I am the late Dauphin!"

You bet you Jim and me stared, this time. Then the duke says:

"You are what?"

"Yes, my friend, it is too true—your eyes is lookin' at this very moment on the pore disappeared Dauphin, Looy the Seventeen, son of Looy the Sixteen and Marry Antonette."

"You! At your age! No! You mean you're the late Charlemagne;[8] you must be six or seven hundred years old, at the very least."

"Trouble has done it, Bilgewater, trouble has done it; trouble has brung these gray hairs and this premature balditude. Yes, gentlemen, you see before you, in blue jeans and misery, the wanderin', exiled, trampled-on and sufferin' rightful King of France."

Well, he cried and took on so, that me and Jim didn't know hardly what to do, we was so sorry—and so glad and proud we'd got him with us, too. So we set in, like we done before with the duke, and tried to

"I AM THE LATE DAUPHIN!"

comfort *him*. But he said it warn't no use, nothing but to be dead and done with it all could do him any good; though he said it often made him feel easier and better for a while if people treated him according to

8. Louis XVII died in 1795, and Charlemagne in 814.

his rights, and got down on one knee to speak to him, and always called him "Your Majesty," and waited on him first at meals, and didn't set down in his presence till he asked them. So Jim and me set to majestying him, and doing this and that and t'other for him, and standing up till he told us we might set down. This done him heaps of good, and so he got cheerful and comfortable. But the duke kind of soured on him, and didn't look a bit satisfied with the way things was going; still, the king acted real friendly towards him, and said the duke's great-grandfather and all the other Dukes of Bilgewater was a good deal thought of by *his* father and was allowed to come to the palace considerable; but the duke staid huffy a good while, till by and by the king says:

"Like as not we got to be together a blamed long time, on thish-yer raft, Bilgewater, and so what's the use o' your bein' sour? It'll only make things oncomfortable. It ain't my fault I warn't born a duke, it ain't your fault you warn't born a king—so what's the use to worry? Make the best o' things the way you find 'em, says I—that's my motto. This ain't no bad thing that we've struck here—plenty grub and an easy life—come, give us your hand, Duke, and less all be friends."

The duke done it, and Jim and me was pretty glad to see it. It took away all the uncomfortableness, and we felt mighty good over it, because it would a been a miserable business to have any unfriendliness on the raft; for what you want, above all things, on a raft, is for everybody to be satisfied, and feel right and kind towards the others.

It didn't take me long to make up my mind that these liars warn't no kings nor dukes, at all, but just low-down humbugs and frauds. But I never said nothing, never let on; kept it to myself; it's the best way; then you don't have no quarrels, and don't get into no trouble. If they wanted us to call them kings and dukes, I hadn't no objections, long as it would keep peace in the family; and it warn't no use to tell Jim, so I didn't tell him. If I never learnt nothing else out of pap, I learnt that the best way to get along with his kind of people is to let them have their own way.

Chapter XX

ON THE RAFT.

THEY ASKED US considerable many questions; wanted to know what we covered up the raft that way for, and laid by in the day-time instead of running—was Jim a runaway nigger? Says I—

"Goodness sakes, would a runaway nigger run *south*?"

No, they allowed he wouldn't. I had to account for things some way, so I says:

"My folks was living in Pike County, in Missouri, where I was born, and they all died off but me and pa and my brother Ike. Pa, he 'lowed he'd break up and go down and live with uncle Ben, who's got a little one-horse place on the river, forty-four mile below Orleans. Pa was pretty poor, and had some debts; so when he'd squared up there warn't nothing left but sixteen dollars and our nigger, Jim. That warn't enough to take us fourteen hundred mile, deck passage nor no other way. Well, when the river rose, pa had a streak of luck one day; he ketched this piece of a raft; so we reckoned we'd go down to Orleans on it. Pa's luck didn't hold out; a steamboat run over the forrard corner of the raft, one night, and we all went overboard and dove under the wheel; Jim and me come up, all right, but pa was drunk, and Ike was only four years old, so they never come up no more. Well, for the next day or two we had considerable trouble, because people was always coming out in skiffs and trying to take Jim away from me, saying they believed he was a runaway nigger. We don't run day-times no more, now; nights they don't bother us."

The duke says—

"Leave me alone to cipher out a way so we can run in the day-time if we want to. I'll think the thing over—I'll invent a plan that'll fix it. We'll let it alone for to-day, because of course we don't want to go by that town yonder in daylight—it mightn't be healthy."

Towards night it begun to darken up and look like rain; the heat lightning was squirting around, low down in the sky, and the leaves was beginning to shiver—it was going to be pretty ugly, it was easy to see that. So the duke and the king went to overhauling our wigwam, to see what the beds was like. My bed was a straw tick—better than Jim's, which was a corn-shuck tick; there's always cobs around about in a shuck tick, and they poke into you and hurt; and when you roll over, the dry shucks sound like you was rolling over in a pile of dead leaves; it makes such a rustling that you wake up. Well, the duke allowed he would take my bed; but the king allowed he wouldn't. He says—

"I should a reckoned the difference in rank would a sejested to you that a corn-shuck bed warn't just fitten for me to sleep on. Your Grace'll take the shuck bed yourself."

Jim and me was in a sweat again, for a minute, being afraid there was going to be some more trouble amongst them; so we was pretty glad when the duke says—

" 'Tis my fate to be always ground into the mire under the iron heel of oppression. Misfortune has broken my once haughty spirit; I yield, I submit; 'tis my fate. I am alone in the world—let me suffer; I can bear it."

We got away as soon as it was good and dark. The king told us to stand well out towards the middle of the river, and not show a light till we got a long ways below the town. We come in sight of the little bunch of lights by and by—that was the town, you know—and slid by, about a half a mile out, all right. When we was three-quarters of a mile below, we hoisted up our signal lantern; and about ten o'clock it come on to rain and blow and thunder and lighten like everything; so the king told us to both stay on watch till the weather got better; then him and the duke crawled into the wigwam and turned in for the night. It was my watch below, till twelve, but I wouldn't a turned in, anyway, if I'd had a bed; because a body don't see such a storm as that every day in the week, not by a long sight. My souls, how the wind did scream along! And every second or two there'd come a glare that lit up the white-caps for a half a mile around, and you'd see the islands looking dusty through the rain, and the trees thrashing around in the wind; then comes a *h-wack!*—bum! bum! bumble-umble-um-bum-bum-bum-bum—and the thunder would go rumbling and grumbling away, and quit—and then *rip* comes another flash and another sockdolager.[1] The waves most washed me off the raft, sometimes, but I hadn't any clothes on, and didn't mind. We didn't have no trouble about snags; the lightning was glaring and flittering around so constant that we could see them plenty soon enough to throw her head this way or that and miss them.

I had the middle watch, you know, but I was pretty sleepy by that time, so Jim he said he would stand the first half of it for me; he was always mighty good, that way, Jim was. I crawled into the wigwam, but the king and the duke had their legs sprawled around so there warn't no show for me; so I laid outside—I didn't mind the rain, because it was warm, and the waves warn't running so high, now. About two they come up again, though, and Jim was going to call me, but he changed his mind because he reckoned they warn't high enough yet to do any harm; but he was mistaken about that, for pretty soon all of a sudden along comes a regular ripper, and washed me overboard. It most killed Jim a-laughing. He was the easiest nigger to laugh that ever was, anyway.

1. A humdinger of a thunderclap.

I took the watch, and Jim he laid down and snored away; and by and by the storm let up for good and all; and the first cabin-light that showed, I rousted him out and we slid the raft into hiding-quarters for the day.

The king got out an old ratty deck of cards, after breakfast, and him and the duke played seven-up[2] a while, five cents a game. Then they got tired of it, and allowed they would "lay out a campaign," as they called it. The duke went down into his carpet-bag and fetched up a lot of little printed bills, and read them out loud. One bill said "The celebrated Dr. Armand de Montalban of Paris," would "lecture on the Science of Phrenology" at such and such a place, on the blank day of blank, at ten cents admission, and "furnish charts of character at twenty-five cents apiece." The duke said that was *him*. In another bill he was the "world renowned Shaksperean tragedian, Garrick the Younger, of Drury Lane, London."[3] In other bills he had a lot of other names and done other wonderful things, like finding water and gold with a "divining rod," "dissipating witch-spells," and so on. By and by he says—

"But the histrionic muse is the darling. Have you ever trod the boards, Royalty?"

"No," says the king.

"You shall, then, before you're three days older, Fallen Grandeur," says the duke. "The first good town we come to, we'll hire a hall and do the sword-fight in Richard III. and the balcony scene in Romeo and Juliet. How does that strike you?"

"I'm in, up to the hub, for anything that will pay, Bilgewater, but you see I don't know nothing about play-actn', and hain't ever seen much of it. I was too small when pap used to have 'em at the palace. Do you reckon you can learn me?"

"Easy!"

"All right. I'm jist a-freezn' for something fresh, anyway. Less commence, right away."

So the duke he told him all about who Romeo was, and who Juliet was, and said he was used to being Romeo, so the king could be Juliet.

"But if Juliet's such a young gal, Duke, my peeled head and my white whiskers is goin' to look oncommon odd on her, maybe."

"No, don't you worry—these country jakes won't ever think of that. Besides, you know, you'll be in costume, and that makes all the difference in the world; Juliet's in a balcony, enjoying the moonlight before she goes to bed, and she's got on her night-gown and her ruffled night-cap. Here are the costumes for the parts."

He got out two or three curtain-calico suits, which he said was meedyevil armor for Richard III. and t'other chap, and a long white cotton night-shirt and a ruffled night-cap to match. The king was satisfied; so the duke got out his book and read the parts over in the most splendid spread-eagle way, prancing around and acting at the same time, to

---

2. A trumping game, also called "All Fours" and "Old Sledge."
3. Here and in the next two chapters the duke confuses three famous British actors: David Garrick (1717–1779), Edmund Kean (1787–1833), and his son Charles John Kean (1811?–1868). The original Theatre Royal in Drury Lane was built in 1663.

THE KING AS JULIET.

show how it had got to be done; then he give the book to the king and told him to get his part by heart.

There was a little one-horse town about three mile down the bend, and after dinner the duke said he had ciphered out his idea about how to run in daylight without it being dangersome for Jim; so he allowed he would go down to the town and fix that thing. The king allowed he would go too, and see if he couldn't strike something. We was out of coffee, so Jim said I better go along with them in the canoe and get some.

When we got there, there warn't nobody stirring; streets empty, and perfectly dead and still, like Sunday. We found a sick nigger sunning himself in a back yard, and he said everybody that warn't too young or too sick or too old, was gone to camp-meeting, about two mile back in the woods. The king got the directions, and allowed he'd go and work that camp-meeting for all it was worth, and I might go, too.

The duke said what he was after was a printing office. We found it; a little bit of a concern, up over a carpenter shop—carpenters and printers all gone to the meeting, and no doors locked. It was a dirty, littered-up place, and had ink marks, and handbills with pictures of horses and runaway niggers on them, all over the walls. The duke shed his coat and said he was all right, now. So me and the king lit out for the camp-meeting.

We got there in about a half an hour, fairly dripping, for it was a most awful hot day. There was as much as a thousand people there, from twenty mile around. The woods was full of teams and wagons, hitched everywheres, feeding out of the wagon troughs and stomping to keep off the flies. There was sheds made out of poles and roofed over with branches, where they had lemonade and gingerbread to sell, and piles of watermelons and green corn and such-like truck.

The preaching was going on under the same kinds of sheds, only they was bigger and held crowds of people. The benches was made out of outside slabs of logs, with holes bored in the round side to drive sticks into for legs. They didn't have no backs. The preachers had high platforms to stand on, at one end of the sheds. The women had on sun-bon-

"COURTING ON THE SLY."

nets; and some had linsey-woolsey[4] frocks, some gingham ones, and a few of the young ones had on calico. Some of the young men was bare-footed, and some of the children didn't have on any clothes but just a tow-linen shirt. Some of the old women was knitting, and some of the young folks was courting on the sly.

The first shed we come to, the preacher was lining out a hymn. He lined out two lines, everybody sung it, and it was kind of grand to hear it, there was so many of them and they done it in such a rousing way; then he lined out two more for them to sing—and so on. The people woke up more and more, and sung louder and louder; and towards the end, some begun to groan, and some begun to shout. Then the preacher begun to preach; and begun in earnest, too; and went weaving first to one side of the platform and then the other, and then a leaning down over the front of it, with his arms and his body going all the time, and shouting his words out with all his might; and every now and then he would hold up his Bible and spread it open, and kind of pass it around this way and that, shouting, "It's the brazen serpent in the wilderness! Look upon it and live!" And people would shout out, "Glory!—A-a-*men!*" And so he went on, and the people groaning and crying and saying amen:

"Oh, come to the mourners' bench![5] come, black with sin! (*amen!*) come, sick and sore! (*amen!*) come, lame and halt, and blind! (*amen!*) come, pore and needy, sunk in shame! (*a-a-men!*) come all that's worn, and soiled, and suffering!—come with a broken spirit! come with a con-

4. Coarse cloth made of linen and wool or cotton and wool.
5. Front-row seats reserved for penitents.

trite heart! come in your rags and sin and dirt! the waters that cleanse is free, the door of heaven stands open—oh, enter in and be at rest!" (*a-a-men! glory, glory hallelujah!*)

And so on. You couldn't make out what the preacher said, any more, on account of the shouting and crying. Folks got up, everywheres in the crowd, and worked their way, just by main strength, to the mourners' bench, with the tears running down their faces; and when all the mourners had got up there to the front benches in a crowd, they sung, and shouted, and flung themselves down on the straw, just crazy and wild.

Well, the first I knowed, the king got agoing; and you could hear him over everybody; and next he went a-charging up on to the platform and the preacher he begged him to speak to the people, and he done it. He told them he was a pirate—been a pirate for thirty years, out in the Indian Ocean, and his crew was thinned out considerable, last spring, in a fight, and he was home now, to take out some fresh men, and thanks to goodness he'd been robbed last night, and put ashore off of a steamboat without a cent, and he was glad of it, it was the blessedest thing that ever happened to him, because he was a changed man now, and happy for the first time in his life; and poor as he was, he was going

"A PIRATE FOR THIRTY YEARS."

to start right off and work his way back to the Indian Ocean and put in the rest of his life trying to turn the pirates into the true path; for he could do it better than anybody else, being acquainted with all the pirate crews in that ocean; and though it would take him a long time to get there, without money, he would get there anyway, and every time he convinced a pirate he would say to him, "Don't you thank me, don't you give me no credit, it all belongs to them dear people in Pokeville camp-meeting, natural brothers and benefactors of the race—and that dear preacher there, the truest friend a pirate ever had!"

And then he busted into tears, and so did everybody. Then somebody sings out, "Take up a collection for him, take up a collection!" Well, a half a dozen made a jump to do it, but somebody sings out, "Let *him* pass the hat around!" Then everybody said it, the preacher too.

So the king went all through the crowd with his hat, swabbing his eyes, and blessing the people and praising them and thanking them for being so good to the poor pirates away off there; and every little while the prettiest kind of girls, with the tears running down their cheeks, would up and ask him would he let them kiss him, for to remember him by; and he always done it; and some of them he hugged and kissed as many as five or six times—and he was invited to stay a week; and everybody wanted him to live in their houses, and said they'd think it was an honor; but he said as this was the last day of the camp-meeting he couldn't do no good, and besides he was in a sweat to get to the Indian Ocean right off and go to work on the pirates.

When we got back to the raft and he come to count up, he found he had collected eighty-seven dollars and seventy-five cents. And then he had fetched away a three-gallon jug of whisky, too, that he found under a wagon when we was starting home through the woods. The king said, take it all around, it laid over any day he'd ever put in in the missionarying line. He said it warn's no use talking, heathens don't amount to shucks, alongside of pirates, to work a camp-meeting with.

The duke was thinking *he'd* been doing pretty well, till the king come to show up, but after that he didn't think so so much. He had set up and printed off two little jobs for farmers, in that printing office—horse bills—and took the money, four dollars. And he had got in ten dollars' worth of advertisements for the paper, which he said he would put in for four dollars if they would pay in advance—so they done it. The price of the paper was two dollars a year, but he took in three subscriptions for half a dollar apiece on condition of them paying him in advance; they were going to pay in cord-wood and onions, as usual, but he said he had just bought the concern and knocked down the price as low as he could afford it, and was going to run it for cash. He set up a little piece of poetry, which he made, himself, out of his own head—three verses— kind of sweet and saddish—the name of it was, "Yes, crush, cold world, this breaking heart"—and he left that all set up and ready to print in the paper and didn't charge nothing for it. Well, he took in nine dollars and a half, and said he'd done a pretty square day's work for it.

Then he showed us another little job he'd printed and hadn't charged for, because it was for us. It had a picture of a runaway nigger, with a bundle on a stick, over his shoulder, and "$200 reward" under it. The reading was all about Jim, and just described him to a dot. It said he run away from St. Jacques' plantation, forty mile below New Orleans, last winter, and likely went north, and whoever would catch him and send him back, he could have the reward and expenses.

"Now," says the duke, "after to-night we can run in the daytime if we want to. Whenever we see anybody coming, we can tie Jim hand and foot with a rope, and lay him in the wigwam and show this handbill and

ANOTHER LITTLE JOB.

say we captured him up the river, and were too poor to travel on a steamboat, so we got this little raft on credit from our friends and are going down to get the reward. Handcuffs and chains would look still better on Jim, but it wouldn't go well with the story of us being so poor. Too much like jewelry. Ropes are the correct thing—we must preserve the unities, as we say on the boards."

We all said the duke was pretty smart, and there couldn't be no trouble about running daytimes. We judged we could make miles enough that night to get out of the reach of the pow-wow we reckoned the duke's work in the printing office was going to make in that little town—then we could boom right along, if we wanted to.

We laid low and kept still, and never shoved out till nearly ten o'clock; then we slid by, pretty wide away from the town, and didn't hoist our lantern till we was clear out of sight of it.

When Jim called me to take the watch at four in the morning, he says—

"Huck, does you reck'n we gwyne to run acrost any mo' kings on dis trip?"

"No," I says, "I reckon not."

"Well," says he, "dat's all right, den. I doan' mine one er two kings, but dat's enough. Dis one's powerful drunk, en de duke ain' much better."

I found Jim had been trying to get him to talk French, so he could hear what it was like; but he said he had been in this country so long, and had so much trouble, he'd forgot it.

Chapter XXI

PRACTICING.

IT was after sun-up, now, but we went right on, and didn't tie up. The king and the duke turned out, by and by, looking pretty rusty; but after they'd jumped overboard and took a swim, it chippered them up a good deal. After breakfast the king he took a seat on a corner of the raft, and pulled off his boots and rolled up his britches, and let his legs dangle in the water, so as to be comfortable, and lit his pipe, and went to getting his Romeo and Juliet by heart. When he had got it pretty good, him and the duke begun to practice it together. The duke had to learn him over and over again, how to say every speech; and he made him sigh, and put his hand on his heart, and after a while he said he done it pretty well; "only," he says, "you mustn't bellow out *Romeo!* that way, like a bull—you must say it soft, and sick, and languishy, so—R-o-o-meo! that is the idea; for Juliet's a dear sweet mere child of a girl, you know, and she don't bray like a jack-ass."

Well, next they got out a couple of long swords that the duke made out of oak laths, and begun to practice the sword-fight—the duke called himself Richard III.; and the way they laid on, and pranced around the raft was grand to see. But by and by the king tripped and fell overboard, and after that they took a rest, and had a talk about all kinds of adventures they'd had in other times along the river.

After dinner, the duke says:

"Well, Capet,[1] we'll want to made this a first-class show, you know, so I guess we'll add a little more to it. We want a little something to answer encores with, anyway."

"What's onkores, Bilgewater?"

The duke told him, and then says:

"I'll answer by doing the Highland fling or the sailor's hornpipe; and you—well, let me see—oh, I've got it—you can do Hamlet's soliloquy."

"Hamlet's which?"

---

1. When convicting Louis XVI, the National Convention used his family name, Louis Capet. The duke may also be garbling Juliet's family name, Capulet.

"Hamlet's soliloquy, you know; the most celebrated thing in Shakespeare. Ah, it's sublime, sublime! Always fetches the house. I haven't got it in the book—I've only got one volume—but I reckon I can piece it out from memory. I'll just walk up and down a minute, and see if I can call it back from recollection's vaults."

So he went to marching up and down, thinking, and frowning horrible every now and then; then he would hoist up his eye-brows; next he would squeeze his hand on his forehead and stagger back and kind of moan; next he would sigh, and next he'd let on to drop a tear. It was beautiful to see him. By and by he got it. He told us to give attention. Then he strikes a most noble attitude, with one leg shoved forwards, and his arms stretched away up, and his head tilted back, looking up at the sky; and then he begins to rip and rave and grit his teeth; and after that, all through his speech he howled, and spread around, and swelled up his chest, and just knocked the spots out of any acting ever I see before. This is the speech—I learned it, easy enough, while he was learning it to the king:[2]

> To be, or not to be; that is the bare bodkin
> That makes calamity of so long life;
> For who would fardels bear, till Birnam Wood do come to
> Dunsinane,
> But that the fear of something after death
> Murders the innocent sleep,
> Great nature's second course,
> And makes us rather sling the arrows of outrageous fortune
> Than fly to others that we know not of.
> There's the respect must give us pause:
> Wake Duncan with thy knocking! I would thou couldst;
> For who would bear the whips and scorns of time,
> The oppressor's wrong, the proud man's contumely,
> The law's delay, and the quietus which his pangs might take,
> In the dead waste and middle of the night, when churchyards
> yawn
> In customary suits of solemn black,
> But that the undiscovered country from whose bourne no traveler
> returns,
> Breathes forth contagion on the world,
> And thus the native hue of resolution, like the poor cat i' the
> adage,
> Is sicklied o'er with care,
> And all the clouds that lowered o'er our housetops,
> With this regard their currents turn awry,
> And lose the name of action.
> 'Tis a consummation devoutly to be wished. But soft you, the fair
> Ophelia:
> Ope not thy ponderous and marble jaws,
> But get thee to a nunnery—go!

2. The duke is supposed to be reciting the soliloquy from *Hamlet*, Act III, scene ii, but his fractured Shakespeare distorts lines from several other plays, particularly *Macbeth* and *Richard III*.

HAMLET'S SOLILOQUY.

Well, the old man he liked that speech, and he mighty soon got it so he could do it first rate. It seemed like he was just born for it; and when he had his hand in and was excited, it was perfectly lovely the way he would rip and tear and rair up behind when he was getting it off.

The first chance we got, the duke he had some show bills printed; and after that, for two or three days as we floated along, the raft was a most uncommon lively place, for there warn't nothing but sword-fighting and rehearsing—as the duke called it—going on all the time. One morning, when we was pretty well down the State of Arkansaw, we come in sight of a little one-horse town in a big bend;[3] so we tied up about three-quarters of a mile above it, in the mouth of a crick which was shut in like a tunnel by the cypress trees, and all of us but Jim took the canoe and went down there to see if there was any chance in that place for our show.

We struck it mighty lucky; there was going to be a circus there that afternoon, and the country people was already beginning to come in, in all kinds of old shackly wagons, and on horses. The circus would leave before night, so our show would have a pretty good chance. The duke he hired the court house, and we went around and stuck up our bills. They read like this:

---

3. "Bricksville," based on Napoleon, Arkansas, at the confluence of the Arkansas and Mississippi rivers.

Shaksperean Revival!!!
Wonderful Attraction!
For One Night Only!
The world renowned tragedians,
David Garrick the younger, of Drury Lane Theatre, London,
and
Edmund Kean the elder, of the Royal Haymarket Theatre, White-
chapel, Pudding Lane, Piccadilly, London, and the
Royal Continental Theatres, in their sublime
Shaksperean Spectacle entitled
The Balcony Scene
in
Romeo and Juliet!!!
Romeo . . . . Mr. Garrick.
Juliet . . . . Mr. Kean.
Assisted by the whole strength of the company!
New costumes, new scenery, new appointments!
Also:
The thrilling, masterly, and blood-curdling
Broad-sword conflict
In Richard III.!!!
Richard III . . . . Mr. Garrick.
Richmond . . . . Mr. Kean.
also:
(by special request,)
Hamlet's Immortal Soliloquy!!
By the Illustrious Kean!
Done by him 300 consecutive nights in Paris!
For One Night Only,
On account of imperative European engagements!
Admission 25 cents; children and servants, 10 cents.

Then we went loafing around the town. The stores and houses was most all old shackly dried-up frame concerns that hadn't ever been painted; they was set up three or four foot above ground on stilts, so as to be out of reach of the water when the river was overflowed. The houses had little gardens around them, but they didn't seem to raise hardly anything in them but jimpson weeds, and sunflowers, and ash-piles, and old curled-up boots and shoes, and pieces of bottles, and rags, and played-out tin-ware. The fences was made of different kinds of boards, nailed on at different times; and they leaned every which-way, and had gates that didn't generly have but one hinge—a leather one. Some of the fences had been whitewashed, some time or another, but the duke said it was in Clumbus's time, like enough. There was gen-erly hogs in the garden, and people driving them out.

All the stores was along one street. They had white-domestic awnings in front, and the country people hitched their horses to the awning-posts. There was empty dry-goods boxes under the awnings, and loafers roosting on them all day long, whittling them with their Barlow knives; and chawing tobacco, and gaping and yawning and stretching—a mighty ornery lot. They generly had on yellow straw hats most as wide as an umbrella, but didn't wear no coats nor waistcoats; they called one another Bill, and Buck, and Hank, and Joe, and Andy, and talked lazy and drawly, and used considerable many cuss-words. There was as many as one loafer leaning up against every awning-post, and he most always had his hands in his britches pockets, except when he fetched them out to lend a chaw of tobacco or scratch. What a body was hearing amongst them, all the time was—

"Gimme a chaw 'v tobacker, Hank."

"Cain't—I hain't got but one chaw left. Ask Bill."

Maybe Bill he gives him a chaw; maybe he lies and says he ain't got none. Some of them kinds of loafers never has a cent in the world, nor a chaw of tobacco of their own. They get all their chawing by borrowing—they say to a fellow, "I wisht you'd len' me a chaw, Jack, I jist this minute give Ben Thompson the last chaw I had"—which is a lie, pretty much every time; it don't fool nobody but a stranger; but Jack ain't no stranger, so he says—

"GIMME A CHAW."

"*You* give him a chaw, did you? so did your sister's cat's grandmother. You pay me back the chaws you've aweady borry'd off'n me, Lafe Buckner, then I'll loan you one or two ton of it, and won't charge you no back intrust, nuther."

"Well, I *did* pay you back some of it wunst."

"Yes, you did—'bout six chaws. You borry'd store tobacker and paid back nigger-head."

Store tobacco is flat black plug, but these fellows mostly chaws the natural leaf twisted. When they borrow a chaw, they don't generly cut it off with a knife, but they set the plug in between their teeth, and gnaw with their teeth and tug at the plug with their hands till they get it in two—then sometimes the one that owns the tobacco looks mournful at it when it's handed back, and says, sarcastic—

"Here, gimme the *chaw*, and you take the *plug*."

All the streets and lanes was just mud, they warn't nothing else *but* mud—mud as black as tar, and nigh about a foot deep in some places; and two or three inches deep in *all* the places. The hogs loafed and grunted around, everywheres. You'd see a muddy sow and a litter of pigs come lazying along the street and whollop herself right down in the way, where folks had to walk around her, and she'd stretch out, and shut her eyes, and wave her ears, whilst the pigs was milking her, and look as happy as if she was on salary. And pretty soon you'd hear a loafer sing out, "Hi! *so* boy! sick him, Tige!" and away the sow would go, squealing most horrible, with a dog or two swinging to each ear, and three or four dozen more a-coming; and then you would see all the loafers get up and watch the thing out of sight, and laugh at the fun and look grateful for the noise. Then they'd settle back again till there was a dog-fight. There couldn't anything wake them up all over, and make them happy all over, like a dog-fight—unless it might be putting turpentine on a stray dog and setting fire to him, or tying a tin pan to his tail and see him run himself to death.

On the river front some of the houses was sticking out over the bank, and they was bowed and bent, and about ready to tumble in. The people had moved out of them. The bank was caved away under one corner of some others, and that corner was hanging over. People lived in them yet, but it was dangersome, because sometimes a strip of land as wide as a house caves in at a time. Sometimes a belt of land a quarter of a mile deep will start in and cave along and cave along till it all caves into the river in one summer. Such a town as that has to be always moving back, and back, and back, because the river's always gnawing at it.

The nearer it got to noon that day, the thicker and thicker was the wagons and horses in the streets, and more coming all the time. Families fetched their dinners with them, from the country, and eat them in the wagons. There was considerable whisky drinking going on, and I seen three fights. By and by somebody sings out—

"Here comes old Boggs!—in from the country for his little old monthly drunk—here he comes, boys!"

All the loafers looked glad—I reckoned they was used to having fun out of Boggs. One of them says—

"Wonder who he's a gwyne to chaw up this time. If he'd a chawed up all the men he's ben a gwyne to chaw up in the last twenty year, he'd have considerble ruputation, now."

Another one says, "I wisht old Boggs'd threaten me, 'cuz then I'd know I warn't gwyne to die for a thousan' year."

Boggs comes a-tearing along on his horse, whooping and yelling like an Injun, and singing out—

"Cler the track, thar. I'm on the waw-path, and the price uv coffins is a gwyne to raise."

He was drunk, and weaving about in his saddle; he was over fifty year old, and had a very red face. Everybody yelled at him, and laughed at him, and sassed him, and he sassed back, and said he'd attend to them and lay them out in their regular turns, but he couldn't wait now, because he'd come to town to kill old Colonel Sherburn, and his motto was, "meat first, and spoon vittles to top off on."

He see me, and rode up and says—

"Whar'd you come f'm, boy? You prepared to die?"

Then he rode on. I was scared; but a man says—

"He don't mean nothing; he's always a carryin' on like that, when he's drunk. He's the best-naturedest old fool in Arkansaw—never hurt nobody, drunk nor sober."

A LITTLE MONTHLY DRUNK.

Boggs rode up before the biggest store in town and bent his head down so he could see under the curtain of the awning, and yells—

"Come out here, Sherburn! Come out and meet the man you've swindled. You're the houn' I'm after, and I'm a gwyne to have you, too!"

And so he went on, calling Sherburn everything he could lay his tongue to, and the whole street packed with people listening and laughing and going on. By and by a proud-looking man about fifty-five—and he was a heap the best dressed man in that town, too—steps out of the store, and the crowd drops back on each side to let him come. He says to Boggs, mighty ca'm and slow—he says:

"I'm tired of this; but I'll endure it till one o'clock. Till one o'clock, mind—no longer. If you open your mouth against me only once, after that time, you can't travel so far but I will find you."

Then he turns and goes in. The crowd looked mighty sober; nobody stirred, and there warn't no more laughing. Boggs rode off blackguarding Sherburn as loud as he could yell, all down the street; and pretty soon back he comes and stops before the store, still keeping it up. Some men crowded around him and tried to get him to shut up, but he wouldn't; they told him it would be one o'clock in about fifteen minutes, and so he *must* go home—he must go right away. But it didn't do no good. He cussed away, with all his might, and throwed his hat down in the mud and rode over it, and pretty soon away he went a-raging down the street again, with his gray hair a-flying. Everybody that could get a chance at him tried their best to coax him off of his horse so they could lock him up and get him sober; but it warn't no use—up the street he would tear again, and give Sherburn another cussing. By and by somebody says—

"Go for his daughter!—quick, go for his daughter; sometimes he'll listen to her. If anybody can persuade him, she can."

So somebody started on a run. I walked down street a ways, and stopped. In about five or ten minutes, here comes Boggs again—but not on his horse. He was a-reeling across the street towards me, bareheaded, with a friend on both sides of him aholt of his arms and hurrying him along. He was quiet, and looked uneasy; and he warn't hanging back any, but was doing some of the hurrying himself. Somebody sings out—

"Boggs!"

I looked over there to see who said it, and it was that Colonel Sherburn. He was standing perfectly still, in the street, and had a pistol raised in his right hand—not aiming it, but holding it out with the barrel tilted up towards the sky. The same second I see a young girl coming on the run, and two men with her. Boggs and the men turned round, to see who called him, and when they see the pistol the men jumped to one side, and the pistol barrel come down slow and steady to a level—both barrels cocked. Boggs throws up both of his hands, and says, "O Lord, don't shoot!" Bang! goes the first shot, and he staggers back claw-

THE DEATH OF BOGGS.

ing at the air—bang! goes the second one, and he tumbles backwards onto the ground, heavy and solid, with his arms spread out. That young girl screamed out, and comes rushing, and down she throws herself on her father, crying, and saying, "Oh, he's killed him, he's killed him!" The crowd closed up around them, and shouldered and jammed one another, with their necks stretched, trying to see, and people on the inside trying to shove them back, and shouting, "Back, back! give him air, give him air!"

Colonel Sherburn he tossed his pistol onto the ground, and turned around on his heels and walked off.[4]

They took Boggs to a little drug store, the crowd pressing around, just the same, and the whole town following, and I rushed and got a good place at the window, where I was close to him and could see in. They laid him on the floor, and put one large Bible under his head, and opened another one and spread it on his breast—but they tore open his shirt first, and I seen where one of the bullets went in. He made about a dozen long gasps, his breast lifting the Bible up when he drawed in his breath, and letting it down again when he breathed it out—and after that he laid still; he was dead. Then they pulled his daughter away from him, screaming and crying, and took her off. She was about sixteen, and very sweet and gentle-looking, but awful pale and scared.

Well, pretty soon the whole town was there, squirming and scrouging and pushing and shoving to get at the window and have a look but people that had the places wouldn't give them up, and folks behind them was saying all the time, "Say, now, you've looked enough, you fellows; 'taint right and 'taint fair, for you to stay thar all the time, and never give nobody a chance; other folks has their rights as well as you."

There was considerable jawing back, so I slid out, thinking maybe there was going to be trouble. The streets was full, and everybody was excited. Everybody that seen the shooting was telling how it happened, and there was a big crowd packed around each one of these fellows, stretching their necks and listening. One long lanky man, with long hair and a big white fur stove-pipe hat on the back of his head, and a crooked-handled cane, marked out the places on the ground where Boggs stood, and where Sherburn stood, and the people following him around from one place to t'other and watching everything he done, and bobbing their heads to show they understood, and stooping a little and resting their hands on their thighs to watch him mark the places on the ground with his cane; and then he stood up straight and stiff where Sherburn had stood, frowning and having his hat-brim down over his eyes, and sung out, "Boggs!" and then fetched his cane down slow to a level, and says "Bang!" staggered backwards, says "Bang!" again, and fell down flat on his back. The people that had seen the thing said he done it perfect; said it was just exactly the way it all happened. Then as much as a dozen people got out their bottles and treated him.

4. This episode is based on the actual murder, in Hannibal in 1845 when Clemens was ten years old, of Sam Smarr by William Owsley. As justice of the peace, John M. Clemens, the author's father, took down twenty-eight depositions from witnesses, for which he was paid $13.50. A jury later acquitted Owsley.

Well, by and by somebody said Sherburn ought to be lynched. In about a minute everybody was saying it; so away they went, mad and yelling, and snatching down every clothes-line they come to, to do the hanging with.[5]

5. At approximately this point, Mark Twain broke off writing again, having added only about four chapters (from the feud to the "lynching") in four years. Then, in a creative burst in 1883, he picked up the book again and finished a first draft between summer and autumn.

Chapter XXII

SHERBURN STEPS OUT.

They swarmed up the street, towards Sherburn's house, a-whooping and yelling and raging like Injuns, and everything had to clear the way or get run over and tromped to mush, and it was awful to see. Children was heeling it ahead of the mob, screaming and trying to get out of the way; and every window along the road was full of women's heads, and there was nigger boys in every tree, and bucks and wenches looking over every fence; and as soon as the mob would get nearly to them they would break and skaddle back out of reach. Lots of the women and girls was crying and taking on, scared most to death.

They swarmed up in front of Sherburn's palings as thick as they could jam together, and you couldn't hear yourself think for the noise. It was a little twenty-foot yard. Some sung out, "Tear down the fence! tear down the fence!" Then there was a racket of ripping and tearing and smashing, and down she goes, and the front wall of the crowd begins to roll in like a wave.

Just then Sherburn steps out onto the roof of his little front porch, with a double-barrel gun in his hand, and takes his stand, perfectly ca'm and deliberate, not saying a word. The racket stopped, and the wave sucked back.

Sherburn never said a word—just stood there, looking down. The stillness was awful creepy and uncomfortable. Sherburn run his eye slow along the crowd; and wherever it struck, the people tried a little to outgaze him, but they couldn't; they dropped their eyes and looked sneaky. Then pretty soon Sherburn sort of laughed; not the pleasant kind, but the kind that makes you feel like when you are eating bread that's got sand in it.

Then he says, slow and scornful:

"The idea of *you* lynching anybody! It's amusing. The idea of you thinking you had pluck enough to lynch a *man!* Because you're brave enough to tar and feather poor friendless cast-out women that come along here, did that make you think you had grit enough to lay your hands on a *man?* Why, a *man's* safe in the hands of ten thousand of your kind—as long as it's daytime and you're not behind him.

"Do I know you? I know you clear through. I was born and raised in the south, and I've lived in the north; so I know the average all around. The average man's a coward. In the north he lets anybody walk over him that wants to, and goes home and prays for a humble spirit to bear it. In the south one man, all by himself, has stopped a stage full of men, in the day-time, and robbed the lot. Your newspapers call you a brave people so much that you think you *are* braver than any other people— whereas you're just *as* brave, and no braver. Why don't your juries hang murderers? Because they're afraid the man's friends will shoot them in the back, in the dark—and it's just what they *would* do.

"So they always acquit; and then a *man* goes in the night, with a hundred masked cowards at his back, and lynches the rascal. Your mistake is, that you didn't bring a man with you; that's one mistake, and the other is that you didn't come in the dark, and fetch your masks. You brought *part* of a man—Buck Harkness, there—and if you hadn't had him to start you, you'd a taken it out in blowing.

"You didn't want to come. The average man don't like trouble and danger. *You* don't like trouble and danger. But if only *half* a man—like Buck Harkness, there—shouts 'Lynch him, lynch him!' you're afraid to back down—afraid you'll be found out to be what you are—*cowards*— and so you raise a yell, and hang yourselves onto that half-a-man's coat tail, and come raging up here, swearing what big things you're going to do. The pitifulest thing out is a mob; that's what an army is—a mob; they don't fight with courage that's born in them, but with courage that's borrowed from their mass, and from their officers. But a mob without any *man* at the head of it, is *beneath* pitifulness. Now the thing for *you* to do, is to droop your tails and go home and crawl in a hole. If any real lynching's going to be done, it will be done in the dark, southern fashion; and when they come, they'll bring their masks, and fetch a *man* along. Now *leave*—and take your half-a-man with you"—tossing his gun up across his left arm and cocking it, when he says this.

The crowd washed back sudden, and then broke all apart and went tearing off every which way, and Buck Harkness he heeled it after them, looking tolerable cheap. I could a staid, if I'd a wanted to, but I didn't want to.

I went to the circus, and loafed around the back side till the watchman went by, and then dived in under the tent. I had my twenty-dollar gold piece and some other money, but I reckoned I better save it, because there ain't no telling how soon you are going to need it, away from home and amongst strangers, that way. You can't be too careful. I ain't opposed to spending money on circuses, when there ain't no other way, but there ain't no use in *wasting* it on them.

It was a real bully circus. It was the splendidest sight that ever was, when they all come riding in, two and two, a gentleman and lady, side by side, the men just in their drawers and undershirts, and no shoes nor stirrups, and resting their hands on their thighs, easy and comfortable,—there must a been twenty of them—and every lady with a lovely complexion, and perfectly beautiful, and looking just like a gang of real

A DEAD HEAD.

sure-enough queens, and dressed in clothes that cost millions of dollars, and just littered with dimonds. It was a powerful fine sight; I never see anything so lovely. And then one by one they got up and stood, and went a-weaving around the ring so gentle, and wavy and graceful, the men looking ever so tall and airy and straight, with their heads bobbing and skimming along, away up there under the tent-roof, and every lady's rose-leafy dress flapping soft and silky around her hips, and she looking like the most loveliest parasol.

And then faster and faster they went, all of them dancing, first one foot stuck out in the air and then the other, the horses leaning more and more, and the ring-master going round and round the centre-pole, cracking his whip and shouting "Hi!—hi!" and the clown cracking jokes behind him; and by and by, all hands dropped the reins, and every lady put her knuckles on her hips and every gentleman folded his arms, and then how the horses did lean over and hump themselves! And so, one after the other they all skipped off into the ring, and made the sweetest bow I ever see, and then scampered out, and everybody clapped their hands and went just about wild.

Well, all through the circus they done the most astonishing things; and all the time, that clown carried on so it most killed the people. The ring-master couldn't ever say a word to him but he was back at him quick as a wink with the funniest things a body ever said; and how he ever *could* think of so many of them, and so sudden and so pat, was what I couldn't no way understand. Why, I couldn't a thought of them in a year. And by and by a drunk man tried to get into the ring—said he wanted to ride; said he could ride as well as anybody that ever was. They argued and tried to keep him out, but he wouldn't listen, and the whole show come to a standstill. Then the people begun to holler at him and make fun of him, and that made him mad, and he begun to rip and tear; so that stirred up the people, and a lot of men begun to pile down off of the benches and swarm towards the ring, saying, "Knock him down! throw him out!" and one or two women begun to scream. So, then, the ring-master he made a little speech, and said he hoped there wouldn't be no disturbance, and if the man would promise he wouldn't make no more trouble, he would let him ride, if he thought he could stay on the horse. So everybody laughed and said all right, and the man got on. The minute he was on, the horse begun to rip and tear and jump, and cavort around, with two circus men hanging on to his bridle trying to hold him, and the drunk man hanging onto his neck, and his heels flying in the air every jump, and the whole crowd of people standing up shouting and laughing till the tears rolled down. And at last, sure enough, all the circus men could do, the horse broke loose, and away he went like the very nation, round and round the ring, with that sot laying down on him and hanging to his neck, with first one leg hanging most to the ground on one side, and then t'other one on t'other side, and the people just crazy. It warn't funny to me, though; I was all of a tremble to see his danger. But pretty soon he struggled up astraddle and grabbed the bridle, a-reeling this way and that; and the next minute he sprung up and dropped the bridle and stood! and the horse agoing like a house afire, too. He just stood up there, a-sailing around as easy and comfortable as if he warn't ever drunk in his life—and then he begun to pull off his clothes and fling them. He shed them so thick they kind of clogged up the air, and altogether he shed seventeen suits. And then, there he was, slim and handsome, and dressed the gaudiest and prettiest you ever saw, and he lit into that horse with his whip and made him fairly hum—and finally skipped off, and made his bow and danced off to the dressing room, and everybody just a-howling with pleasure and astonishment.

Then the ring-master he see how he had been fooled, and he *was* the sickest ring-master you ever see, I reckon. Why, it was one of his own

HE SHED SEVENTEEN SUITS.

men! He had got up that joke all out of his own head, and never let on to nobody. Well, I felt sheepish enough, to be took in so, but I wouldn't a been in that ring-master's place, not for a thousand dollars. I don't know; there may be bullier circuses than what that one was, but I never struck them yet. Anyways it was plenty good enough for *me*; and wherever I run across it, it can have all of *my* custom, every time.

Well, that night we had *our* show, but there warn't only about twelve people there; just enough to pay expenses. And they laughed all the time, and that made the duke mad; and everybody left, anyway, before the show was over, but one boy which was asleep. So the duke said these Arkansaw lunkheads couldn't come up to Shakspeare: what they wanted was low comedy—and maybe something ruther worse than low comedy, he reckoned. He said he could size their style. So next morning he got some big sheets of wrapping paper and some black paint, and drawed off some handbills and stuck them up all over the village. The bills said:

AT THE COURT HOUSE!

FOR 3 NIGHTS ONLY!
The World-Renowned Tragedians
DAVID GARRICK THE YOUNGER!
AND
EDMUND KEAN THE ELDER!
*Of the London and Continental
Theatres,*
In their Thrilling Tragedy of
THE KING'S CAMELOPARD
OR
THE ROYAL NONESUCH!!!
Admission 50 cents.

Then at the bottom was the biggest line of all—which said:

LADIES AND CHILDREN NOT ADMITTED.

"There," says he, "if that line don't fetch them, I don't know Arkansaw!"

Chapter XXIII

Kemble.

TRAGEDY.

Well all day him and the king was hard at it, rigging up a stage, and a curtain, and a row of candles for footlights; and that night the house was jam full of men in no time. When the place couldn't hold no more, the duke he quit tending door and went around the back way and come onto the stage and stood up before the curtain, and made a little speech, and praised up this tragedy, and said it was the most thrillingest one that ever was; and so he went on, a-bragging about the tragedy, and about Edmund Kean the Elder, which was to play the main principal part in it; and at last when he'd got everybody's expectations up high enough, he rolled up the curtain, and the next minute the king come a-prancing out on all fours, naked; and he was painted, all over, ring-streaked-and-striped, all sorts of colors, as splendid as a rain-bow. And—but never mind the rest of his outfit, it was just wild, but it was awful funny. The people most killed themselves laughing; and when the king got done capering, and capered off behind the scenes, they roared and clapped and stormed and haw-hawed till he come back and done it over again; and after that, they made him do it another time. Well, it would a made a cow laugh, to see the shines that old idiot cut.[1]

Then the duke he lets the curtain down, and bows to the people, and says the great tragedy will be performed only two nights more, on accounts of pressing London engagements, where the seats is all sold already for it in Drury Lane; and then he makes them another bow, and says if he has succeeded in pleasing them and instructing them, he will be deeply obleeged if they will mention it to their friends and get them to come and see it.

Twenty people sings out:

"What, is it over? Is that *all*?"

1. This is the "pale" version, mentioned in Mark Twain's *Autobiography*, of "The Tragedy of the Burning Shame," an "unprintable" folk story probably involving a lighted candle inserted in the performer's posterior.

166

The duke says yes. Then there was a fine time. Everybody sings out "Sold!"and rose up mad, and was agoing for that stage and them tragedians. But a big fine looking man jumps up on a bench and shouts:

"Hold on! Just a word, gentlemen." They stopped to listen. "We are sold—mighty badly sold. But we don't want to be the laughing-stock of this whole town, I reckon, and never hear the last of this thing as long as we live. *No.* What we want, is to go out of here quiet, and talk this show up, and sell the *rest* of the town! Then we'll all be in the same boat. Ain't that sensible?" ["You bet it is!—the jedge is right!" everybody sings out.] "All right, then—not a word about any sell. Go along home, and advise everybody to come and see the tragedy."

Next day you couldn't hear nothing around that town but how splendid that show was. House was jammed again, that night, and we sold this crowd the same way. When me and the king and the duke got home to the raft, we all had a supper; and by and by, about midnight, they made Jim and me back her out and float her down the middle of the river and fetch her in and hide her about two mile below town.

The third night the house was crammed again—and they warn't newcomers, this time, but people that was at the show the other two nights. I stood by the duke at the door, and I see that every man that went in had his pockets bulging, or something muffled up under his coat—and I see it warn't no perfumery, neither, not by a long sight. I smelt sickly eggs by the barrel, and rotten cabbages, and such things; and if I know the signs of a dead cat being around, and I bet I do, there was sixty-four of them went in. I shoved in there for a minute, but it was too various for me, I couldn't stand it. Well, when the place couldn't hold no more people, the duke he give a fellow a quarter and told him to tend door for him a minute, and then he started around for the stage door, I after him; but the minute we turned the corner and was in the dark, he says:

"Walk fast, now, till you get away from the houses, and then shin for the raft like the dickens was after you!"

I done it, and he done the same. We struck the raft at the same time, and in less than two seconds we was gliding down stream, all dark and still, and edging towards the middle of the river, nobody saying a word. I reckoned the poor king was in for a gaudy time of it with the audience; but nothing of the sort: pretty soon he crawls out from under the wigwam, and says:

THEIR POCKETS BULGED.

"Well, how'd the old thing pan out this time, duke?"

He hadn't been up town at all.

We never showed a light till we was about ten mile below that village. Then we lit up and had a supper, and the king and the duke fairly laughed their bones loose over the way they'd served them people. The duke says:

"Greenhorns, flatheads! *I* knew the first house would keep mum and let the rest of the town get roped in; and I knew they'd lay for us the third night, and consider it was *their* turn now. Well, it *is* their turn, and I'd give something to know how much they'd take for it. I *would* just like to know how they're putting in their opportunity. They can turn it into a picnic, if they want to—they brought plenty provisions."

Them rapscallions took in four hundred and sixty-five dollars in that three nights. I never see money hauled in by the wagon load like that, before.

By and by, when they was asleep and snoring, Jim says:

"Don't it sprise you, de way dem kings carries on, Huck?"

"No," I says, "it don't."

"Why don't it, Huck?"

"Well, it don't, because it's in the breed. I reckon they're all alike."

"But Huck, dese kings o' ourn is reglar rapscallions; dat's jist what dey is; dey's reglar rapscallions."

"Well, that's what I'm a-saying; all kings is mostly rapscallions, as fur as I can make out."

"Is dat so?"

"You read about them once—you'll see. Look at Henry the Eight; this'n 's a Sunday School superintendent to *him*.[2] And look at Charles Second, and Louis Fourteen, and Louis Fifteen, and James Second, and Edward Second, and Richard Third, and forty more; besides all them Saxon heptarchies that used to rip around so in old times and raise Cain. My, you ought to seen old Henry the Eight when he was in bloom. He *was* a blossom. He used to marry a new wife every day, and chop off her head next morning. And he would do it just as indifferent as if he was ordering up eggs. 'Fetch up Nell Gwynn,' he says. They fetch her up. Next morning, 'Chop off her head!' And they chop it off. 'Fetch up Jane Shore,' he says; and up she comes. Next morning, 'Chop off her head'—and they chop it off. 'Ring up Fair Rosamun.' Fair Rosamun answers the bell. Next morning, 'Chop off her head.' And he made every one of them tell him a tale every night; and he kept that up till he had hogged a thousand and one tales that way, and then he put them all in a book, and called it Domesday Book—which was a good name, and stated the case. You don't know kings, Jim, but I know them; and this old rip of ourn is one of the cleanest I've struck in history. Well, Henry he takes a notion he wants to get up some trouble with

2. Huck's description of Henry VIII (1491–1547) grandly confuses the historical *Domesday Book*, a census and land survey completed for William the Conqueror in 1086, with the fictional *Arabian Nights' Entertainments*, and it conflates persons, incidents, and even centuries that had no connection with Henry. He makes the sixteenth-century king the son of the nineteenth-century Duke of Wellington, whom he confuses with the fifteenth-century Duke of Clarence (supposedly drowned in a butt of malmsey wine). Fair Rosamond Clifford was mistress to twelfth-century Henry II, Jane Shore to fifteenth-century Edward IV, and Eleanor (Nell) Gwyn to seventeenth-century Charles II.

this country. How does he go at it—give notice?—give the country a show? No. All of a sudden he heaves all the tea in Boston harbor overboard, and whacks out a declaration of independence, and dares them to come on. That was *his* style—he never give anybody a chance. He had suspicions of his father, the duke of Wellington. Well, what did he

HENRY THE EIGHTH IN BOSTON HARBOR.

do?—ask him to show up? No—drownded him a butt of mamsey, like a cat. Spose people left money laying around where he was—what did he do? He collared it. Spose he contracted to do a thing; and you paid him, and didn't set down there and see that he done it—what did he do? He always done the other thing. Spose he opened his mouth—what then? If he didn't shut it up powerful quick, he'd lose a lie, every time. That's the kind of a bug Henry was; and if we'd a had him along stead of our kings, he'd a fooled that town a heap worse than ourn done. I don't say that ourn is lambs, because they ain't, when you come right down to the cold facts; but they ain't nothing to *that* old ram, anyway. All I say, is, kings is kings, and you got to make allowances. Take them all around, they're a mighty ornery lot. It's the way they're raised."

"But dis one do *smell* so like de nation, Huck."

"Well, they all do, Jim. *We* can't help the way a king smells; history don't tell no way."

"Now de duke, he's a tolerble likely man, in some ways."

"Yes, a duke's different. But not very different. This one's a middling hard lot,—for a duke. When he's drunk, there ain't no near-sighted man could tell him from a king."

"Well, anyways, I doan hanker for no mo' un um, Huck. Dese is all I kin stan'."

"It's the way I feel, too, Jim. But we've got them on our hands, and we got to remember what they are, and make allowances. Sometimes I wish we could hear of a country that's out of kings."

What was the use to tell Jim these warn't real kings and dukes? It wouldn't a done no good; and besides, it was just as I said; you couldn't tell them from the real kind.

I went to sleep, and Jim didn't call me when it was my turn. He often done that. When I waked up, just at daybreak, he was setting there with his head down betwixt his knees, moaning and mourning to himself. I didn't take notice, nor let on. I knowed what it was about. He was think-ing about his wife and his children, away up yonder, and he was low and homesick; because he hadn't ever been away from home before in his life; and I do believe he cared just as much for his people as white folks does for theirn. It don't seem natural, but I reckon it's so. He was often moaning and mourning, that way, nights, when he judged I was asleep, and saying "Po' little 'Lizabeth! po' little Johnny! it mighty hard; I spec' I ain't ever gwyne to see you no mo', no mo'!" He was a mighty good nig-ger, Jim was.

But this time I somehow got to talking to him about his wife and young ones; and by and by he says:

"What make me feel so bad dis time, 'uz bekase I hear sumpn over yonder on de bank like a whack, er a slam, while ago, en it mine me er de time I treat my little 'Lizabeth so ornery. She warn't on'y 'bout fo' year ole, en she tuck de sk'yarlet fever, en had a powful rough spell; but she got well, en one day she was a-stannin' aroun', en I says to her, I says:

" 'Shet de do'.'

"She never done it; jis' stood dah, kiner smilin' up at me. It make me mad; en I says agin, mighty loud! I says:

" 'Doan you hear me?—shet de do'!'

"She jis' stood de same way, kiner smilin' up. I was a-bilin'! I says:

" 'I lay I *make* you mine!'

"En wid dat I fetch' her a slap side de head dat sont her a-sprawlin'. Den I went into de yuther room, en 'uz gone 'bout ten minutes; en when I come back, dah was dat do' a-stannin' open *yit*, en dat chile stannin' mos' right in it, a-lookin' down en mournin', en de tears runnin' down. My, but I *wuz* mad. I was agwyne for de chile, but jis' den—it was a do' dat open' innerds—jis' den, 'long come de wind en slam it to, behine de chile, ker-*blam!*—en my lan', de chile never move'! My breff mos' hop outer me; en I feel so—so—I doan know *how* I feel. I crope out, all a-tremblin', en crope aroun' en open de do' easy en slow, en poke my head in behine de chile, sof' en still, en all uv a sudden I says *pow!* jis' as loud as I could yell. *She never budge!* O, Huck, I bust out a-cryin', en grab her up in my arms en say, 'O de po' little thing! de Lord God Amighty fogive po' ole Jim, kaze he never gwyne to fogive hisseff as long's he live!' O, she was plumb deef en dumb, Huck, plumb deef en dumb—en I'd ben a treat'n her so!"

Chapter XXIV

Sick Arab — but harmless when not out of his head

HARMLESS.

NEXT day, towards night, we laid up under a little willow towhead out in the middle, where there was a village on each side of the river, and the duke and the king begun to lay out a plan for working them towns. Jim he spoke to the duke, and said he hoped it wouldn't take but a few hours, because it got mighty heavy and tiresome to him when he had to lay all day in the wigwam tied with the rope. You see, when we left him all alone we had to tie him, because if anybody happened on him all by himself and not tied, it wouldn't look much like he was a runaway nigger, you know. So the duke said it *was* kind of hard to have to lay roped all day, and he'd cipher out some way to get around it.

He was uncommon bright, the duke was, and he soon struck it. He dressed Jim up in King Leer's outfit—it was a long curtain-calico gown, and a white horse-hair wig and whiskers; and then he took his theatre-paint and painted Jim's face and hands and ears and neck all over a dead dull solid blue, like a man that's been drownded nine days. Blamed if he warn't the horriblest looking outrage I ever see. Then the duke took and wrote out a sign on a shingle, so—

Sick Arab—but harmless when not out of his head.

And he nailed that shingle to a lath, and stood the lath up four or five foot in front of the wigwam. Jim was satisfied. He said it was a sight better than laying tied a couple of years every day, and trembling all over every time there was a sound. The duke told him to make himself free and easy, and if anybody ever come meddling around, he must hop out of the wigwam, and carry on a little, and fetch a howl or two like a wild beast, and he reckoned they would light out and leave him alone. Which was sound enough judgment; but you take the average man, and he wouldn't wait for him to howl. Why, he didn't only look like he was dead, he looked considerable more than that.

These rapscallions wanted to try the Nonesuch again, because there was so much money in it, but they judged it wouldn't be safe, because

171

maybe the news might a worked along down by this time. They couldn't hit no project that suited, exactly; so at last the duke said he reckoned he'd lay off and work his brains an hour or two and see if he couldn't put up something on the Arkansaw village; and the king he allowed he would drop over to t'other village, without any plan, but just trust in Providence to lead him the profitable way—meaning the devil, I reckon. We had all bought store clothes where we stopped last; and now the king put his'n on, and he told me to put mine on. I done it, of course. The king's duds was all black, and he did look real swell and starchy. I never knowed how clothes could change a body before. Why, before, he looked like the orneriest old rip that ever was; but now, when he'd take off his new white beaver and make a bow and do a smile, he looked that grand and good and pious that you'd say he had walked right out of the ark, and maybe was old Leviticus[1] himself. Jim cleaned up the canoe, and I got my paddle ready. There was a big steamboat laying at the shore away up under the point, about three mile above town—been there a couple of hours—taking on freight. Says the king:

"Seein' how I'm dressed, I reckon maybe I better arrive down from St. Louis or Cincinnati, or some other big place. Go for the steamboat, Huckleberry; we'll come down to the village on her."

I didn't have to be ordered twice, to go and take a steamboat ride. I fetched the shore a half a mile above the village, and then went scooting along the bluff bank in the easy water. Pretty soon we come to a nice innocent looking young country jake setting on a log swabbing the sweat off of his face, for it was powerful warm weather; and he had a couple of big carpet bags by him.

"Run her nose in shore," says the king. I done it. "Wher' you bound for, young man?"

"For the steamboat; going to Orleans."

"Git aboard," says the king. "Hold on a minute, my servant 'll he'p you with them bags. Jump out and he'p the gentleman, Adolphus"—meaning me, I see.

I done so, and then we all three started on again. The young chap was mighty thankful; said it was tough work toting his baggage such weather. He asked the king where he was going, and the king told him he'd come down the river and landed at the other village this morning, and now he was going up a few mile to see an old friend on a farm up there. The young fellow says:

"When I first see you, I says to myself, 'It's Mr. Wilks, sure, and he come mighty near getting here in time.' But then I says, again, 'No, I reckon it ain't him, or else he wouldn't be paddling up the river.' You *ain't* him, are you?"

"No, my name's Blodgett—Elexander Blodgett—*Reverend* Elexander Blodgett, I spose I must say, as I'm one o' the Lord's poor servants. But still I'm jest as able to be sorry for Mr. Wilks for not arriving in time, all the same, if he's missed anything by it—which I hope he hasn't."

"Well, he don't miss any property by it, because he'll get that, all right; but he's missed seeing his brother Peter die—which he mayn't mind,

1. A book of the Old Testament.

ADOLPHUS.

nobody can tell, as to that—but his brother would a give anything in this world to see *him* before he died; never talked about nothing else all these three weeks; hadn't seen him since they was boys together—and hadn't ever seen his brother William, at all—that's the deef and dumb one—William ain't more than thirty or thirty-five. Peter and George was the only ones that come out here; George was the married brother; him and his wife both died last year. Harvey and William's the only ones that's left, now; and as I was saying, they haven't got here in time."

"Did anybody send 'em word?"

"O, yes; a month or two ago, when Peter was first took; because Peter said, then, that he sorter felt like he wasn't going to get well this time. You see, he was pretty old, and George's g'yirls was too young to be much company for him, except Mary Jane the red-headed one; and so he was kinder lonesome after George and his wife died, and didn't seem to care much to live. He most desperately wanted to see Harvey—and William too, for that matter—because he was one of them kind that can't bear to make a will. He left a letter behind, for Harvey, and said he'd told in it where his money was hid, and how he wanted the rest of the property divided up so George's g'yirls would be all right—for George didn't leave nothing. And that letter was all they could get him to put a pen to."

"Why do you reckon Harvey don't come? Wher' does he live?"

"O, he lives in England—Sheffield—preaches there—hasn't ever been in this country. He hasn't had any too much time—and besides he mightn't a got the letter at all, you know."

"Too bad, too bad he couldn't a lived to see his brothers, poor soul. You going to Orleans, you say?"

"Yes, but that ain't only a part of it. I'm going in a ship, next Wednesday, for Ryo Janeero,[2] where my uncle lives."

2. Rio de Janeiro in southeastern Brazil. Sam Clemens himself planned such a trip in 1856 when he was twenty years old.

"It's a pretty long journey. But it'll be lovely; I wisht I was agoing. Is Mary Jane the oldest? How old is the others?"

"Mary Jane's nineteen, Susan's fifteen, and Joanna's about fourteen—that's the one that gives herself to good works and has a harelip."

"Poor things! to be left alone in the cold world, so."

"Well, they could be worse off. Old Peter had friends, and they ain't going to let them come to no harm. There's Hobson, the Babtis' preacher; and deacon Lot Hovey, and Ben Rucker, and Abner Shackleford; and Levi Bell, the lawyer; and Dr. Robinson; and their wives; and the widow Bartley, and—well, there's a lot of them; but these are the ones that Peter was thickest with, and used to write about, sometimes, when he wrote home; so Harvey'll know where to look for friends when he gets here."

Well, the old man he went on asking questions till he just fairly emptied that young fellow. Blamed if he didn't inquire about everybody and every thing in that blessed town, and all about all the Wilkses; and about Peter's business—which was a tanner; and about George's—which was a carpenter; and about Harvey's—which was a dissentering minister; and so on, and so on. Then he says:

"What did you want to walk all the way up to the steamboat, for?"

"Because she's a big Orleans boat, and I was afeard she mightn't stop there. When they're deep they won't stop for a hail. A Cincinnati boat will, but this is a St. Louis one."

"Was Peter Wilks well off?"

"O, yes, pretty well off. He had houses and land, and it's reckoned he left three or four thousand in cash hid up som'ers."

"When did you say he died?"

"I didn't say; but it was last night."

"Funeral to-morrow, likely?"

HE FAIRLY EMPTIED THAT YOUNG FELLOW.

"Yes, 'bout the middle of the day."

"Well, it's all terrible sad; but we've all got to go, one time or another. So what we want to do is to be prepared; then we're all right."

"Yes, sir, it's the best way. Ma used to always say that."

When we struck the boat, she was about done loading, and pretty soon she got off. The king never said nothing about going aboard, so I lost my ride, after all. When the boat was gone, the king made me paddle up another mile, to a lonesome place, and then he got ashore and says:

"Now hustle back, right off, and fetch the duke up here, and the new carpet-bags. And if he's gone over to t'other side, go over there and git him. And tell him to git himself up regardless. Shove along, now."

I see what *he* was up to; but I never said nothing, of course. When I got back with the duke, we hid the canoe, and then they set down on a log, and the king told him everything, just like the young fellow had said it—every last word of it. And all the time he was a doing it, he tried to talk like an Englishman; and he done it pretty well, too, for a slouch. I can't imitate him, and so I ain't agoing to try to; but he really done it pretty good. Then he says:

"How are you on the deef and dumb, Bilgewater?"

The duke said, leave him alone for that; said he had played a deef and dumb person on the histrionic boards. So then they waited for a steamboat.

About the middle of the afternoon a couple of little boats come along, but they didn't come from high enough up the river; but at last there was a big one, and they hailed her. She sent out her yawl, and we went aboard, and she was from Cincinnati; and when they found we only wanted to go four or five mile, they was booming mad, and give us a cussing, and said they wouldn't land us. But the king was ca'm. He says:

"If gentlemen kin afford to pay a dollar a mile, apiece, to be took on and put off in a yawl, a steamboat kin afford to carry 'em, can't it?"

So they softened down and said it was all right; and when we got to the village, they yawled us ashore. About two dozen men flocked down, when they see the yawl a coming; and when the king says—

"Kin any of you gentlemen tell me wher' Mr. Peter Wilks lives?" they give a glance at one another, and nodded their heads, as much as to say, "What d' I tell you?" Then one of them says, kind of soft and gentle:

"I'm sorry, sir, but the best we can do is to tell you where he *did* live, yesterday evening."

Sudden as winking, the ornery old cretur went all to smash, and fell up against the man, and put his chin on his shoulder, and cried down his back, and says:

"Alas, alas, our poor brother—gone, and we never got to see him; oh, it's too, *too* hard!"

Then he turns around, blubbering, and makes a lot of idiotic signs to the duke on his hands, and blamed if *he* didn't drop a carpet-bag and bust out a-crying. If they warn't the beatenest lot, them two frauds, that ever I struck.

Well, the men gethered around, and sympathized with them, and said all sorts of kind things to them, and carried their carpet bags up the hill

"ALAS, OUR POOR BROTHER."

for them, and let them lean on them and cry, and told the king all about his brother's last moments, and the king he told it all over again on his hands to the duke, and both of them took on about that dead tanner like they'd lost the twelve disciples. Well, if ever I struck anything like it, I'm a nigger. It was enough to make a body ashamed of the human race.

Chapter XXV

The news was all over town in two minutes, and you could see the people tearing down on the run, from every which way, some of them putting on their coats as they come. Pretty soon we was in the middle of a crowd, and the noise of the tramping was like a soldier-march. The windows and door-yards was full; and every minute somebody would say, over a fence:

"Is it *them*?"

And somebody trotting along with the gang would answer back and say:

"You bet it is."

When we got to the house, the street in front of it was packed, and the three girls was standing in the door. Mary Jane *was* red-headed, but that don't make no difference, she was most awful beautiful, and her face and her eyes was all lit up like glory, she was so glad her uncles was come. The king he spread his arms, and Mary Jane she jumped for them, and the hare-lip jumped for the duke, and there they *had* it! Everybody, most, leastways women, cried for joy to see them meet at last and have such good times.

Then the king he hunched the duke, private—I see him do it—and then he looked around and see the coffin, over in the corner on two chairs; so then, him and the duke, with a hand across each other's shoulder, and t'other hand to their eyes, walked slow and solemn over there, everybody dropping back to give them room, and all the talk and noise stopping, people saying "Sh!" and all the men taking their hats off and drooping their heads, so you could a heard a pin fall. And when they got there, they bent over and looked in the coffin, and took one sight, and then they bust out a crying so you could a heard them to Orleans, most; and then they put their arms around each other's necks, and hung their chins over each other's shoulders; and then for three minutes, or maybe four, I never see two men leak the way they done. And mind you, everybody was doing the same; and the place was that damp I never see anything like it. Then one of them got on one side of the coffin, and t'other on t'other side, and they kneeled down and rested

"YOU BET IT IS."

their foreheads on the coffin, and let on to pray, all to their selves. Well, when it come to that, it worked the crowd like you never see anything like it, and so everybody broke down and went to sobbing right out loud—the poor girls, too; and every woman, nearly, went up to the girls, without saying a word, and kissed them, solemn, on the forehead, and then put their hand on their head, and looked up towards the sky, with the tears running down, and then busted out and went off sobbing and swabbing, and give the next woman a show. I never see anything so disgusting.

LEAKING.

Well, by and by the king he gets up and comes forward a little, and works himself up and slobbers out a speech, all full of tears and flapdoodle about its being a sore trial for him and his poor brother to lose the diseased, and to miss seeing diseased alive, after the long journey of four thousand mile, but it's a trial that's sweetened and sanctified to us by this dear sympathy and these holy tears, and so he thanks them out of his heart and out of his brother's heart, because out of their mouths they can't, words being too weak and cold, and all that kind of rot and slush, till it was just sickening; and then he blubbers out a pious goodygoody Amen, and turns himself loose and goes to crying fit to bust.

And the minute the words was out of his mouth somebody over in the crowd struck up the doxolojer,[1] and everybody joined in with all their might, and it just warmed you up and made you feel as good as church letting out. Music *is* a good thing; and after all that soul-butter and hogwash, I never see it freshen up things so, and sound so honest and bully.

1. The Doxology, beginning "Praise God, from whom all blessings flow."

Then the king begins to work his jaw again, and says how him and his nieces would be glad if a few of the main principal friends of the family would take supper here with them this evening, and help set up with the ashes of the diseased; and says if his poor brother laying yonder could speak, he knows who he would name, for they was names that was very dear to him, and mentioned often in his letters; and so he will name the same, to-wit, as follows, vizz:—Rev. Mr. Hobson, and deacon Lot Hovey, and Mr. Ben Rucker, and Abner Shackleford, and Levi Bell, and Dr. Robinson, and their wives, and the widow Bartley.

Rev. Hobson and Dr. Robinson was down to the end of the town, a-hunting together; that is, I mean the doctor was shipping a sick man to t'other world, and the preacher was pinting him right. Lawyer Bell was away up to Louisville on some business. But the rest was on hand, and so they all come and shook hands with the king and thanked him and talked to him; and then they shook hands with the duke, and didn't say nothing, but just kept a-smiling and bobbing their heads like a passel of sapheads whilst he made all sorts of signs with his hands and said "Goo-goo—goo-goo-goo," all the time, like a baby that can't talk.

So the king he blatted along, and managed to inquire about pretty much everybody and dog in town, by his name, and mentioned all sorts of little things that happened one time or another in the town, or to George's family, or to Peter; and he always let on that Peter wrote him the things, but that was a lie, he got every blessed one of them out of that young flathead that we canoed up to the steamboat.

Then Mary Jane she fetched the letter her uncle left behind, and the king he read it out loud and cried over it. It give the dwelling house and three thousand dollars, gold, to the girls; and it give the tanyard, (which was doing a good business,) along with some other houses and land (worth about seven thousand,) and three thousand dollars in gold, to Harvey and William, and told where the six thousand cash was hid, down cellar. So these two frauds said they'd go and fetch it up, and have everything square and aboveboard; and told me to come with a candle. We shut the cellar door behind us, and when they found the bag they spilt it out on the floor, and it was a lovely sight, all them yaller-boys.[2] My, the way the king's eyes did shine! He slaps the duke on the shoulder, and says:

"O, *this* ain't bully nor noth'n! O, no, I reckon not! Why, Biljy, it beats the Nonesuch, *don't* it!"

The duke allowed it did. They pawed the yaller-boys, and sifted them through their fingers and let them jingle down on the floor; and the king says:

"It ain't no use talkin': bein' brothers to a rich dead man, and representatives of furrin heirs that's got left, is the line for you and me, Bilge. Thish-yer comes of trust'n to Providence. It's the best way, in the long run. I've tried 'em all, and ther' ain't no better way."

Most everybody would a been satisfied with the pile, and took it on trust; but no, they must count it. So they counts it, and it comes out four hundred and fifteen dollars short. Says the king:

2. Gold coins.

"Dern him, I wonder what he done with that four hunderd and fifteen dollars?"

They worried over that, a while, and ransacked all around for it. Then the duke says:

"Well, he was a pretty sick man, and likely he made a mistake—I reckon that's the way of it. The best way's to let it go, and keep still about it. We can spare it."

"Oh, shucks, yes, we can *spare* it. I don't k'yer noth'n'bout that—it's the *count* I'm thinkin' about. We want to be awful square and open and aboveboard, here, you know. We want to lug thish-yer money up stairs and count it before everybody—then ther' ain't noth'n suspicious. But when the dead man says ther's six thous'n dollars, you know, we don't want to—"

"Hold on," says the duke. "Less make up the deffisit"—and he begun to haul out yaller-boys out of his pocket.

"It's a most amaz'n' good idea, duke—you *have* got a rattlin' clever head on you," says the king. "Blest if the old Nonesuch ain't a heppin' us out agin"—and *he* begun to haul out yaller-jackets and stack them up.

It most busted them, but they made up the six thousand clean and clear.

MAKING UP THE "DEFFISIT."

"Say," says the duke, "I got another idea. Le's go up stairs and count this money, and then take and *give it to the girls.*"

"Good land, duke, lemme hug you! It's the most dazzling idea 'at ever a man struck. You have cert'nly got the most astonishin' head I ever see.

O, this is the boss dodge, ther' ain't no mistake 'bout it. Let 'em fetch along their suspicions, now, if they want to—this'll lay 'em out."

When we got up stairs, everybody gethered around the table, and the king he counted it and stacked it up, three hundred dollars in a pile— twenty elegant little piles. Everybody looked hungry at it, and licked their chops. Then they raked it into the bag again, and I see the king begin to swell himself up for another speech. He says:

"Friends all, my poor brother that lays yonder, has done generous by them that's left behind in the vale of sorrers. He has done generous by these-yer poor little lambs that he loved and sheltered, and that's left fatherless and motherless. Yes, and we that knowed him, knows that he would a done *more* generous by 'em if he hadn't ben afeard o' woundin' his dear William and me. Now, *wouldn't* he? Ther' ain't no question 'bout it, in *my* mind. Well, then—what kind o'brothers would it be, that 'd stand in his way at sech a time? And what kind o' uncles would it be that 'd rob—yes, *rob*—sech poor sweet lambs as these 'at he loved so, at sech a time? If I know William—and I *think* I do—he—well, I'll jest ask him." He turns around and begins to make a lot of signs to the duke with his hands; and the duke he looks at him stupid and leatherheaded a while, then all of a sudden he seems to catch his meaning, and jumps for the king goo-gooing with all his might for joy, and hugs him about fifteen times before he lets up. Then the king says, "I knowed it; I reckon *that*'ll convince anybody the way *he* feels about it. Here, Mary Jane, Susan, Joanner, take the money—take it *all*. It's the gift of him that lays yonder, cold but joyful."

Mary Jane she went for him, Susan and the hare-lip went for the duke, and then such another hugging and kissing I never see yet. And

GOING FOR HIM.

everybody crowded up, with the tears in their eyes, and most shook the hands off of them frauds, saying all the time:

"You *dear* good souls!—how *lovely!*—how *could* you!"

Well, then, pretty soon all hands got to talking about the diseased again, and how good he was, and what a loss he was, and all that; and before long a big iron-jawed man worked himself in there from outside, and stood a-listening and looking, and not saying anything; and nobody saying anything to him, either, because the king was talking and they was all busy listening. The king was saying—in the middle of something he'd started in on—

"—they bein' partickler friends o' the diseased. That's why they're invited here this evenin'; but to-morrow we want *all* to come—everybody; for he respected everybody, he liked everybody, and so it's fitten that his funeral orgies sh'd be public."

And so he went a-mooning on and on, liking to hear himself talk, and every little while he fetched in his funeral orgies again, till the duke he couldn't stand it no more; so he writes on a little scrap of paper, "*obsequies*, you old fool," and folds it up and goes to goo-gooing and reaching it over people's heads to him. The king he reads it, and puts it in his pocket, and says:

"Poor William, afflicted as he is, his *heart's* aluz right. Asks me to invite everybody to come to the funeral—wants me to make 'em all welcome. But he needn't a worried—it was jest what I was at."

Then he weaves along, again, perfectly ca'm, and goes to dropping in his funeral orgies again every now and then, just like he done before. And when he done it the third time, he says:

"I say orgies, not because it's the common term, because it ain't—obsequies bein' the common term—but because orgies is the right term. Obsequies ain't used in England no more, now—it's gone out. We say orgies, now, in England. Orgies is better, because it means the thing you're after, more exact. It's a word that's made up out'n the Greek *orgo*, outside, open, abroad; and the Hebrew *jeesum*, to plant, cover up; hence in*ter*. So, you see, funeral orgies is an open er public funeral."

He was the *worst* I ever struck. Well, the iron-jawed man he laughed right in his face. Everybody was shocked. Everybody says, "Why *doctor!*" and Abner Shackleford says:

"Why, Robinson, hain't you heard the news? This is Harvey Wilks."

The king he smiled, eager, and shoved out his flapper, and says:

"*Is* it my poor brother's dear good friend and physician? I—"

THE DOCTOR.

"Keep your hands off of me!" says the doctor. "*You* talk like an Englishman—*don't* you? It's the worst imitation I ever heard. *You* Peter Wilks's brother. You're a fraud, that's what you are!"

Well, how they all took on! They crowded around the doctor, and tried to quiet him down, and tried to explain to him, and tell him how Harvey'd showed in forty ways that he *was* Harvey, and knowed everybody by name, and the names of the very dogs, and begged and *begged* him not to hurt Harvey's feelings and the poor girls' feelings, and all that; but it warn't no use, he stormed right along, and said any man that pretended to be an Englishman and couldn't imitate the lingo no better than what he did, was a fraud and a liar. The poor girls was hanging to the king and crying; and all of a sudden the doctor ups and turns on *them*. He says:

"I was your father's friend, and I'm your friend; and I warn you *as* a friend, and an honest one, that wants to protect you and keep you out of harm and trouble, to turn your backs on that scoundrel, and have nothing to do with him, the ignorant tramp, with his idiotic Greek and Hebrew as he calls it. He is the thinnest kind of an imposter—has come here with a lot of empty names and facts which he has picked up somewheres, and you take them for *proofs*, and are helped to fool yourselves by these foolish friends here, who ought to know better. Mary Jane Wilks, you know me for your friend, and for your unselfish friend, too. Now listen to me; turn this pitiful rascal out—I *beg* you to do it. Will you?"

Mary Jane straightened herself up, and my, but she was handsome! She says:

"*Here* is my answer." She hove up the bag of money, and put it in the king's hands, and says, "Take this six thousand dollars, and invest for me and my sisters any way you want to, and don't give us no receipt for it."

Then she put her arm around the king on one side, and Susan and the hare-lip done the same on the other. Everybody clapped their hands and stomped on the floor like a perfect storm, whilst the king held up his head and smiled proud. The doctor says:

"All right, I wash *my* hands of the matter. But I warn you all that a time's coming when you're going to feel sick whenever you think of this day"—and away he went.

"All right, doctor" says the king, kinder mocking him, "we'll try and git 'em to send for you"—which made them all laugh, and they said it was a prime good hit.

THE BAG OF MONEY.

Chapter XXVI

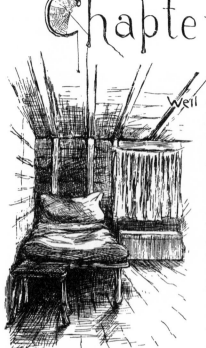

THE CUBBY.

Well when they was all gone, the king he asks Mary Jane how they was off for spare rooms, and she said she had one spare room, which would do for uncle William, and she'd give her own room to uncle Harvey, which was a little bigger, and she would turn into the room with her sisters and sleep on a cot; and up garret was a little cubby, with a pallet in it. The king said the cubby would do for his valley—meaning me.

So Mary Jane took us up, and she showed them their rooms, which was plain but nice. She said she'd have her frocks and a lot of other traps took out of her room if they was in uncle Harvey's way, but he said they warn't. The frocks was hung along the wall, and before them was a curtain made out of calico that hung down to the floor. There was an old hair trunk in one corner, and a guitar box in another, and all sorts of little knick-knacks and jim-cracks around, like girls brisken up a room with. The king said it was all the more homely and more pleasanter for these fixings, and so don't disturb them. The duke's room was pretty small, but plenty good enough, and so was my cubby.

That night they had a big supper, and all them men and women was there, and I stood behind the king and the duke's chairs and waited on them, and the niggers waited on the rest. Mary Jane she set at the head of the table, with Susan alongside of her, and said how bad the biscuits was, and how mean the preserves was, and how ornery and tough the fried chickens was,—and all that kind of rot, the way women always do for to force out compliments; and the people all knowed everything was tip-top, and said so—said "How *do* you get biscuits to brown so nice?" and "Where, for the land's sake *did* you get these amaz'n pickles?" and all that kind of humbug talky-talk, just the way people always does at a supper, you know.

And when it was all done, me and the hare-lip had supper in the kitchen off of the leavings, whilst the others was helping the niggers clean up the things. The hare-lip she got to pumping me about England, and blest if I didn't think the ice was getting mighty thin, some-times. She says:

"Did you ever see the king?"

"Who? William Fourth? Well, I bet I have—he goes to our church." I knowed he was dead years ago, but I never let on. So when I says he goes to our church, she says:

"What—regular?"

"Yes—regular. His pew's right over opposite ourn—on t'other side the pulpit."

"I thought he lived in London?"

"Well, he does. Where *would* he live?"

"But I thought *you* lived in Sheffield?"

I see I was up a stump. I had to let on to get choked with a chicken bone, so as to get time to think how to get down again. Then I says:

"I mean he goes to our church regular when he's in Sheffield. That's only in the summer time, when he comes there to take the sea baths."

"Why, how you talk—Sheffield ain't on the sea."

"Well, who said it was?"

"Why, you did."

"I *didn't*, nuther."

"You did!"

"I didn't."

"You did."

"I never said nothing of the kind."

"Well, what *did* you say, then?"

"Said he come to take the sea *baths*—that's what I said."

"Well, then!—how's he going to take the sea baths if it ain't on the sea?"

SUPPER WITH THE HARE-LIP.

"Looky here," I says; "did you ever see any Congress-water?"[1]

"Yes."

"Well, did you have to go to Congress to get it?"

"Why, no."

"Well, neither does William Fourth have to go to the sea to get a sea bath."

"How does he get it, then?"

"Gets it the way people down here gets Congress-water—in barrels. There in the palace at Sheffield they've got furnaces, and he wants his water hot. They can't bile that amount of water away off there at the sea. They haven't got no conveniences for it."

"O, I see, now. You might a said that in the first place, and saved time."

When she said that, I see I was out of the woods again, and so I was comfortable and glad. Next, she says:

"Do you go to church, too?"

"Yes—regular."

"Where do you set?"

"Why, in our pew."

"*Whose* pew?"

"Why, *ourn*—your uncle Harvey's."

"His'n? What does *he* want with a pew?"

"Wants it to set in. What did you *reckon* he wanted with it?"

"Why, I thought he'd be in the pulpit."

Rot him, I forgot he was a preacher. I see I was up a stump again; so I played another chicken bone and got another think. Then I says:

"Blame it, do you suppose there ain't but one preacher to a church?"

"Why, what do they want with more?"

"What!—to preach before a king? I never see such a girl as you. They don't have no less than seventeen."

"Seventeen! My land! Why, I wouldn't set out such a string as that, not if I *never* got to glory. It must take 'em a week."

"Shucks, they don't *all* of 'em preach the same day—only *one* of 'em."

"Well, then, what does the rest of 'em do?"

"Oh, nothing much. Loll around, pass the plate—and one thing or another. But mainly they don't do nothing."

"Well, then, what are they *for*?"

"Why, they're for *style*. Don't you know nothing?"

"Well, I don't *want* to know no such foolishness as that. How is servants treated in England? Do they treat 'em better'n we treat our niggers?"

"*No!* A servant ain't nobody, there. They treat them worse than dogs."

"Don't they give 'em holidays, the way we do, Christmas, and New Year's week, and fourth of July?"

"Oh, just listen! A body could tell *you* hadn't ever been to England, by that. Why, Hare-l—why, Joanna, they never see a holiday from year's end to year's end; never go to the circus, nor theatre, nor nigger shows, nor nowheres."

---

1. Mineral water from the Congress Spring at Saratoga, New York.

"Nor church?"

"Nor church."

"But *you* always went to church."

Well, I was gone up again. I forgot I was the old man's servant. But next minute I whirled in on a kind of an explanation how a valley was different from a common servant, and *had* to go to church whether he wanted to or not, and set with the family, on account of it's being the law. But I didn't do it pretty good, and when I got done I see she warn't satisfied. She says:

"Honest injun, now, hain't you been telling me a lot of lies?"

"Honest injun," says I.

"None of it at all?"

"None of it at all. Not a lie in it," says I.

"Lay your hand on this book and say it."

"HONEST INJUN."

I see it warn't nothing but a dictionary, so I laid my hand on it and said it. So then she looked a little better satisfied, and says:

"Well, then, I'll believe some of it; but I hope to gracious if I'll believe the rest."

"What is it you won't believe, Joe?" says Mary Jane, stepping in, with Susan behind her. "It ain't right nor kind for you to talk so to him, and him a stranger and so far from his people. How would you like to be treated so?"

"That's always your way, Maim—always sailing in to help somebody before they're hurt. I hain't done nothing to him. He's told some stretchers, I reckon; and I said I wouldn't swallow it all; and that's every bit and grain I *did* say. I reckon he can stand a little thing like that, can't he?"

"I don't care whether 'twas little or whether 'twas big, he's here in our house and a stranger, and it wasn't good of you to say it. If you was in his place, it would make you feel ashamed; and so you oughtn't to say a thing to another person that will make *them* feel ashamed."

"Why, Maim, he said—"

"It don't make no difference what he *said*—that ain't the thing. The thing is for you to treat him *kind*, and not be saying things to make him remember he ain't in his own country and amongst his own folks."

I says to myself, *This* is a girl that I'm letting that old reptile rob her of her money!

Then Susan *she* waltzed in; and if you'll believe me, she did give Hare-Lip hark from the tomb![2]

Says I to myself, And this is *another* one that I'm letting him rob her of her money!

Then Mary Jane she took another inning, and went in sweet and lovely again—which was her way—but when she got done there warn't hardly anything left o' poor Hare-Lip. So she hollered.

"All right, then," says the other girls, "you just ask his pardon."

She done it, too. And she done it beautiful. She done it so beautiful it was good to hear; and I wished I could tell her a thousand lies, so she could do it again.

I says to myself, This is *another* one that I'm letting him rob her of her money. And when she got through, they all jest laid theirselves out to make me feel at home and know I was amongst friends. I felt so ornery and low down and mean, that I says to myself, My mind's made up; I'll hive[3] that money for them or bust.

So then I lit out—for bed, I said, meaning some time or another. When I got by myself, I went to thinking the thing over. I says to myself, Shall I go to that doctor, private, and blow on these frauds? No—that won't do. He might tell who told him; then the king and the duke would make it warm for me. Shall I go, private, and tell Mary Jane? No—I dasn't do it. Her face would give them a hint, sure; they've got the money, and they'd slide right out and get away with it. If she was to fetch in help, I'd get mixed up in the business, before it was done with, I judge. No, there ain't no good way but one: I got to steal that money, somehow; and I got to steal it some way that they won't suspicion that I done it. They've got a good thing, here; and they ain't agoing to leave till they've played this family and this town for all they're worth, so I'll find a chance time enough. I'll steal it, and hide it; and by and by, when I'm away down the river, I'll write a letter and tell Mary Jane where it's hid. But I better hive it to-night, if I can, because the doctor maybe hasn't let up as much as he lets on he has; he might scare them out of here, yet.

So, thinks I, I'll go and search them rooms. Up stairs the hall was dark, but I found the duke's room, and started to paw around it with my

2. A talking-to, a scolding.
3. Store up, secure.

hands; but I recollected it wouldn't be much like the king to let anybody else take care of that money but his own self; so then I went to his room and begun to paw around there. But I see I couldn't do nothing without a candle, and I dasn't light one, of course. So I judged I'd got to do the other thing—lay for them, and eavesdrop. About that time, I hears their footsteps coming, and was going to skip under the bed; I reached for it, but it wasn't where I thought it would be; but I touched the curtain that hid Mary Jane's frocks, so I jumped in behind that and snuggled in amongst the gowns, and stood there perfectly still.

They come in and shut the door; and the first thing the duke done was to get down and look under the bed. Then I was glad I hadn't found the bed when I wanted it. And yet you know it's kind of natural to hide under the bed when you are up to anything private. They sets down, then, and the king says:

"Well, what is it? And cut it middlin' short, because it's better for us to be down there a whoopin'-up the mournin', than up here givin' 'em a chance to talk us over."

"Well, this is it, Capet. I ain't easy; I ain't comfortable. That doctor lays on my mind. I wanted to know your plans. I've got a notion, and I think it's a sound one."

"What is it, duke?"

"That we better glide out of this, before three in the morning, and clip it down the river with what we've got. Specially, seeing we got it so easy—*given* back to us, flung at our heads, as you may say, when of course we allowed to have to steal it back. I'm for knocking off and lighting out."

That made me feel pretty bad. About an hour or two ago, it would a been a little different, but now it made me feel bad and disappointed. The king rips out and says:

THE DUKE LOOKS UNDER THE BED.

"What! And not sell out the rest o' the property? March off like a passel o' fools and leave eight or nine thous'n' dollars' worth o' property layin' around jest sufferin' to be scooped in?—and all good saleable stuff, too."

The duke he grumbled; said the bag of gold was enough, and he didn't want to go no deeper—didn't want to rob a lot of orphans of *everything* they had.

"Why, how you talk!" says the king. "We shan't rob 'em of nothing at all but jest this money. The people that *buys* the property is the suff'r-ers; because as soon's it's found out 'at we didn't own it—which won't be long after we've slid—the sale won't be valid, and it'll all go back to the estate. These-yer orphans 'll git their house back agin, and that's enough for *them*: they're young, and spry, and k'n easy earn a livin'. *They* ain't agoing to suffer. Why, jest think—there's thous'n's and thous'n's that ain't nigh so well off. Bless you, *they* ain't got noth'n to complain of."

Well, the king he talked him blind; so at last he give in, and said all right, but said he believed it was blame' foolishness to stay, and that doctor hanging over them: But the king says:

"Cuss the doctor! What do we k'yer for *him*? Hain't we got all the fools in town on our side? and ain't that a big enough majority in any town?"

So they got ready to go down stairs again. The duke says:

"I don't think we put that money in a good place."

That cheered me up. I'd begun to think I warn't going to get a hint of no kind to help me. The king says:

"Why?"

"Because Mary Jane'll be in mourning from this out; and first you know the nigger that does up the rooms will get an order to box these duds up and put 'em away; and do you reckon a nigger can run across money and not borrow some of it?"

"Your head's level, agin, duke," says the king; and he come a fumbling under the curtain two or three foot from where I was. I stuck tight to the wall, and kept mighty still, though quivery; and I wondered what them fellows would say to me if they catched me; and I tried to think what I'd better do if they did catch me. But the king he got the bag before I could think more than about a half a thought, and he never suspicioned I was around. They took and shoved the bag through a rip in the straw tick that was under the feather bed, and crammed it in a foot or two amongst the straw, and said it was all right, now, because a nigger only makes up the feather bed, and don't turn over the straw tick only about twice a year, and so it warn't in no danger of getting stole, now.

But I knowed better. I had it out of there before they was half way down stairs. I groped along up to my cubby, and hid it there till I could get a chance to do better. I judged I better hide it outside of the house somewheres, because if they missed it they would give the house a good ransacking, I knowed that very well. Then I turned in, with my clothes all on; but I couldn't a gone to sleep, if I'd a wanted to, I was in such a sweat to get through with the business. By and by I heard the king and the duke come up; so I rolled off of my pallet and laid with my chin at the top of my ladder and waited to see if anything was going to happen. But nothing did.

So I held on till all the late sounds had quit and the early ones hadn't begun, yet; and then I slipped down the ladder.

HUCK TAKES THE MONEY.

Chapter XXVII.

A CRACK IN THE
DINING ROOM DOOR.

I crept to their doors and listened; they was snoring, so I tip-toed along, and got down stairs all right. There warn't a sound anywheres. I peeped through a crack of the dining room door, and see the men that was watching the corpse all sound asleep on their chairs. The door was open into the parlor, where the corpse was laying, and there was a candle in both rooms. I passed along, and the parlor door was open; but I see there warn't nobody in there but the remainders of Peter; so I shoved on by; but the front door was locked, and the key wasn't there. Just then I heard somebody coming down the stairs, back behind me. I run in the parlor, and took a swift look around, and the only place I see to hide the bag, was in the coffin. The lid was shoved along about a foot, showing the dead man's face down in there, with a wet cloth over it, and his shroud on. I tucked the money bag in under the lid, just down beyond where his hands was crossed, which made me creep, they was so cold, and then I run back across the room and in behind the door.

The person coming was Mary Jane. She went to the coffin, very soft, and kneeled down and looked in; then she put up her handkerchief and I see she begun to cry, though I couldn't hear her, and her back was to me. I slid out, and as I passed the dining room I thought I'd make sure them watchers hadn't seen me; so I looked through the crack and everything was all right. They hadn't stirred.

I slipped up to bed, feeling ruther blue, on accounts of the thing playing out that way after I had took so much trouble and run so much resk about it. Says I, if it could stay where it is, all right; because when we get down the river a hundred mile or two, I could write back to Mary Jane, and she could dig him up again and get it; but that ain't the thing that's going to happen; the thing that's going to happen, is, the money'll be found when they come to screw on the lid. Then the king'll get it again, and it'll be a long day before he gives anybody another chance to smouch it from him. Of course I *wanted* to slide down and get it out of

192

there, but I dasn't try it. Every minute it was getting earlier, now, and pretty soon some of them watchers would begin to stir, and I might get catched—catched with six thousand dollars in my hands that nobody hadn't hired me to take care of. I don't wish to be mixed up in no such business as that, I says to myself.

When I got down stairs in the morning, the parlor was shut up, and the watchers was gone. There warn't nobody around but the family and the widow Bartley and our tribe. I watched their faces to see if anything had been happening, but I couldn't tell.

Towards the middle of the day the undertaker come, with his man, and they set the coffin in the middle of the room on a couple of chairs, and then set all our chairs in rows, and borrowed more from the neighbors till the hall and the parlor and the dining room was full. I see the coffin lid was the way it was before, but I dasn't go to look in under it, with folks around.

Then the people begun to flock in, and the beats[1] and the girls took seats in the front row at the head of the coffin, and for a half an hour the people filed around slow, in single rank, and looked down at the dead man's face a minute, and some dropped in a tear, and it was all very still and solemn, only the girls and the beats holding handkerchiefs to their eyes and keeping their heads bent, and sobbing a little. There warn't no other sound but the scraping of the feet on the floor, and blowing noses—because people always blows them more at a funeral than they do at other places except church.

When the place was packed full, the undertaker he slid around in his black gloves with his softy soothering ways, putting on the last touches, and getting people and things all ship-shape and comfortable, and making no more sound than a cat. He never spoke; he moved people around, he squeezed in late ones, he opened up passage-ways, and done it all with nods, and signs with his hands. Then he took his place over against the wall. He was the softest, glidingest, stealthiest man I ever see; and there warn't no more smile to him than there is to a ham.

They had borrowed a melodeum[2]—a sick one; and when everything was ready, a young woman set down and worked it, and it was pretty skreeky and colicky, and everybody joined in and sung, and Peter was the only one that had a good thing, according to my notion. Then the Reverend Hobson opened up, slow and solemn, and begun to talk; and straight off the most outrageous row busted out in

THE UNDERTAKER.

1. Deadbeats, cheats; the duke and the king.
2. Melodeon, a small reed organ.

the cellar a body ever heard; it was only one dog, but he made a most powerful racket, and he kept it up, right along; the parson he had to stand there, over the coffin, and wait—you couldn't hear yourself think. It was right down awkward, and nobody didn't seem to know what to do. But pretty soon they see that long-legged undertaker make a sign to the preacher as much as to say "Don't you worry—just depend on me." Then he stooped down and begun to glide along the wall, just his shoulders showing over the people's heads. So he glided along, and the pow-wow and racket getting more and more outrageous all the time; and at last, when he had gone around two sides of the room, he disappears down cellar. Then, in about two seconds we heard a whack, and the dog he finished up with a most amazing howl or two and then everything was dead still, and the parson begun his solemn talk where he left off. In a minute or two here comes this undertaker's back and shoulders gliding along the wall again; and so he glided, and glided, around three sides of the room, and then rose up, and shaded his mouth with his hands, and stretched his neck out towards the preacher, over the people's heads, and says, in a kind of a coarse whisper, *"He had a rat!"* Then he drooped down and glided along the wall again, to his place. You could see it was a great satisfaction to the people, because naturally they wanted to know. A little thing like that don't cost nothing, and it's just the little things that makes a man to be looked up to and liked. There warn't no more popular man in town than what that undertaker was.

"HE HAD A RAT!"

Well, the funeral sermon was very good, but pison-long and tiresome; and then the king he shoved in and got off some of his usual rubbage, and at last the job was through, and the undertaker begun to sneak up on the coffin with his screw-driver. I was in a sweat, then, and watched him pretty keen. But he never meddled at all; just slid the lid along, as soft as mush, and screwed it down tight and fast. So there I was! I didn't know whether the money was in there or not. So, says I, spose somebody has hogged that bag, on the sly?—now how do *I* know whether to write to Mary Jane or not? Spose she dug him up and didn't find nothing—

what would she think of me? Blame it, I says, I might get hunted up and jailed; I'd better lay low and keep dark, and not write at all; the thing's awful mixed, now; trying to better it, I've worsened it a hundred times, and I wish to goodness I'd just let it alone, dad fetch the whole business!

They buried him, and we come back home, and I went to watching faces again—I couldn't help it, and I couldn't rest easy. But nothing come of it; the faces didn't tell me nothing.

The king he visited around, in the evening, and sweetened everybody up, and made himself ever so friendly; and he give out the idea that his congregation over in England would be in a sweat about him, so he must hurry and settle up the estate right away, and leave for home. He was very sorry he was so pushed, and so was everybody; they wished he could stay longer, but they said they could see it couldn't be done. And he said of course him and William would take the girls home with them; and that pleased everybody too, because then the girls would be well fixed, and amongst their own relations; and it pleased the girls, too—tickled them so they clean forgot they ever had a trouble in the world; and told him to sell out as quick as he wanted to, they would be ready. Them poor things was that glad and happy it made my heart ache to see them getting fooled and lied to, so, but I didn't see no safe way for me to chip in and change the general tune.

Well, blamed if the king didn't bill the house and the niggers and all the property for auction straight off—sale two days after the funeral; but anybody could buy private beforehand if they wanted to.

So the next day after the funeral, along about noontime, the girls' joy got the first jolt: a couple of nigger traders come along, and the king sold them the niggers reasonable, for three-day drafts as they called it, and away they went—the two sons up the river to Memphis, and their mother down the river to Orleans. I thought them poor girls and them niggers would break their hearts for grief; they cried around each other, and took on so it most made me down sick to see it. The girls said they hadn't ever dreamed of seeing the family separated or sold away from the town. I can't ever get it out of my memory, the sight of them poor miserable girls and niggers hanging around each other's necks and crying; and I reckon I couldn't a stood it all but would a had to bust out and tell on our gang if I hadn't knowed the sale warn't no account and the niggers would be back home in a week or two.

The thing made a big stir in the town, too, and a good many come out flatfooted and said it was scandalous to separate the mother and the children that way. It injured the frauds some, but the old fool he bulled right along, spite of all the duke could say or do, and I tell you the duke was powerful uneasy.

Next day was auction day. About broad-day in the morning, the king and the duke come up in the garret and woke me up, and I see by their look that there was trouble. The king says:

"Was you in my room night before last?"

"No, your majesty"—which was the way I always called him when nobody but our gang warn't around.

"Was you in there yesterday er last night?"

"No, your majesty."

"WAS YOU IN MY ROOM?

"Honor bright, now—no lies."

"Honor bright, your majesty, I'm telling you the truth. I hain't been anear your room since Miss Mary Jane took you and the duke and showed it to you."

The duke says:

"Have you seen anybody else go in there?"

"No, your grace, not as I remember, I believe."

"Stop and think."

I studied a while, and see my chance; then I says:

"Well, I see the niggers go in there several times."

Both of them give a little jump; and looked like they hadn't ever expected it, and then like they *had*. Then the duke says:

"What, *all* of them?"

"No—leastways not all at once. That is, I don't think I ever see them all come *out* at once but just one time."

"Hello—when was that?"

"It was the day we had the funeral. In the morning. It warn't early, because I overslept. I was just starting down the ladder, and I see them."

"Well, go on, *go* on—what did they do? how'd they act?"

"They didn't do nothing. And they didn't act anyway, much, as fur as I see. They tip-toed away; so, I seen, easy enough, that they'd shoved in there to do up your majesty's room, or something, sposing you was up; and found you *warn't* up, and so they was hoping to slide out of the way of trouble without waking you up, if they hadn't already waked you up."

"Great guns, *this* is a go!" says the king; and both of them looked pretty sick, and tolerable silly. They stood there a thinking and scratching their heads, a minute, and then the duke he bust into a kind of a little raspy chuckle, and says:

"It does beat all, how neat the niggers played their hand. They let on to be *sorry* they was going out of this region! and I believed they *was* sorry. And so did you, and so did everybody. Don't ever tell *me*, any more, that a nigger ain't got any histrionic talent. Why, the way they played that thing, it would fool *anybody*. In my opinion, there's a fortune in 'em. If I had capital and a theatre, I wouldn't want a better layout than that—and here we've gone and sold 'em for a song. Yes, and ain't privileged to sing the song, yet. Say, where *is* that song?—that draft."

"In the bank for to be collected. Where *would* it be?"

"Well, *that's* all right, then, thank goodness."

Says I, kind of timid-like:

"Is something gone wrong?"

The king whirls on me and rips out:

"None o' your business! You keep your head shet, and mind y'r own affairs—if you got any. Long as you're in this town, don't you forgit *that*, you hear?" Then he says to the duke, "We got to jest swaller it, and say noth'n: mum's the word, for *us*."

As they was starting down the ladder, the duke he chuckles again, and says:

"Quick sales *and* small profits! It's a good business—yes."

The king snarls around on him and says:

"I was trying to do for the best, in sellin' 'm out so quick. If the profits has turned out to be none, lackin' considable, and none to carry, is it my fault any more'n it's yourn?"

"Well, *they*'d be in this house yet, and we *wouldn't*, if I could a got my advice listened to."

The king sassed back, as much as was safe for him, and then swapped around and lit into *me* again. He give me down the banks for not coming and *telling* him I see the niggers come out of his room acting that way—said any fool would a *knowed* something was up. And then waltzed in and cussed *himself* a while; and said it all come of him not laying late and taking his natural rest that morning, and he'd be blamed if he'd ever do it again. So they went off a-jawing; and I felt dreadful glad I'd worked it all off onto the niggers and yet hadn't done the niggers no harm by it.

JAWING.

Chapter XXVIII

IN TROUBLE.

By and by it was getting-up time; so I come down the ladder and started for down stairs, but as I come to the girls' room, the door was open, and I see Mary Jane setting by her old hair trunk, which was open and she'd been packing things in it—getting ready to go to England. But she had stopped, now, with a folded gown in her lap, and had her face in her hands, crying. I felt awful bad to see it; of course anybody would. I went in there, and says:

"Miss Mary Jane, you can't abear to see people in trouble, and I can't—most always. Tell me about it."

So she done it. And it was the niggers—I just expected it. She said the beautiful trip to England was most about spoiled for her; she didn't know *how* she was ever going to be happy there, knowing the mother and the children warn't ever going to see each other no more—and then busted out bitterer than ever, and flung up her hands and says:

"O, dear, dear, to think they ain't *ever* going to see each other any more!"

"But they *will*—and inside of two weeks—and I *know* it!" says I.

Laws, it was out before I could think!—and before I could budge, she throws her arms around my neck, and told me to say it *again*, say it *again*, say it *again*!

I see I had spoke too sudden, and said too much, and was in a close place. I asked her to let me think, a minute; and she set there, very impatient and excited and handsome, but looking kind of happy and eased-up, like a person that's had a tooth pulled out. So I went to studying it out. I says to myself, I reckon on a body that ups and tells the truth when he is in a tight place, is taking considerable many resks; though I ain't had no experience, and can't say for certain; but it looks so to me, anyway; and yet here's a case where I'm blest if it don't look to me like the truth is better, and actuly *safer*, than a lie. I must lay it by in my mind, and think it over some time or other, it's so kind of strange and unregular. I never see nothing like it. Well, I says to myself, at last, I'm agoing to chance it; I'll up and tell the truth this time, though it does seem most like setting down on a kag of powder and touching it off, just to see where you'll go to. Then I says:

"Miss Mary Jane, is there any place, out of town a little ways, where you could go and stay three or four days?"

"Yes—Mr. Lothrop's. Why?"

"Never mind why, yet. If I'll tell you how I know the niggers will see each other again—inside of two weeks—here in this house— *prove* how I know it—will you go to Mr. Lothrop's and stay four days?"

"Four days!" she says; "I'll stay a year!"

"All right," I says, "I don't want nothing more out of *you* than just your word—I druther have it than another man's kiss-the-Bible." She smiled, and reddened up very sweet, and I says, "if you don't mind it, I'll shut the door—and bolt it."

Then I come back and set down again, and says:

"Don't you holler. Just set still, and take it like a man. I got to tell the truth, and you want to brace up, Miss Mary, because it's a bad kind, and going to be hard to take, but there ain't no help for it. These uncles of yourn ain't no uncles at all—they're a couple of frauds—regular dead-beats. There, now, we're over the worst of it—you can stand the rest middling easy."

It jolted her up, like everything, of course; but I was over the shoal water, now, so I went right along,—her eyes a-blazing higher and higher all the time—and told her every blame thing, from where we first struck that young fool going up to the steamboat, clear through to where she flung herself onto the king's breast at the front door and he kissed her sixteen or seventeen times—and then up she jumps, with her face afire like sunset, and says:

"The brute! Come—don't waste a minute—not a *second*—we'll have them tarred and feathered, and flung in the river!"

Says I:

"Cert'nly. But do you mean, *before* you go to Mr. Lothrop's, or—"

"O," she says, "what am I *thinking* about!" she says, and set right down again. "Don't mind what I said—please

Kemble

INDIGNATION.

don't—you *won't*, now, *will* you?" laying her silky hand on mine in that kind of a way that I said I would die first. "I never thought, I was so stirred up," she says; "now go on, and I won't do so any more. You tell me what to do, and whatever you say, I'll do it."

"Well," I says, "it's a rough gang, them two frauds, and I'm fixed so I got to travel with them a while longer, whether I want to or not—I druther not tell you why—and if you was to blow on them this town would get me out of their claws, and I'd be all right, but there'd be another person that you don't know about who'd be in big trouble. Well, we got to save *him* hain't we? Of course. Well then, we won't blow on them."

Saying them words put a good idea in my head. I see how maybe I could get me and Jim rid of the frauds: get them jailed, here, and then leave. But I didn't want to run the raft in daytime, without anybody aboard to answer questions but me; so I didn't want the plan to begin working till pretty late to-night. I says:

"Miss Mary Jane, I'll tell you what we'll do—and you won't have to stay at Mr. Lothrop's so long, nuther. How fur is it?"

"A little short of four miles—right out in the country, back here."

"Well, that'll answer. Now you go along out there, and lay low till nine or half-past, to-night, and then get them to fetch you home again—tell them you've thought of something. If you get here before eleven, put a candle in this window, and if I don't turn up, wait *till* eleven, and *then* if I don't turn up, it means I'm gone, and out of the way, and safe. Then you come out and spread the news around, and get these beats jailed."

"Good," she says, "I'll do it."

"And if it just happens so that I don't get away, but get took up, along with them, you must up and say I told you the whole thing beforehand, and you must stand by me all you can."

"Stand by you, indeed I will. They shan't touch a hair of your head!" she says, and I see her nostrils spread and her eyes snap when she said it, too.

"If I get away, I shan't be here," I says, "to prove these rapscallions ain't your uncles, and I couldn't do it if I *was* here. I could swear they was beats and bummers, that's all; though that's worth something. Well, there's others can do that, better than what I can—and they're people that ain't going to be doubted as quick as I'd be. I'll tell you how to find them. Gimme a pencil and a piece of paper. There—'*Royal Nonesuch, Bricksville.*' Put it away, and don't lose it. When the court wants to find out something about these two, let them send up to Bricksville and say they've got the men that played the Royal Nonesuch, and ask for some

HOW TO FIND THEM.

witnesses—why, you'll have that entire town down here before you can hardly wink, Miss Mary. And they'll come a-biling, too."

I judged we had got everything fixed about right, now. So I says:

"Just let the auction go right along, and don't worry. Nobody don't have to pay for the things they buy till a whole day after the auction, on accounts of the short notice, and they ain't going out of this till they get that money—and the way we've fixed it the sale ain't going to count, and they ain't going to get no money. It's just like the way it was with the niggers—it warn't no sale, and the niggers will be back before long. Why, they can't collect the money for the *niggers*, yet—they're in the worst kind of a fix, Miss Mary."

"Well," she says, "I'll run down to breakfast, now, and then I'll start straight for Mr. Lothrop's."

" 'Deed, *that* ain't the ticket, Miss Mary Jane," I says, "by no manner of means; go *before* breakfast."

"Why?"

"What did you reckon I wanted you to go at all, for, Miss Mary?"

"Well, I never thought—and come to think, I don't know. What was it?"

"Why, it's because you ain't one of these leather-face people. I don't want no better book than what your face is. A body can set down and read it off like coarse print. Do you reckon you can go and face your uncles, when they come to kiss you good-morning, and never—"

"There, there, don't! Yes, I'll go before breakfast—I'll be glad to. And leave my sisters with them?"

"Yes—never mind about them. They've got to stand it yet awhile. They might suspicion something if all of you was to go. I don't want you to see them, nor your sisters, nor nobody in this town—if a neighbor was to ask how is your uncles this morning, your face would tell something. No, you go right along, Miss Mary Jane, and I'll fix it with all of them. I'll tell Miss Susan to give your love to your uncles and say you've went away for a few hours for to get a little rest and change, or to see a friend, and you'll be back to-night or early in the morning."

"Gone to see a friend is all right, but I won't have my love given to them."

"Well, then, it shan't be." It was well enough to tell *her* so—no harm in it. It was only a little thing to do, and no trouble; and it's the little things that smoothes people's roads the most, down here below; it would make Mary Jane comfortable, and it wouldn't cost nothing. Then I says: "There's one more thing—that bag of money."

"Well, they've got that; and it makes me feel pretty silly to think *how* they got it."

"No, you're out, there. They hain't got it."

"Why, who's got it?"

"I wish I knowed, but I don't. I *had* it, because I stole it from them; and I stole it to give to you; and I know where I hid it, but I'm afraid it ain't there no more. I'm awful sorry, Miss Mary Jane, I'm just as sorry as I can be; but I done the best I could; I did, honest. I come nigh getting caught, and I had to shove it into the first place I come to, and run— and it warn't a good place."

"O, stop blaming yourself—it's too bad to do it, and I won't allow it—you couldn't help it; it wasn't your fault. Where did you hide it?"

I didn't want to set her to thinking about her troubles again; and I couldn't seem to get my mouth to tell her what would make her see that corpse laying in the coffin with that bag of money on his stomach. So, for a minute I didn't say nothing—then I says:

"I'd ruther not *tell* you where I put it, Miss Mary Jane, if you don't mind letting me off; but I'll write it for you on a piece of paper, and you can read it along the road to Mr. Lothrop's, if you want to. Do you reckon that'll do?"

"O, yes."

HE WROTE.

So I wrote: "I put it in the coffin. It was in there when you was crying there, away in the night. I was behind the door, and I was mighty sorry for you, Miss Mary Jane."

It made my eyes water a little, to remember her crying there all by herself in the night, and them devils laying there right under her own roof, shaming her and robbing her; and when I folded it up and give it to her, I see the water come into her eyes, too; and she shook me by the hand, hard, and says:

"*Good*-bye—I'm going to do everything just as you've told me; and if I don't ever see you again, I shan't ever forget you, and I'll think of you a many and a many a time, and I'll *pray* for you, too!"—and she was gone.

Pray for me! I reckoned if she knowed me she'd take a job that was more nearer her size. But I bet she done it, just the same—she was just that kind. She had the grit to pray for Judus if she took the notion—there warn't no back-down to her, I judge. You may say what you want to, but in my opinion she had more sand in her than any girl I ever see; in my opinion she was just full of sand. It sounds like flattery, but it ain't no flattery. And when it comes to beauty—and goodness too—she lays over them all. I hain't ever seen her since that time that I see her go out of that door; no, I hain't ever seen her since; but I reckon I've thought of her a many and a many a million times, and of her saying she would pray for me; and if ever I'd a thought it would do any good for me to pray for *her*, blamed if I wouldn't a done it or bust.

Well, Mary Jane she lit out the back way, I reckon, because nobody see her go. When I struck Susan and the hare-lip, I says:

"What's the name of them people over on t'other side of the river that you-all goes to see sometimes?"

They says:

"There's several; but it's the Proctors, mainly."

"That's the name," I says; "I most forgot it. Well, Miss Mary Jane she told me to tell you she's gone over there in a dreadful hurry—one of them's sick."

"Which one?"

"I don't know; leastways I kinder forget; but I think it's—"

"Sakes alive, I hope it ain't *Hanner*?"

"I'm sorry to say it," I says, "but Hanner's the very one."

"My goodness—and she so well only last week! Is she took bad?"

"It ain't no name for it. They set up with her all night, Miss Mary Jane said, and they don't think she'll last many hours."

"Only think of that, now! What's the matter with her?"

I couldn't think of anything reasonable, right off that way, so I says: "Mumps."

"Mumps your granny!—they don't set up with people that's got the mumps."

HANNER WITH THE MUMPS.

"They don't, don't they? You better bet they do with *these* mumps. These mumps is different. It's a new kind, Miss Mary Jane said."

"How's it a new kind?"

"Because it's mixed up with other things."

"What other things?"

"Well, measles, and whooping cough, and erysiplas, and consumption, and yallerjanders, and brain fever, and I don't know what all."[1]

"My land! And they call it the *mumps*?"

1. Erysipelas, a severe skin disease; consumption, tuberculosis; yellow jaundice, a liver disease.

"That's what Miss Mary Jane said."

"Well, what in the nation do they call it the *mumps* for?"

"Why, because it *is* the mumps. That's what it starts with."

"Well, ther' ain't no sense in it. A body might stump his toe, and take pison, and fall down the well, and break his neck, and bust his brains out, and somebody come along and ask what killed him, and some numskull up and say, 'Why, he stumped his *toe.*' Would ther' be any sense in that? *No.* And ther' ain't no sense in *this,* nuther. Is it ketching?"

"Is it *ketching?* Why, how you talk. Is a *harrow* catching?—in the dark? If you don't hitch onto one tooth, you're bound to on another, ain't you? And you can't get away with that tooth without fetching the whole harrow along, can you? Well, these kind of mumps is a kind of a harrow, as you may say—and it ain't no slouch of a harrow, nuther, you come to get it hitched on good."

"Well, it's awful, *I* think," says the hare-lip. "I'll go to uncle Harvey and—"

"O, yes," I says, "I *would.* Of *course* I would. I wouldn't lose no time."

"Well, why wouldn't you?"

"Just look at it a minute, and maybe you can see. Hain't your uncles obleeged to get along home to England as fast as they can? And do you reckon they'd be mean enough to go off and leave you to go all that journey by yourselves? *You* know they'll wait for you. So fur, so good. Your uncle Harvey's a preacher, ain't he? Very well, then; is a *preacher* going to deceive a steamboat clerk? is he going to deceive a *ship clerk?*—so as to get them to let Miss Mary Jane go aboard? Now *you* know he ain't. What *will* he do, then? Why, he'll say, 'It's a great pity, but my church matters has got to get along the best way they can; for my niece has been exposed to the dreadful pluribus-unum mumps,[2] and so it's my bounden duty to set down here and wait the three months it takes to show on her if she's got it.' But never mind, if you think it's best to tell your uncle Harvey—"

"Shucks, and stay fooling around here when we could all be having good times in England whilst we was waiting to find out whether Mary Jane's got it or not? Why, you talk like a muggins."[3]

"Well, anyway, maybe you better tell some of the neighbors."

"Listen at that, now. You do beat all, for natural stupidness. Can't you *see* that *they'*d go and tell? Ther' ain't no way but just to not tell anybody at *all.*"

"Well, maybe you're right—yes, I judge you *are* right."

"But I reckon we ought to tell uncle Harvey she's gone out a while, anyway, so he won't be uneasy about her?"

"Yes, Miss Mary Jane she wanted you to do that. She says, 'Tell them to give uncle Harvey and William my love and a kiss, and say I've run over the river to see Mr.—Mr.—what *is* the name of that rich family your uncle Peter used to think so much of?—I mean the one that—"

"Why, you must mean the Apthorps, ain't it?"

"Of course; bother them kind of names, a body can't ever seem to remember them, half the time, somehow. Yes, she said, say she has run

2. Like the United States, whose motto Huck misappropriates, this fearful disease makes "one out of many."
3. A fool.

over for to ask the Apthorps to be sure and come to the auction and buy this house, because she allowed her uncle Peter would ruther they had it than anybody else; and she's going to stick to them till they say they'll come; and then if she ain't too tired, she's coming home; and if she is, she'll be home in the morning, anyway. She said, don't say nothing about the Proctors, but only about the Apthorps—which'll be perfectly true, because she *is* going there to speak about their buying the house; I know it, because she told me so, herself."

"All right," they said, and cleared out to lay for their uncles, and give them the love and the kisses, and tell them the message.

Everything was all right, now. The girls wouldn't say nothing, because they wanted to go to England; and the king and the duke would ruther Mary Jane was off working for the auction than around in reach of doctor Robinson. I felt very good; I judged I had done it pretty neat—I reckoned Tom Sawyer couldn't a done it no neater, himself. Of course he would a throwed more style into it, but I can't do that very handy, not being brung up to it.

Well, they held the auction, in the public square, along towards the end of the afternoon, and it strung along, and strung along, and the old man he was on hand and looking his level piousest, up there longside of the auctioneer, and chipping in a little Scripture, now and then, or a little goody-goody saying, of some kind, and the duke he was around goo-gooing for sympathy all he knowed how, and just spreading himself gen-erly.

THE AUCTION.

But by and by the thing dragged through, and everything was sold. Everything but a little old trifling lot in the graveyard. So they'd got to work *that* off—I never see such a girafft as the king was for wanting to swallow *everything*. Well, whilst they was at it, a steamboat landed, and in about two minutes, up comes a crowd a whooping and yelling and laughing and carrying on, and singing out:

"*Here's* your opposition line! Here's your two sets o'heirs to old Peter Wilks—and you pays your money and you takes your choice!"

Chapter XXIX

THE TRUE BROTHERS.

They was fetching a very nice looking old gentleman along, and a nice looking younger one, with his right arm in a sling. And my souls, how the people yelled, and laughed, and kept it up. But I didn't see no joke about it, and I judged it would strain the duke and the king some, to see any. I reckoned they'd turn pale. But no, nary a pale did they turn. The duke he never let on he suspicioned what was up, but just went a goo-gooing around, happy and satisfied, like a jug that's googling out buttermilk; and as for the king, he just gazed and gazed down sorrowful on them newcomers like it give him the stomachache in his very heart to think there could be such frauds and rascals in the world. O, he done it admirable. Lots of the principal people gethered around the king, to let him see they was on his side. That old gentleman that had just come, looked all puzzled to death. Pretty soon he begun to speak, and I see, straight off, he pronounced like an Englishman; not the king's way, though the king's was pretty good, for an imitation. I can't give the old gent's words, nor I can't imitate him; but he turned around to the crowd, and says, about like this:

"This is a surprise to me which I wasn't looking for; and I'll acknowledge, candid and frank, I ain't very well fixed to meet it and answer it; for my brother and me has had misfortunes: he's broke his arm, and our baggage got put off at a town above here, last night in the night, by a mistake. I am Peter Wilks's brother Harvey, and this is his brother William, which can't hear nor speak—and can't even make signs to amount to much, now 't he's only got one hand to work them with. We are who we say we are; and in a day or two, when I get the baggage, I can prove it. But, up till then, I won't say nothing more, but go to the hotel and wait."

So him and the new dummy started off; and the king he laughs, and blethers out:

"Broke his arm—*very* likely, *ain't* it?—and very convenient, too, for a fraud that's got to make signs, and hain't learnt how. Lost their baggage! That's *mighty* good!—and mighty ingenious—under the *circumstances!*"

So he laughed again; and so did everybody else, except three or four, or maybe half a dozen. One of these was that doctor; another one was a sharp looking gentleman, with a carpet bag of the old-fashioned kind made out of carpet-stuff, that had just come off of the steamboat and was talking to him in a low voice, and glancing towards the king now and then and nodding their heads—it was Levi Bell, the lawyer that was gone up to Louisville; and another one was a big rough husky that come along and listened to all the old gentleman said, and was listening to the king, now. And when the king got done, this husky up and says:

"Say, looky-here; if you are Harvey Wilks, when'd you come to this town?"

"The day before the funeral, friend," says the king.

"But what time o' day?"

"In the evenin'—'bout an hour er two before sundown."

"*How'd* you come?"

"I come down on the Susan Powell, from Cincinnati."

"Well, then, how'd you come to be up at the Pint in the *mornin'*—in a canoe?"

"I warn't up at the Pint in the mornin'."

"It's a lie."

Several of them jumped for him and begged him not to talk that way to an old man and a preacher.

"Preacher be hanged, he's a fraud and a liar. He was up at the Pint that mornin'. I live up there, don't I? Well, I was up there, and he was up there. I *see* him there. He come in a canoe, along with Tim Collins and a boy."

The doctor he up and says:

"Would you know the boy again if you was to see him, Hines?"

"I reckon I would, but I don't know. Why, yonder he is, now. I know him perfectly easy."

It was me he pointed at. The doctor says:

"Neighbors, I don't know whether the new couple is frauds or not; but if *these* two ain't frauds, I am an idiot, that's all. I think it's our duty to see that they don't get away from here till we've looked into this thing. Come along, Hines; come along, the rest of you. We'll take these fellows to the tavern and affront them with t'other couple, and I reckon we'll find out *something* before we get through."

It was nuts for the crowd, though maybe not for the king's friends; so we all started. It was about sundown. The doctor he led me along by the hand, and was plenty kind enough, but he never let *go* my hand.

We all got in a big room in the hotel, and lit up some candles, and fetched in the new couple.

First, the doctor says:

"I don't wish to be too hard on these two men, but *I* think they're frauds, and they may have complices that we don't know nothing about. If they have, won't the complices get away with that bag of gold Peter Wilks left? It ain't unlikely. If these men ain't frauds, they won't object to sending for that money and letting us keep it till they prove they're all right—ain't that so?"

THE DOCTOR LEADS HUCK.

Everybody agreed to that. So I judged they had our gang in a pretty tight place, right at the outstart. But the king he only looked sorrowful, and says:

"Gentlemen, I wish the money was there, for I ain't got no disposition to throw anything in the way of a fair, open, out-and-out investigation o' this misable business; but alas, the money ain't there; you k'n send and see, if you want to."

"Where is it, then?"

"Well, when my niece give it to me to keep for her, I took and hid it inside o' the straw tick o' my bed, not wishin' to bank it for the few days we'd be here, and considerin' the bed a safe place, we not bein' used to niggers, and suppos'n' 'em honest, like servants in England. The niggers stole it the very next mornin', after I had went down stairs; and when I sold 'em, I hadn't missed the money yit, so they got clean away with it. My servant here k'n tell you 'bout it, gentlemen."

The doctor and several said "Shucks!" and I see nobody didn't altogether believe him. One man asked me if I see the niggers steal it. I said no, but I see them sneaking out of the room and hustling away, and I never thought nothing, only I reckoned they was afraid they had waked up my master and was trying to get away before he made trouble with them. That was all they asked me. Then the doctor whirls on me and says:

"Are *you* English, too?"

I says yes; and him and some others laughed, and said, "Stuff!"

Well, then they sailed in on the general investigation, and there we had it, up and down, hour in, hour out, and nobody never said a word about supper, nor ever seemed to think about it—and so they kept it up, and kept it up; and it *was* the worst mixed-up thing you ever see. They made the king tell his yarn, and they made the old gentleman tell his'n; and anybody but a lot of prejudiced chuckleheads would a *seen* that the old gentleman was spinning truth and t'other one lies. And by and by they had me up to tell what I knowed. The king he give me a left-handed look out of the corner of his eye, and so I knowed enough to talk on the right side. I begun to tell about Sheffield, and how we lived there, and all about the English Wilkses, and so on; but I didn't get pretty fur till the doctor begun to laugh; and Levi Bell, the lawyer, says:

"Set down, my boy, I wouldn't strain myself, if I was you. I reckon you ain't used to lying, it don't seem to come handy; what you want is prac- tice. You do it pretty awkward."

I didn't care nothing for the compliment, but I was glad to be let off, any way.

The doctor he started to say something, and turns and says:

"If you'd been in town at first, Levi Bell—"

The king broke in and reached out his hand and says:

"Why, is this my poor dead brother's old friend that he's wrote so often about?"

The lawyer and him shook hands, and the lawyer smiled, and looked pleased, and they talked right along, a while, and then got to one side and talked low; and at last the lawyer speaks up and says:

"That'll fix it. I'll take the order and send it, along with your brother's, and then they'll know it's all right."

So they got some paper and a pen, and the king he set down and twisted his head to one side, and chawed his tongue, and scrawled off something; and then they give the pen to the duke—and then for the first time, the duke looked sick. But he took the pen and wrote. So then the lawyer turns to the new old gentleman and says:

"You and your brother please write a line or two and sign your names."

The old gentleman wrote, but nobody couldn't read it. The lawyer looked powerful astonished, and says:

"Well, it beats *me*"—and snaked a lot of old letters out of his pocket, and examined them, and then examined the old man's writing, and then

THE DUKE WROTE.

them again; and then says: "These old letters is from Harvey Wilks; and here's *these* two's handwritings, and anybody can see *they* didn't write them" (the king and the duke looked sold and foolish, I tell you, to see how the lawyer had took them in), "and here's *this* old gentleman's handwriting, and anybody can tell, easy enough, *he* didn't write them— fact is, the scratches he makes ain't properly *writing*, at all. Now here's some letters from—"

The new old gentleman says:

"If you please, let me explain. Nobody can read my hand but my brother there—so he copies for me. It's *his* hand you've got there, not mine."

"*Well!*" says the lawyer, "this *is* a state of things. I've got some of William's letters, too; so if you'll get him to write a line or so we can com—"

"He *can't* write with his left hand," says the old gentleman. "If he could use his right hand, you would see that he wrote his own letters and mine too. Look at both, please—they're by the same hand."

The lawyer done it, and says:

"I believe it's so—and if it ain't so there's a heap stronger resemblance than I'd noticed before, anyway. Well, well, well! I thought we was right on the track of a slution, but it's gone to grass, partly. But anyway, *one* thing is proved—*these* two ain't either of 'em Wilkses"—and he wagged his head towards the king and the duke.

Well, what do you think?—that muleheaded old fool wouldn't give in *then!* Indeed he wouldn't. Said it warn't no fair test. Said his brother William was the cussedest joker in the world, and hadn't *tried* to write— *he* see William was going to play one of his jokes the minute he put the pen to paper. And so he warmed up and went warbling and warbling right along, till he was actuly beginning to believe what he was saying, *himself*—but pretty soon the new old gentleman broke in and says:

"I've thought of something. Is there anybody here that helped to lay out my br—helped to lay out the late Peter Wilks for burying?"

"Yes" says somebody, "me and Ab Turner done it. We're both here."

Then the old man turns towards the king and says:

"Peraps this gentleman can tell me what was tattooed on his breast?"

Blamed if the king didn't have to brace up mighty quick, or he'd a squshed down like a bluff bank that the river has cut under, it took him so sudden—and mind you it was a thing that was calculated to make most *anybody* sqush, to get fetched such a solid one as that without any notice—because how was *he* going to know what was tattooed on the man? He whitened a little; he couldn't help it; and it was mighty still, in there, and everybody bending a little forward and gazing at him. Says I to myself, *Now* he'll throw up the sponge—there ain't no more use. Well, did he? A body can't hardly believe it, but he didn't. I reckon he thought he'd keep the thing up till he tired them people out, so they'd thin out and him and the duke could break loose and get away. Anyway, he set there, and pretty soon he begun to smile, and says:

"Mf! It's a *very* tough question, *ain't it!* *Yes*, sir, I k'n tell you what's tat-tooed on his breast. It's jest a small, thin, blue arrow—that's what it is; and if you don't look clost, you can't see it. *Now* what do you say—hey?"

Well, *I* never see anything like that old blister, for clean out-and-out cheek.

The new old gentleman turns brisk towards Ab Turner and his pard, and his eye lights up like he judged he'd got the king *this* time, and says:

"There—you've heard what he said! Was there any such mark on Peter Wilks's breast?"

Both of them spoke up and says:

"We didn't see no such mark."

"Good!" says the old gentleman. "Now what you *did* see on his breast was a small dim P, and a B, (which is an initial he dropped when he was young,) and a W, with dashes between them, so: P—B—W"—and he marked them that way on a piece of paper. "Come—ain't that what you saw?"

Both of them spoke up again, and says:

"No, we *didn't*. We never seen any marks, at all."

Well, everybody *was* in a state of mind, now; and they sings out:

"The whole *bilin'* of 'm 's frauds! Le's duck 'em! le's drown 'em! le's ride 'em on a rail!" and everybody was whooping at once, and there was a rattling pow-wow. But the lawyer he jumps on the table and yells, and says:

"Gentlemen—gentle*men*! Hear me just a word—just a *single* word—

"GENTLEMEN—GENTLE*MEN*!"

if you PLEASE! There's one way, yet—let's go and dig up the corpse and look."

That took them.

"Hooray!" they all shouted, and was starting right off; but the lawyer and the doctor sung out:

"Hold on, hold on! Collar all these four men and the boy, and fetch *them* along, too!"

"We'll do it!" they all shouted; "and if we don't find them marks, we'll lynch the whole gang!"

I *was* scared, now, I tell you. But there warn't no getting away, you know. They gripped us all, and marched us right along, straight for the graveyard, which was a mile and a half down the river, and the whole town at our heels, for we made noise enough, and it was only nine in the evening.

As we went by our house I wished I hadn't sent Mary Jane out of town; because now if I could tip her the wink, she'd light out and save me, and blow on our dead-beats.

Well, we swarmed along down the river road, just carrying on like wild-cats; and to make it more scary, the sky was darking up, and the lightning beginning to wink and flitter, and the wind to shiver amongst the leaves. This was the most awful trouble and most dangersome I ever was in; and I was kinder stunned, everything was going so different from what I had allowed for: 'stead of being fixed so I could take my own time, if I wanted to, and see all the fun, and have Mary Jane at my back to save me and set me free when the close-fit come, here was nothing in the world betwixt me and sudden death but just them tattoo-marks. If they didn't find them—

I couldn't bear to think about it; and yet, somehow, I couldn't think about nothing else. It got darker and darker, and it was a beautiful time to give the crowd the slip; but that big husky had me by the wrist— Hines—and a body might as well try to give Goliar[1] the slip. He dragged me right along, he was so excited; and I had to run to keep up.

When they got there they swarmed into the graveyard, and washed over it like an overflow. And when they got to the grave, they found they had about a hundred times as many shovels as they wanted, but nobody hadn't thought to fetch a lantern. But they sailed into digging, anyway, by the flicker of the lightning, and sent a man to the nearest house a half a mile off, to borrow one.

So they dug and dug, like everything; and it got awful dark, and the rain started, and the wind swished and swushed along, and the lightning come brisker and brisker, and the thunder boomed; but them people never took no notice of it, they was so full of this business; and one minute you could see every thing and every face in that big crowd, and the shovelfuls of dirt sailing up out of the grave, and the next second the dark wiped it all out, and you couldn't see nothing at all.

At last they got out the coffin, and begun to unscrew the lid, and then such another crowding, and shouldering and shoving as there was, to scrouge in and get a sight, you never see; and in the dark, that way, it was awful. Hines he hurt my wrist dreadful, pulling and tugging so, and I reckon he clean forgot I was in the world, he was so excited and panting.

All of a sudden the lightning let go a perfect sluice of white glare, and somebody sings out:

"By the living jingo, here's the bag of gold on his breast!"

Hines let out a whoop, like everybody else, and dropped my wrist and give a big surge to bust his way in and get a look, and the way I lit out and shinned for the road in the dark, there ain't nobody can tell.

---

1. Goliath.

I had the road all to myself, and I fairly flew—leastways I had it all to myself except the solid dark, and the now-and-then glares, and the buzzing of the rain, and the thrashing of the wind, and the splitting of the thunder; and sure as you are born I did clip it along!

When I struck the town, I see there warn't nobody out in the storm, so I never hunted for no back steets, but humped it straight through the main one; and when I begun to get towards our house I aimed my eye and set it. No light there; the house all dark—which made me feel sorry and disappointed, I didn't know why. But at last, just as I was sailing by, *flash* comes the light in Mary Jane's window! and my heart swelled up sudden, like to bust, and the same second the house and all was behind me in the dark, and wasn't ever going to be before me no more in this world. She *was* the best girl I ever see, and had the most sand.

The minute I was far enough above the town to see I could make the towhead, I begun to look sharp for a boat to borrow; and the first time the lightning showed me one that wasn't chained, I snatched it and shoved. It was a canoe, and warn't fastened with nothing but a rope. The towhead was a rattling big distance off, away out there in the middle of the river, but I didn't lose no time; and when I struck the raft at last, I was so fagged I would a just laid down to blow and gasp if I could afforded it. But I didn't. As I sprung aboard I sung out:

"Out with you Jim, and set her loose! Glory be to goodness, we're shut of them!"

Jim lit out, and was a coming for me with both arms spread, he was so full of joy, but when I glimpsed him in the lightning, my heart shot up in my mouth, and I went overboard backwards; for I forgot he was

"JIM LIT OUT."

old King Leer and a drownded A-rab all in one, and it most scared the livers and lights out of me. But Jim fished me out, and was going to hug me and bless me, and so on, he was so glad I was back and we was shut of the king and the duke, but I says:

"Not now—have it for breakfast, have it for breakfast! Cut loose and let her slide!"

So, in two seconds, away we went, a sliding down the river, and it *did* seem so good to be free again and all by ourselves on the big river and nobody to bother us. I had to skip around a bit, and jump up and crack my heels a few times, I couldn't help it; but about the third crack, I noticed a sound that I knowed mighty well,—and held my breath, and listened and waited—and sure enough, when the next flash busted out over the water, here they come!—and just a laying to their oars and making their skiff hum! It was the king and the duke.

So I wilted right down onto the planks, then, and give up; and it was all I could do to keep from crying.

Chapter XXX

THE KING SHAKES HUCK.

When they got aboard, the king went for me, and shook me by the collar, and says:

"Tryin' to give us the slip, was ye, you pup! Tired of our company—hey?"

I says:

"No, your majesty, we warn't—*please* don't, your majesty!"

"Quick, then, and tell us what *was* your idea, or I'll shake the insides out o' you!"

"Honest, I'll tell you everything, just as it happened, your majesty. The man that had aholt of me was very good to me, and kept saying he had a boy about as big as me, that died last year, and he was sorry to see a boy in such a dangerous fix; and when they was all took by surprise by finding the gold, and made a rush for the coffin, he lets go of me and whispers, 'Heel it, now, or they'll hang ye, sure!' and I lit out. It didn't seem no good for *me* to stay—I couldn't do nothing, and I didn't want to be hung if I could get away. So I never stopped running till I found the canoe; and when I got here I told Jim to hurry, or they'd catch me and hang me, yet, and said I was afeard you and the duke wasn't alive, now, and I was awful sorry, and so was Jim, and was awful glad when we see you coming, you may ask Jim if I didn't."

Jim said it was so; and the king told him to shut up, and said, "O, yes, it's *mighty* likely!" and shook me up again, and said he reckoned he'd drownd me. But the duke says:

"Leggo the boy, you old idiot! Would *you* a done any different? Did you inquire around for *him*, when you got loose? *I* don't remember it."

So the king let go of me, and begun to cuss that town, and everybody in it. But the duke says:

"You better a blame sight give *yourself* a good cussing, for you're the one that's entitled to it most. You hain't done a thing, from the start, that had any sense in it, except coming out so cool and cheeky with that imaginary blue-arrow mark. That *was* bright—it was right down bully; and it was the thing that saved us. For if it hadn't been for that, they'd a jailed us till them Englishmen's baggage come, and then—the penitentiary, you bet! But that trick took 'em to the graveyard, and the gold done us a still bigger kindness; for if the excited fools hadn't let go all holts and made that rush to get a look, we'd a slept in our cravats to-night—cravats warranted to *wear*,[1] too—longer than *we'd* need 'em."

They was still a minute—thinking—then the king says, kind of absent-minded like:

"Mf! And we reckoned the *niggers* stole it!"

That made me squirm!

"Yes," says the duke, kinder slow, and deliberate, and sarcastic. "*We* did."

After about a half a minute, the king drawls out:

"Leastways—*I* did."

The duke says, the same way:

"On the contrary—*I* did."

The king kind of ruffles up, and says:

"Looky here, Bilgewater, what'r you referrin' to?"

The duke says, pretty brisk:

"When it comes to that, maybe you'll let me ask, what was *you* refer-ring to?"

"Shucks!" says the king, very sarcastic; "but *I* don't know—maybe you was asleep, and didn't know what you was about."

The duke bristles right up, now, and says:

"O, let *up* on this cussed nonsense—do you take me for a blame' fool? Don't you reckon *I* know who hid that money in that coffin?"

"*Yes* sir! I know you *do* know—because you done it yourself!"

"It's a lie!"—and the duke went for him. The king sings out:

"Take y'r hands off!—leggo my throat!—I take it all back!"

THE DUKE WENT FOR HIM.

The duke says:

"Well, you just own up, first, that you *did* hide that money there, intending to give me the slip one of these days, and come back and dig it up, and have it all to yourself."

---

1. Hangman's nooses; *cravat*: necktie or scarf.

"Wait jest a minute, duke—answer me this one question, honest and fair: if you didn't put the money there, say it, and I'll b'lieve you, and take back everything I said."

"You old scoundrel, I didn't, and you know I didn't. There, now!"

"Well then, I b'lieve you. But answer me only jest this one more— now *don't* git mad: didn't you have it in your *mind* to hook the money and hide it?"

The duke never said nothing for a little bit; then he says:

"Well—I don't care if I *did*, I didn't *do* it, anyway. But you not only had it in mind to do it, but you *done* it."

"I wisht I may never die if I done it, duke, and that's honest. I won't say I warn't *goin'* to do it, because I *was*; but you—I mean somebody— got in ahead o' me."

"It's a lie! You done it, and you got to *say* you done it, or—"

The king begun to gurgle, and then he gasps out:

" 'Nough!—*I own up!*"

I was very glad to hear him say that, it made me feel much more easier than what I was feeling before. So the duke took his hands off, and says:

"If you ever deny it again, I'll drown you. It's *well* for you to set there and blubber like a baby—it's fitten for you, after the way you've acted. I never see such an old ostrich for wanting to gobble everything—and I a trusting you all the time, like you was my own father. You ought to been ashamed of yourself to stand by and hear it saddled onto a lot of poor niggers and you never say a word for 'em. It makes me feel ridiculous to think I was soft enough to *believe* that rubbage. Cuss you, I can see, now, why you was so anxious to make up the deffesit—you wanted to get what money I'd got out of the Nonesuch and one thing or another, and scoop it *all*!"

The king says, timid, and still a snuffling:

"Why, duke, it was you that said make up the deffersit, it warn't me."

"Dry up! I don't want to hear no more *out* of you!" says the duke. "And *now* you see what you *got* by it. They've got all their own money back, and all of *ourn* but a shekel or two, *besides*. G'long to bed—and don't you deffersit *me* no more deffersits, long's *you* live!"

So the king sneaked into the wigwam, and took to his bottle for comfort; and before long the duke tackled *his* bottle; and so in about a half an hour they was as thick as thieves again, and the tighter they got the lovinger they got; and went off a-snoring in each other's arms. They both got powerful mellow, but I noticed the king didn't get mellow enough to forget to remember to not deny about hiding the money-bag, again. That made me feel easy and satisfied. Of course when they got to snoring, we had a long gabble, and I told Jim everything.

Chapter XXXI

SPANISH MOSS.

We dasn't stop again at any town, for days and days; kept right along down the river. We was down south in the warm weather, now, and a mighty long ways from home. We begun to come to trees with Spanish moss on them, hanging down from the limbs like long gray beards. It was the first I ever see it growing, and it made the woods look solemn and dismal. So now the frauds reckoned they was out of danger, and they begun to work the villages again.

First they done a lecture on temperance; but they didn't make enough for them both to get drunk on. Then in another village they started a dancing school; but they didn't know no more how to dance than a kangaroo does; so the first prance they made, the general public jumped in and pranced them out of town. Another time they tried a go at yellocution; but they didn't yellocute long till the audience got up and give them a solid good cussing and made them skip out. They tackled missionarying, and mesmerizering, and doctoring, and telling fortunes, and a little of everything; but they couldn't seem to have no luck. So at last they got just about dead broke, and laid around the raft, as she floated along, thinking, and thinking, and never saying nothing, by the half a day at a time, and dreadful blue and desperate.

And at last they took a change and begun to lay their heads together in the wigwam and talk low and confidential two or three hours at a time. Jim and me got uneasy. We didn't like the look of it. We judged they was studying up some kind of worse deviltry than ever. We turned it over and over, and at last we made up our minds they was going to break into somebody's house or store, or was going into the counterfeit money business, or something. So then we was pretty scared, and made up an agreement that we wouldn't have nothing in the world to do with such actions, and if we ever got the least show we would give them the cold shake, and clear out and leave them behind. Well, early one morning we hid the raft in a good safe place about two mile below a little bit of a shabby village, named Pikesville, and the king he went ashore, and told us all to stay hid whilst he went up to town and smelt around to see if anybody had got any wind of the Royal Nonesuch there yet. ("House to rob, you *mean*," says I to myself; "and when you get through robbing it you'll come back here and wonder what's become of me and Jim and the raft—and you'll have to take it out in wondering.") And he said if he warn't back by midday, the duke and me would know it was all right, and we was to come along.

So we staid where we was. The duke he fretted and sweated around, and was in a mighty sour way. He scolded us for everything, and we couldn't seem to do nothing right; he found fault with every little thing. Something was a-brewing, sure. I was good and glad when midday come and no king; we could have a change, anyway—and maybe a chance for *the* change, on top of it. So me and the duke went up to the village, and hunted around there for the king, and by and by we found him in the back room of a little low doggery,[1] very tight, and a lot of loafers bullyragging him for sport, and he a cussing and threatening with all his might, and so tight he couldn't walk, and couldn't do nothing to them. The duke he begun to abuse him for an old fool, and the king begun to sass back; and the minute they was fairly at it, I lit out, and shook the reefs[2] out of my hind legs, and spun down the river road like a deer—for I see our chance; and I made up my mind that it would be a long day before they ever see me and Jim again. I got down there all out of breath but loaded up with joy, and sung out—

"Set her loose, Jim, we're all right, now!"

But there warn't no answer, and nobody come out of the wigwam. Jim was gone! I set up a shout,—and then another—and then another one; and run this way and that in the woods, whooping and screeching; but it warn't no use—old Jim was gone. Then I set down and cried; I couldn't help it. But I couldn't set still long. Pretty soon I went out on the road, trying to think what I better do, and I run across a boy walking, and asked him if he'd seen a strange nigger, dressed so and so, and he says:

"Yes."

"Whereabouts?" says I.

"Down to Silas Phelps's place, two mile below here. He's a runaway nigger, and they've got him. Was you looking for him?"

"You bet I ain't! I run across him in the woods about an hour or two ago, and he said if I hollered he'd cut my livers out—and told me to lay down and stay where I was; and I done it. Been there ever since; afeard to come out."

"Well," he says, "you needn't be afeard no more, becuz they've got him. He run off f'm down south, som'ers."

"It's a good job they got him."

"Well, I *reckon*! There's two hunderd dollars reward on him. It's like picking up money out'n the road."

"Yes, it is—and *I* could a had it if I'd been big enough: I see him *first*. Who nailed him?"

---

1. Saloon.
2. Folds, kinks.

"WHO NAILED HIM?"

"It was an old fellow—a stranger—and he sold out his chance in him for forty dollars, becuz he's got to go up the river and can't wait. Think o' that, now! You bet I'd wait, if it was seven year."

"That's me, every time," says I. "But maybe his chance ain't worth no more than that, if he'll sell it so cheap. Maybe there's something ain't straight about it."

"But it *is*, though—straight as a string. I see the handbill myself. It tells all about him, to a dot—paints him like a picture, and tells the plantation he's frum, below Newr*leans*. No-sir-ree-*bob*, they ain't no trouble 'bout *that* speculation, you bet you. Say, gimme a chaw tobacker, won't ye?"

I didn't have none, so he left. I went to the raft, and set down in the wigwam to think. But I couldn't come to nothing. I thought, till I wore my head sore, but I couldn't see no way out of the trouble. After all this long journey, and after all we'd done for them scoundrels, here was it all come to nothing, everything all busted up and ruined, because they could have the heart to serve Jim such a trick as that, and make him a slave again all his life, and amongst strangers, too, for forty dirty dollars.

Once I said to myself it would be a thousand times better for Jim to be a slave at home where his family was, as long as he'd *got* to be a slave, and so I'd better write a letter to Tom Sawyer and tell him to tell Miss Watson where he was. But I soon give up that notion, for two things: she'd be mad and disgusted at his rascality and ungratefulness for leaving her, and so she'd sell him straight down the river again; and if she didn't, everybody naturally despises an ungrateful nigger, and they'd make Jim feel it all the time, and so he'd feel ornery and disgraced. And

then think of *me*! It would get all around, that Huck Finn helped a nigger to get his freedom; and if I was to ever see anybody from that town
again, I'd be ready to get down and lick his boots for shame. That's just
the way: a person does a low-down thing, and then he don't want to take
no consequences of it. Thinks as long as he can hide it, it ain't no dis-
grace. That was my fix exactly. The more I studied about this, the more
my conscience went to grinding me, and the more wicked, and low-
down and ornery I got to feeling. And at last, when it hit me all of a sudden that here was the plain hand of Providence slapping me in the face
and letting me know my wickedness was being watched all the time
from up there in heaven, whilst I was stealing a poor old woman's nigger that hadn't ever done me no harm, and now was showing me there's
One that's always on the lookout, and ain't agoing to allow no such miserable doings to go only just so fur and no further, I most dropped in my
tracks I was so scared. Well, I tried the best I could to kinder soften it
up somehow for myself, by saying I was brung up wicked, and so I
warn't so much to blame; but something inside of me kept saying,
"There was the Sunday School, you could a gone to it; and if you'd a
done it they'd a learnt you, there, that people that acts as I'd been acting about that nigger goes to everlasting fire."

It made me shiver. And I about made up my mind to pray; and see
if I couldn't try to quit being the kind of a boy I was, and be better. So
I kneeled down. But the words wouldn't come. Why wouldn't they? It
warn't no use to try and hide it from Him. Nor from *me*, neither. I
knowed very well why they wouldn't come. It was because my heart
warn't right; it was because I warn't square; it was because I was playing double. I was letting *on* to give up sin, but away inside of me I was
holding on to the biggest one of all. I was trying to make my mouth
say I would do the right thing and the clean thing, and go and write
to that nigger's owner and tell where he was; but deep down in me I
knowed it was a lie—and He knowed it. You can't pray a lie—I found
that out.

So I was full of trouble, full as I could be; and didn't know what to
do. At last I had an idea; and I says, I'll go and write the letter—and
then see if I can pray. Why, it was astonishing, the way I felt as light
as a feather, right straight off, and my troubles all gone. So I got a
piece of paper and a pencil, all glad and excited, and set down and
wrote:

Miss Watson your runaway nigger Jim is down here two mile below
Pikesville and Mr. Phelps has got him and he will give him up for the
reward if you send. HUCK FINN.

I felt good and all washed clean of sin for the first time I had ever felt
so in my life, and I knowed I could pray, now. But I didn't do it straight
off, but laid the paper down and set there thinking; thinking how good
it was all this happened so, and how near I come to being lost and
going to hell. And went on thinking. And got to thinking over our trip
down the river; and I see Jim before me, all the time, in the day, and in
the night-time, sometimes moonlight, sometimes storms, and we a
floating along, talking, and singing, and laughing. But somehow I

couldn't seem to strike no places to harden me against him, but only the other kind. I'd see him standing my watch on top of his'n, stead of calling me—so I could go on sleeping; and see him how glad he was when I come back out of the fog; and when I come to him again in the swamp, up there where the feud was; and such-like times; and would always call me honey, and pet me, and do everything he could think of

THINKING.

for me, and how good he always was; and at last I struck the time I saved him by telling the men we had small-pox aboard, and he was so grateful, and said I was the best friend old Jim ever had in the world, and the *only* one he's got now; and then I happened to look around, and see that paper.

It was a close place. I took it up, and held it in my hand. I was a trembling, because I'd got to decide, forever, betwixt two things, and I knowed it. I studied a minute, sort of holding my breath, and then says to myself:

"All right, then, I'll *go* to hell"—and tore it up.[3]

It was awful thoughts, and awful words, but they was said. And I let them stay said; and never thought no more about reforming. I shoved the whole thing out of my head; and said I would take up wickedness again, which was in my line, being brung up to it, and the other warn't. And for a starter, I would go to work and steal Jim out of slavery again; and if I could think up anything worse, I would do that, too; because as long as I was in, and in for good, I might as well go the whole hog.

3. This is Huck's celebrated crisis of conscience. Mark Twain apparently worked on the passage with great care, lengthening it by about 150 words when revising the manuscript. By pushing Huck the "wrong" way in a tug-of-war between feeling and conscience, he inverts a stock device of Christian rhetoric that goes back at least to St. Augustine's *Confessions* of the fourth century.

Then I set to thinking over how to get at it, and turned over considerable many ways in my mind; and at last fixed up a plan that suited me. So then I took the bearings of a woody island that was down the river a piece, and as soon as it was fairly dark I crept out with my raft and went for it, and hid it there, and then turned in. I slept the night through, and got up before it was light, and had my breakfast, and put on my store clothes, and tied up some others and one thing or another in a bundle, and took the canoe and cleared for shore. I landed below where I judged was Phelps's place, and hid my bundle in the woods, and then filled up the canoe with water, and loaded rocks into her and sunk her where I could find her again when I wanted her, about a quarter of a mile below a little steam sawmill that was on the bank.

Then I struck up the road, and when I passed the mill I see a sign on it, "Phelps's Sawmill," and when I come to the farm houses, two or three hundred yards further along, I kept my eyes peeled, but didn't see nobody around, though it was good daylight, now. But I didn't mind, because I didn't want to see nobody just yet—I only wanted to get the lay of the land. According to my plan, I was going to turn up there from the village, not from below. So I just took a look, and shoved along, straight for town. Well, the very first man I see, when I got there, was the duke. He was sticking up a bill for the Royal Nonesuch—three-night performance, like that other time. *They* had the cheek, them frauds! I was right on him, before I could shirk. He looked astonished, and says:

"Hel-*lo*! Where'd *you* come from?" Then he says, kind of glad, and eager, "Where's the raft?—got her in a good place?"

I says:

"Why, that's just what I was agoing to ask your grace."

Then he didn't look so joyful—and says:

"What was your idea for asking *me*?" he says.

"Well," I says, "when I see the king in that doggery, yesterday, I says to myself, we can't get him home for hours, till he's soberer; so I went a loafing around town to put in the time, and wait. A man up and offered me ten cents to help him pull a skiff over the river and back to fetch a sheep, and so I went along; but when we was dragging him to the boat, and the man left me aholt of the rope and went behind him to shove him along, he was too strong for me, and jerked loose and run, and we after him. We didn't have no dog, and so we had to chase him all over the country till we tired him out. We never got him till dark, then we fetched him over, and I started down for the raft. When I got there and see it was gone, I says to myself, 'They've got into trouble and had to leave; and they've took my nigger, which is the only nigger I've got in the world, and now I'm in a strange country, and ain't got no property no more, nor nothing, and no way to make my living;' so I set down and cried. I slept in the woods all night. But what *did* become of the raft, then?—and Jim, poor Jim!"

"Blamed if *I* know—that is, what's become of the raft. That old fool had made a trade and got forty dollars, and when we found him in the doggery, the loafers had matched half dollars with him and got every cent but what he'd spent for whisky; and when I got him home late last night and found the raft gone, we said, 'That little rascal has stole our raft and shook us, and run off down the river.'"

"I wouldn't shake my *nigger*, would I?—the only nigger I had in the world, and the only property."

"We never thought of that. Fact is, I reckon we'd come to consider him *our* nigger; yes, we did consider him so—goodness knows we had trouble enough for him. So, when we see the raft was gone, and we flat broke, there warn't anything for it but to try the Royal Nonesuch another shake. And I've pegged along ever since, dry as a powder horn. Where's that ten cents? Give it here."

I had considerable money, so I give him ten cents, but begged him to spend it for something to eat, and give me some, because it was all the

HE GAVE HIM TEN CENTS.

money I had, and I hadn't had nothing to eat since yesterday. He never said nothing. The next minute he whirls on me and says:

"Do you reckon that nigger would blow on us? We'd skin him if he done that!"

"How can he blow? Hain't he run off?"

"No! That old fool sold him, and never divided with me, and the money's gone."

"*Sold* him?" I says, and begun to cry: "Why, he was *my* nigger, and that was my money. Where is he?—I want my nigger."

"Well, you can't *get* your nigger, that's all—so dry up your blubbering. Looky-here—do you think *you'd* venture to blow on us? Blamed if I think I'd trust you. Why, if you *was* to blow on us—"

He stopped, but I never see the duke look so ugly out of his eyes before. I went on a-whimpering, and says:

"I don't want to blow on nobody; and I ain't got no time to blow, nohow. I got to turn out and find my nigger."

He looked kinder bothered, and stood there with his bills fluttering on his arm, thinking, and wrinkling up his forehead. At last he says:

"I'll tell you something. We got to be here three days. If you'll promise you won't blow, and won't let the nigger blow, I'll tell you where to find him."

So I promised, and he says:

"A farmer by the name of Silas Ph—" and then he stopped. You see, he started to tell me the truth; but when he stopped, that way, and begun to study and think, again, I reckoned he was changing his mind. And so he was. He wouldn't trust me; he wanted to make sure of having me out of the way the whole three days. So pretty soon he says:

"The man that bought him is named Abram Foster—Abram G. Foster—and he lives forty mile back here in the country, on the road to Lafayette."

"All right," I says, "I can walk it in three days. And I'll start this very afternoon."

"No you won't, you'll start *now*; and don't you lose any time about it, neither, nor do any gabbling by the way. Just keep a tight tongue in your head and move right along, and then you won't get into trouble with *us*, d'ye hear?"

That was the order I wanted, and that was the one I played for. I wanted to be left free to work my plans.

"So clear out," he says; "and you can tell Mr. Foster whatever you want to. Maybe you can get him to believe that Jim *is* your nigger—some idiots don't require documents—leastways I've heard there's such down South here. And when you tell him the handbill and the reward's bogus, maybe he'll believe you when you explain to him what the idea was for getting 'em out. Go 'long, now, and tell him anything you want to; but mind you don't work your jaw any *between* here and there."

So I left, and struck for the back country. I didn't look around, but I kinder felt like he was watching me. But I knowed I could tire him out

STRIKING FOR THE BACK COUNTRY

at that. I went straight out in the country as much as a mile, before I stopped; then I doubled back through the woods towards Phelps's. I reckoned I better start in on my plan straight off, without fooling around, because I wanted to stop Jim's mouth till these fellows could get away. I didn't want no trouble with their kind. I'd seen all I wanted to of them, and wanted to get entirely shut of them.

Chapter XXXII

STILL AND SUNDAY-LIKE.

When I got there it was all still and Sunday-like, and hot and sunshiny—the hands was gone to the fields; and there was them kind of faint dronings of bugs and flies in the air that makes it seem so lonesome and like everybody's dead and gone; and if a breeze fans along and quivers the leaves, it makes you feel mournful, because you feel like it's spirits whispering—spirits that's been dead ever so many years—and you always think they're talking about *you*. As a general thing, it makes a body wish *he* was dead, too, and done with it all.

Phelps's was one of these little one-horse cotton plantations; and they all look alike.[1] A rail fence round a two-acre yard; a stile, made out of logs sawed off and up-ended, in steps, like barrels of a different length, to climb over the fence with, and for the women to stand on when they are going to jump onto a horse; some sickly grass-patches in the big yard, but mostly it was bare and smooth, like an old hat with the nap rubbed off; big double log house for the white folks,—hewed logs, with the chinks stopped up with mud or mortar, and these mud-stripes been whitewashed some time or another; round-log kitchen, with a big broad, open, but roofed passage, joining it to the house; log smoke-house back of the kitchen; three little log nigger-cabins in a row t'other side the smoke-house; one little hut all by itself, away down against the back fence, and some out-buildings down a piece the other side; ash-hopper,[2] and big kettle to bile soap in, by the little hut; bench by the kitchen door, with bucket of water and a gourd; hound asleep there, in the sun; more hounds asleep, round about; about three shade trees, away off in a corner; some currant bushes and gooseberry bushes in one place by the fence; outside of the fence, a garden and a watermelon patch; then the cotton fields begins; and after the fields, the woods.

I went around and clumb over the back stile by the ash-hopper, and started for the kitchen. When I got a little ways, I heard the dim hum of

1. The Phelps plantation resembles the farm of his uncle John Quarles near Florida, Missouri, that Mark Twain describes in his *Autobiography* (see p. 302).
2. Containing lye for making soap.

a spinning wheel wailing along up and sinking along down again: and then I knowed for certain I wished I was dead—for that *is* the lone-somest sound in the whole world.

I went right along, not fixing up any particular plan, but just trusting to Providence to put the right words in my mouth when the time come; for I'd noticed that Providence always did put the right words in my mouth, if I left it alone.

When I got half way, first one hound and then another got up and went for me, and of course I stopped, and faced them, and kept still. And such another pow-wow as they made! in a quarter of a minute I was a kind of a hub of a wheel, as you may say—spokes made out of dogs—circle of fifteen of them packed together around me, with their necks and noses stretched up towards me, a-barking and howling; and more a-coming; you could see them sailing over fences and around corners, from everywheres.

A nigger woman come tearing out of the kitchen, with a rolling-pin in her hand, singing out, "Begone! *you* Tige! you Spot! bedone, sah!" and she fetched first one and then another of them a clip and sent him howling, and then the rest followed; and the next second, half of them come back, wagging their tails around me, and making friends with me. There ain't no harm in a hound, nohow.

And behind the woman comes a little nigger girl and two little nigger boys, without anything on but tow-linen shirts, and they hung onto their mother's gown, and peeped out from behind her at me, bashful, the way they always do. And here comes the white woman running from the house, about forty-five or fifty year old, bareheaded, and her spin-ning-stick in her hand; and behind her comes her little white children, acting the same way the little niggers was doing. She was smiling all over so she could hardly stand—and says:

"It's *you*, at last!—*ain't* it?"

I out with a "Yes'm," before I thought.

She grabbed me and hugged me tight; and then gripped me by both hands, and shook and shook; and the tears come in her eyes, and run down over; and she couldn't seem to hug and shake enough, and kept saying, "You don't look as much like your mother as I reckoned you would, but law sakes, I don't care for that, I'm *so* glad to see you! Dear, dear, it does seem like I could eat you up! Children, it's your cousin Tom!—tell him howdy."

But they ducked their heads, and put their fingers in their mouths, and hid behind her. So she run on:

"Lize, hurry up and get him a hot breakfast, right away—or did you get your breakfast on the boat?"

I said I had got it on the boat. So then she started for the house, lead-ing me by the hand, and the children tagging after. When we got there, she set me down in a split-bottomed chair, and set herself down on a lit-tle low stool in front of me, holding both of my hands, and says:

"Now I can have a *good* look at you; and laws-a-me, I've been hungry for it a many and a many a time, all these long years, and it's come at last! We been expecting you a couple of days and more. What's kep' you?—boat get aground?"

"Yes'm—she—"

"Don't say yes'm—say Aunt Sally. Where'd she get aground?"

I didn't rightly know what to say, because I didn't know whether the boat would be coming up the river, or down. But I go a good deal on instinct; and my instinct said she would be coming up—from down towards Orleans. That didn't help me much, though; for I didn't know

SHE HUGGED HIM TIGHT.

the names of bars down that way. I see I'd got to invent a bar, or forget the name of the one we got aground on—or—. Now I struck an idea, and fetched it out:

"It wasn't the grounding—that didn't keep us back but a little. We blowed out a cylinder-head."

"Good gracious! anybody hurt?"

"No'm. Killed a nigger."

"Well, it's lucky; because sometimes people do get hurt. Two years ago last Christmas, your uncle Silas was coming up from Newrleans on the old Lally Rook,[3] and she blowed out a cylinder-head and crippled a man. And I think he died, afterwards. He was a Babtist. Your uncle Silas knowed a family in Baton Rouge that knowed his people very well. Yes, I remember, now, he *did* die. Mortification set in, and they had to amputate him. But it didn't save him. Yes, it was mortification—that was it. He turned blue all over, and died in the hope of a glorious resurrection. They say he was a sight to look at. Your uncle's been up to the town every day to fetch you. And he's gone again, not more'n an hour ago; he'll be back any minute, now. You must a met him on the road, didn't you—oldish man, with a—"

3. Named after the emperor's daughter in Thomas Moore's *Lalla Rookh* (1817).

"No, I didn't see nobody, aunt Sally. The boat landed just at daylight, and I left my baggage on the wharfboat and went looking around the town and out a piece in the country, to put in the time and not get here too soon; and so I come down the back way."

"Who'd you give the baggage to?"

"Nobody."

"Why, child, it'll be stole!"

"Not where *I* hid it I reckon it won't," I says.

"How'd you get your breakfast so early on the boat?"

It was kinder thin ice, but I says:

"The captain see me standing around, and told me I better have something to eat before I went ashore; so he took me in the texas to the officers' lunch, and give me all I wanted."

I was getting so uneasy I couldn't listen good. I had my mind on the children all the time; I wanted to get them out to one side, and pump them a little, and find out who I was. But I couldn't get no show, Mrs. Phelps kept it up and run on so. Pretty soon she made the cold chills streak all down my back; because she says:

"But here we're a running on, this way, and you hain't told me a word about Sis, nor any of them. Now I'll rest my works a little, and you start-up yourn; just tell me *everything*—tell me all about 'm all—every one of 'm; and how they are, and what they're doing, and what they told you to tell me; and every last thing you can think of."

Well, I see I was up a stump—and up it good. Providence had stood by me this fur, all right, but I was hard and tight aground, now. I see it warn't a bit of use to try to go ahead—I'd *got* to throw up my hand. So I says to myself, here's another place where I got to resk the truth. I opened my mouth to begin; but she grabbed me and hustled me in behind the bed, and says:

"Here he comes! Stick your head down lower—there, that'll do; you can't be seen, now. Don't you let on you're here: I'll play a joke on him. Childern, don't you say a word."

I see I was in a fix, now. But it wasn't no use to worry; there wasn't nothing to do but just hold still, and try and be ready to stand from under when the lightning struck.

I had just one little glimpse of the old gentleman when he come in,—then the bed hid him. Mrs. Phelps she jumps for him and says:

"Has he come?"

"No," says her husband.

"Good-*ness* gracious!" she says, "what in the world *can* have become of him?"

"I can't imagine," says the old gentleman; "and I must say, it makes me dreadful uneasy."

"Uneasy!" she says, "I'm ready to go distracted! he *must* a come; and you've missed him along the road. I *know* it's so—something *tells* me so."

"Why Sally, I *couldn't* miss him along the road—*you* know that."

"But oh, dear, dear, what *will* Sis say! He must a come! You must a missed him. He—"

"Oh, don't distress me any more'n I'm already distressed. I don't know what in the world to make of it. I'm at my wit's end, and I don't mind acknowledging 't I'm right down scared. But there's no hope that he's come; for he *couldn't* come and me miss him. Sally it's terrible—just terrible—something's happened to the boat, sure!"

"Why, Silas! Look yonder!—up the road!—ain't that somebody coming?"

He sprung to the window at the head of the bed, and that give Mrs. Phelps the chance she wanted. She stooped down quick, at the foot of the bed, and give me a pull, and out I come; and when he turned back from the window, there she stood, a-beaming and a-smiling like a house afire, and I standing pretty meek and sweaty alongside. The old gentleman stared, and says:

"Why, who's that?"

"Who do you reckon 't is?"

"I hain't no idea. Who *is* it?"

"It's *Tom Sawyer*!"

"WHO DO YOU RECKON 'T IS?"

By jings, I most slumped through the floor. But there warn't no time to swap knives: the old man grabbed me by the hand and shook, and kept on shaking; and all the time, how the woman did dance around and laugh and cry; and then how they both did fire off questions about Sid, and Mary, and the rest of the tribe.

But if they was joyful, it warn't nothing to what I was; for it was like being born again, I was so glad to find out who I was. Well, they froze to me for two hours; and at last when my chin was so tired it couldn't hardly go, any more, I had told them more about my family—I mean the Sawyer family—than ever happened to any six Sawyer families. And I explained all about how we blowed out a cylinder-head at the mouth of White river and it took us three days to fix it. Which was all right, and worked first-rate; because *they* didn't know but what it would take three days to fix it. If I'd a called it a bolt-head it would a done just as well.

Now I was feeling pretty comfortable all down one side, and pretty uncomfortable all up the other. Being Tom Sawyer was easy and comfortable; and it staid easy and comfortable till by and by I hear a steamboat coughing along down the river—then I says to myself, spose Tom Sawyer come down on that boat?—and spose he steps in here, any minute, and sings out my name before I can throw him a wink to keep quiet? Well, I couldn't *have* it that way—it wouldn't do, at all. I must go up the road and waylay him. So I told the folks I reckoned I would go up to the town and fetch down my baggage. The old gentleman was for going along with me, but I said no, I could drive the horse myself, and I druther he wouldn't take no trouble about me.

Chapter XXXIII.

"IT WAS TOM SAWYER."

So I started for town, in the wagon, and when I was half way I see a wagon coming, and sure enough it was Tom Sawyer, and I stopped and waited till he come along. I says "Hold on!" and it stopped alongside, and his mouth opened up like a trunk, and staid so; and he swallowed two or three times, like a person that's got a dry throat, and then says:

"I hain't ever done you no harm. You know that. So then, what you want to come back and ha'nt *me*, for?"

I says:

"I hain't come back—I hain't been *gone*."

When he heard my voice, it righted him up, some, but he warn't quite satisfied, yet. He says:

"Don't you play nothing on me, because I wouldn't on you. Honest injun, now, you ain't a ghost?"

"Honest injun, I ain't," I says.

"Well—I—I—well, that ought to settle it, of course; but I can't somehow seem to understand it, no way. Lookyhere, warn't you ever murdered *at all*?"

"No. I warn't ever murdered at all—I played it on them. You come in here and feel of me if you don't believe me."

So he done it; and it satisfied him; and he was that glad to see me again, he didn't know what to do. And he wanted to know all about it, right off; because it was a grand adventure, and mysterious, and so it hit him where he lived. But I said, leave it alone till by and by; and told his driver to wait, and we drove off a little piece, and I told him the kind of a fix I was in, and what did he reckon we better do? He said, let him alone a minute, and don't disturb him. So he thought and thought, and pretty soon he says:

"It's all right, I've got it. Take my trunk in your wagon, and let on it's your'n; and you turn back and fool along slow, so as to get to the house about the time you ought to; and I'll go towards town a piece, and take a fresh start, and get there a quarter or a half an hour after you; and you needn't let on to know me, at first."

I says:

"All right; but wait a minute. There's one more thing—a thing that *nobody* don't know but me. And that is, there's a nigger here that I'm trying to steal out of slavery—and his name is *Jim*—old Miss Watson's Jim."

He says:

"What! Why Jim is—"

He stopped, and went to studying. I says:

"*I* know what you'll say. You'll say it's dirty low-down business; but what if it is?—*I'm* low-down; and I'm agoing to steal him, and I want you to keep mum and not let on. Will you?"

His eye lit up, and he says:

"I'll *help* you steal him!"

Well, I let go all holts, then, like I was shot. It was the most astonishing speech I ever heard—and I'm bound to say Tom Sawyer fell, considerable, in my estimation. Only I couldn't believe it. Tom Sawyer a *nigger stealer*!

"Oh, shucks," I says, "you're joking."

"I ain't joking, either."

"Well, then," I says, "joking or no joking, if you hear anything said about a runaway nigger, don't forget to remember that *you* don't know nothing about him, and *I* don't know nothing about him."

Then we took the trunk and put it in my wagon, and he drove off his way, and I drove mine. But of course I forgot all about driving slow, on accounts of being glad and full of thinking; so I got home a heap too quick for that length of a trip. The old gentleman was at the door, and he says:

"Why, this is wonderful. Who ever would a thought it was in that mare to do it. I wish we'd a timed her. And she hain't sweated a hair— not a hair. It's wonderful. Why, I wouldn't take a hundred dollars for that horse now; I wouldn't honest; and yet I'd a sold her for fifteen, before, and thought 'twas all she was worth."

That's all he said. He was the innocentest best old soul I ever see. But it warn't surprising; because he warn't only just a farmer, he was a preacher, too, and had a little one-horse log church down back of the plantation, which he built it himself at his own expense, for a church and school house, and never charged nothing for his preaching, and it was worth it, too. There was plenty other farmer-preachers like that, and done the same way, down South.

In about half an hour Tom's wagon drove up to the front stile, and aunt Sally she see it through the window—because it was only about fifty yards—and says:

"Why, there's somebody come! I wonder who 'tis? Why, I do believe it's a stranger. Jimmy," (that's one of the children,) "run and tell Lize to put on another plate for dinner."

Everybody made a rush for the front door—because, of course, a stranger don't come *every* year, and so he lays over the yaller fever, for interest, when he does come. Tom was over the stile and starting for the house; the wagon was spinning up the road for the village, and we was all bunched in the front door. Tom had his store clothes on, and an audience—and that was always nuts for Tom Sawyer. In them circumstances it warn't no trouble to him to throw in an amount of style that was suitable. He warn't a boy to meeky[1] along up that yard like a sheep, no, he come ca'm and important, like the ram. When he got afront of us, he lifts his hat ever so gracious and dainty, like it was the lid of a box that had butterflies asleep in it and he didn't want to disturb them, and says:

"Mr. Archibald Nichols, I presume?"

"No, my boy," says the old gentleman, "I'm sorry to say 't your driver has deceived you; Nichols's place is down a matter of three mile more. Come in, come in."

Tom he took a look back over his shoulder, and says, "Too late—he's out of sight."

"Yes, he's gone, my son, and you must come in and eat your dinner with us; and then we'll hitch up and take you down to Nichols's."

"MR. ARCHIBALD NICHOLS, I PRESUME?"

"Oh, I can't make you so much trouble, I couldn't think of it. I'll walk—I don't mind the distance."

"But we won't let you walk—it wouldn't be southern hospitality to do it. Come right in."

"Oh, do," says aunt Sally; "it ain't a bit of trouble to us, not a bit in the world. You must stay. It's a long, dusty three mile, and we can't let you walk. And besides, I've already told 'em to put on another plate, when I see you coming; so you mustn't disappoint us. Come right in, and make yourself at home."

1. Come meekly.

So Tom he thanked them very hearty and handsome, and let himself be persuaded, and come in; and when he was in, he said he was a stranger from Hicksville, Ohio, and his name was William Thompson— and he made another bow.

Well, he run on, and on, and on, making up stuff about Hicksville and everybody in it he could invent, and I getting a little previous, and wondering how this was going to help me out of my scrape; and at last, still talking along, he reached over and kissed aunt Sally right on the mouth, and then settled back again, in his chair, comfortable, and was going on talking; but she jumped up and wiped it off with the back of her hand, and says:

"You owdacious puppy!"

He looked kind of hurt, and says:

"I'm surprised at you, m'am."

"You're s'rp—Why, what do you reckon *I* am? I've a good notion to take and—say, what do you mean by kissing me?"

He looked kind of humble, and says:

"I didn't mean nothing, m'am. I didn't mean no harm. I—I—thought you'd like it."

"Why, you born fool!" She took up the spinning-stick, and it looked like it was all she could do to keep from giving him a crack with it. "What made you think I'd like it?"

"Well, I don't know. Only, they—they—told me you would."

"*They* told you I would. Whoever told you, 's *another* lunatic. I never heard the beat of it. Who's *they*?"

"Why—everybody. They all said so, m'am."

It was all she could do to hold in; and her eyes snapped, and her fingers worked like she wanted to scratch him; and she says:

"Who's 'everybody?' Out with their names—or ther'll be an idiot short."

He got up and looked distressed, and fumbled his hat, and says:

"I'm sorry, and I warn't expecting it. They told me to. They all told me to. They all said kiss her; and said, she'll like it. They all said it—every one of them. But I'm sorry, m'am, and I won't do it no more—I won't, honest."

"You won't, won't you? Well, I sh'd *reckon* you won't!"

"No'm, I'm honest about it; I won't ever do it again. Till you ask me."

"Till I *ask* you! Well, I never see the beat of it in my born days! I lay you'll be the Methusalem-numskull[2] of creation before ever *I* ask you— or the likes of you."

"Well," he says, "it does surprise me so. I can't make it out, somehow. They said you would, and I thought you would. But—" He stopped, and looked around slow, like he wished he could run across a friendly eye, somewheres; and fetched up on the old gentleman's, and says, "Didn't *you* think she'd like me to kiss her, sir?"

"Why, no, I—I—well, no, I b'lieve I didn't."

Then he looks on around, the same way, to me—and says:

"Tom, didn't *you* think aunt Sally'd open out her arms and say, 'Sid Sawyer'—"

2. An imbecile as old as Methuselah.

"My land!" she says, breaking in and jumping for him, "you impudent young rascal, to fool a body so—" and was going to hug him, but he fended her off, and says:

"No, not till you've asked me, first."

So she didn't lose no time, but asked him; and hugged him and kissed him, over and over again, and then turned him over to the old man, and he took what was left. And after they got a little quiet again, she says:

"Why dear me, I never see such a surprise. We warn't looking for *you*, at all, but only Tom. Sis never wrote to me about anybody coming but him."

"It's because it warn't *intended* for any of us to come but Tom," he says; "but I begged and begged, and at the last minute she let me come, too; so, coming down the river, me and Tom thought it would be a first rate surprise for him to come here to the house first, and for me to by and by tag along and drop in and let on to be a stranger. But it was a mistake, aunt Sally. This ain't no healthy place for a stranger to come."

"No—not impudent whelps, Sid. You ought to had your jaws boxed; I hain't been so put out since I don't know when. But I don't care, I don't mind the terms—I'd be willing to stand a thousand such jokes to have you here. Well, to think of that performance! I don't deny it, I was most putrefied with astonishment when you give me that smack."

We had dinner out in that broad open passage betwixt the house and the kitchen; and there was things enough on that table for seven families—and all hot, too; none of your flabby tough meat that's laid in a cupboard in a damp cellar all night and tastes like a hunk of old cold cannibal in the morning. Uncle Silas he asked a pretty long blessing over it, but it was worth it; and it didn't cool it a bit, neither, the way I've seen them kind of interruptions do, lots of times.

There was a considerable good deal of talk, all the afternoon, and me and Tom was on the lookout all the time, but it warn't no use, they didn't happen to say nothing about any runaway nigger, and we was afraid to try to work up to it. But at supper, at night, one of the little boys says:

A PRETTY LONG BLESSING.

"Pa, mayn't Tom and Sid and me go to the show?"

"No," says the old man, "I reckon there ain't going to be any; and you couldn't go if there was; because the runaway nigger told Burton and me all about that scandalous show, and Burton said he would tell the people; so I reckon they've drove the owdacious loafers out of town before this time."

So there it was!—but *I* couldn't help it. Tom and me was to sleep in the same room and bed; so, being tired, we bid good night and went up to bed, right after supper, and clumb out of the window and down the lightning rod, and shoved for the town; for I didn't believe anybody was going to give the king and the duke a hint, and so if I didn't hurry up and give them one they'd get into trouble, sure.

On the road Tom he told me all about how it was reckoned I was murdered, and how pap disappeared, pretty soon, and didn't come back no more, and what a stir there was when Jim run away; and I told Tom all about our Royal Nonesuch rapscallions, and as much of the raft-voyage as I had time to; and as we struck into the town and up through the middle of it—it was as much as half after eight, then— here comes a raging rush of people, with torches, and an awful whooping and yelling, and banging tin pans and blowing horns; and we jumped to one side to let them go by; and as they went by, I see they had the king and the duke astraddle of a rail—that is, I knowed it *was* the king and the duke, though they was all over tar and feathers, and didn't look like nothing in the world that was human—just looked like a couple of monstrous big soldier-plumes. Well, it made me sick to see it; and I was sorry for them poor pitiful rascals, it seemed like I couldn't ever feel any hardness against them any more in the world. It was a dreadful thing to see. Human beings *can* be awful cruel to one another.

We see we was too late—couldn't do no good. We asked some stragglers about it, and they said everybody went to the show looking very innocent; and laid low and kept dark till the poor old king was in the

TRAVELING BY RAIL.

middle of his cavortings on the stage; then somebody give a signal, and the house rose up and went for them.

So we poked along back home, and I warn't feeling so brash as I was before, but kind of ornery, and humble, and to blame, somehow—though I hadn't done nothing. But that's always the way: it don't make no difference whether you do right or wrong, a person's conscience ain't got no sense, and just goes for him *anyway*. If I had a yaller dog that didn't know no more than a person's conscience does, I would pison him. It takes up more room than all the rest of a person's insides, and yet ain't no good, nohow. Tom Sawyer he says the same.

Chapter XXXIV.

VITTLES.

We stopped talking, and got to thinking. By and by, Tom says:

"Looky-here, Huck, what fools we are, to not think of it before! I bet I know where Jim is."

"No! Where?"

"In that hut down by the ash-hopper. Why, looky-here. When we was at dinner, didn't you see a nigger man go in there with some vittles?"

"Yes."

"What did you think the vittles was for?"

"For a dog."

"So'd I. Well, it warn't for a dog."

"Why?"

"Because part of it was watermelon."

"So it was—I noticed it. Well, it does beat all, that I never thought about a dog not eating watermelon. It shows how a body can see and don't see, at the same time."

"Well, the nigger unlocked the padlock when he went in, and he locked it again when he come out. He fetched uncle a key, about the time we got up from table—same key, I bet. Watermelon shows man, lock shows prisoner; and it ain't likely there's two prisoners on such a little plantation, and where the people's all so kind and good. Jim's the prisoner. All right—I'm glad we found it out detective fashion; I wouldn't give shucks for any other way. Now you work your mind and study out a plan to steal Jim, and I will study out one, too; and we'll take the one we like the best."

What a head for just a boy to have! If I had Tom Sawyer's head, I wouldn't trade it off to be a duke, nor mate of a steamboat, nor clown in a circus, nor nothing I can think of. I went to thinking out a plan, but only just to be doing something: I knowed very well where the right plan was going to come from. Pretty soon, Tom says:

"Ready?"

"Yes," I says.

"All right,—bring it out."

"My plan is this," I says. "We can easy find out if it's Jim in there. Then get up my canoe to-morrow night, and fetch my raft over from the

241

island. Then the first dark night that comes, steal the key out of the old man's britches, after he goes to bed, and shove off down the river on the raft, with Jim, hiding daytimes and running nights, the way me and Jim used to do before. Wouldn't that plan work?"

"*Work?* Why cert'nly, it would work, like rats a-fighting. But it's too blame' simple; there ain't nothing *to* it. What's the good of a plan that ain't no more trouble than that? It's as mild as goose-milk. Why, Huck, it wouldn't make no more talk than breaking into a soap factory."

I never said nothing, because I warn't expecting nothing different; but I knowed mighty well that whenever he got *his* plan ready it wouldn't have none of them objections to it.

And it didn't. He told me what it was, and I see in a minute it was worth fifteen of mine, for style, and would make Jim just as free a man as mine would, and maybe get us all killed, besides. So I was satisfied, and said we would waltz in on it. I needn't tell what it was, here, because I knowed it wouldn't stay the way it was. I knowed he would be changing it around, every which way, as we went along, and heaving in new bullinesses wherever he got a chance. And that is what he done.

Well, one thing was dead sure; and that was, that Tom Sawyer was in earnest, and was actuly going to help steal that nigger out of slavery. That was the thing that was too many for me. Here was a boy that was respectable, and well brung up; and had a character to lose; and folks at home that had characters; and he was bright and not leather-headed; and knowing, and not ignorant; and not mean, but kind; and yet here he was, without any more pride, or rightness, or feeling, than to stoop to this business, and make himself a shame, and his family a shame, before everybody. I *couldn't* understand it, no way at all. It was outrageous, and I knowed I ought to just up and tell him so; and so be his true friend, and let him quit the thing right where he was, and save himself. And I *did* start to tell him; but he shut me up, and says:

"Don't you reckon I know what I'm about? Don't I generly know what I'm about?"

"Yes."

"Didn't I *say* I was going to help steal the nigger?"

"Yes."

"*Well*, then."

That's all he said, and that's all I said. It warn't no use to say any more; because when he said he'd do a thing, he always done it. But *I* couldn't make out how he was willing to go into this thing; so I just let it go, and never bothered no more about it. If he was bound to have it so, *I* couldn't help it.

When we got home, the house was all dark and still; so we went on down to the hut by the ash-hopper, for to examine it. We went through the yard, so as to see what the hounds would do. They knowed us, and didn't make no more noise than country dogs is always doing when anything comes by in the night. When we got to the cabin, we took a look at the front and the two sides; and on the side I warn't acquainted with—which was the north side—we found a square window-hole, up tolerable high, with just one stout board nailed across it. I says:

"Here's the ticket. This hole's big enough for Jim to get through, if we wrench off the board."

Tom says:

"It's as simple as tit-tat-toe, three-in-a-row, and as easy as playing hookey. I should *hope* we can find a way that's a little more complicated than *that*, Huck Finn."

A SIMPLE JOB.

"Well, then," I says, "how'll it do to saw him out, the way I done before I was murdered, that time?"

"That's more *like*," he says. "It's real mysterious, and troublesome, and good," he says; "but I bet we can find a way that's twice as long. There ain't no hurry; le's keep on looking around."

Betwixt the hut and the fence, on the backside, was a lean-to, that joined the hut at the eaves, and was made out of plank. It was as long as the hut, but narrow—only about six foot wide. The door to it was at the south end, and was padlocked. Tom he went to the soap kettle, and searched around and fetched back the iron thing they lift the lid with; so he took it and prized out one of the staples. The chain fell down, and we opened the door and went in, and shut it and struck a match, and see the shed was only built against the cabin and hadn't no connection with it; and there warn't no floor to the shed, nor nothing in it but some old rusty played-out hoes, and spades, and picks and a crippled plow. The match went out, and so did we, and shoved in the staple again, and the door was locked as good as ever. Tom was joyful. He says:

"Now we're all right. We'll *dig* him out. It'll take about a week!"

Then we started for the house, and I went in the back door—you only have to pull a buckskin latch-string, they don't fasten the doors—but that warn't romantical enough for Tom Sawyer: no way would do him but he must climb up the lightning rod. But after he got up half way about three times, and missed fire and fell every time, and the last time most busted his brains out, he thought he'd got to give it up; but after he was rested, he allowed he would give her one more turn for luck, and this time he made the trip.

In the morning we was up at break of day, and down to the nigger cabins to pet the dogs and make friends with the nigger that fed Jim—if it *was* Jim that was being fed. The niggers was just getting through breakfast and starting for the fields; and Jim's nigger was piling up a tin pan with bread and meat and things; and whilst the others was leaving, the key come from the house.

This nigger had a good-natured chuckleheaded face, and his wool was all tied up in little bunches with thread. That was to keep witches off. He said the witches was pestering him awful, these nights, and making him see all kinds of strange things, and hear all kinds of strange words and noises, and he didn't believe he was ever witched so long, before, in his life. He got so worked up, and got to running on so, about his troubles, he forgot all about what he'd been agoing to do. So Tom says:

"What's the vittles for? Going to feed the dogs?"

The nigger kind of smiled around gradully over his face like when you heave a brickbat in a mud puddle, and he says:

"Yes, mars Sid, *a* dog. Cur'us dog, too. Does you want to go en look at 'im?"

"Yes."

I hunched Tom, and whispers:

"You going, right here in the daybreak? *That* warn't the plan."

"No, it warn't—but it's the plan *now*."

So, drat him, we went along, but I didn't like it much. When we got in, we couldn't hardly see anything, it was so dark; but Jim was there, sure enough, and could see us; and he sings out:

"Why *Huck*! En good *lan'*! ain' dat Misto Tom?"

I just knowed how it would be; I just expected it. *I* didn't know nothing to do; and if I had, I couldn't a done it; because that nigger busted in and says:

"Why, de gracious sakes! do he know you genlmen?"

We could see pretty well, now. Tom he looked at the nigger, steady and kind of wondering, and says:

"Does *who* know us?"

"Why, dish-yer runaway nigger."

"I don't reckon he does; but what put that into your head?"

"What *put* it dar? Didn' he jis' dis minute sing out like he knowed you?"

Tom says, in a puzzled-up kind of way:

"Well, that's mighty curious. *Who* sung out? *When* did he sing out? *What* did he sing out?" And turns to me, perfectly ca'm, and says, "Did *you* hear anybody sing out?"

Of course there warn't nothing to be said but the one thing; so I says:

"No; *I* ain't heard nobody say nothing."

Then he turns to Jim, and looks him over like he never see him before; and says:

"Did you sing out?"

"No, sah," says Jim, "*I* hain't said nothing, sah."

"Not a word?"

"No, sah, I hain't said a word."

"Did you ever see us before?"

"No, sah; not as *I* knows on."

So Tom turns to the nigger, which was looking wild and distressed, and says, kind of severe:

"What do you reckon's the matter with you, anyway? What made you think somebody sung out?"

WITCHES.

"O, it's de dad-blame' witches, sah, en I wisht I was dead, I do. Dey's awluz at it, sah, en dey do mos' kill me, dey sk'y-ers me so. Please to don't tell nobody 'bout it, sah, er ole mars Silas he'll scole me; 'kase he say dey *ain'* no witches. I jis' wish to goodness he was heah now—*den* what would he say! I jis' bet he couldn' fine no way to git aroun' it *dis* time. But it's awluz jis' so: people dat's *sot*, stays sot; dey won't look into noth'n en fine it out f'r deyselves, en when *you* fine it out en tell um 'bout it, dey doan b'lieve you."

Tom give him a dime, and said we wouldn't tell nobody; and told him to buy some more thread to tie up his wool with; and then looks at Jim and says:

"I wonder if uncle Silas is going to hang this nigger. If I was to catch a nigger that was ungrateful enough to run away, *I* wouldn't give him up, I'd hang him." And whilst the nigger stepped to the door to look at the dime and bite it to see if it was good, he whispers to Jim, and says:

"Don't ever let on to know us. And if you hear any digging going on, nights, it's us: we're going to set you free."

Jim only had time to grab us by the hand and squeeze it, then the nigger come back, and we said we'd come again some time if the nigger wanted us to; and he said he would, more particular if it was dark, because the witches went for him mostly in the dark, and it was good to have folks around, then.

Chapter XXXV:

GETTING WOOD.

It would be most an hour, yet, till breakfast, so we left, and struck down into the woods; because Tom said we got to have *some* light to see how to dig by, and a lantern makes too much, and might get us into trouble; what we must have was a lot of them rotten chunks that's called fox-fire, and just makes a soft kind of a glow when you lay them in a dark place. We fetched an armful and hid it in the weeds, and set down to rest, and Tom says, kind of dissatisfied:

"Blame it, this whole thing is just as easy and awkard as it can be. And so it makes it so rotten difficult to get up a difficult plan. There ain't no watchman to be drugged—now there *ought* to be a watchman. There ain't even a dog, to give a sleeping-mixture to. And there's Jim chained by one leg, with a ten-foot chain, to the leg of his bed: why, all you got to do is to lift up the bedstead and slip off the chain. And uncle Silas he trusts everybody; sends the key to the punkinheaded nigger, and don't send nobody to watch the nigger. Jim could a got out of that window-hole, before this, only there wouldn't be no use trying to travel with a ten-foot chain on his leg. Why, drat it, Huck, it's the stupidest arrangement I ever see: You got to invent *all* the difficulties. Well, we can't help it, we got to do the best we can with the materials we've got. Anyhow, there's one thing—there's more honor in getting him out through a lot of difficulties and dangers, where there warn't one of them furnished to you by the people who it was their duty to furnish them, and you had to contrive them all out of your own head. Now look at just that one thing of the lantern. When you come down to the cold facts, we simply got to *let* on that a lantern's resky. Why, we could work with a torch-light procession if we wanted to, I believe. Now whilst I think of it, we got to hunt up something to make a saw out of, the first chance we get."

"What do we want of a saw?"

"What do we *want* of it? Hain't we got to saw the leg of Jim's bed off, so as to get the chain loose?"

246

"Why, you just said a body could lift up the bedstead and slip the chain off."

"Well, if that ain't just like you, Huck Finn. You *can* get up the infant-schooliest ways of going at a thing. Why, hain't you ever read any books at all?—Baron Trenck, nor Casanova, nor Benvenuto Chelleeny, nor Henri IV, nor none of them heroes?[1] Whoever heard of getting a prisoner loose in such an old-maidy way as that? No; the way all the best authorities does, is to saw the bed-leg in two, and leave it just so, and swallow the sawdust, so it can't be found, and put some dirt and grease around the sawed place so the very keenest seneskal[2] can't see no sign of its being sawed, and thinks the bed-leg is perfectly sound. Then, the night you're ready, fetch the leg a kick, down she goes; slip off your chain, and there you are: nothing to do but hitch your rope-ladder to the battlements, shin down it, break your leg in the moat—because a rope-ladder is nineteen foot too short, you know—and there's your horses and your trusty vassles, and they scoop you up and fling you across a saddle and away you go, to your native Langudoc,[3] or Navarre, or wherever it is. It's gaudy, Huck. I wish there was a moat to this cabin. If we get time, the night of the escape, we'll dig one."

I says:

"What do we want of a moat, when we're going to snake him out from under the cabin?"

But he never heard me. He had forgot me and everything else. He had his chin in his hand, thinking. Pretty soon, he sighs, and shakes his head; then sighs again, and says:

"No, it wouldn't do—there ain't necessity enough for it."

"For what?" I says.

"Why, to saw Jim's leg off," he says.

"Good land!" I says, "Why, there ain't *no* necessity for it. And what would you want to saw his leg off, for, anyway?"

"Well, some of the best authorities has done it. They couldn't get the chain off, so they just cut their hand off, and shoved. And a leg would be better still. But we got to let that go. There ain't necessity enough in this case; and besides, Jim's a nigger and wouldn't understand the reasons for it, and how it's the custom in Europe; so we'll let it go. But there's one thing—he can have a rope ladder; we can tear up our sheets and make him a rope ladder easy enough. And we can send it to him in a pie; it's mostly done that way. And I've et worse pies."

"Why, Tom Sawyer, how you talk," I says; "Jim ain't got no use for a rope ladder."

"He *has* got use for it. How *you* talk, you better say: you don't know nothing about it. He's *got* to have a rope ladder: they all do."

"What in the nation can he *do* with it?"

"*Do* with it? He can hide it in his bed, can't he? That's what they all do; and *he's* got to, too. Huck, you don't ever seem to want to do anything that's regular: you want to be starting something fresh all the

---

1. All of Tom's models attempted daring escapes—Friedrich von der Trenck (1726–1794), staff officer of Frederick the Great; Giovanni Jacopo Casanova (1725–1798), Italian lover-adventurer; Benvenuto Cellini (1500–1571), goldsmith and sculptor; and King Henry IV of France (1553–1610).
2. Seneschal, powerful steward of a medieval lord.
3. Languedoc, formerly a province in southern France.

time. Spose he *don't* do nothing with it? ain't it there in his bed, for a clew, after he's gone? and don't you reckon they'll want clews? Of course they will. And you wouldn't leave them any? That would be a *pretty* howdy-do, *wouldn't* it! I never heard of such a thing."

ONE OF THE BEST AUTHORITIES.

"Well," I says, "if it's in the regulations, and he's got to have it, all right, let him have it; because I don't wish to go back on no regulations; but there's one thing, Tom Sawyer—if we go to tearing up our sheets to make Jim a rope ladder, we're going to get into trouble with aunt Sally, just as sure as you're born. Now the way I look at it, a hickry bark ladder don't cost nothing, and don't waste nothing, and is just as good to load up a pie with, and hide in a straw tick, as any rag-ladder you can start; and as for Jim, he ain't had no experience, and so *he* don't care what kind of a—"

"O shucks, Huck Finn, if I was as ignorant as you, I'd keep still— that's what *I'd* do. Who ever heard of a state prisoner escaping by a hickry bark ladder? Why, it's perfectly ridiculous."

"Well, all right, Tom, fix it your own way; but if you'll take my advice, you'll let me borrow a sheet off of the clothes line."

He said that would do. And that give him another idea, and he says:

"Borrow a shirt, too."

"What do we want of a shirt, Tom?"

"Want it for Jim to keep a journal on."

"Journal your granny—*Jim* can't write."

"Spose he *can't* write— he can make marks on the shirt, can't he, if we make him a pen out of an old pewter spoon or a piece of an old iron barrel-hoop?"

"Why, Tom, we can pull a feather out of a goose and make him a better one; and quicker, too."

"*Prisoners* don't have geese running around the donjon-keep to pull pens out of, you muggins. They *always* make their pens out of the hardest, toughest, troublesomest piece of old brass candlestick or something like that they can get their hands on; and it takes them weeks and weeks, and months and months to file it out, too, because they've got to do it by rubbing it on the wall. *They* wouldn't use a goose-quill if they had it. It ain't regular."

"Well, then, what'll we make him the ink out of?"

"Many makes it out of iron-rust and tears; but that's the common sort and women; the best authorities uses their own blood. Jim can do that; and when he wants to send any little common ordinary mysterious message to let the world know where he's captivated, he can write it on the bottom of a tin plate with a fork and throw it out of the window. The Iron Mask[4] always done that, and it's a blame' good way, too."

"Jim ain't got no tin plates. They feed him in a pan."

"That ain't anything; we can get him some."

"Can't nobody *read* his plates."

"That ain't got nothing to *do* with it, Huck Finn. All *he*'s got to do is to write on the plate and throw it out. You don't *have* to be able to read it. Why, half the time you can't read anything a prisoner writes on a tin plate, or anywhere else."

"Well, then, what's the sense in wasting the plates?"

"Why, blame it all, it ain't the *prisoner's* plates."

"But it's *somebody's* plates, ain't it?"

"Well, spos'n it is? What does the *prisoner* care whose—"

THE BREAKFAST HORN.

---

4. The mysterious masked prisoner in Alexandre Dumas's *Le Vicomte de Bragelonne* (1848–50), translated in part as *The Man in the Iron Mask*.

He broke off there, because we heard the breakfast horn blowing. So we cleared out for the house.

Along during that morning I borrowed a sheet and a white shirt off of the clothes line; and I found an old sack and put them in it, and we went down and got the fox-fire, and put that in, too. I called it borrowing, because that was what pap always called it; but Tom said it warn't borrowing, it was stealing. He said we was representing prisoners; and prisoners don't care how they get a thing so they get it, and nobody don't blame them for it, either. It ain't no crime in a prisoner to steal the thing he needs to get away with, Tom said; it's his right; and so, as long as we was representing a prisoner, we had a perfect right to steal anything on this place we had the least use for, to get ourselves out of prison with. He said if we warn't prisoners it would be a very different thing, and nobody but a mean ornery person would steal when he warn't a prisoner. So we allowed we would steal everything there was that come handy. And yet he made a mighty fuss, one day, after that, when I stole a watermelon out of the nigger patch and eat it; and he made me go and give the niggers a dime, without telling them what it was for. Tom said that what he meant was, we could steal anything we *needed*. Well, I says, I needed the watermelon. But he said I didn't need it to get out of prison with, there's where the difference was. He said if I'd a wanted it to hide a knife in, and smuggle it to Jim to kill the seneskal with, it would a been all right. So I let it go at that, though I couldn't see no advantage in my representing a prisoner, if I got to set down and chaw over a lot of gold-leaf distinctions like that, every time I see a chance to hog a watermelon.

Well, as I was saying, we waited, that morning, till everybody was settled down to business, and nobody in sight around the yard; then Tom he carried the sack into the lean-to whilst I stood off a piece to keep watch. By and by he come out, and we went and set down on the woodpile, to talk. He says:

"Everything's all right, now, except tools; and that's easy fixed."

"Tools?" I says.

"Yes."

"Tools for what?"

"Why, to dig with. We ain't agoing to *gnaw* him out, are we?"

"Ain't them old crippled picks and things in there good enough to dig a nigger out with?" I says.

He turns on me looking pitying enough to make a body cry; and says:

"Huck Finn, did you *ever* hear of a prisoner having picks and shovels and all the modern conveniences in his wardrobe to dig himself out with? Now I want to ask you—if you got any reasonableness in you at all—what kind of a show would *that* give him to be a hero? Why they might as well lend him the key, and done with it. Picks and shovels— why they wouldn't furnish 'em to a king."

"Well, then," I says, "if we don't want the picks and shovels, what do we want?"

"A couple of caseknives."

"To dig the foundations out from under that cabin with?"

"Yes."

"Consound it, it's foolish, Tom."

"It don't make no difference how foolish it is, it's the *right* way—and it's the regular way. And there ain't no *other* way, that ever *I* heard of; and I've read all the books that gives any information about these things. They always dig out with a caseknife—and not through dirt, mind you; generly it's through solid rock. And it takes them weeks and weeks and weeks, and forever and ever. Why, look at one of them prisoners in the bottom dungeon of the Castle Deef,[5] in the harbor of Marseilles, that dug himself out that way: how long was *he* at it, you reckon?"

"I don't know."

"Well, guess."

"I don't know. A month and a half?"

"*Thirty-seven year*—and he come out in China. *That's* the kind. I wish the bottom of *this* fortress was solid rock."

"*Jim* don't know nobody in China."

"What's *that* got to do with it? Neither did that other fellow. But you're always a-wandering off on a side issue. Why can't you stick to the main point?"

"All right—*I* don't care where he comes out, so he *comes* out; and Jim don't, either, I reckon. But there's one thing, anyway—Jim's too old to be dug out with a caseknife. He won't last."

"Yes he will *last*, too. You don't reckon it's going to take thirty-seven years to dig out through a *dirt* foundation, do you?"

"How long will it take, Tom?"

"Well, we can't resk being as long as we ought to, because it mayn't take very long for uncle Silas to hear from down there by New Orleans. He'll hear Jim ain't from there. Then his next move will be to advertise Jim, or something like that. So we can't resk being as long digging him out as we ought to. By rights I reckon we ought to

SMOUCHING THE KNIVES.

be a couple of years; but we can't. Things being so uncertain, what I recommend is this: that we really dig right in, as quick as we can; and after that, we can *let on*, to ourselves, that we was at it thirty-seven years. Then we can snatch him out and rush him away the first time there's an alarm. Yes, I reckon that'll be the best way."

5. Chateau d'If; the hero of Dumas's *Count of Monte Cristo* was imprisoned there.

"Now there's *sense* in that," I says. "Letting-on don't cost nothing; letting-on ain't no trouble; and if it's any object, I don't mind letting on we was at it a hundred and fifty year. It wouldn't strain me none, after I got my hand in. So I'll mosey along, now, and smouch a couple of caseknives."

"Smouch three," he says; "we want one to make a saw out of."

"Tom, if it ain't unregular and irreligious to sejest it," I says, "there's an old rusty saw-blade around yonder sticking under the weatherboarding behind the smokehouse."

He looked kind of weary and discouraged-like, and says:

"It ain't no use to try to learn you nothing, Huck. Run along and smouch the knives—three of them." So I done it.

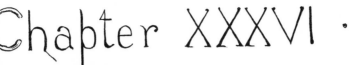

Chapter XXXVI

**GOING DOWN
THE LIGHTNING ROD.**

As soon as we reckoned everybody was asleep, that night, we went down the lightning rod, and shut ourselves up in the lean-to, and got out our pile of fox-fire, and went to work. We cleared everything out of the way, about four or five foot along the middle of the bottom log. Tom said we was right behind Jim's bed, now, and we'd dig in under it, and when we got through, there couldn't nobody in the cabin ever know there was any hole there, because Jim's counterpin[1] hung down most to the ground, and you'd have to raise it up and look under, to see the hole. So we dug and dug, with the caseknives, till most midnight; and then we was dog-tired, and our hands was blistered, and yet you couldn't see we'd done anything, hardly. At last I says:

"This ain't no thirty-seven year job, this is a thirty-eight year job, Tom Sawyer."

He never said nothing. But he sighed, and pretty soon he stopped digging, and then for a good little while I knowed he was thinking. Then he says:

"It ain't no use, Huck, it ain't agoing to work. If we was prisoners, it would, because then we'd have as many years as we wanted, and no hurry; and we wouldn't get but a few minutes to dig, every day, while they was changing watches, and so our hands wouldn't get blistered, and we could keep it up right along, year in and year out, and do it right and the way it ought to be done. But *we* can't fool along, we got to rush; we ain't got no time to spare. If we was to put in another night this way, we'd have to knock off for a week to let our hands get well—couldn't touch a caseknife with them sooner."

"Well, then, what we going to do, Tom?"

"I'll tell you. It ain't right, and it ain't moral, and I wouldn't like it to get out—but there ain't only just the one way: we got to dig him out with the picks, and *let on* it's case-knives."

1. Counterpane, bedspread.

"*Now* you're *talking!*" I says; "your head gets leveler and leveler all the time, Tom Sawyer," I says. "Picks is the thing, moral or no moral; and as for me, I don't care shucks for the morality of it, nohow. When I start in to steal a nigger, or a watermelon, or a Sunday school book, I ain't no ways particular how it's done, so it's done. What I want is my nigger; or what I want is my watermelon; or what I want is my Sunday school book: and if a pick's the handiest thing, that's the thing I'm agoing to dig that nigger or that watermelon or that Sunday school book out with; and I don't give a dead rat what the authorities thinks about it, nuther."

"Well," he says, "there's excuse for picks and letting-on, in a case like this; if it warn't so, I wouldn't approve of it, nor I wouldn't stand by and see the rules broke—because right is right, and wrong is wrong, and a body ain't got no business doing wrong when he ain't ignorant and knows better. It might answer for *you* to dig Jim out with a pick, *without* any letting-on, because you don't know no better; but it wouldn't for me, because I do know better. Gimme a caseknife."

He had his own by him, but I handed him mine. He flung it down, and says:

"Gimme a *caseknife.*"

I didn't know just what to do—but then I thought. I scratched around amongst the old tools, and got a pick-axe and give it to him, and he took it and went to work, and never said a word.

He was always just that particular. Full of principle.

So then I got a shovel, and then we picked and shoveled, turn about, and made the fur fly. We stuck to it about a half an hour, which was as long as we could stand up; but we had a good deal of a hole to show for it. When I got up stairs, I looked out at the window and see Tom doing his level best with the lightning rod, but he couldn't come it, his hands was so sore. At last he says:

"It ain't no use, it can't be done. What you reckon I better do? Can't you think up no way?"

"Yes," I says, "but I reckon it ain't regular. Come up the stairs, and let on it's a lightning rod."

So he done it.

Next day Tom stole a pewter spoon and a brass candlestick in the house, for to make some pens for Jim out of, and six tallow candles; and I hung around the nigger cabins, and laid for a chance, and stole three tin plates. Tom said it wasn't enough; but I said nobody wouldn't ever see the plates that Jim throwed out, because they'd fall in the dog-fennel and jimpson weeds under the window-hole—then we could tote them back and he could use them over again. So Tom was satisfied. Then he says:

"Now, the thing to study out, is, how to get the things to Jim."

"Take them in through the hole," I says, "when we get it done."

He only just looked scornful, and said something about nobody ever heard of such an idiotic idea, and then he went to studying. By and by he said he had ciphered out two or three ways, but there warn't no need to decide on any of them, yet. Said we'd got to post Jim, first.

That night we went down the lightning rod a little after ten, and took one of the candles along, and listened under the window-hole, and

STEALING SPOONS.

heard Jim snoring; so we pitched it in, and it didn't wake him. Then we whirled in with the pick and shovel, and in about two hours and a half the job was done. We crept in under Jim's bed and into the cabin, and pawed around and found the candle and lit it, and stood over Jim awhile, and found him looking hearty and healthy, and then we woke him up, gentle and gradual. He was so glad to see us he most cried; and called us honey, and all the pet names he could think of; and was for having us hunt up a cold chisel to cut the chain off of his leg with, right away, and clearing out without losing any time. But Tom he showed him how unregular it would be, and set down and told him all about our plans, and how we could alter them in a minute any time there was an alarm; and not to be the least afraid, because we would see he got away, *sure*. So Jim he said it was all right, and we set there and talked over old times a while, and then Tom asked a lot of questions, and when Jim told him uncle Silas come in every day or two to pray with him, and aunt Sally come in to see if he was comfortable and had plenty to eat, and both of them was kind as they could be, Tom says:

"*Now* I know how to fix it. We'll send you some things by them."

I said, "Don't do nothing of the kind; it's one of the most jackass ideas I ever struck;" but he never paid no attention to me; went right on. It was his way when he'd got his plans set.

So he told Jim how we'd have to smuggle in the rope-ladder pie, and other large things, by Nat, the nigger that fed him, and he must be on the lookout, and not be surprised, and not let Nat see him open them; and we would put small things in uncle's coat pockets and he must steal them out; and we would tie things to aunt's apron strings or put them in her apron pocket, if we got a chance; and told him what they would be and what they was for. And told him how to keep a journal on the shirt with his blood, and all that. He told him everything. Jim he couldn't see no sense in the most of it, but he allowed we was white folks and knowed better than him; so he was satisfied and said he would do it all just as Tom said.

Jim had plenty corn-cob pipes and tobacco; so we had a right down good sociable time; then we crawled out through the hole, and so home to bed, with hands that looked like they'd been chawed by a dog. Tom was in high spirits. He said it was the best fun he ever had in his life, and the most intellectural; and said if he only could see his way to it we would keep it up all the rest of our lives and leave Jim to our children to get out; for he believed Jim would come to like it better and better the more he got used to it. He said that in that way it could be strung out to as much as eighty year, and would be the best time on record. And he said it would make us all celebrated that had a hand in it.

In the morning we went out to the woodpile and chopped up the brass candlestick into handy sizes, and Tom put them and the pewter spoon in his pocket. Then we went to the nigger cabins, and while I got Nat's notice off, Tom shoved a piece of candlestick into the middle of a corn-pone that was in Jim's pan, and we went along with Nat to see how it would work, and it just worked noble: when Jim bit into it it most mashed all his teeth out; and there warn't ever anything could a worked better. Tom said so himself. Jim he never let on but what it was only just a piece of rock or something like that that's always getting into bread, you know, but after that he never bit into nothing but what he jabbed his fork into it in three or four places, first.

And whilst we was a standing there in the dimmish light, here comes a couple of the hounds bulging in, from under Jim's bed; and they kept on piling in till there was eleven of them, and there warn't hardly room in there to get your breath. By jings we forgot to fasten that lean-to door. The nigger Nat he only just hollered "witches!" once, and keeled over onto the floor amongst the dogs and begun to groan like he was dying. Tom jerked the door open and flung out a slab of Jim's meat, and the dogs went for it; and in two seconds he was out himself and back again and shut the door, and I knowed he'd fixed the other door, too. Then he went to work on the nigger, coaxing him and petting him, and asking him if he'd been imagining he saw something again. He raised up, and blinked his eyes around, and says:

"Mars Sid, you'll say I's a fool, but if I didn't b'lieve I see most a million dogs, er devils, er some'n, I wisht I may die right heah in dese tracks. I did, mos'sholy. Mars Sid, I *felt* um—I *felt* um, sah; dey was all over me. Dad fetch it, I jis' wisht I could git my han's on one er dem witches jis' wunst—on'y jis' wunst—it's all I'd ast. But mos'ly I wisht dey'd lemme 'lone, I does."

Tom says:

"Well, I tell you what *I* think. What makes them come here just at this runaway nigger's breakfast time? It's because they're hungry; that's the reason. You make them a witch pie; that's the thing for *you* to do."

TOM ADVISES A WITCH PIE.

"But my lan', mars Sid, how's *I* gwyne to make 'm a witch pie? I doan know how to make it. I hain't ever hearn er sich a thing b'fo'."

"Well, then, I'll have to make it myself."

"Will you do it, honey?—will you? I'll wusshup de groun' und' yo' foot, I will!"

"All right, I'll do it, seeing it's you, and you've been good to us and showed us the runaway nigger. But you got to be mighty careful. When we come around, you turn your back; and then whatever we've put in the pan, don't you let on you see it at all. And don't you look, when Jim unloads the pan—something might happen, I don't know what. And above all, don't you *handle* the witch-things."

"*Hannel* 'm, mars Sid? What *is* you a talkin' 'bout? I wouldn' lay de weight er my finger on um, not f'r ten hund'd thous'n' billion dollars, I wouldn't."

Chapter XXXVII.

THE RUBBAGE PILE.

That was all fixed. So then we went away, and went to the rubbage pile in the back yard where they keep the old boots, and rags, and pieces of bottles, and wore-out tin things, and all such truck, and scratched around and found an old tin wash-pan and stopped up the holes as well as we could, to bake the pie in, and took it down cellar and stole it full of flour, and started for breakfast, and found a couple of shingle nails that Tom said would be handy for a prisoner to scrabble his name and sorrows on the dungeon walls with, and dropped one of them in aunt Sally's apron pocket which was hanging on a chair, and t'other we stuck in the band of uncle Silas's hat, which was on the bureau, because we heard the children say their pa and ma was going to the runaway nigger's house this morning, and then went to breakfast, and Tom dropped the pewter spoon in uncle Silas's coat pocket, and aunt Sally wasn't come yet, so we had to wait a little while.

And when she come she was hot, and red, and cross, and couldn't hardly wait for the blessing, and then she went to sluicing out coffee with one hand and cracking the handiest child's head with her thimble with the other, and says:

"I've hunted high, and I've hunted low, and it does beat all, what *has* become of your other shirt."

My heart fell down amongst my lungs and livers and things, and a hard piece of corn-crust started down my throat after it and got met on the road with a cough and was shot across the table and took one of the children in the eye and curled him up like a fishing-worm, and let a cry out of him the size of a war-whoop, and Tom he turned kinder blue around the gills, and it all amounted to a considerable state of things for about a quarter of a minute or as much as that, and I would a sold out for half price if there was a bidder. But after that, we was all right again—it was the sudden surprise of it that knocked us so kind of cold. Uncle Silas he says:

"It's most uncommon curious, I can't understand it. I know perfectly well I took it *off*, because—"

"Because you hain't got but one *on.* Just *listen* at the man! I know you took it off, and know it by a better way than your wool-gethering memory, too, because it was on the clo'es line yesterday—I see it there myself. But it's gone—that's the long and the short of it, and you'll just have to change to a red flann'l one till I can get time to make a new one. And it'll be the third I've made in two years; it just keeps a body on the jump to keep you in shirts; and whatever you do manage to *do* with 'm all, is more'n I can make out. A body'd think you *would* learn to take some sort of care of 'em, at your time of life."

"I know it, Sally, and I do try, all I can. But it oughtn't to be altogether my fault, because you know I don't see them nor have nothing to do with them except when they're on me; and I don't believe I've ever lost one of them *off* of me."

"Well, it ain't *your* fault if you haven't, Silas—you'd a done it if you could, I reckon. And the shirt ain't all that's gone, nuther. Ther's a spoon gone; and *that* ain't all. There was ten, and now ther's only nine. The calf got the shirt, I reckon, but the calf never took the spoon, *that's* certain."

"Why, what else is gone, Sally?"

"Ther's six *candles* gone—that's what. The rats could a got the candles, and I reckon they did; I wonder they don't walk off with the whole place, the way you're always going to stop their holes and don't do it; and if they warn't fools they'd sleep in your hair, Silas—*you'*d never find it out; but you can't lay the *spoon* on the rats, and that I *know.*"

"Well, Sally, I'm in fault, and I acknowledge it; I've been remiss; but I won't let to-morrow go by without stopping up them holes."

"O, I wouldn't hurry, next year'll do. Matilda Angelina Araminta *Phelps!*"

Whack comes the thimble, and the child snatches her claws out of the sugar bowl without fooling around any. Just then, the nigger woman steps onto the passage, and says:

"Missus, dey's a sheet gone."

"A *sheet* gone! Well, for the land's sake!"

"I'll stop up them holes *to-day,*" says uncle Silas, looking sorrowful.

"O, *do* shet up!—Spose the rats took the *sheet? Where's* it gone, Lize?"

"MISSUS, DEY'S A SHEET GONE."

"Clah to goodness I hain't no notion, Miss Sally. She wuz on de clo's line yistiddy, but she done gone; she ain' dah no mo', now."

"I reckon the world *is* coming to an end. I *never* see the beat of it, in all my born days. A shirt, and a sheet, and a spoon, and six can—"

"Missus," comes a young yaller wench, "dey's a brass cannelstick mis-s'n."

"Cler out from here, you hussy, er I'll take a skillet to ye!"

Well, she was just a biling. I begun to lay for a chance; I reckoned I would sneak out and go for the woods till the weather moderated. She kept a-raging right along, running her insurrection all by herself, and everybody else mighty meek and quiet; and at last uncle Silas, looking kind of foolish, fishes up that spoon out of his pocket. She stopped, with her mouth open and her hands up; and as for me, I wished I was in Jeruslem or somewheres. But not long; because she says:

"It's *just* as I expected. So you had it in your pocket all the time; and like as not you've got the other things there, too. How'd it get there?"

"I reely don't know, Sally," he says, kind of apologizing, "or you know I would tell. I was a-studying over my text in Acts seventeen,[1] before breakfast, and I reckon I put it in there, not noticing, meaning to put my Testament in, and it must be so, because my Testament ain't in, but I'll go and see, and if the Testament is where I had it, I'll know I didn't put it in, and that will show that I laid the Testament down and took up the spoon, and—"

"O, for the land's sake! Give a body a rest! Go 'long, now, the whole kit and biling of ye; and don't come nigh me again till I've got back my peace of mind."

I'd a heard her, if she'd a said it to herself, let alone speaking it out; and I'd a got up and obeyed her, if I'd a been dead. As we was passing through the setting room, the old man he took up his hat, and the shingle nail fell out on the floor, and he just merely picked it up and laid it on the mantel shelf, and never said nothing, and went out. Tom see him do it, and remembered about the spoon, and says:

"Well, it ain't no use to send things by *him* no more, he ain't reliable." Then he says: "But he done us a good turn with the spoon, anyway, without knowing it, and so we'll go and do him one without *him* knowing it—stop up his rat holes."

There was a noble good lot of them, down cellar, and it took us a whole hour, but we done the job tight and good, and ship-shape. Then we heard steps on the stairs, and blowed out our light, and hid; and here comes the old man, with a candle in one hand and a bundle of stuff in t'other, looking as absent-minded as year before last. He went a mooning around, first to one rat hole and then another, till he'd been to them all. Then he stood about five minutes, picking tallow-drip off of his candle and thinking. Then he turns off slow and dreamy towards the stairs, saying:

"Well, for the life of me I can't remember when I done it. I could show her, now, that I warn't to blame on account of the rats. But never mind—let it go. I reckon it wouldn't do no good."

And so he went on a-mumbling up stairs, and then we left. He was a mighty nice old man. And always is.

---

1. In Acts 17, Silas and Paul are persecuted for their eloquent preaching. Uncle Silas, who imprisons Jim, seems not to have lingered, however, over the preceding book, in which the biblical Silas is himself imprisoned by slaveholders.

Tom was a good deal bothered about what to do for a spoon, but he said we'd got to have it; so he took a think. When he had ciphered it out, he told me how we was to do; then we went and waited around the spoon-basket till we see aunt Sally coming, and then Tom went to counting the spoons and laying them out to one side, and I slid one of them up my sleeve, and Tom says:

"Why, aunt Sally, there ain't but nine spoons, *yet.*"

She says:

"Go 'long to your play, and don't bother me. I know better, I counted 'm myself."

"Well, I've counted them twice, aunty, and *I* can't make but nine."

She looked out of all patience, but of course she come to count—anybody would.

"I declare to gracious ther' *ain't* but nine!" she says. "Why, what in the world—plague *take* the things, I'll count 'm again."

So I slipped back the one I had, and when she got done counting, she says:

"Hang the troublesome rubbage, ther's *ten*, now!" and she looked huffy and bothered both. But Tom says:

"Why, aunty, *I* don't think there's ten."

"You numscull, didn't you see me *count* 'm?"

"I know, but—"

"Well, I'll count 'm *again.*"

So I smouched one, and they come out nine, same as the other time. Well, she *was* in a tearing way—just a trembling all over, she was so mad. But she counted, and counted, till she got that addled she'd start to count-in the *basket* for a spoon, sometimes: and so, three times they

IN A TEARING WAY.

come out right, and three times they come out wrong. Then she grabbed up the basket and slammed it across the house and knocked the cat galley-west;[2] and she said "cle'r out and let her have some peace, and if we come bothering around her again betwixt that and dinner, she'd skin us." So we had the odd spoon; and dropped it in her apron pocket whilst she was a-giving us our sailing-orders, and Jim got it, all right, along with her shingle-nail, before noon. We was very well satisfied with this business, and Tom allowed it was worth twice the trouble it took, because he said *now* she couldn't ever count them spoons twice alike again to save her life; and wouldn't believe she'd counted them right, if she *did*; and said that after she'd about counted her head off, for the next three days, he judged she'd give it up and offer to kill anybody that wanted her to ever count them any more.

So we put the sheet back on the line, that night, and stole one out of her closet; and kept on putting it back and stealing it again, for a couple of days, till she didn't know how many sheets she had, any more, and said she didn't *care*, and warn't agoing to bullyrag[3] the rest of her soul out about it, and wouldn't count them again not to save her life, she druther die first.

So we was all right, now, as to the shirt and the sheet and the spoon and the candles, by the help of the calf and the rats and the mixed-up counting; and as to the candlestick, it warn't no consequence, it would blow over by and by.

But that pie was a job; we had no end of trouble with that pie. We fixed it up away down in the woods, and cooked it there; and we got it done, at last, and very satisfactory, too; but not all in one day; and we had to use up three washpans full of flour, before we got through, and we got burnt pretty much all over, in places, and eyes put out with the smoke; because, you see, we didn't want nothing but a crust, and we couldn't prop it up, right, and she would always cave in. But of course we thought of the right way at last; which was, to cook the ladder, too, in the pie. So then we laid in with Jim, the second night, and tore up the sheet all in little strings, and twisted them together, and long before daylight we had a lovely rope, that you could a hung a person with. We let on it took nine months to make it.

And in the forenoon we took it down to the woods, but it wouldn't go in the pie. Being made of a whole sheet, that way, there was rope enough for forty pies, if we'd a wanted them, and plenty left over for soup, or sausage, or anything you choose. We could a had a whole dinner.

But we didn't need it. All we needed was just enough for the pie, and so we throwed the rest away. We didn't cook none of the pies in the washpan, afraid the solder would melt; but uncle Silas he had a noble brass warming pan which he thought considerable of, because it belonged to one of his ancestors with a long wooden handle that come over from England with William the Conqueror in the Mayflower or one of them early ships and was hid away up garret with a lot of other

---

2. Out of kilter, cockeyed.
3. Abuse, threaten.

old pots and things that was valuable, not on account of being any account, because they warn't, but on account of them being relicts, you know, and we snaked her out, private, and took her down there, but she failed on the first pies, because we didn't know how, but she come up smiling on the last one. We took and lined her with dough, and set her in the coals, and loaded her up with rag-rope, and put on a dough roof, and shut down the lid, and put hot embers on top, and stood off five foot, with the long handle, cool and comfortable, and in fifteen minutes she turned out a pie that was a satisfaction to look at. But the person that et it would want to fetch a couple of kags of tooth-

ONE OF HIS ANCESTERS.

picks along, for if that rope ladder wouldn't cramp him down to business, I don't know nothing what I'm talking about, and lay him in enough stomach-ache to last him till next time, too.

Nat didn't look, when we put the witch-pie in Jim's pan; and we put the three tin plates in the bottom of the pan under the vittles; and so Jim got everything all right, and as soon as he was by himself he busted into the pie and hid the rope ladder inside of his straw tick, and scratched some marks on a tin plate and throwed it out of the window-hole.

Chapter XXXVIII

JIM'S COAT OF ARMS.

Making them pens was a distressid tough job, and so was the saw; and Jim allowed the inscription was going to be the toughest of all. That's the one which the prisoner has to scrabble on the wall. But we had to have it; Tom said we'd *got* to: there warn't no case of a state prisoner not scrabbling his inscription to leave behind, and his coat of arms.

"Look at lady Jane Grey," he says; "look at Gilford Dudley; look at old Northumberland![1] Why, Huck, spose it *is* considerble trouble?—what you going to do?—how you going to get around it? Jim's *got* to do his inscription and coat of arms. They all do."

Jim says:

"Why, mars Tom, I hain't got no coat o' arms; I hain't got nuffn but dish-yer ole shirt, en you knows I got to keep de journal on dat."

"O, you don't understand, Jim; a coat of arms is very different."

"Well," I says, "Jim's right, anyway, when he says he hain't got no coat of arms, because he hain't."

"I reckon *I* knowed that," Tom says, "but you bet he'll have one before he goes out of this—because he's going out *right*, and there ain't going to be no flaws in his record."

So whilst me and Jim filed away at the pens on a brickbat apiece, Jim a making his'n out of the brass and I making mine out of the spoon, Tom set to work to think out the coat of arms. By and by he said he'd struck so many good ones he didn't hardly know which to take, but there was one which he reckoned he'd decide on. He says:

"On the scutcheon we'll have a bend *or* in the dexter base, a saltire *murrey* in the fess, with a dog, couchant, for common charge, and under his foot a chain embattled, for slavery, with a chevron *vert* in a chief engrailed, and three invected lines on a field *azure*, with the nombril points rampant on a dancette indented; crest, a runaway nigger, *sable*, with his bundle over his shoulder on a bar sinister; and a couple

---

1. Lady Jane Grey (1537–1554), briefly a claimant to the British throne, was imprisoned in the Tower of London along with her husband, Guildford Dudley, and his father, the Duke of Northumberland. All three were executed.

of gules for supporters, which is you and me; motto, *Maggiore fretta, minore atto.* Got it out of a book—means, the more haste, the less speed."[2]

"Geewhillikins," I says, "but what does the rest of it mean?"

"We ain't got no time to bother over that," he says, "we got to dig in like all git-out."

"Well, anyway," I says, "what's *some* of it? What's a fess?"

"A fess—a fess is—*you* don't need to know what a fess is: I'll show him how to make it when he gets to it."

"Shucks, Tom," I says, "I think you might tell a person. What's a bar sinister?"

"Oh, *I* don't know. But he's got to have it. All the nobility does."

That was just his way. If it didn't suit him to explain a thing to you, he wouldn't do it. You might pump at him a week, it wouldn't make no difference.

He'd got all that coat of arms business fixed, so now he started in to finish up the rest of that part of the work, which was to plan out a mournful inscription—said Jim got to have one, like they all done. He made up a lot, and wrote them out on a paper, and read them off, so:

1. *Here a captive heart busted.*

2. *Here a poor prisoner, forsook by the world and friends, fretted out his sorrowful life.*

3. *Here a lonely heart broke, and a worn spirit went to its rest, after thirty-seven years of solitary captivity.*

4. *Here, homeless and friendless, after thirty-seven years of bitter captivity, perished a noble stranger, natural son of Louis XIV.*

Tom's voice trembled, whilst he was reading them, and he most broke down. When he got done, he couldn't no way make up his mind which one for Jim to scrabble onto the wall, they was all so good; but at last he allowed he would let him scrabble them all on. Jim said it would take him a year to scrabble such a lot of truck onto the logs with a nail, and he didn't know how to make letters, besides; but Tom said he would block them out for him, and then he wouldn't have nothing to do but just follow the lines. Then pretty soon he says:

"Come to think, the logs ain't agoing to do; they don't have log walls in a dungeon: we got to dig the inscriptions into a rock. We'll fetch a rock."

Jim said the rock was worse than the logs; he said it would take him such a pison long time to dig them into a rock, he wouldn't ever get out. But Tom said he would let me help him do it. Then he took a look to see how me and Jim was getting along with the pens. It was most pesky tedious hard work and slow, and didn't give my hands no show to get well of the sores, and we didn't seem to make no headway, hardly. So Tom says:

"I know how to fix it. We got to have a rock for the coat of arms and mournful inscriptions, and we can kill two birds with that same rock.

2. Jim's shield is even more crowded than Kemble's illustration. Divided into thirds (chief, fess, base), it is crisscrossed with bars and emblazoned with six colors, the figures of a dog and a slave, and a motto appropriate to Tom's leisurely conduct of the escape.

There's a gaudy big grindstone down at the mill, and we'll smouch it, and carve the things on it, and file out the pens and the saw on it, too."

It warn't no slouch of an idea; and it warn't no slouch of a grindstone, nuther; but we allowed we'd tackle it. It warn't quite midnight, yet, so we cleared out for the mill, leaving Jim at work. We smouched the grindstone, and set out to roll her home, but it was a most nation tough job. Sometimes, do what we could, we couldn't keep her from falling over, and she come mighty near mashing us, every time. Tom said she was going to get one of us, sure, before we got through. We got her half way; and then we was plumb played out, and most drownded with sweat. We see it warn't no use, we got to go and fetch Jim. So he raised up his bed and slid the chain off of the bed-leg, and wrapt it round and round his neck, and we crawled out through our hole and down there, and Jim and me laid into that grindstone and walked her along like nothing; and Tom superintended. He could out-superintend any boy I ever see. He knowed how to do everything.

A TOUGH JOB.

Our hole was pretty big, but it warn't big enough to get the grindstone through; but Jim he took the pick and soon made it big enough. Then Tom marked out them things on it with the nail, and set Jim to work on them, with the nail for a chisel and an iron bolt from the rubbage in the lean-to for a hammer, and told him to work till the rest of his candle quit on him, and then he could go to bed, and hide the grindstone under his straw tick and sleep on it. Then we helped him fix his chain back, on the bedleg, and was ready for bed ourselves. But Tom thought of something, and says:

"You got any spiders in here, Jim?"

"No, sah, thanks to goodness I hain't, mars Tom."

"All right, we'll get you some."

"But bless you, honey, I doan *want* none. I's afeard un um. I jis' 's soon have rattlesnakes aroun'."

Tom thought a minute or two, and says:

"It's a good idea. And I reckon it's been done. It *must* a been done: it stands to reason. Yes, it's a prime good idea. Where could you keep it?"

"Keep what, mars Tom?"

"Why, a rattlesnake."

"De goodness gracious alive, mars Tom! Why, if dey was a rattlesnake to come in heah, I'd take en bust right out thoo dat log wall, I would, wid my head."

"Why, Jim, you wouldn't be afraid of it, after a little. You could tame it."

"*Tame* it!"

"Yes—easy enough. Every animal is grateful for kindness and petting, and they wouldn't *think* of hurting a person that pets them. Any book will tell you that. You try—that's all I ask; just try for two or three days. Why, you can get him so, in a little while, that he'll love you; and sleep with you; and won't stay away from you a minute; and will let you wrap him round your neck and put his head in your mouth."

"*Please*, mars Tom—*doan'* talk so! I can't *stan'* it! He'd *let* me shove his head in my mouf—fer a favor, hain't it? I lay he'd wait a pow'ful long time 'fo' I *ast* him. En mo' em dat, I doan' *want* him to sleep wid me."

"Jim, don't act so foolish. A prisoner's *got* to have some kind of a dumb pet, and if a rattlesnake hain't ever been tried, why there's more glory to be gained in your being the first to ever try it than any other way you could ever think of to save your life."

"Why, mars Tom, I doan' *want* no sich glory. Snake take 'n bite Jim's chin off, den *whah* is de glory? No, sah, I doan' want no sich doin's."

"Blame it, can't you *try*? I only *want* you to try—you needn't keep it up if it don't work."

"But de trouble all *done*, ef de snake bite me while I's a-tryin' him. Mars Tom, I's willin' to tackle mos' anything 'at ain't onreasonable, but ef you en Huck fetches a rattlesnake in heah for me to tame, I's gwyne to *leave*, dat's *shore*."

"Well, then, let it go, let it go, if you're so bullheaded about it. We can get you some garter-snakes and you can tie some buttons on their tails, and let on they're rattlesnakes, and I reckon that'll have to do."

"I k'n stan' *dem*, mars Tom, but blame' 'f I couldn' git along widout um, I tell you dat. I never knowed, b'fo', 't was so much bother and trouble to be a prisoner."

"Well, it *always* is, when it's done right. You got any rats around here?"

"No, sah, I hain't seed none."

"Well, we'll get you some rats."

"Why, mars Tom, I doan *want* no rats. Dey's de dad-blamedest creturs to 'sturb a body, en rustle roun' over 'im, en bite his feet, when he's tryin' to sleep, I ever see. No, sah, gimme g'yarter snakes, 'f I's got to have 'm, but doan' gimme no rats, I ain' got no use f'r um, skasely."

"But Jim, you *got* to have 'em,—they all do. So don't make no more fuss about it. Prisoners ain't ever without rats. There ain't no instance

BUTTONS ON THEIR TAILS.

of it. And they train them, and pet them, and learn them tricks, and they get to be as sociable as flies. But you got to play music to them. You got anything to play music on?"

"I ain' got nuffn but a coase comb en a piece o' paper, en a juice-harp; but I reck'n dey wouldn' take no stock in a juice-harp."

"Yes they would. *They* don't care what kind of music 'tis. A jewsharp's plenty good enough for a rat. All animals likes music—in a prison; they dote on it. Specially, painful music; and you can't get no other kind out of a jewsharp. It always interests them; they come out to see what's the matter with you. Yes, you're all right; you're fixed very well. You want to set on your bed, nights, before you go to sleep, and early in the mornings, and play your jewsharp; play The Last Link is Broken—that's the thing that'll scoop a rat, quicker'n anything else: and when you've played about two minutes, you'll see all the rats, and the snakes, and spiders, and things begin to feel worried about you, and come. And they'll just fairly swarm over you, and have a noble good time."

"Yes, *dey* will, I reck'n, mars Tom, but what kine er time is *Jim* havin'? Blest if I kin see de pint. But I'll do it, ef I got to. I reck'n I better keep de animals satisfied, en not have no trouble in de house."

Tom waited to think over, and see if there wasn't nothing else; and pretty soon he says:

"Oh—there's one thing I forgot. Could you raise a flower here, do you reckon?"

"I doan' know but maybe I could, mars Tom; but it's tolable dark in heah, en I ain' got no use f'r no flower, nohow, en she'd be a powful sight o' trouble."

"Well, you try it, anyway. Some other prisoners has done it."

"One er dem big cat-tail-lookin' mullen-stalks would grow in heah, mars Tom, I reck'n, but she wouldn' be wuth half de trouble she'd coss."

"Don't you believe it. We'll fetch you a little one, and you plant it in the corner, over there, and raise it. And don't call it mullen, call it Pitchiola—that's its right name, when it's in a prison. And you want to water it with your tears."

"Why, I got plenty spring water, mars Tom."

"You don't *want* spring water; you want to water it with your tears. It's the way they always do."

"Why mars Tom, I lay I kin raise one er dem mullen-stalks twyste wid spring water whiles another man's a *start*'n one wid tears."

"That ain't the idea. You *got* to do it with tears."

"She'll die on my han's, mars Tom, she sholy will; kase I doan' skasely ever cry."

IRRIGATION.

So Tom was stumped. But he studied it over, and then said Jim would have to worry along the best he could with an onion. He promised he would go to the nigger cabins and drop one, private, in Jim's coffee pot, in the morning. Jim said he would "jis' 's soon have tobacker in his coffee"; and found so much fault with it, and with the work and bother of raising the mullen, and jewsharping the rats, and petting and flattering up the snakes and spiders and things, on top of all the other work he had to do on pens, and inscriptions, and journals, and things, which made it more trouble and worry and responsibility to be a prisoner than anything he ever undertook, that Tom most lost all patience with him; and said he was just loadened down with more gaudier chances than a prisoner ever had in the world to make a name for himself, and yet he didn't know enough to appreciate them, and they was just about wasted on him. So Jim he was sorry, and said he wouldn't behave so no more, and then me and Tom shoved for bed.

Chapter XXXIX

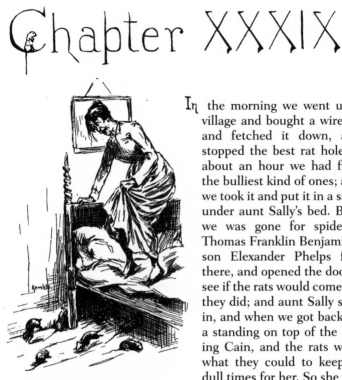

KEEPING OFF DULL TIMES.

In the morning we went up to the village and bought a wire rat trap and fetched it down, and unstopped the best rat hole, and in about an hour we had fifteen of the bulliest kind of ones; and then we took it and put it in a safe place under aunt Sally's bed. But while we was gone for spiders, little Thomas Franklin Benjamin Jefferson Elexander Phelps found it there, and opened the door of it to see if the rats would come out, and they did; and aunt Sally she come in, and when we got back she was a standing on top of the bed raising Cain, and the rats was doing what they could to keep off the dull times for her. So she took and dusted us both with the hickry, and we was as much as two hours catching another fifteen or sixteen, drat that meddlesome cub, and they warn't the likeliest, nuther, because the first haul was the pick of the flock. I never see a likelier lot of rats than what that first haul was.

We got a splendid stock of sorted spiders, and bugs, and frogs, and caterpillars, and one thing or another; and we like-to got a hornet's nest, but we didn't. The family was at home. We didn't give it right up, but staid with them as long as we could; because we allowed we'd tire them out or they'd got to tire us out, and they done it. Then we got ally-cumpain[1] and rubbed on the places, and was pretty near all right, again, but couldn't set down convenient. And so we went for the snakes, and grabbed a couple of dozen garters and house-snakes, and put them in a bag, and put it in our room, and by that time it was supper time, and a rattling good honest day's work; and hungry?—oh, no, I reckon not! And there warn't a blessed snake up there, when we went back—we didn't half tie the sack, and they worked out, somehow, and left. But it didn't matter much, because they was still on the premises somewheres. So we judged we could get some of them again. No, there warn't no real scarcity of snakes about the house for a considerble spell. You'd see them dripping from the rafters and places, every now and then; and

1. Elecampane, a medicinal herb.

they generly landed in your plate, or down the back of your neck, and most of the time where you didn't want them. Well, they was handsome, and striped, and there warn't no harm in a million of them; but that never made no difference to aunt Sally, she despised snakes, be the breed what they might, and she couldn't stand them, no way you could fix it; and every time one of them flopped down on her, it didn't make no difference what she was doing, she would just lay that work down and light out. I never see such a woman. And you could hear her whoop to Jericho. You couldn't get her to take aholt of one of them with the tongs. And if she turned over and found one in bed, she would scramble out and lift a howl that you would think the house was afire. She disturbed the old man so, that he said he could most wish there hadn't ever been no snakes created. Why, after every last snake had been gone clear out of the house for as much as a week, aunt Sally warn't over it yet; she warn't near over it; when she was setting thinking about something, you could touch her on the back of her neck with a feather and she would jump right out of her stockings. It was very curious. But Tom said all women was just so. He said they was made that way; for some reason or other.

We got a licking every time one of our snakes come in her way; and she allowed these lickings warn't nothing to what she would do if we ever loaded up the place again with them. I didn't mind the lickings, because they didn't amount to nothing; but I minded the trouble we had, to lay in another lot. But we got them laid in, and all the other things; and you never see a cabin as blithesome as Jim's was when they'd all swarm out for music and go for him. Jim didn't like the spiders, and the spiders didn't like Jim; and so they'd lay for him and make it mighty warm for him. And he said that between the rats, and the snakes, and the grindstone, there warn't no room in bed for him, skasely; and when there was, a body couldn't sleep, it was so lively, and it was always lively, he said, because *they* never all slept at one time, but took turn about, so when the snakes was asleep the rats was on deck, and when the rats turned in the snakes come on watch, so he always had one gang under him, in his way, and t'other gang having a circus over him, and if he got up to hunt a new place, the spiders would take a chance at him as he crossed over. He said if he ever got out, this time, he wouldn't ever be a prisoner again, not for a salary.

Well, by the end of three weeks, everything was in pretty good shape. The shirt was sent in early, in a pie, and every time a rat bit Jim he would get up and write a little in his journal, whilst the ink was fresh; the pens was made, the inscriptions and so-on was all carved on the grindstone; the bed-leg was sawed in two, and we had et up the saw-dust, and it give us a most amazing stomach-ache. We reckoned we was all going to die, but didn't. It was the most undigestible sawdust I ever see; and Tom said the same. But as I was saying, we'd got all the work done, now, at last; and we was all pretty much fagged out, too, but mainly Jim. The old man had wrote a couple of times to the plantation below Orleans to come and get their runaway nigger, but hadn't got no answer, because there warn't no such plantation; so he allowed he would advertise Jim in the St. Louis and New Orleans papers; and when

SAWDUST DIET.

he mentioned the St. Louis ones, it give me the cold shivers, and I see we hadn't no time to lose. So Tom said, now for the nonnamous letters.

"What's them?" I says.

"Warnings to the people that something is up. Sometimes it's done one way, sometimes another. But there's always somebody spying around, that gives notice to the governor of the castle. When Louis XVI was going to light out of the Tooleries,[2] a servant girl done it. It's a very good way, and so is the nonnamous letters. We'll use them both. And it's usual for the prisoner's mother to change clothes with him, and she stays in, and he slides out in her clothes. We'll do that, too."

"But lookyhere, Tom, what do we want to *warn* anybody for, that something's up? Let them find it out for themselves—it's their lookout."

"Yes, I know; but you can't depend on them. It's the way they've acted from the very start—left us to do *everything*. They're so confiding and mullet-headed[3] they don't take notice of nothing at all. So if we don't *give* them notice, there won't be nobody nor nothing to interfere with us, and so after all our hard work and trouble this escape 'll go off perfectly flat: won't amount to nothing—won't be nothing *to* it."

"Well, as for me, Tom, that's the way I'd like."

"Shucks," he says, and looked disgusted. So I says:

"But I ain't going to make no complaint. Any way that suits you suits me. What you going to do about the servant girl?"

"You'll be her. You slide in, in the middle of the night, and hook that yaller girl's frock."

"Why, Tom, that'll make trouble, next morning, because of course she prob'ly hain't got any but that one."

2. The Tuileries, a royal palace in Paris, burned in 1871; it is now the site of a park near the Louvre.
3. Trusting and stupid.

"I know; but you don't want it but fifteen minutes, to carry the non-namous letter and shove it under the front door."

"All right, then, I'll do it; but I could carry it just as handy in my own togs."

"You wouldn't look like a servant girl *then*, would you?"

"No, but there won't be nobody to see what I look like, *anyway*."

"That ain't got nothing to do with it. The thing for us to do, is just to do our *duty*, and not worry about whether anybody *sees* us do it or not. Hain't you got no principle at all?"

"All right, I ain't saying nothing: I'm the servant girl. Who's Jim's mother?"

"I'm his mother. I'll hook a gown from aunt Sally."

"Well, then, you'll have to stay in the cabin when me and Jim leaves."

"Not much. I'll stuff Jim's clothes full of straw and lay it on his bed to represent his mother in disguise, and Jim'll take aunt Sally's gown off of me and wear it, and we'll all evade together. When a prisoner of style escapes, it's called an evasion.[4] It's always called so when a king escapes, frinstance. And the same with a king's son; it don't make no difference whether he's a natural one or an unnatural one."

TROUBLE IS BREWING.

So Tom he wrote the nonnamous letter, and I smouched the yaller wench's frock, that night, and put it on, and shoved it under the front door, the way Tom told me to. It said:

---

4. Escape; as in the title of Dumas's romance *L'évasion du duc de Beaufort*.

Beware. Trouble is brewing. Keep a sharp lookout. UNKNOWN FRIEND.

Next night, we stuck a picture which Tom drawed in blood, of a skull and crossbones, on the front door; and next night another one of a coffin, on the back door. I never see a family in such a sweat. They couldn't a been worse scared if the place had a been full of ghosts laying for them behind everything and under the beds and shivering through the air. If a door banged, aunt Sally she jumped, and said "ouch!" if anything fell, she jumped and said "ouch!" if you happened to touch her, when she warn't noticing, she done the same; she couldn't face noway and be satisfied, because she allowed there was something behind her every time—so she was always a whirling around, sudden, and saying "ouch," and before she'd get two-thirds around, she'd whirl back again, and say it again; and she was afraid to go to bed, but she dasn't set up. So the thing was working very well, Tom said; he said he never see a thing work more satisfactory. He said it showed it was done right.

So he said, now for the grand bulge! So the very next morning at the streak of dawn we got another letter ready, and was wondering what we better do with it, because we heard them say at supper they was going to have a nigger on watch at both doors all night. Tom he went down the lightning rod to spy around; and the nigger at the back door was asleep, and he stuck it in the back of his neck and come back. This letter said:

Don't betray me, I wish to be your friend. There is a desprate gang of cutthroats from over in the Ingean Territory[5] going to steal your runaway nigger to-night, and they have been trying to scare you so as you will stay in the house and not bother them. I am one of the gang, but have got religgion and wish to quit it and lead a honest life again, and will betray the helish design. They will sneak down from northards, along the fence, at midnight exact, with a false key, and go in the nigger's cabin to get him. I am to be off a piece and blow a tin horn if I see any danger; but stead of that, I will BA *like a sheep soon as they get in and not blow at all; then whilst they are getting his chains loose, you slip there and lock them in, and can kill them at your leasure. Don't do anything but just the way I am telling you, if you do they will suspicion something and raise whoopjamboreehoo. I do not wish any reward but to know I have done the right thing.* UNKNOWN FRIEND.

---

5. Land in what is now Oklahoma granted to native Americans by the federal government.

Chapter XL

FISHING.

"We was feeling pretty good, after breakfast, and took my canoe and went over the river a-fishing, with a lunch, and had a good time, and took a look at the raft and found her all right, and got home late to supper, and found them in such a sweat and worry they didn't know which end they was standing on, and made us go right off to bed the minute we was done supper, and wouldn't tell us what the trouble was, and never let on a word about the new letter, but didn't need to, because we knowed as much about it as anybody did, and as soon as we was half up stairs and her back was turned, we slid for the cellar cubboard and loaded up a good lunch and took it up to our room and went to bed, and got up about half past eleven, and Tom put on aunt Sally's dress that he stole and was going to start with the lunch, but says:

"Where's the butter?"

"I laid out a hunk of it," I says, "on a piece of a corn-pone."

"Well, you *left* it laid out, then—it ain't here."

"We can get along without it," I says.

"We can get along *with* it, too," he says; "just you slide down cellar and fetch it. And then mosey right down the lightning rod and come along. I'll go and stuff the straw into Jim's clothes to represent his mother in disguise, and be ready to *ba* like a sheep and shove, soon as you get there."

So out he went, and down cellar went I. The hunk of butter, big as a person's fist, was where I had left it, so I took up the slab of corn-pone with it on, and blowed out my light, and started up stairs, very stealthy, and got up to the main floor all right, but here comes aunt Sally with a candle, and I clapped the truck in my hat, and clapped my hat on my head, and the next second she see me; and she says:

"You been down cellar?"

"Yes'm."

"What you been doing down there?"

"Noth'n."

"*Noth'n!*"

"No'm."

"Well, then, what possessed you to go down there, this time of night?"

"I don't know'm."

"You don't *know*? Don't answer me that way, Tom, I want to know what you been *doing* down there?"

"I hain't been doing a single thing, aunt Sally, I hope to gracious if I have."

I reckoned she'd let me go, now, and as a generl thing she would; but I spose there was so many strange things going on she was just in a sweat about every little thing that warn't yard-stick straight; so she says, very decided:

"You just march into that setting-room and stay there till I come. You been up to something you no business to, and I lay I'll find out what it is before *I'm* done with you."

So she went away as I opened the door and walked into the setting room. My, but there was a crowd there! Fifteen farmers, and every one of them had a gun. I was most powerful sick, and slunk to a chair and set down. They was setting around, some of them talking a little, in a low voice, and all of them fidgety and uneasy, but trying to look like they warn't; but I knowed they was, because they was always taking off their hats, and putting them on, and scratching their heads, and changing their seats, and fumbling with their buttons. I warn't easy, myself, but I didn't take my hat off, all the same.

EVERY ONE HAD A GUN.

I did wish aunt Sally would come, and get done with me, and lick me, if she wanted to, and let me get away and tell Tom how we'd overdone this thing, and what a thundering hornet's nest we'd got ourselves into, so we could stop fooling around, straight off, and clear out with Jim before these rips got out of patience and come for us.

At last she come, and begun to ask me questions, but I *couldn't* answer them straight, I didn't know which end of me was up; because these men was in such a fidget, now, that some was wanting to start right *now* and lay for them desperadoes, and saying it warn't but a few minutes to midnight; and others was trying to get them to hold on and wait for the sheep-signal; and here was aunty pegging away at the questions, and me a shaking all over and ready to sink down in my tracks I was that scared; and the place getting hotter and hotter, and the butter beginning to melt and run down my neck and behind my ears; and pretty soon, when one of them says, "*I'm* for going and getting in the cabin *first*, and right *now*, and catching them when they come," I most dropped; and a streak of butter come a trickling down my forehead, and aunt Sally she see it, and turns white as a sheet, and says:

"For the land's sake what *is* the matter with the child!— he's got the brain fever as shore as you're born, and they're oozing out!"

And everybody runs to see, and she snatches off my hat, and out comes the bread, and what was left of the butter, and she grabbed me, and hugged me, and says:

"Oh, what a turn you did give me! and how glad and grateful I am it ain't no worse; for luck's against us, and it never rains but it pours, and when I see that truck I thought we'd lost you, for I knowed by the color and all, it was just like your brains would be if—Dear, dear, whydn't you *tell* me that was what you'd been down there for, *I* wouldn't a cared. Now cler out to bed, and don't lemme see no more of you till morning!"

I was up stairs in a second, and down the lightning rod in another one, and shinning through the dark for the lean-to. I couldn't hardly get my words out, I was so anxious; but I told Tom as quick as I could, we must jump for it, now, and not a minute to lose—the house full of men, yonder, with guns!

His eyes just blazed; and he says:

"No!—is that so? *Ain't* it bully! Why, Huck, if it was to do over again, I bet I could fetch two hundred! If we could put it off till—"

"Hurry! *hurry!*" I says; "where's Jim?"

"Right at your elbow; if you reach out your arm you can touch him. He's dressed, and everything's ready. Now we'll slide out and give the sheep-signal."

But then we heard the tramp of men, coming to the door, and heard them begin to fumble with the padlock; and heard a man say:

"I *told* you we'd be too soon; they haven't come—the door is locked. Here—I'll lock some of you into the cabin and you lay for 'em in the dark and kill 'em when they come; and the rest scatter around a piece, and listen if you can hear 'em coming."

So in they come, but couldn't see us in the dark, and most trod on us whilst we was hustling to get under the bed. But we got under, all right, and out through the hole, swift but soft—Jim first, me next, and Tom last, which was according to Tom's orders. Now we was in the lean-to, and heard trampings close by, outside. So we crept to the door, and Tom stopped us there and put his eye to the crack, but couldn't make out nothing, it was so dark; and whispered and said he would listen for the steps to get further, and when he nudged us Jim must glide out first, and him last. So he set his ear to the crack and listened, and listened, and listened, and the steps a scraping around, out there, all the time; and at last he nudged us, and we slid out, and stooped down, not

breathing, and not making the least noise, and slipped stealthy towards
the fence, in Injun file, and got to it, all right, and me and Jim over it;
but Tom's britches catched fast on a splinter on the top rail, and then
he hear the steps coming, so he had to pull loose, which snapped the
splinter and made a noise; and as he dropped in our tracks and started,
somebody sings out:

"Who's that? Answer, or I'll shoot!"

TOM CAUGHT ON A SPLINTER.

But we didn't answer; we just unfurled our heels and shoved. Then
there was a rush, and a *bang, bang, bang!* and the bullets fairly whizzed
around us! We heard them sing out:

"Here they are! They've broke for the river! after 'em, boys! And turn
loose the dogs!"

So here they come, full tilt. We could hear them, because they wore
boots, and yelled, but we didn't wear no boots, and didn't yell. We was
in the path to the mill; and when they got pretty close onto us, we
dodged into the bush and let them go by, and then dropped in behind
them. They'd had all the dogs shut up, so they wouldn't scare off the
robbers; but by this time somebody had let them loose, and here they
come, making pow-wow enough for a million; but they was our dogs; so
we stopped in our tracks till they catched up; and when they see it
warn't nobody but us, and no excitement to offer them, they only just
said howdy, and tore right ahead towards the shouting and clattering;
and then we up steam again and whizzed along after them till we was
nearly to the mill, and then struck up through the bush to where my

canoe was tied, and hopped in and pulled for dear life towards the middle of the river, but didn't make no more noise than we was obleeged to. Then we struck out, easy and comfortable, for the island where my raft was; and we could hear them yelling and barking at each other all up and down the bank, till we was so far away the sounds got dim and died out. And when we stepped onto the raft, I says:

"*Now*, old Jim, you're a free man *again*, and I bet you won't ever be a slave no more."

"En a mighty good job it wuz, too, Huck. It 'uz planned beautiful, en it 'uz *done* beautiful; en dey ain't *nobody* kin git up a plan dat's mo' mixed-up en splendid den what dat one wuz."

We was all as glad as we could be, but Tom was the gladdest of all, because he had a bullet in the calf of his leg.

When me and Jim heard that, we didn't feel so brash as what we did before. It was hurting him considerble, and bleeding; so we laid him in the wigwam and tore up one of the duke's shirts for to bandage him; but he says:

"Gimme the rags, I can do it myself. Don't stop, now; don't fool around here, and the evasion booming along so handsome: man the sweeps, and set her loose! Boys, we done it elegant!—'deed we did. I wish *we*'d a had the handling of Louis XVI, there wouldn't a been no 'Son of Saint Louis, ascend to heaven!'[1] wrote down in *his* biography: no, sir, we'd a whooped him over the *border*—that's what we'd a done with *him*—and done it just as slick as nothing at all, too. Man the sweeps—man the sweeps!"

But me and Jim was consulting—and thinking. And after we'd thought a minute, I says:

"Say it, Jim."

So he says:

"Well, den, dis is de way it look to me, Huck. Ef it wuz *him* dat 'uz bein' sot free, en one er de boys wuz to git shot, would he say, 'Go on en save me, nemmine 'bout a doctor f'r to save dis one?' Is dat like mars Tom Sawyer? Would he say dat? You *bet* he wouldn't! *Well* den—is *Jim* gwyne to say it? No, sah—I doan' budge a step out'n dis place, 'dout a *doctor*; not ef it's forty year!"

I knowed he was white inside, and I reckoned he'd say what he did say—so it was all right, now, and I told Tom I was agoing for a doctor. He raised considerble row about it, but me and Jim stuck to it and wouldn't budge; so he was for crawling out and setting the raft loose himself; but we wouldn't let him. Then he give us a piece of his mind—but it didn't do no good.

So when he see me getting the canoe ready, he says:

"Well, then, if you're bound to go, I'll tell you the way to do, when you get to the village. Shut the door, and blindfold the doctor tight and fast, and make him swear to be silent as the grave, and put a purse full of gold in his hand, and then take and lead him all around the back alleys and everywheres, in the dark, and then fetch him here in the canoe, in a roundabout way amongst the islands, and search him and take his

---

1. Tom is quoting Thomas Carlyle's account of Louis XVI's execution in *The French Revolution* (1837), a book Mark Twain knew well.

chalk away from him, and don't give it back to him till you get him back to the village, or else he will chalk this raft so he can find it again. It's the way they all do."

So I said I would, and left, and Jim was to hide in the woods when he see the doctor coming, till he was gone again.

JIM ADVISES A DOCTOR.

Chapter XLI •

THE DOCTOR.

The doctor was an old man; a very nice, kind looking old man, when I got him up. I told him me and my brother was over on Spanish island hunting, yesterday after noon, and camped on a piece of a raft we found, and about midnight he must a kicked his gun in his dreams, for it went off and shot him in the leg; and we wanted him to go over there and fix it and not say nothing about it, nor let anybody know, because we wanted to come home this evening, and surprise the folks.

"Who is your folks?" he says.

"The Phelpses, down yonder."

"Oh," he says. And after a minute, he says: "How'd you say he got shot?"

"He had a dream," I says, "and it shot him."

"Singular dream," he says.

So he lit up his lantern, and got his saddlebags, and we started. But when he see the canoe, he didn't like the look of her—said she was big enough for one, but didn't look pretty safe for two. I says:

"O, you needn't be afeard, sir, she carried the three of us, easy enough."

"What three?"

"Why, me and Sid, and—and—and *the guns*; that's what I mean."

"Oh," he says.

But he put his foot on the gunnel, and rocked her; and shook his head, and said he reckoned he'd look around for a bigger one. But they was all locked and chained; so he took my canoe, and said for me to wait till he come back, or I could hunt around further, or maybe I better go down home and get them ready for the surprise, if I wanted to. But I said I didn't; so I told him just how to find the raft, and then he started.

I struck an idea, pretty soon. I says to myself, spos'n he can't fix that leg just in three shakes of a sheep's tail, as the saying is? spos'n it takes him three or four days? What are we going to do?—lay around there till he lets the cat out of the bag? No, sir, I know what I'll do: I'll wait, and when he comes back, if he says he's got to go any more, I'll get down there, too, if I swim; and we'll take and tie him, and keep him, and shove out down the river; and when Tom's done with him, we'll give him what it's worth, or all we got, and then let him get ashore.

So then I crept into a lumber pile to get some sleep; and next time I waked up the sun was away up over my head! I shot out and went for the doctor's house, but they told me he'd gone away in the night, some time or other, and warn't back yet. Well, thinks I, that looks powerful bad for Tom, and I'll dig out for the island, right off. So away I shoved, and turned the corner, and nearly rammed my head into uncle Silas's stomach! He says:

"Why, *Tom*! Where you been, all this time, you rascal?"

"*I* hain't been nowheres," I says, "only just hunting for the runaway nigger—me and Sid."

UNCLE SILAS IN DANGER.

"Why, where ever did you go?" he says. "Your aunt's been mighty uneasy."

"She needn't," I says, "because we was all right. We followed the men and the dogs, but they outrun us, and we lost them; but we thought we heard them on the water, so we got a canoe and took out after them, and crossed over, but couldn't find nothing of them; so we cruised along up shore till we got kind of tired and beat out; and tied up the canoe and went to sleep, and never waked up till about an hour ago, then we paddled over here to hear the news, and Sid's at the postoffice to see what he can hear, and I'm a-branching out to get something to eat for us, and then we're going home."

So then we went to the postoffice to get 'Sid'; but, just as I suspicioned, he warn't there; so the old man he got a letter out of the office, and we waited a while longer, but Sid didn't come; so the old man said come along, let Sid foot it home, or canoe-it, when he got done fooling around—but we would ride. I couldn't get him to let me stay and wait for Sid; and he said there warn't no use in it, and I must come along, and let aunt Sally see we was all right.

When we got home, aunt Sally was that glad to see me she laughed and cried both, and hugged me, and give me one of them lickings of hern that don't amount to shucks, and said she'd serve Sid the same when he come.

And the place was plumb full of farmers and farmers' wives, to dinner; and such another clack a body never heard. Old Mrs. Hotchkiss was the worst; her tongue was agoing all the time. She says:

"Well, sister Phelps, I've ransacked that-air cabin over, an' I b'lieve the nigger was crazy. I says so to sister Damrell—didn't I, sister Damrell?—s'I, he's crazy, s'I—them's the very words I said. You all hearn me: he's crazy, s'I; everything shows it, s'I. Look at that-air grindstone, s'I: want to tell *me* 't any cretur 'ts in his right mind 's agoin' to scrabble all them crazy things onto a grindstone, s'I? Here sich 'n' sich a person busted his heart; 'n' here so 'n' so pegged along for thirty-seven year, 'n' all that—natcherl son o' Louis somebody, 'n' sich everlast'n rubbage. He's plumb crazy, s'I; it's what I says in the fust place, it's what I says in the middle, 'n' it's what I says last 'n' all the time—the nigger's crazy—crazy's Nebokoodneezer, s'I."[1]

"An' look at that-air ladder made out'n rags, sister Hotchkiss," says old Mrs. Damrell, "what in the name o' goodness *could* he ever want of—"

OLD MRS. HOTCHKISS.

"The very words I was a-sayin' no longer ago th'n this minute to sister Utterback, 'n' she'll tell you so herself. Sh-she, look at that-air rag ladder, sh-she; 'n' s'I, yes, *look* at it, s'I—what *could* he a wanted of it, s'I. Sh-she, sister Hotchkiss, sh-she—"

"But how in the nation'd they ever *git* that grindstone *in* there, *any*way? 'n' who dug that-air *hole*? 'n' who—"

1. Nebuchadnezzar, king of Babylon, loses his sanity in Daniel 4.33.

"My very *words*, Brer Penrod! I was a-sayin'—pass that-air sasser o' m'lasses, won't ye?—I was a-sayin' to sister Dunlap, jist this minute, how *did* they git that grindstone in there, s'I. Without *help*, mind you— 'thout *help! Thar's* wher' 'tis. Don't tell *me*, s'I; there *wuz* help, s'I; 'n' ther' wuz a *plenty* help, too, s'I; ther's ben a *dozen* a-helpin' that nigger, 'n' I lay I'd skin every last nigger on this place, but *I'd* find out who done it, s'I; 'n' moreover, s'I—"

"A *dozen*, says you!—*forty* couldn't a done everything that's been done. Look at them caseknife saws and things, how tedious they've been made; look at that bed-leg sawed off with 'm, a week's work for six men; look at that nigger made out'n straw on the bed; and look at—"

"You may *well* say it, Brer Hightower! It's jist as I was a-sayin' to Brer Phelps, his own self. S'e, what do *you* think of it, sister Hotchkiss, s'e? think o' what, Brer Phelps, s'I? think o' that bed-leg sawed off that a way, s'e? *think* of it, s'I? I lay it never sawed *itself* off, s'I—somebody *sawed* it, s'I; that's my opinion, take it or leave it, it mayn't be no 'count, s'I, but sich as't is, it's my opinion, s'I, 'n' if anybody k'n start a better one, s'I, let him *do* it, s'I, that's all. I says to sister Dunlap, s'I—"

"Why, dog my cats, they must a ben a house-full o' niggers in there every night for four weeks, to a done all that work, sister Phelps. Look at that shirt—every last inch of it kivered over with secret African writ'n, done with blood! Must a ben a raft uv 'm at it right along, all the time, amost. Why, I'd give two dollars to have it read to me; 'n' as for the niggers that wrote it, I 'low I'd take 'n' lash 'm t'll—"

"People to *help* him, Brother Marples! Well, I reckon you'd *think* so, if you'd a been in this house for a while back. Why, they've stole everything they could lay their hands on—and we a watching, all the time, mind you. They stole that shirt right off o' the line! and as for that sheet they made the rag ladder out of, ther' ain't no telling how many times they *didn't* steal that; and flour, and candles, and candlesticks, and spoons, and the old warming pan, and most a thousand things that I disremember, now, and my new calico dress; and me, and Silas, and my Sid and Tom on the constant watch day *and* night, as I was a-telling you, and not a one of us could catch hide nor hair, nor sight nor sound of them; and here at the last minute, lo and behold you, they slides right in under our noses, and fools us, and not only fools *us* but the Injun Territory robbers too, and actuly gets *away* with that nigger, safe and sound, and that with sixteen men and twenty-two dogs right on their very heels at that very time! I tell you, it just bangs anything I ever *heard* of. Why, *sperits* couldn't a done better, and been no smarter. And I reckon they must a *been* sperits—because, *you* know our dogs, and ther' ain't no better: well, them dogs never even got on the *track* of 'm, once! You explain *that* to me, if you can!—*any* of you!"

"Well, it does beat—"

"Land alive, I never—"

"So help me, I wouldn't a be—"

"*House*-thieves as well as—"

"Goodnessgracioussakes, I'd a ben afeard to *live* in sich a—"

" 'Fraid to *live*!—why, I was that scared I dasn't hardly go to bed, or get up, or lay down, or *set* down, sister Ridgeway. Why, they'd steal the very—why, goodness sakes, you can guess what kind of a fluster *I* was in by the time midnight come, last night: I hope to gracious if I warn't afraid they'd steal some o' the family! I was just to that pass, I didn't have no reasoning faculties no more. It looks foolish enough, *now*, in the daytime; but I says to myself, there's my two poor boys asleep, 'way up stairs in that lonesome room, and I declare to goodness I was that uneasy 't I crep' up there and locked 'em in! I *did*. And anybody would. Because, you know, when you get scared, that way, and it keeps running on, and getting worse and worse, all the time, and your wits gets to addling, and you get to doing all sorts o' wild things, and by and by you think to yourself, spos'n *I* was a boy, and was away up there, and the door ain't locked, and you—" She stopped, looking kind of wondering, and then she turned her head around slow, and when her eye lit on me—I got up and took a walk.

Says I to myself, I can explain better how we come to not be in that room this morning, if I go out to one side and study over it a little. So I done it. But I dasn't go fur, or she'd a sent for me. And when it was late in the day, the people all went, and then I come in and told her the noise and shooting waked up me and 'Sid,' and the door was locked, and we wanted to see the fun, so we went down the lightning rod, and both of us got hurt a little, and we didn't never want to try *that* no more. And then I went on and told her all what I told uncle Silas before; and then she said she'd forgive us, and maybe it was all right enough, anyway, and about what a body might expect of boys, for all boys was a pretty harum-scarum lot, as fur as she could see; and so, as long as no harm hadn't come of it, she judged she better put in her time being grateful we was alive and well and she had us still, stead of fretting over what was past and done. So then she kissed me, and patted me on the head, and dropped into a kind of a brown study; and pretty soon jumps up and says:

"Why, lawsamercy, it's most night, and Sid not come yet! What *has* become of that boy?"

I see my chance; so I skips up and says:

"I'll run right up to town and get him," I says.

"No you won't," she says. "You'll stay right wher' you are; *one's* enough to be lost at a time. If he ain't here to supper, your uncle'll go."

Well, he warn't there to supper; so right after supper, uncle went.

He come back about ten, a little bit uneasy; hadn't run across Tom's track. Aunt Sally was a good *deal* uneasy; but uncle Silas he said there warn't no occasion to be—boys will be boys, he said, and you'll see this one turn up in the morning, all sound and right. So she had to be satisfied. But she said she'd set up for him a while, anyway, and keep a light burning, so he could see it.

And then when I went up to bed, she come up with me, and fetched her candle, and tucked me in, and mothered me so good I felt mean and like I couldn't look her in the face; and she set down on the bed and talked with me a long time, and said what a splendid boy Sid was, and didn't seem to want to ever stop talking about him; and kept asking me every now and then, if I reckoned he could a got lost, or hurt, or maybe drownded, and might be laying at this minute, somewheres, suffering or

AUNT SALLY TALKS TO HUCK.

dead, and she not by him to help him; and so the tears would drip down, silent, and I would tell her that Sid was all right, and would be home in the morning, sure; and she would squeeze my hand, or maybe kiss me, and tell me to say it again, and keep on saying it, because it done her good, and she was in so much trouble. And when she was going away, she looked down in my eyes, so steady and gentle, and says:

"The door ain't going to be locked, Tom; and there's the window and the rod; but you'll be good, *won't* you? And you won't go? For *my* sake."

Laws knows I *wanted* to go, bad enough, to see about Tom, and was all intending to go; but after that, I wouldn't a went, not for kingdoms.

But she was on my mind, and Tom was on my mind; so I slept very restless. And twice I went down the rod, away in the night, and slipped around front, and see her setting there by her candle in the window with her eyes towards the road and the tears in them; and I wished I could do something for her, but I couldn't, only to swear that I wouldn't never do nothing to grieve her any more. And the third time, I waked up at dawn, and slid down, and she was there yet, and her candle was most out, and her old gray head was resting on her hand, and she was asleep.

Chapter XLII

TOM SAWYER WOUNDED.

The old man was up town again, before breakfast, but couldn't get no track of Tom; and both of them set at the table, thinking, and not saying nothing, and looking mournful, and their coffee getting cold, and not eating anything. And by and by the old man says:

"Did I give you the letter?"

"What letter?"

"The one I got yesterday, out of the postoffice."

"No, you didn't give me no letter."

"Well, I must a forgot it."

So he rummaged his pockets, and then went off somewheres where he had laid it down, and fetched it, and give it to her. She says:

"Why, it's from St. Petersburg—it's from Sis."

I allowed another walk would do me good; but I couldn't stir. But before she could break it open, she dropped it and run—for she see something. And so did I. It was Tom Sawyer on a mattrass; and that old doctor; and Jim, in *her* calico dress, with his hands tied behind him; and a lot of people. I hid the letter behind the first thing that come handy, and rushed. She flung herself at Tom, crying, and says:

"O, he's dead, he's dead, I know he's dead!"

And Tom he turned his head a little, and muttered something or other, which showed he warn't in his right mind; then she flung up her hands, and says:

"He's alive, thank God! And that's enough!" and she snatched a kiss of him, and flew for the house, to get the bed ready, and scattering orders right and left at the niggers and everybody else, as fast as her tongue could go, every jump of the way.

I followed the men to see what they was going to do with Jim; and the old doctor and uncle Silas followed after Tom into the house. The men was very huffy, and some of them wanted to hang Jim, for an example to all the other niggers around there, so they wouldn't be trying to run away, like Jim done, and making such a raft of trouble, and keeping a whole family scared most to death for days and nights. But the others said, don't do it, it wouldn't answer at all, he ain't our nigger, and his

287

owner would turn up and make us pay for him, sure. So that cooled
them down a little, because the people that's always the most anxious
for to hang a nigger that hadn't done just right, is always the very ones
that ain't the most anxious to pay for him when they've got their satisfaction out of him.

They cussed Jim considerble, though, and give him a cuff or two, side
the head, once in a while, but Jim never said nothing, and he never let
on to know me, and they took him to the same cabin, and put his own
clothes on him, and chained him again, and not to no bed-leg, this time,
but to a big staple drove into the bottom log, and chained his hands,
too, and both legs, and said he warn't to have nothing but bread and
water to eat, after this, till his owner come or he was sold at auction,
because he didn't come in a certain length of time, and filled up our
hole, and said a couple of farmers with guns must stand watch around
about the cabin every night, and a bulldog tied to the door in the daytime, and about this time they was through with the job and was taper-
ing off with a kind of generl goodbye cussing, and then the old doctor
comes, and takes a look, and says:

"Don't be no rougher on him than you're obleeged to, because he
ain't a bad nigger. When I got to where I found the boy, I see I couldn't
cut the bullet out without some help, and he warn't in no condition for
me to leave, to go and get help; and he got a little worse and a little

THE DOCTOR SPEAKS FOR JIM.

worse, and after a long time he went out of his head, and wouldn't let
me come anigh him, any more, and said if I chalked his raft he'd kill me,
and no end of wild foolishness like that, and I see I couldn't do anything
at all with him; so I says, I got to have *help*, somehow; and the minute
I says it, out crawls this nigger from somewheres, and says he'll help;

and he done it, too, and done it very well. Of course I jud

be a runaway nigger, and there I *was*! and there I had t(

straight along, all the rest of the day, and all night. It was a

I had a couple of patients with the chills, and of course I'

run up to town and see them, but I dasn't, because the nigg

away, and then I'd be to blame; and yet never a skiff come close enough

for me to hail. So there I had to stick, plumb till daylight this morning;

and I never see a nigger that was a better nuss or faithfuller, and yet he

was resking his freedom to do it, and was all tired out, too, and I see

plain enough he'd been worked main hard, lately. I liked the nigger for

that; I tell you, gentlemen, a nigger like that is worth a thousand dol-

lars—and kind treatment, too. I had everything I needed, and the boy

was doing as well there as he would a done at home—better, maybe,

because it was so quiet; but there I *was*, with both of 'm on my hands;

and there I had to stick, till about dawn this morning; then some men

in a skiff come by, and as good luck would have it, the nigger was set-

ting by the pallet with his head propped on his knees, sound asleep; so

I motioned them in, quiet, and they slipped up on him and grabbed him

and tied him before he knowed what he was about, and we never had no

trouble. And the boy being in a kind of a flighty sleep, too, we muffled

the oars and hitched the raft on, and towed her over very nice and quiet,

and the nigger never made the least row nor said a word, from the start.

He ain't no bad nigger, gentlemen; that's what I think about him."

Somebody says:

"Well, it sounds very good, doctor, I'm obleeged to say."

Then the others softened up a little, too, and I was mighty thankful

to that old doctor for doing Jim that good turn; and I was glad it was

according to my judgement of him, too; because I thought he had a

good heart in him and was a good man, the first time I see him. Then

they all agreed that Jim had acted very well, and was deserving to have

some notice took of it, and reward. So every one of them promised,

right out and hearty, that they wouldn't cuss him no more.

Then they come out and locked him up. I hoped they was going to say

he could have one or two of the chains took off, because they was rot-

ten heavy, or could have meat and greens with his bread and water, but

they didn't think of it, and I reckoned it warn't best for me to mix in, but

I judged I'd get the doctor's yarn to aunt Sally, somehow or other, as

soon as I'd got through the breakers that was laying just ahead of me.

Explanations, I mean, of how I forgot to mention about 'Sid' being shot,

when I was telling how him and me put in that dratted night paddling

around hunting the runaway nigger.

But I had plenty time. Aunt Sally she stuck to the sick room all day

and all night; and every time I see uncle Silas mooning around, I

dodged him.

Next morning I heard Tom was a good deal better, and they said aunt

Sally was gone to get a nap. So I slips to the sick room and if I found

him awake I reckoned we could put up a yarn for the family that would

wash. But he was sleeping, and sleeping very peaceful, too; and pale,

not fire-faced the way he was when he come. So I set down and laid for

him to wake. In about a half an hour, aunt Sally comes gliding in, and d ere I was, up a stump again! She motioned me to be still, and set down by me, and begun to whisper, and said we could all be joyful, now, because all the symptoms was first rate, and he'd been sleeping like that for ever so long, and looking better and peacefuller all the time, and ten to one he'd wake up in his right mind.

So we set there watching, and by and by, he stirs a bit, and opens his eyes very natural, and takes a look, and says:

"Hello, why I'm at *home!* How's that? Where's the raft?"

"It's all right," I says.

"And *Jim?*"

"The same," I says, but couldn't say it pretty brash. But he never noticed, but says:

"Good! Splendid! *Now* we're all right and safe! Did you tell aunty?"

I was going to say yes; but she chipped in and says:

"About what, Sid?"

"Why, about the way the whole thing was done."

"What whole thing?"

"Why, *the* whole thing—there ain't but one: how we set the runaway nigger free—me and Tom."

"Good land! Set the run— What *is* the child talking about! Dear, dear, out of his head again!"

"*No* I ain't out of my HEAD, I know all what I'm talking about. We *did* set him free—me and Tom. We laid out to do it and we *done* it. And we done it elegant, too." He'd got a start, and she never checked him up, just set and stared and stared, and let him clip along, and I see it warn't no use for *me* to put in. "Why, aunty, it cost us a power of work—weeks of it—hours and hours, every night, whilst you was all asleep. And we had to steal candles, and the sheet and the shirt, and your dress, and spoons, and tin plates, and caseknives, and the warming pan, and the grindstone, and flour, and just no end of things, and you can't think what work it was, to make the saws, and pens, and inscriptions, and one thing or another, and you can't think *half* the fun it was. And we had to make up the pictures of coffins and things, and nonnamous letters from the robbers, and get up and down the lightning rod, and dig the hole into the cabin, and make the rope-ladder and send it in, cooked up in a pie, and send in spoons and things to work with, in your apron pocket"—

"Mercy sakes!"

—"and load up the cabin with rats and snakes and so-on, for company for Jim; and then you kept Tom here so long with the butter in his hat that you come near spiling the whole business, because the men come before we was out of the cabin, and we had to rush, and they heard us and let drive at us, and I got my share, and we dodged out of the path and let them go by, and when the dogs come they warn't interested in us, but went for the most noise, and we got our canoe, and made for the raft, and was all safe, and Jim was a free man, and we done it all by ourselves, and *wasn't* it bully, aunty!"

"Well, I never heard the likes of it in all my born days! So it was *you,* you little rapscallions, that's been making all this trouble, and turned everybody's wits clean inside out and scared us all most to death. I've as good a notion as ever I had in my life, to take it out o' you this very minute. To think, here I've been, night after night, a—*you* just get well, once, you young scamp, and I lay I'll tan the Old Harry out o' both o' ye!"

But Tom, he *was* so proud and joyful, he just *couldn't* hold in, and his tongue just *went* it—she a-chipping in, and spitting fire all along, and both of them going it at once, like a cat-convention; and she says:

"*Well*, you get all the enjoyment you can out of it *now*, for mind I tell you if I catch you meddling with him again—"

"Meddling with *who*?" Tom says, dropping his smile and looking surprised.

"With *who*? Why, the runaway nigger, of course. Who'd you reckon?"

Tom looks at me very grave, and says:

"Tom, didn't you just tell me he was all right? Hasn't he got away?"

"*Him*?" says aunt Sally; "the runaway nigger? 'Deed he hasn't. They've got him back, safe and sound, and he's in that cabin again, on bread and water, and loaded down with chains, till he's claimed or sold!"

Tom rose square up in bed, with his eye hot, and his nostrils opening and shutting like gills, and sings out to me:

"They hain't no *right* to shut him up! *Shove!*—and don't you lose a minute. Turn him loose! he ain't no slave, he's as free as any cretur that walks this earth!"

TOM ROSE SQUARE UP IN BED.

"What *does* the child mean!"

"I mean every word I *say*, aunt Sally, and if somebody don't go, *I'll* go. I've knowed him all his life, and so has Tom, there. Old Miss Watson died two months ago, and she was ashamed she ever was going to sell him down the river, and *said* so; and she set him free in her will."

"Then what on earth did *you* want to set him free for, seeing he was already free?"

"Well that *is* a question, I must say; and *just* like women! Why, I wanted the *adventure* of it; and I'd a waded neck-deep in blood to—goodness alive, AUNT POLLY!"

If she warn't standing right there, just inside the door, looking as sweet and contented as an angel half-full of pie, I wish I may never!

Aunt Sally jumped for her, and most hugged the head off of her, and cried over her, and I found a good enough place for me under the bed, for it was getting pretty sultry for *us*, seemed to me. And I peeped out, and in a little while Tom's aunt Polly shook herself loose and stood there looking across at Tom over her spectacles—kind of grinding him into the earth, you know. And then she says:

"Yes, you *better* turn y'r head away—I would if I was you, Tom."

"Oh, deary me!" says aunt Sally, "*is* he changed so? Why, that ain't *Tom*, it's Sid; Tom's—Tom's—why, where is Tom? He was here a minute ago."

"You mean where's Huck *Finn*—that's what you mean! I reckon I hain't raised such a scamp as my Tom all these years, not to know him when I *see* him. That *would* be a pretty howdy-do. Come out from under that bed, Huck Finn."

So I done it. But not feeling brash.

Aunt Sally she was one of the mixed-upest looking persons I ever see; except one, and that was uncle Silas, when he come in, and they told it all to him. It kind of made him drunk, as you may say, and he didn't know nothing at all the rest of the day, and preached a prayer meeting sermon that night that give him a rattling ruputation, because the oldest man in the world couldn't a understood it. So Tom's aunt Polly she told all about who I was, and what; and I had to up and tell how I was in such a tight place that when Mrs. Phelps took me for Tom Sawyer—she chipped in and says, "O, go on and call me aunt Sally, I'm used to it, now, and 't ain't no need to change"—that when aunt Sally took me for Tom Sawyer, I had to stand it—there warn't no other way, and I knowed he wouldn't mind, because it would be nuts for him, being a mystery, and he'd make an adventure out of it and be perfectly satisfied. And so it turned out, and he let on to be Sid, and made things as soft as he could for me.

And his aunt Polly she said Tom was right about old Miss Watson setting Jim free in her will; and so, sure enough, Tom Sawyer had gone and took all that trouble and bother to set a free nigger free! and I couldn't ever understand, before, until that minute and that talk, how he *could* help a body set a nigger free, with his bringing-up.

Well, aunt Polly she said that when aunt Sally wrote to her that Tom and *Sid* had come, all right and safe, she says to herself:

"Look at that, now! I might have expected it, letting him go off that way without anybody to watch him. So now I got to go and trapse all the way down the river eleven hundred mile, and find out what that cretur's up to, *this* time; as long as I couldn't seem to get any answer out of *you* about it."

"Why, I never heard nothing from you," says aunt Sally.

"Well, I wonder! Why, I wrote to you twice, to ask you what you could mean by Sid being here."

"Well, I never got 'em, Sis."

Aunt Polly she turns around slow and severe, and says:

"You, Tom!"

"Well—*what?*" he says, kind of pettish.

"Don't you what *me*, you impudent thing—hand out them letters."

"What letters?"

"*Them* letters. I be bound, if I have to take aholt of you I'll—"

"They're in the trunk. There, now. And they're just the same as they was when I got them out of the office. I hain't looked into them, I hain't touched them. But I knowed they'd make trouble, and I thought if you warn't in no hurry, I'd—"

"Well, you *do* need skinning, there ain't no mistake about it. And I wrote another one to tell you I was coming; and I spose he—"

"No, it come yesterday; I hain't read it yet, but *it's* all right, I've got that one."

"HAND OUT THEM LETTERS."

I wanted to offer to bet two dollars she hadn't, but I reckoned maybe it was just as safe to not to. So I never said nothing.

Chapter the Last

The first time I catched Tom, private, I asked him what was his idea, time of the evasion?—what it was he'd planned to do if the evasion worked all right and he managed to set a nigger free that was already free before? And he said, what he had planned in his head, from the start, if we got Jim out, all safe, was for us to run him down the river, on the raft, and have adventures plumb to the mouth of the river, and then tell him about his being free, and take him back up home on a steamboat, in style, and pay him for his lost time, and write word ahead, and get out all the niggers around, and have them waltz him into town with a torchlight procession, and a brass band, and then he would be a hero, and so would we. But I reckoned it was about as well the way it was.

OUT OF BONDAGE.

We had Jim out of the chains in no time, and when aunt Polly and uncle Silas and aunt Sally found out how good he helped the doctor nurse Tom, they made a heap of fuss over him, and fixed him up prime, and give him all he wanted to eat, and a good time, and nothing to do. And we had him up to the sick room; and had a high talk; and Tom give Jim forty dollars for being prisoner for us so patient, and doing it up so good, and Jim was pleased most to death, and busted out, and says:

"*Dah*, now, Huck, what I tell you?—what I tell you up dah on Jackson islan'? I *tole* you I got a hairy breas', en what's de sign un it; en I *tole* you I ben rich wunst, en gwineter be rich *agin*; en it's come true; en heah she *is*! *Dah*, now! doan' talk to *me*—signs is *signs*, mine I tell you;

294

en I knowed jis' 's well 'at I 'uz gwineter be rich agin as I's a stannin' heah dis minute!"

And then Tom he talked along, and talked along, and says, le's all three slide out of here, one of these nights, and get an outfit, and go for howling adventures amongst the Injuns,[1] over in the Territory, for a couple of weeks or two; and I says, all right, that suits me, but I ain't got no money for to buy the outfit, and I reckon I couldn't get none from home, because it's likely pap's been back before now, and got it all away from Judge Thatcher and drunk it up.

"No he hain't," Tom says; "it's all there, yet—six thousand dollars and more; and your pap hain't ever been back since. Hadn't when I come away, anyhow."

Jim says, kind of solemn:

"He ain't a comin' back no mo', Huck."

I says:

"Why, Jim?"

"Nemmine why, Huck—but he ain't comin' back no mo'. "

But I kept at him; so at last he says:

"Doan' you 'member de house dat was float'n down de river, en dey wuz a man in dah, kivered up, en I went in en unkivered him en didn' let you come in? Well, den, you k'n git yo' money when you wants it; kase dat wuz him."

TOM'S LIBERALITY.

Tom's most well, now, and got his bullet around his neck on a watch-guard for a watch, and is always seeing what time it is, and so there ain't nothing more to write about, and I am rotten glad of it, because if I'd a knowed what a trouble it was to make a book I wouldn't a tackled it and

1. Mark Twain began a narrative of "Huck Finn and Tom Sawyer among the Indians" in the summer of 1884 but never finished it.

ain't agoing to no more. But I reckon I got to light out for the Territory ahead of the rest, because aunt Sally she's going to adopt me and sivilize me and I can't stand it. I been there before.

THE END, YOURS TRULY HUCK FINN.

CONTEXTS
AND
SOURCES

MARK TWAIN

[Letters about *Huckleberry Finn*]†
To W. D. Howells

[Hartford] July 5, [1875]

I have finished the story [*Tom Sawyer*] & didn't take the chap beyond boyhood. I believe it would be fatal to do it in any shape but autobiographically—like Gil Blas.¹ I perhaps made a mistake in not writing it in the first person. If I went on, now, & took him into manhood, he would just be like all the one-horse men in literature & the reader would conceive a hearty contempt for him. It is *not* a boy's book, at all. It will only be read by adults. It is only written for adults.

* * *

By & by I shall take a boy of twelve & run him on through life (in the first person) but not Tom Sawyer—he would not be a good character for it.

* * *

Elmira, Aug[ust] 9, [1876]

* * *

The double-barreled novel [perhaps *The Prince and the Pauper*] lies torpid. I found I could not go on with it. The chapters I had written were still too new and familiar to me. I may take it up next winter, but cannot tell yet; I waited and waited to see if my interest in it would not revive, but gave it up a month ago and began another boys' book—more to be at work than anything else. I have written 400 pages on it—therefore it is very nearly half done. It is Huck Finn's Autobiography. I like it only tolerably well, as far as I have got, and may possibly pigeonhole or burn the MS when it is done.

* * *

Elmira, July 21, [18]83

* * *

I haven't piled up MS so in years as I have done since we came here to the farm three weeks & a half ago. Why, it's like old times, to step

† The following excerpts from letters about the composition and publication of *Huckleberry Finn* are reprinted in chronological order. "Letter to W. D. Howells, Aug. 9 [1876]" and "Letter to Orion Clemens and family, in Keokuk, Ia., Elmira, July 21, '83," ("Private—Dear Ma and Orion and Mollie") in *Mark Twain's Letters*, Vol. 1, arranged by Albert Bigelow Paine. Copyright© 1917 by Mark Twain Company. By permission of Harper & Row, Publishers, Inc. The letter to Charles L. Webster is quoted from Hamlin Hill, ed., *Mark Twain's Letters to His Publishers* (Berkeley and Los Angeles: University of California Press, 1967). Copyright© 1967 by The Mark Twain Company; reprinted by permission of the Regents of the University of California Press. The rest, to Howells, appear in Frederick Anderson, William M. Gibson, and Henry Nash Smith, eds., *Selected Mark Twain–Howells Letters: 1872–1910* (Cambridge, Massachusetts: Harvard University Press, 1967). Reprinted by permission of the Mark Twain Foundation.
1. Hero of Alain René Le Sage's picaresque classic *The History of Gil Blas de Santillane* (1715–35). This letter indicates that Mark Twain was concerned with narrative point of view from the inception of *Huckleberry Finn*.

straight into the study, damp from the breakfast table, & sail right in & sail right on, the whole day long, without thought of running short of stuff or words. I wrote 4000 words to-day & I touch 3000 & upwards pretty often, & don't fall below 2600 on any working day. And when I get fagged out, I lie abed a couple of days & read & smoke, & then go it again for 6 or 7 days. I have finished one small book, & am away along in a big one that I half-finished two or three years ago. I expect to complete it in a month or six weeks or two months more. And *I* shall *like* it, whether anybody else does or not. It's a kind of companion to Tom Sawyer. There's a raft episode from it in second or third chapter of Life on the Mississippi.

* * *

To Jane Lampton Clemens

Elmira, July 21, [18]83

* * *

I haven't had such booming working-days for many years. I am piling up manuscript in a really astonishing way. I believe I shall complete, in two months, a book which I have been fooling over for 7 years. This summer it is no more trouble to me to write than it is to lie.

* * *

To W. D. Howells

Elmira, Aug[ust] 22, [18]83

How odd it seems, to sit down to write a letter with the feeling that you've got *time* to do it. But I'm done work, for this season, & so have got time. I've done two seasons' work in one, & haven't anything left to do, now, but revise. I've written eight or nine hundred MS pages in such a brief space of time that I mustn't name the number of days; *I* shouldn't believe it myself, & therefore of course couldn't expect you to. I used to restrict myself to 4 & 5 hours a day & 5 days in the week; but this time I've wrought from breakfast till 5.15 p.m. six days in the week; & once or twice I smouched a Sunday when the boss wasn't looking. Nothing is half so good as literature hooked on Sunday on the sly.

* * *

Hartford, Ap[ri]l 8, [18]84

It took my breath away, & I haven't recovered it yet, entirely—I mean the generosity of your proposal to read the proofs of Huck Finn.

Now if you *mean* it, old man—if you are in *earnest*—proceed, in God's name, & be by me forever blest. I cannot conceive of a rational man deliberately piling such an atrocious job upon himself; but if there is such a man, & you be that man, why then *pile it on*. It will cost me a pang every time I think of it. * * * The proofreading on the P & Pauper [*The Prince and the Pauper*] cost me the last rags of my religion.

To Charles L. Webster[2]

[Hartford], April 14, 1884

*   *   *

Get at your canvassing early, and drive it with all your might, with the intent and purpose of issuing on the 10th (or 15th) of next December (the best time in the year to tumble a big pile into the trade)—but if we haven't 40,000 orders then, we simply postpone publication till we've *got* them. It is a plain, simple policy, and would have saved both of my last books if it had been followed. There is not going to be any reason whatever, why this book should not succeed—and it shall and *must*.

*   *   *

To W. D. Howells

Elmira, Aug[ust] 31, [18]84

Thank you ever so much for reading that batch of the proof. It was a relief & respite, & I cursed my way through the rest & survived. I was most heavenly glad to get done with it. The sight of a proof-slip is always exasperating to me; but on this book it was maddening.

*   *   *

MARK TWAIN

From the *Autobiography*†

Tom Blankenship

In *Huckleberry Finn* I have drawn Tom Blankenship exactly as he was. He was ignorant, unwashed, insufficiently fed; but he had as good a heart as ever any boy had. His liberties were totally unrestricted. He was the only really independent person—boy or man—in the community, and by consequence he was tranquilly and continuously happy, and was envied by all the rest of us. We liked him; we enjoyed his society. And as his society was forbidden us by our parents, the prohibition trebled and quadrupled its value, and therefore we sought and got more of his society than of any other boy's. I heard, four years ago, that he was justice of the peace in a remote village in Montana, and was a good citizen and greatly respected.

[11, 174–75]

---

2. Clemens's nephew, and manager of the publishing company he established in New York under Webster's name. The firm sold books by subscription, a method some writers considered unfashionable but which helped make Mark Twain the best-paid writer of his day.
† From *Mark Twain's Autobiography*, ed. Albert Bigelow Paine (New York, 1924). Copyright © 1924 by Clara Gabrilowitsch. Reprinted by permission of Harper and Brothers. The bracketed volume and page numbers following each excerpt refer to the Harper edition.

The Quarles Farm

My uncle, John A. Quarles, was a farmer, and his place was in the country four miles from Florida. He had eight children and fifteen or twenty negroes, and was also fortunate in other ways, particularly in his character. I have not come across a better man than he was. I was his guest for two or three months every year, from the fourth year after we removed to Hannibal till I was eleven or twelve years old. I have never consciously used him or his wife in a book, but his farm has come very handy to me in literature once or twice. In *Huck Finn* and in *Tom Sawyer, Detective* I moved it down to Arkansas. It was all of six hundred miles, but it was no trouble; it was not a very large farm—five hundred acres, perhaps—but I could have done it if it had been twice as large. And as for the morality of it, I cared nothing for that; I would move a state if the exigencies of literature required it.

It was a heavenly place for a boy, that farm of my uncle John's. The house was a double log one, with a spacious floor (roofed in) connecting it with the kitchen. In the summer the table was set in the middle of that shady and breezy floor, and the sumptuous meals—well, it makes me cry to think of them. Fried chicken, roast pig; wild and tame turkeys, ducks, and geese; venison just killed; squirrels, rabbits, pheasants, partridges, prairie-chickens; biscuits, hot batter cakes, hot buckwheat cakes, hot "wheat bread," hot rolls, hot corn pone; fresh corn boiled on the ear, succotash, butterbeans, stringbeans, tomatoes, peas, Irish potatoes, sweet potatoes; buttermilk, sweet milk, "clabber"; watermelons, muskmelons, cantaloupes—all fresh from the garden; apple pie, peach pie, pumpkin pie, apple dumplings, peach cobbler—I can't remember the rest. The way that the things were cooked was perhaps the main splendor—particularly a certain few of the dishes. For instance, the corn bread, the hot biscuits and wheat bread, and the fried chicken. These things have never been properly cooked in the North—in fact, no one there is able to learn the art, so far as my experience goes. The North thinks it knows how to make corn bread, but this is mere superstition. Perhaps no bread in the world is quite so good as Southern corn bread, and perhaps no bread in the world is quite so bad as the Northern imitation of it. The North seldom tries to fry chicken, and this is well; the art cannot be learned north of the line of Mason and Dixon, nor anywhere in Europe. This is not hearsay; it is experience that is speaking. In Europe it is imagined that the custom of serving various kinds of bread blazing hot is "American," but that is too broad a spread; it is custom in the South, but is much less than that in the North. In the North and in Europe hot bread is considered unhealthy. This is probably another fussy superstition, like the European superstition that ice-water is unhealthy. Europe does not need ice-water and does not drink it; and yet, notwithstanding this, its word for it is better than ours, because it describes it, whereas ours doesn't. Europe calls it "iced" water. Our word describes water made from melted ice—a drink which has a characterless taste and which we have but little acquaintance with.

It seems a pity that the world should throw away so many good things merely because they are unwholesome. I doubt if God has given us any refreshment which, taken in moderation, is unwholesome, except microbes. Yet there are people who strictly deprive themselves of each and every eatable, drinkable, and smokable which has in any way acquired a shady reputation. They pay this price for health. And health is all they get for it. How strange it is! It is like paying out your whole fortune for a cow that has gone dry.

The farmhouse stood in the middle of a very large yard, and the yard was fenced on three sides with rails and on the rear side with high palings; against these stood the smoke-house; beyond the palings was the orchard; beyond the orchard were the negro quarters and the tobacco fields. The front yard was entered over a stile made of sawed-off logs of graduated heights; I do not remember any gate. In a corner of the front yard were a dozen lofty hickory trees and a dozen black walnuts, and in the nutting season riches were to be gathered there.

Down a piece, abreast the house, stood a little log cabin against the rail fence; and there the woody hill fell sharply away, past the barns, the corn-crib, the stables, and the tobacco-curing house, to a limpid brook which sang along over its gravelly bed and curved and frisked in and out and here and there and yonder in the deep shade of overhanging foliage and vines—a divine place for wading, and it had swimming pools, too, which were forbidden to us and therefore much frequented by us. For we were little Christian children and had early been taught the value of forbidden fruit.

[I, 90–99]

THE "POET LARIAT," THE "SWEET SINGER OF MICHIGAN," AND YOUNG SAM CLEMENS†

BLOODGOOD H. CUTTER: On the Death of His Beloved Wife, March 24, 1881

The tyrant, Death did my home invade,
In his cold embrace my wife he laid;
So sudden and fatal was the blow,
She had to yield and from me go.

---

† Emmeline Grangerford's "Ode to Stephen Dowling Bots, Dec'd." imitates the sentimental and only semiliterate effusions of such versifiers as Bloodgood Haviland Cutter (1817–1906) and Julia A. Moore (1847–1920). Cutter, the "poet lariat" of the *Quaker City* excursion to the Holy Land as reported in *Innocents Abroad* (1869), was inspired by every aspect of the trip, including seasickness, the health authorities at Naples, and his fellow passengers. Of these last, he wrote: "One droll person there was on board / The passengers called him 'Mark Twain;' / He'd talk and write all sort of stuff, / In his queer way, would it explain." Clemens gleefully encouraged Cutter to publish *The Long Island Farmer's Poems, Lines Written on the "Quaker City" Excursion to Palestine, and other Poems* (New York, 1886), the source of the present selection. Julia A. Moore, known as the "Sweet Singer of Michigan," was moved to verse by the deaths of little children, such perils as choking on roast beef, and the Ashtabula bridge disaster. One of her "admirers," Clemens said that she had "the touch that makes an intentionally humorous episode pathetic and an intentionally pathetic one funny." "Little Andrew" is taken from *The Sentimental Song Book* (Cleveland, 1877). "To Jennie" and "To Mollie" are reprinted from *The Works of Mark Twain*, Vol. 15, edited by Edgar Marquess Branch, Robert H. Hirst, and Harriet Elinor Smith (Berkeley: University of California Press, 1979).

When the doctor said her end was near,
It did affect me so severe;
It seemed to paralyze my brains,
And the circulation of my veins.

When I went up into her room,
I quickly did perceive her doom;
So fatal, then, did seem her case,
The mark of death was in her face.

Oh! 'twas the sad agony of my life,
To see the death gasping of my wife;
Then calmly yielding up her breath,
There in the cold embrace of death.

So quietly she seemed to rest,
With her cold hands across her breast;
Free from all pain and sorrow too,
Her face still looked lovely to my view.

As if her spirit was at rest
In the pure regions of the blest;
That, I sincerely do believe,
Though for my loss I sadly grieve.

In sadness now I mourn! I mourn,
For her who never will return;
Wife of my youth, my heart's delight,
Forever banished from my sight.

After I bade my last adieu,
The grave soon hid her from my view;
Tears from my eyes like fountains run,
When I did lose this faithful one.

If the Lord who gave took her away,
I must submit and to Him pray;
To enable me this trial to bear,
And trust to His Almighty care.

For forty years He did her spare,
And in my trials she did share;
When sick, to me she was so kind,
To ease my pain, to cheer my mind.

Bind up my wounds, to bathe my head,
Sit up by night by my sick bed;
Try many ways to me relieve—
Till that was done, would sit and grieve.

Now she is taken from the earth,
More keenly I do feel her worth!

On none like her I can depend,
I've lost! I've lost my dearest friend.

Perhaps my loss is now her gain:
She's free from sickness, care and pain;
But the debt of nature all must pay,
At a sooner or a later day.

Her spirit seems whispering in my ear,
"Weep not for me, my husband dear;
O! do your duty there below,
Until the Lord call you also."
(Little Neck, L. I., April, 1881)

JULIA A. MOORE: Little Andrew

Andrew was a little infant,
And his life was two years old;
He was his parents' eldest boy,
And he was drowned, I was told.
His parents never more can see him
In this world of grief and pain,
And Oh! they will not forget him
While on earth they do remain.

On one bright and pleasant morning
His uncle thought it would be nice
To take his dear little nephew
Down to play upon a raft,
Where he was to work upon it,
And this little child would company be—
The raft the water rushed around it,
Yet he the danger did not see.

This little child knew no danger—
Its little soul was free from sin—
He was looking in the water,
When, alas, this child fell in.
Beneath the raft the water took him,
For the current was so strong,
And before they could rescue him
He was drowned and was gone.

Oh! how sad were his kind parents
When they saw their drowned child,
As they brought him from the water,
It almost made their hearts grow wild.

Oh! how mournful was the parting
From that little infant son.

Friends, I pray you, all take warning,
Be careful of your little ones.

SAM CLEMENS: To Jennie[1]

Good-bye! a kind good-bye,
  I bid you now, my friend,
And though 'tis sad to speak the word,
  To destiny I bend.

And though it be decreed by Fate,
  That we ne'er meet again,
Your image, graven on my heart,
  Forever shall remain.

Aye, in my heart thoult have a place,
  Among the friends held dear,—
Nor shall the hand of Time efface
The *memories* written there.
                              Good-bye,
                              S. L. C.

To Mollie

All the earth with buds is teeming,—
  Bursting into life and light,—
The morning sun is kindly beaming,
  And lingering Winter takes his flight.

Long absent Spring, to Earth returning,
  Is welcomed by the *bowing* trees,
While soaring birds, the forest spurning,
  Are greeting her with songs of praise.

Green is the earth, and cloudless is the sky—
  Peace reigns within the hearts of men;
Clouds and Winter, vanquished, fly—
  Oh, may they ne'er return again!

Years of sorrow and trouble will over you pass,
  And the ties of your Earth-home be riven,
But your *Winter* of Woe will give place at the last,
  To a *Spring* everlasting in Heaven!
                              S. C.

---

1. Mark Twain, or rather Sam Clemens, had not always been immune to the deadly conventional-ism of the verse he parodies in *Huckleberry Finn*. As a young man in Keokuk, Iowa, Clemens himself wrote, without apparent irony, these effusions to young ladies in times of distress. "Jen-nie" was Ann Virginia Ruffner, with whom Clemens socialized briefly in 1853 before she left town; "Mollie" was Mary Eleanor Stotts, who married Clemens's older brother Orion in Decem-ber 1854.

CONFIDENTIAL TERMS TO AGENTS.

MARK TWAIN'S NEW BOOK.

Adventures of Huckleberry Finn.

Tom Sawyer's Companion.

☞MAGNIFICENT AND UNPARALLED OFFER TO CANVASSERS.☜

A CHANCE TO MAKE MONEY FOR ALL.

TO EVERY CANVASSER selling **50** copies of the book, we will send FIVE additional copies **FREE**.
TO EVERY CANVASSER selling **100** copies of the book, we will send TEN additional copies **FREE**.
TO EVERY CANVASSER selling **150** copies of the book, we will send FIFTEEN additional **FREE**.
TO EVERY CANVASSER selling **200** copies of the book, we will send TWENTY additional **FREE**.
FOR ALL sales above two hundred copies, agents will receive FIVE COPIES FREE for every FIFTY copies sold. To take advantage of the above unprecedented offer, the books must be sold to bona fide subscribers, at the full retail price. The above premiums are entirely in addition to the liberal discounts offered below.

HARD FACTS.

Five Hundred and Twenty-Five Thousand, over Half Million Copies Mark Twain's Books

Have been sold in this country alone; to say nothing of the immense sales in England and Germany.

Mark Twain's Books are the Quickest Selling in the World.

☞AGENTS: Secure Easy Work and Sure Pay by Getting a Mark Twain Agency.

HOW TO GET AN AGENCY.

Among the circulars sent, you will notice one in blank, headed "APPLICATION FOR AGENCY." You will fill this out, naming the amount enclosed and the book and territory wanted. To each agent is given a certain field, and he must not canvass outside the prescribed limits. His first choice of territory is given him if it is not already assigned; if it is, his second or third choice is given; provided he gives us satisfactory evidence of his ability and experience to work the territory, and conduct the agency successfully—we reserving the right to cancel the agency if not so conducted. Upon the receipt of this "APPLICATION FOR AGENCY" properly filled out, with proper amount inclosed for outfit, the territory asked for is assigned, the outfit forwarded and the applicant informed that he has an agency and the sole and the exclusive sale of the book in the territory assigned. If he is a new agent, advice is given him how to get to work, and such other instruction as will guarantee success.

OUTFIT FOR CANVASSING.

This consists of a Bound Prospectus Book, fully representing the work; Showing the style of Binding, Paper Size of Page, Type, Engravings, etc. Also Circulars. Blanks. Notices and Private Instruction-Book teaching the agent how to proceed with the business. **These are sent Post-Paid for 75 Cents,** which must invariably accompany all orders for Canvassing Books.

POSITIVELY NO PROSPECTUSES GIVEN AWAY.

The amount paid for outfit deducted on first order of ten or more copies.

We Furnish Books to Agents as Follows:

			Retail Prices.	To Agents.	Agents' Profit
In Fine English Cloth Binding,	Plain Edges	....	$3.50 Style.	$2.10.	$1.40.
In Leather Library,	" Sprinkled,	"	$4.00 "	$2.40.	$1.60.
In Half Morocco,	" Marbled,	"	$5.50 "	$3.30.	$2.20.

Although this is a companion book to "Adventures of Tom Sawyer," yet each book is complete in itself.

☞SPECIAL ADDITIONAL INDUCEMENTS.☜

WE WILL CHARGE YOU NOTHING FOR PACKING BOXES. We will furnish all books given to editors for notices at one-half agents' prices; but in every instance a copy of the paper containing the notice, for which a book is wanted, must be received by us.

We allot agents certain specified territory to canvass. No other agent is allowed to go into that territory so long as the agent to whom it is assigned canvasses satisfactorily, and abides by rules and regulations. We sell the book exclusively by subscription, and every agent pledges to do the same. Finally, we give you a book the people want, by the greatest living humorist in the world.

If you can act as agent for us, please signify your willingness at your earliest possible convenience. If unable to do so, PLEASE OBLIGE US by handing this to some INTELLIGENT PERSON of your acquaintance whom you think might be willing to act in your stead. The very reasonable price of this work brings it within the reach of all classes. Those applying immediately, with remittances, will secure a choice territory.

When you write to us, please give your POST OFFICE address in full, naming the TOWNSHIP as well as the COUNTY in which you live. Please name the territory you prefer to canvass.

Hoping that you will at once engage with us in the sale of this, the most popular and salable book of the age, we remain very respectfully yours,

OCCIDENTAL PUBLISHING CO.

120 Sutter Street,   **San Francisco, Cal.**

† Issued by the publisher who served as Mark Twain's general agent for the Pacific Coast, this circular, written and designed by Webster and Company, illustrates how subscription publication was financed in the nineteenth century. It is reprinted from *The Works of Mark Twain*, Vol. 8, edited by Walter Blair and Victor Fischer (Berkeley: University of California Press, 1988).

A BANNED BOOK: ONE HUNDRED YEARS OF "TROUBLE" FOR HUCK'S BOOK†

Boston *Transcript*, March 1885

The Concord (Mass.) Public Library committee has decided to exclude Mark Twain's latest book from the library. One member of the committee says that, while he does not wish to call it immoral, he thinks it contains but little humor, and that of a very coarse type. He regards it as the veriest trash. The librarian and the other members of the committee entertain similar views, characterizing it as rough, coarse and inelegant, dealing with a series of experiences not elevating, the whole book being more suited to the slums than to intelligent, respectable people.

Springfield *Republican*, March 1885

The Concord public library committee deserves well of the public by their action in banishing Mark Twain's new book, 'Huckleberry Finn,' on the ground that it is trashy and vicious. It is time that this influential pseudonym should cease to carry into homes and libraries unworthy productions. Mr. Clemens is a genuine and powerful humorist, with a bitter vein of satire on the weaknesses of humanity which is sometimes wholesome, sometimes only grotesque, but in certain of his works degenerates into a gross trifling with every fine feeling. The trouble with Mr. Clemens is that he has no reliable sense of propriety. His notorious speech at an *Atlantic* dinner, marshalling Longfellow and Emerson and Whittier in vulgar parodies in a Western miner's cabin, illustrated this, but not in much more relief than the 'Adventures of Tom Sawyer' did, or these Huckleberry Finn stories, do. . . . They are no better in tone than the dime novels which flood the blood-and-thunder reading population. Mr. Clemens has made them smarter, for he has an inexhaustible fund of 'quips and cranks and wanton wiles,' and his literary skill is, of course, superior; but their moral level is low, and their perusal cannot be anything less than harmful.

MARK TWAIN: Replies to the Newspapers

"Prefatory Remark"†

Huckleberry Finn is not an imaginary person. He still lives; or rather, *they* still live; for Huckleberry Finn is two persons in one— namely, the author's two uncles, the present editors of the Boston

---

† On April 4, 1885, Clemens instructed Charles L. Webster to include in future editions of *Huckleberry Finn* a "Prefatory Remark" aimed at newspaper attacks like those quoted above. Mrs. Clemens, however, vetoed the retort, reprinted here from Hamlin Hill, ed., *Mark Twain's Letters to His Publishers: 1867–1894* (Berkeley and Los Angeles, University of California Press, 1967). Copyright © 1967 by The Mark Twain Company; reprinted by permission of the University of California Press.

Advertiser and the Springfield *Republican.* In character, language, clothing, education, instinct, and origin, he is the painstakingly and truthfully drawn photograph and counterpart of these two gentlemen as they were in the time of their boyhood, forty years ago. The work has been most carefully and conscientiously done, and is exactly true to the originals, in even the minutest particulars, with but one exception, and that a trifling one: this boy's language has been toned down and softened, here and there, in deference to the taste of a more modern and fastidious day.

Letter to the Omaha *World-Herald*

York Beach, M[ain]e, August 23, 1902

Your telegram has arrived, but I have already said all I want to say concerning Huck Finn's new adventures, there is no need to say it over again. . . . I am fearfully afraid this noise is doing much harm. It has started a number of hitherto spotless people to reading "Huck Finn," out of natural human curiosity to learn what this is all about—people who had not heard of him before, people whose morals will go to rack and ruin now.

The publishers are glad, but it makes me want to borrow a handkerchief and cry. I should be sorry to think it was the publishers themselves that got up this entire little flutter to enable them to unload a book that was taking too much room in their cellars, but you never can tell what a publisher will do. I have been one myself.

JOHN H. WALLACE: The Case against *Huck Finn*†

The *Adventures of Huckleberry Finn,* by Mark Twain, is the most grotesque example of racist trash ever written. During the 1981–82 school year, the media carried reports that it was challenged in Davenport, Iowa; Houston, Texas; Bucks County, Pennsylvania; and, of all places, Mark Twain Intermediate School in Fairfax County, Virginia. Parents in Waukegan, Illinois, in 1983 and in Springfield, Illinois, in 1984 asked that the book be removed from the classroom—and there are many challenges to this book that go unnoticed by the press. All of these are coming from black parents and teachers after complaints from their children or students, and frequently they are supported by white teachers, as in the case of Mark Twain Intermediate School.

For the past forty years, black families have trekked to schools in numerous districts throughout the country to say, "This book is not good for our children," only to be turned away by insensitive and

---

† Written by a public school official who opposed the teaching of *Huckleberry Finn* at the Mark Twain Intermediate School (Fairfax County, Virginia), this essay is excerpted from *Satire or Evasion? Black Perspectives on "Huckleberry Finn,"* ed. James S. Leonard, Thomas A. Tenney, and Thadious M. Davis (Durham: Duke University Press, 1992) 16–24. Reprinted by permission of the Duke University Press.

often unwittingly racist teachers and administrators who respond, "This book is a classic." Classic or not, it should not be allowed to continue to cause our children embarrassment about their heritage.

Louisa May Alcott, the Concord Public Library, and others condemned the book as trash when it was published in 1885. The NAACP and the National Urban League successfully collaborated to have *Huckleberry Finn* removed from the classrooms of the public schools of New York City in 1957 because it uses the term "nigger." In 1969 Miami-Dade Junior College removed the book from its classrooms because the administration believed that the book created an emotional block for black students which inhibits learning. It was excluded from the classrooms of the New Trier High School in Winnetka, Illinois, and removed from the required reading list in the state of Illinois in 1976.

My own research indicates that the assignment and reading aloud of *Huckleberry Finn* in our classrooms is humiliating and insulting to black students. It contributes to their feelings of low self-esteem and to the white students' disrespect for black people. It constitutes mental cruelty, harassment, and outright racial intimidation to force black students to sit in the classroom with their white peers and read *Huckleberry Finn*. The attitudes developed by the reading of such literature can lead to tensions, discontent, and even fighting. If this book is removed from the required reading lists of our schools there should be improved student-to-student, student-to-teacher, and teacher-to-teacher relationships.

*   *   *

EARL F. BRIDEN

Kemble's "Specialty" and the Pictorial Countertext of *Huckleberry Finn*†

In a *Colophon* article of February 1930. Edward Windsor Kemble recalled a decisive event in his early career, his commission to illustrate *Adventures of Huckleberry Finn*. It was his drawings for Mark Twain's second book of boyhood, he pointed out, and specifically a picture he had done of Jim, that "started something in my artistic career." For this "Negro Jim" caught the fancy of the *Century Magazine* editors, who engaged Kemble to work exclusively for their magazine. Thus Kemble got to illustrate the works of a number of Southern writers, including George W. Cable, Richard Malcolm Johnson, and Thomas Nelson Page, and in time he became established "as a delineator of the South, the Negro being my specialty." By 1930 Kemble's "specialty" had carried him through a career of some forty-five years.[1] In short, his *Huck Finn* illustrations amounted to a Twainian turning point in Kemble's life as an artist.

† From the *Mark Twain Journal* 26.2 (Fall 1988): 2–14. Reprinted by permission.
1. E. W. Kemble, "Illustrating *Huckleberry Finn*," *Colophon* 1 (1930): 44–45.

However, like Mark Twain's recollections of his past, which often are in fact intriguing fictions, Kemble's account in "Illustrating *Huckleberry Finn*" is both unreliable in its details and provocatively suggestive in what it discloses about Twain's intentions for his second boy-book. A reexamination of the *Huck Finn* illustrations in the context of Kemble's early career will help to straighten out the historical record; more importantly, it will reveal that, in retaining Kemble, Twain was in effect authorizing a pictorial narrative which runs counter to major implications of his verbal text. For Kemble's drawings rewrite the Huck-Jim relationship by reducing Jim, whom Huck gradually recognizes as an individualized human being, to a simple comic type, a stock figure in an emerging pictorial tradition.

In late February 1884, Twain decided to establish his own publishing house and produce *Huck Finn* himself. With his nephew, Charles L. Webster, at the head of the firm, he had complete control, for the first time in his career, over the important choice of an illustrator for his work. On 31 March he wrote to Webster asking about an artist on the staff of *Life* magazine:

> Is that artist's name *Kemble?*—I *cannot* recall that man's name. Is that it? There *is* a Kemble on "Life," but is he the man who illustrated the applying of electrical protectors to door-knobs, door-mats &c & electrical hurriers to messengers, waiters, &c., 4 or 5 weeks ago. *That* is the man I want to try.[2]

The drawing that Twain remembered was "Some Uses for Electricity," a cartoon which had appeared in the 3 March issue of *Life*. For all his uncertainty about the authorship of this picture, however, Twain was clearly acquainted with the work of "a Kemble" on the magazine. Nor is this surprising, since by then Kemble had been a regular contributor to *Life* for a year and had been listed among its staff artists since 29 March 1883, the third month of the new magazine's existence; moreover his cartoons had also appeared regularly in the New York *Daily Graphic* since 1880. Thus, Twain's speedy decision to employ the young artist for the *Huck Finn* pictures was probably a result of his familiarity with Kemble's magazine illustrations. For although Kemble was only 23 years old and had no experience whatever as an illustrator of novels, by 10 April 1884 Twain had looked at samples of his work and selected him for the job, agreeing to his $1200 asking price.[3] By 12 April he was urging Webster to "Let Kemble rush—time is already growing short."[4]

2. Samuel Webster, ed., *Mark Twain: Business Man* (Boston: Little, Brown, 1946), p. 246. In her doctoral dissertation, *Picture and Text: A Theory of Illustrated Fiction in the Nineteenth Century* (Los Angeles: University of California, 1977), Teona Tone Gneiting speculates that, in choosing the cartoonist for the *Huck Finn* drawings, Twain indicated he "wanted an illustrator who could pick up on the comic/satiric elements . . . and interpret them visually for the reader" (p. 200). She adds, however, that Twain did not want "the illustrations to be cartoons or caricatures, but rather . . . to reflect some of the zest and originality he saw in the electricity cartoon" (201). My point, of course, is that Kemble's drawings of Jim are squarely in the cartoon tradition.
3. For details on this sequence of events, see Textual Introduction, *Adventures of Huckleberry Finn*, ed. Walter Blair and Victor Fischer (Berkeley and Los Angeles: University of California Press, 1988), pp. 439–40. As this Introduction notes, Webster in fact bargained Kemble down to $1000 for the job.
4. *Mark Twain: Business Man*, p. 248.

Kemble's narrative of these career-launching events is misleading on a number of points. For example, he recalls negotiating a $2000 commission, largely on the strength of Twain's enthusiastic response to "a small picture of a little boy being stung by a bee," a boy resembling the writer's conception of Huck.[5] It is his reconstruction of the circumstances giving rise to his "speciality," however, that is especially troublesome. In October 1884, Twain had agreed to let *Century Magazine* publish a short—and unspecified—excerpt from *Huck Finn* and had given editor Richard Watson Gilder a set of unbound pages from the forthcoming American edition of the novel from which to make his selection.[6] (*Century* would in fact publish selections from *Huck Finn*, including some of Kemble's drawings, in December 1884 and January and February 1885, i.e., just before the appearance of the first American edition.) According to Kemble, when Gilder and *Century* art director W. Lewis Frazer saw his drawings of Jim, they asked him to call on them and display additional samples of his work. Kemble's story of the ensuing job-landing transaction goes as follows:

> I went to *Life* and borrowed a few originals, but not one picture contained a Negro type.
> "We want to see some of your Negro drawings," Mr. Frazer said.
> "I have none," I replied. "I've never made any until this one in Huck Finn."
> The art editor looked dubious. "I have several stories I would like to have you illustrate, but they are all of the South."
> "Let me try," I urged, "and if they do not suit the text you need not use or pay me for them."
> I made the drawings. Mr. Frazer nodded his head as he looked at them.
> "I guess they'll go. We'll strike off some proofs and send them to the authors and see what they say."[7]

The authors approved, Kemble got the *Century* job, and his black character "types," as he repeatedly calls them in his *Colophon* article, caught on with the magazine-reading public and became his métier in a period of illustrator-specialists. As Francis Martin, Jr., points out, "Kemble became so identified with them [i.e., drawings of black subjects] that there is the erroneous impression that he drew only images of the Negro, when, in fact, he worked with many themes. . . ."[8]

Kemble's remark that he had never made any drawings of a "Negro type" before he did his picture of Jim for *Huck Finn* is wildly erroneous, however. As his obituary in the *New York Times* of 20 September 1933 points out, Kemble had drawn black characters for *Life*, although it is

5. Kemble, 42. My examination of *Life* for this period has turned up no drawing of this description. Kemble may have been thinking of a drawing he contributed to *Mark Twain's Library of Humor*, first published in 1888 and appearing as a photographic reprint in 1969 (New York: Bonanza Books). The drawing of the bee-stung boy appeared on p. 649.
6. See *Huckleberry Finn*, pp. 484–85.
7. Kemble, 44.
8. Francis Martin, "Edward Windsor Kemble, A Master of Pen and Ink," *American Art Review*, 3 (Jan.–Feb. 1976), 58.

not true that "For *Life* he made his first Negro pictures."[9] The fact of the matter is that Kemble had begun to develop his stylistic approach to black subjects—an approach involving comic typification—during his early years on the staff of the *Daily Graphic*. Some of his composite cartoons for the *Graphic* included black subjects; and, as the figure from the cover-piece of 2 October 1882 suggests, these drawings often played on old stereotypes—in this case, of the black as henhouse robber.[1] On occasion, too, the *Graphic* published full-page cartoons which similarly foreshadowed his *Life* drawings. For example, "The First Snow," which appeared in the issue of 28 November 1882, points ahead to the image of the simple, easily impressed black man that would repeatedly find its way into the pages of *Life*. And, as Martin notes, it was during his early years as a staff cartoonist on the *Graphic* that Kemble had introduced his soon-to-be-famous drawings of the "Gold Dust Twins," cherubic black children who appeared in advertisements for Fairbank's Washing Powder.[2]

More importantly, the pictures Kemble borrowed from the files of *Life* to show to the *Century* editors could have included a gallery of black characters. His first contribution of a black cartoon figure to *Life* had appeared on 17 May 1883, and by April 1884, when Twain chose him for the *Huck Finn* job, *Life* had published a dozen drawings of this sort, including Kemble's illustrations for Henry G. Carleton's comic serial, *The Thompson Street Poker Club*, which was also published in book form, complete with Kemble's drawings from *Life*, in 1884.[3] Thus Carleton's book made its appearance several months before the American edition of *Huck Finn*, which was published in February 1885.

In short, Kemble had marked out his area of specialization well in advance of the *Huck Finn* commission. And in view of Twain's acquaintance with the work of "a Kemble" in *Life*, it is difficult to believe that he was unfamiliar with Kemble's stylistic approach to black subjects when the Webster company retained the artist. Certainly a comparison of Kemble's drawings of Jim with his presentation of black characters in *Life* shows an obvious stylistic consistency. In both cases the black figure is treated in essentially the fashion of the *Graphic* pieces, i.e., as a comic type bordering on caricature, his features and postures exaggerated, with the result that any distinct personality and individual reality are absorbed into what amounts to a racial abstraction.

This consistency is most apparent in Kemble's picture of Jim in Chapter 2 of the novel, a drawing which repeats the essential details of a Kemble cartoon which had appeared in *Life* on 6 September 1883.

9. *New York Times*, 20 September 1933, L21. Perhaps the most misleading account of Kemble's early career is provided by his model for the *Huck Finn* drawings, who remarks that "In the early part of 1884 he [Kemble] was famous all over the world as a portrayer of negro characters, and did a lot of work for *Harper's Century, Graphic, Life, McClure's* and *Colliers*." See Courtland Morris, "The Model for Huck Finn," *Mark Twain Quarterly*, 2:4 (Summer/Fall 1938), 22–23.
1. For access to the *Daily Graphic* I am indebted to the New York Public Library Annex and Yale University Library; for use of materials from *Life*, to the Providence Public Library and the Rockefeller Library, Brown University.
2. Martin, 57. For a sample of Kemble's Gold Dust Twins cartoon-advertising see Martin, 55.
3. Henry G. Carleton, *The Thompson Street Poker Club* (London: George Routledge & Sons, 1884).

Complete with bucket, baggy chest-high pants held up by a single gallus, frayed straw hat, and look of comic indignation, Kemble's Jim seems drawn more from his *Life* counterpart than from any information supplied by Twain's text. True, Kemble includes the detail of the five-cent piece that Jim keeps "around his neck with a string"; the text, in other words, is not utterly ignored. But neither here nor in any other drawing of Jim is his most distinguishing physical feature, his prophetically "hairy arms en a hairy breas'," in evidence, as Beverly David rightly notes. Her assessment of this omission suggests its oddity: "Though Jim's hairiness can be dismissed as an oversight on the part of Kemble as a New York illustrator unaware of Negro characteristics, it is a strange error for Mark Twain not to catch if hairiness was his intention for Jim. After all, he knew Negro characteristics well and realized that hair or lack of it would make his Nigger Jim different from the usual Negro."[4]

Further comparisons indicate, however, that Kemble's Jim is indeed the "usual Negro," a repetition, in other words, of the comic stereotypes which had been appearing in *Life* magazine. In the early chapters of the novel Jim is drawn repeatedly as an icon of wide-eyed, slack-jawed astonishment, whether he is seeing what he thinks is a ghost, approaching a cave entrance, talking with Huck, or peering into the window of the House of Death. These pictures are clearly modeled after the open-mouthed, pop-eyed cartoon figures that Kemble had been doing for *Life*—for example, Brer Abe in "New Year's Day in Mokeville," which had appeared in the issue of 27 December 1883, or the character on the viewer's right in "Mr. Dilsey in Hoboken," from the issue of 10 April 1884.

In some measure Jim's affinity with these cartoon figures may be explained in terms of Kemble's methods of composition. In his *Colophon* article he describes how the *Huck Finn* commission induced him, for the first time in his artistic career, to employ a model instead of picking his "types out of the ether." Since his primary concern was his portrayal of Huck, he used a white school-boy, Cort Morris, who tallied with his idea of Twain's boy hero. However, Kemble had Morris sit for all of the novel's characters, man, woman, and child, black as well as white. The artist would simply deck the boy out in a rudimentary costume, ask him to strike an appropriate pose, and use him to make "a simple outline sketch." When he posed as Jim, the boy wore a "little black wool cap."[5] Thus Kemble's procedure in drawing Jim amounted to superimposing a type plucked from the ether of his imagination upon an outline drawn from his live model. The fact that he began the *Huck Finn* illustrations with only a portion of the manuscript and at times went ahead with no manuscript whatever (since he was pressed to meet short deadlines) also helps to explain his resort to stock comic figures.[6]

4. Beverly R. David, "The Pictorial *Huck Finn*: Mark Twain and His Illustrator, E. W. Kemble," *American Quarterly*, 26 (Oct. 1974), 337.
5. Kemble, 43–44.
6. See *Huckleberry Finn*, pp. 448–57, and David, 336–39, for discussion of these difficulties. Such accounts call into question the contention of Tak Sioui (John Hakac) that Kemble "knew the text quite intimately, having sifted some edited and unedited manuscript for his ideas." See *Huckleberry Finn: More Molecules* (Privately Printed, 1962), p. 17.

With no clear idea of the direction of Twain's character development and no time to capture its nuances in any case, Kemble simply called upon his experience as a creator of popular stereotypes. To do his pictures of Jim he evidently saw no need for a black male model.

The reduction of Jim to a comic type entailed a number of sacrifices. For one thing, Kemble threw away his opportunity to capture Jim's complexity in pictorial terms.[7] Generally speaking, Kemble's Jim harks back to his precursors in *Life* magazine in being represented, in virtually every instance, as a childlike figure capable of only the simplest feelings. Thus Jim is flattened out emotionally and intellectually and rendered as an image of whole-souled astonishment, or delight, or earnestness, or humility. This quality of childlike simplicity, of single- and perhaps simple-mindedness, is an essential feature of Kemble's magazine characters. His drawing of Tooter Williams, for example, which appeared in *Life* for 6 March 1884, presents Carleton's Thompson Street character as an embodiment of smugness: hat cocked rakishly over his eyes, arms folded in a congratulatory self-embrace, Tooter is *the* black show-off. In a cartoon in the *Life* issue of 3 April 1884, Kemble similarly depicts Brer Pewter as *the* black windbag, inflated with self-importance and holding forth in the posture of oratorical bombast.

Kemble's typification of Jim also made it impossible for him to chart Huck's shifting perception of his friend and comrade, a perception which moves from the abstract to the concrete, from his view of Jim as generic "nigger" to his recognition of Jim as individual human being. Trapped within a comic idiom, so to speak, Kemble's Jim can only remain a static type, a pictorial reminder of the emphasis of comedy, which is, as Maynard Mack notes, on the "typicality of human experience, as projected in persistent social species whose sufficient destiny is simply to go on revealing themselves to us"; such figures "do not *essentially* change."[8] The problem, however, is that Huck's Jim—and Twain's—is something more than a comic type, though it is certainly arguable that in the much-debated "evasion" chapters (33–43) Jim is returned to his status of the opening chapters, where he is little more than a minstrel-show figure and an object of white boys' pranks. But in Kemble's illustrations Jim never rises above his typicality.[9]

It is interesting that, while Twain found much to dislike about Kemble's pictures for *Huck Finn*, he never singled out the artist's drawings of Jim (or of other black characters, for that matter) for criticism. One explanation, of course, is that he was acquainted with Kemble's magazine pictures of blacks when he retained the artist and therefore found nothing at all surprising or upsetting about Kemble's characterization of blacks in *Huck Finn*. And yet Twain's objections to the pictures Kemble

7. I have in mind episodes such as Jim's subtle manipulation of Huck's feelings in chapter 16; Huck has left the raft intending to act according to his conscience and turn Jim in, but Jim's expressions of gratitude and appreciation deter the boy from his plan of betrayal.
8. Maynard Mack, Introduction to *Joseph Andrews* (New York: Holt, Rinehart, and Winston, 1948); rpt. in *Fielding: A Collection of Critical Essays*, ed. Ronald Paulson (Englewood Cliffs. N.J.: Prentice-Hall, 1962), p. 57.
9. On occasion Kemble does capture the sympathetic in Jim's character; see, for example, his picture of Jim asleep on the raft, a portrait of weariness and sorrow.

had done for roughly the first third of the book focused on the very stylistic qualities—exaggeration and distortion—under discussion here. On
24 May 1884 he continued a line of commentary that he had begun
earlier; having scrutinized some forty-eight of Kemble's drawings, he
wrote to Webster:[1]

> Some of the pictures are good, but none of them are very *very* good.
> The faces are generally ugly, & wrenched into over-expression
> amounting sometimes to distortion. As a rule (though not always)
> the people in these pictures are forbidding and repulsive. . . . An
> artist shouldn't follow a book too literally, perhaps—if this is the
> necessary result. And mind you, much of the drawing, in these pic-
> tures is careless & bad. The pictures will do—they will just barely
> do—& that is the best I can say for them.[2]

By 11 June, however, when he had examined another batch of drawings, Twain felt that Kemble had finally hit the stylistic target he had in
mind: "I *knew* Kemble had it in him," he told Webster, "if he would only
modify his violences & come down to careful, painstaking work. This
batch of pictures is most rattling good."[3]

Together, these letters serve to clarify Twain's intentions for the
Huck Finn illustrations. As David points out, Twain fully understood
that "what his 'genteel' audience saw in the illustrations would shape
their reading of the story and that the illustrations would manipulate
the responses of his readers." Of course, Twain's text bristles with
grotesque characters, acts of brutality, dead bodies, and robust satire
on false piety and gentility. The pictorial text was calculated, then, to
"tone down" the ugliness and violence of the verbal text and to deflect
the reader's attention away from anything offensive by putting in its
place "a comically irrelevant topic."[4] Kemble was decidedly not to follow this book "too literally." Thus Twain ruled out a drawing of the
lecherous old King kissing a girl at the camp meeting and advised Webster against "*any* pictures of the camp meeting," a subject, he judged,
that "won't *bear* illustrating."[5] Nor, apparently, was Kemble to encourage the reader to take Jim—and Huck's relationship with Jim—seriously. The reality of the black-white alliance and of the black hero was
to be suppressed pictorially, with the result that an additional source of
"genteel" uneasiness would be dissolved in pictorial humor. Twain's
choice of Kemble as the novel's illustrator virtually guaranteed this
result.

In selecting Kemble, in other words, Twain welcomed one form of
stereotyping to the pages of *Huck Finn*; he drew the line, however, at
another form. For his reaction to Kemble's rendition of Huck for the book's
cover design was his well-known comment, "All right & good, & will
answer, although the boy's mouth is a trifle more Irishy than necessary."[6]

1. For details see *Adventures of Huckleberry Finn*, pp. 454–55.
2. *Mark Twain: Business Man*, p. 255.
3. *Mark Twain: Business Man*, p. 260.
4. David, 334, 346,
5. *Mark Twain: Business Man*, p. 260.
6. *Mark Twain: Business Man*, p. 253.

Twain's objection to Huck's "Irishy" look probably reflected his awareness of an emerging comic type in magazine illustration of the 1880s. As a contributor to *Life*, Kemble had in fact done several cartoons depicting Irish figures. His drawing in the issue of 22 March 1883, for example, made pictorial capital of the Irishman's well-known fondness for drink, while a similarly disheveled and dissolute figure appeared in *Life* for 21 June 1883. In protesting against Huck's Irish look, then, Twain was almost certainly trying to forestall the reader's assumption, formed on the basis of the cover design, that the humor of *Huck Finn* was in this tradition of Irish stereotyping.

Twain's view of Kemble's market value doubtless induced him to retain the artist for one more production of the Webster Company, *Mark Twain's Library of Humor* (1888), an anthology of work by American comic writers which was assembled by Twain, William Dean Howells, and Charles H. Clark. Although some of Kemble's eight pictures of black characters in the *Library* indicate that he could tone down his style, others show his penchant for distortion carrying him into racist caricature. His illustration for a Josh Billings sketch, "The Alligator," seizes upon two details in the verbal text: Billings' remarks that the alligator is "az ugly to kontemplate az a congo darkey" and that alligators "are grate cowards, but ain't afraid ov yung pork, or little darkeys, and kan eat all the time . . ."[7]

Kemble accordingly depicts two black children struggling with an enormous alligator and expressing terror in what amounts to a comic iconography of bulging eyes and gaping mouths. A similar image appears in one of Kemble's illustrations of William T. Thompson's sketch "Christmas In Pineville," with its slapstick climax in which Major Jones is tumbled from a bag by his servant Cato.[8] Though Thompson provides no description of the black man's astonishment, Kemble saw in the event one more opportunity to serve up comic caricature. It was doubtless this liability to duplication and repetition of stereotypic images that turned Twain against the artist after the *Library of Humor* was produced. For in that book Twain found the "blackboard outlines" finally regrettable: "If Kemble illustrations for my last book were handed me today," he wrote, "I would understand how tiresome to me the sameness would get to be, when distributed through a whole book, and I would put them promptly in the fire."[9]

The *Library of Humor* was not Kemble's swansong, however, as an illustrator of Twain's works. The 1899 Harper & Brothers "Author's National Edition" of Twain's collected works contained five new drawings by Kemble—three for *Huckleberry Finn* and two for *Pudd'nhead Wilson*. Three of these illustrations present black characters and reveal that by the century's end Kemble was more than ever the "specialist" in black caricature. In the frontispiece of *Huck Finn*, for example, there are the familiar black children, all round eyes as they peep from behind

7. *Mark Twain's Library of Humor*, p. 370.
8. *Mark Twain's Library of Humor*, pp. 576–77.
9. *Mark Twain's Letters to His Publishers, 1867–1894*, ed. Hamlin Hill (Berkeley and Los Angeles: University of California Press, 1967), p. 254.

the apron of their mother, a grotesquely grinning, rollingpin-wielding mammy.

And, as Michael Patrick Hearn notes, in this same year Kemble added three more items to his gallery of *Huck Finn* drawings, pictures which appeared in a *New York World* supplement for 10 December 1899, while in 1933, the year of his death, he did one more, this time for the Limited Editions Club edition of the novel.[1]

It was in the late 1890s, certainly, that Kemble was producing those works which would prove especially offensive to the twentieth-century sensibility. By this period he was authoring his own books, with titles such as *Comical Coons* and *A Coon Alphabet* (both published in 1898), books whose hackneyed comic subjects and unequivocally racist illustrations would ironically win Kemble his widest popularity. *A Coon Alphabet* traffics in wearisome stereotypes of blacks as lazy, easily frightened, watermelon-loving children. Yet such drawings are stylistic echoes of earlier pictures. * * * Indeed his 1898 blacks are often of a stylistic piece with his earlier renditions. The figure in the frontispiece of *A Coon Alphabet*, for example, distinctly recalls his picture of the horn-blowing slave child in Chapter 35 of *Huck Finn*.[2]

Anyone who grants this stylistic consistency throughout Kemble's career as a "specialist" in black types must condemn him as a racist by twentieth-century standards and wonder, in light of Twain's choice of the illustrator for *Huck Finn*, about the writer's own racial attitudes. True, Twain's period of enthusiasm for Kemble's work was flanked by times of disappointment—first, in its crudity and, later, in its tiresome monotony. True, too, once Huck's story was written, Twain riveted his attention on business issues, decisions, above all, that would affect sales. Yet in approving Kemble's countertext for *Huck Finn*, a pictorial text that holds the black hero fast in the grip of comic typification, Twain might be said to have sold Jim down the river himself. At any rate, Joel Chandler Harris seems to me to summarize the case against the *Huck Finn* illustrations very aptly. Finding Kemble's work "too doggoned flip"[3] for his taste, Harris flatly repudiated any use of comic types in either literary or pictorial texts and defined the stylistic requirements that I, for one, would set for an illustrator of Huck's story: "Neither fiction nor illustrative art has any business with types," Harris remarked. "It must address itself to life, to the essence of life which is character, which is individuality."[4]

1. Michael Patrick Hearn, "Mark Twain, E. W. Kemble, and *Huckleberry Finn*," *American Book Collector*, 2 (Nov.–Dec. 1981), 18. Hearn reproduced the three *World* pictures and the title-page emblem of the Limited Editions Club *Huck Finn* in *The Annotated Huckleberry Finn* (New York: Clarkson N. Potter, Inc., 1981), pp. 106, 205, 230, and 44, respectively.
2. *Huckleberry Finn*, p. 302. For an examination of Kemble's racist cartoons in *Coon Alphabet*, see Elvin Holt, "*A Coon Alphabet* and the Comic Mask of Racial Prejudice," *Studies in American Humor*, 5 (Winter 1986–87), 307–18.
3. Joel Chandler Harris, letter to A. B. Frost dated 7 June 1892, cited by Beverly David, "Visions of the South: Joel Chandler Harris and His Illustrators," *American Literary Realism* (Summer 1976), 198.
4. In this editorial, which appeared in the Atlanta *Constitution* of 26 September 1892, Harris praised the artistry of A. B. Frost, whose illustrations, Harris felt, captured a distinctly American individuality and atmosphere. The editorial is cited by David, "Visions of the South," 198.

DAVID CARKEET

The Dialects in *Huckleberry Finn*†

*   *   *

Our conclusion, then, is that while it is not the case that there are seven and only seven distinct dialects in *Huckleberry Finn*, is *is* the case that there are seven distinct dialects which Clemens had in mind when he wrote the "Explanatory." These are as follows:

Missouri Negro: Jim (and four other minor characters)
Southwestern: Arkansas Gossips (Sister Hotchkiss et al.)
Ordinary "Pike County": Huck, Tom, Aunt Polly, Ben Rogers, Pap,
    Judith Loftus
Modified "Pike County": Thieves on the *Sir Walter Scott*
Modified "Pike County": King
Modified "Pike County": Bricksville Loafers
Modified "Pike County": Aunt Sally and Uncle Silas Phelps

The fact that intelligent sense can be made out of the preface falsifies the view that Clemens was joking when he wrote it. This view never had much merit anyway. While the last sentence of the "Explanatory" might raise a smile, there is nothing rib-splitting about a list of dialects. The existence of a separate comical preface (called "Notice" and published on a separate page in the first English and American editions) is irrelevant; it is certainly possible for an author to write two prefaces to a work, one comical and one serious.

Clemens's abiding interest in folk speech, his impatience with Harte's use of dialect, and his working notes on the dialects in *Huckleberry Finn* all point to earnestness in the representation of dialects in this novel—as does the evidence of extensive revision of dialect spellings. There are hundreds of corrections of dialect in the manuscript (or discrepancies between a dialect form in the manuscript and the final form in the first edition). A *just* might be corrected to *jest* in the manuscript, for example, and then end up as *jist* in the first edition. Such labored revision makes no sense if the "Explanatory" is frivolous.

Thus Clemens was serious when he wrote the "Explanatory." But he was also partly mistaken about the work he was describing. This makes for a blend of system with chaos which has either confused investigators or discouraged them at the outset. Also, while there is greater differentiation than stated in the "Explanatory" in terms of the number of distinguishable dialects, there is a somewhat smaller degree of differentiation of the dialects than one would expect from such a bold announcement. This is especially true of the varieties of "Pike County" dialect, where the differentiation is so fine that one must wonder what

† By a close linguistic analysis of the speech patterns of all the characters in *Huckleberry Finn*, David Carkeet has conclusively demonstrated that Mark Twain's "Explanatory" preface about dialects is to be taken seriously. This summary of his findings is from "The Dialects in *Huckleberry Finn*," *American Literature* 51.3 (November 1979): 315–32. Copyright 1979, Duke University Press. Reprinted with permission.

the author hoped the novel could gain from it. In this regard it is worth noting that the speakers of three of the four modified varieties of the "Pike County" dialect—the thieves on the *Sir Walter Scott*, the King, and the Bricksville Loafers—are morally reprehensible, and, in addition, that their speech differs from Huck's by virtue of features normally found in the speech of the blacks in the novel. The Bricksville Loafers' *gwyne*, for example, occurs elsewhere in the novel only in the speech of slaves. The same can be said for the King's palatalization, which in the manuscript is also given to the thieves on the *Sir Walter Scott*. This last group also loses *r* in phonetic environments similar to those where *r* is lost in Jim's speech (*befo'*, *yo'*), whereas Huck very rarely loses *r* and never loses it word-finally (e.g., *stabboard, whippowill*). One's first thought is that it is surprising that Clemens, in a novel concerned with exposing weaknesses in the conventional values of society, calls upon those values in the way he taints these characters' dialects—to "lower" them he draws them with features of black speech. But in doing this Clemens was merely reflecting linguistic reality in his time and, indeed, in the present century: the speech of lower-class rural whites in the South shares a great deal with the speech of blacks. In *Huckleberry Finn, gwyne*, palatalization, and *r*-lessness are—for both blacks and whites—physical signals of low social status, and—for whites only—physical signals of "substandard" morals. These white characters may share something of Jim's dialect, but they do not share in his goodness.

Finally, it is important to recognize the showmanship in the ambitious, seven-way dialectal differentiation and in the attention the author calls to it. Clemens composed *Huckleberry Finn* in the heyday of literary dialect in American literature, and no doubt he wanted to show what he too was capable of doing, especially with the "Pike County" dialect that he helped to create.

MARK TWAIN

A True Story, Repeated Word for Word as I Heard It†

It was summer time, and twilight. We were sitting on the porch of the farm-house, on the summit of the hill, and "Aunt Rachel" was sitting respectfully below our level, on the steps,—for she was our servant, and colored. She was of mighty frame and stature; she was sixty years old, but her eye was undimmed and her strength unabated. She was a cheerful, hearty soul, and it was no more trouble for her to laugh than it is for a bird to sing. She was under fire, now, as usual when the day was done. That is to say, she was being chaffed without mercy, and was

---

† Mark Twain's first contribution to the *Atlantic Monthly* (1874) and his first sustained attempt to represent African American speech. "Aunt Rachel" was actually Mary Ann Cord, a former slave, who was a servant at Quarry Farm, the Clemens family's summer home in Elmira, New York. Mark Twain reprinted "A True Story" in *Sketches New and Old* (1875). The 29-page manuscript is in the Barrett Collection of the University of Virginia Library and may be viewed, along with the illustrations by True Williams, at http://etext.lib.virginia.edu/railton/huckfinn/truestl.html.

enjoying it. She would let off peal after peal of laughter, and then sit with her face in her hands and shake with throes of enjoyment which she could no longer get breath enough to express. At such a moment as this a thought occurred to me, and I said:—

"Aunt Rachel, how is it that you've lived sixty years and never had any trouble?"

She stopped quaking. She paused, and there was a moment of silence. She turned her face over her shoulder toward me, and said, without even a smile in her voice:—

"Misto C—, is you in 'arnest?"

It surprised me a good deal; and it sobered my manner and my speech, too. I said:—

"Why, I thought—that is, I meant—why, you *can't* have had any trouble. I've never heard you sigh, and never seen your eye when there wasn't a laugh in it."

She faced fairly around, now, and was full of earnestness.

"Has I had any trouble? Misto C—, I's gwyne to tell you, den I leave it to you. I was bawn down 'mongst de slaves; I knows all 'bout slavery, 'case I been one of 'em my own se'f. Well, sah, my ole man—dat's my husban'—he was lovin' an' kind to me, jist as kind as you is to yo' own wife. An' we had chil'en—seven chil'en—an' we loved dem chil'en jist de same as you loves you' chil'en. Dey was black, but de Lord can't make no chil'en so black but what dey mother loves 'em an' wouldn't give 'em up, no, not for anything dat's in dis whole world.

"Well, sah, I was raised in ole Fo'ginny, but my mother she was raised in Maryland; an' my *souls!* she was turrible when she'd git started! My *lan'*! but she'd make de fur fly! When she'd git into dem tantrums, she always had one word dat she said. She'd straighten herse'f up an' put her fists in her hips an' say, 'I want you to understan' dat I wasn't bawn in de mash to be fool' by trash! I's one o' de ole Blue Hen's Chickens, I is!' 'Ca'se, you see, dat's what folks dat's bawn in Maryland calls deyselves, an' dey's proud of it. Well, dat was her word. I don't ever forgit it, beca'se she said it so much, an' beca'se she said it one day when my little Henry tore his wris' awful, an' most busted his head, right up at de top of his forehead, an' de niggers didn't fly aroun' fas' enough to 'tend to him. An' when dey talk' back at her, she up an' she says, 'Look-a-heah!' she says, 'I want you niggers to understan' dat I wasn't bawn in de mash to be fool' by trash! I's one o' de ole Blue Hen's Chickens, I is!' an' den she clar' dat kitchen an' bandage' up de chile herse'f. So I says dat word, too, when I's riled.

"Well, bymeby my ole mistis say she's broke, an' she got to sell all de niggers on de place. An' when I heah dat dey gwyne to sell us all off at oction in Richmon', oh de good gracious! I know what dat mean!"

Aunt Rachel had gradually risen, while she warmed to her subject, and now she towered above us, black against the stars.

"Dey put chains on us an' put us on a stan' as high as dis po'ch,—twenty foot high,—an' all de people stood aroun', crowds an' crowds. An' dey 'd come up dah an' look at us all roun', an' squeeze our arm, an' make us git up an' walk, an' den say, 'Dis one too ole,' or 'Dis one lame,' or 'Dis one don't 'mount to much.' An' dey sole my ole man, an' took him away, an' dey begin to sell my chil'en an' take *dem* away, an' I begin to cry; an' de man say, 'Shet up yo' dam blubberin',' an' hit me on de mouf wid his han'. An' when de las' one was gone but my little Henry, I grab' *him* clost up to my breas' so, an' I ris up an' says, 'You shan't take him away,' I says; 'I'll kill de man dat fetches him!' I says. But my little Henry whisper an' say, 'I gwyne to run away, an' den I work an' buy yo' freedom.' Oh, bless de chile, he always so good! But dey got him—dey got him, de men did; but I took and tear de clo'es mos' off of 'em, an' beat 'em over de head wid my chain; an' *dey* give it to *me*, too, but I didn't mine dat.

"Well, dah was my ole man gone, an' all my chil'en, all my seven chil'en—an' six of 'em I hadn't set eyes on ag'in to dis day, an' dat's twenty-two year ago las' Easter. De man dat bought me b'long' in New-bern, an' he took me dah. Well, bymeby de years roll on an' de waw come. My marster he was a Confedrit colonel, an' I was his family's cook. So when de Unions took dat town, dey all run away an' lef' me all by myse'f wid de other niggers in dat mons'us big house. So de big Union officers move in dah, an' dey ask me would I cook for *dem*. 'Lord bless you,' says I, 'dat's what I's *for*.'

"Dey wa'n't no small-fry officers, mine you, dey was de biggest dey is; an' de way dey made dem sojers mosey roun'! De Gen'l he tole me to boss dat kitchen; an' he say, 'If anybody come meddlin' wid you, you jist make 'em walk chalk; don't you be afeard,' he say; 'you's 'mong frens, now.'

"Well, I thinks to myse'f, if my little Henry ever got a chance to run away, he'd make to de Norf, o' course. So one day I comes in dah whah de big officers was, in de parlor, an' I drops a kurtchy, so, an' I up an' tole 'em 'bout my Henry, dey a-listenin' to my troubles jist de same as if I was white folks; an' I says, 'What I come for is beca'se if he got away and got up Norf whah you gemmen comes from, you might 'a' seen him, maybe, an' could tell me so as I could fine him ag'in; he was very little, an' he had a sk-yar on his lef' wris', an' at de top of his forehead.' Den dey look mournful, an' de Gen'l say, 'How long sence you los' him?' an' I say, 'Thirteen year.' Den de Gen'l say, 'He wouldn't be little no mo', now—he's a man!'

"I never thought o' dat befo'! He was only dat little feller to *me*, yit. I never thought 'bout him growin' up an' bein' big. But I see it den. None o' de gemmen had run across him, so dey couldn't do nothin' for me. But all dat time, do' I didn't know it, my Henry *was* run off to de Norf, years an' years, an' he was a barber, too, an' worked for hisse'f. An' bymeby, when de waw come, he ups an' he says, 'I's done barberin',' he says; 'I's gwyne to fine my ole mammy, less'n she's dead.' So he sole out an' went to whah dey was recruitin', an' hired hisse'f out to de colonel for his servant; en' den he went all froo de battles everywhah, huntin' for his ole mammy; yes indeedy, he'd hire to fust one officer an' den another, tell he'd ransacked de whole Souf; but you see I didn't know nufffin 'bout *dis*. How was I gwyne to know it?

"Well, one night we had a big sojer ball; de sojers dah at Newbern was always havin' balls an' carryin' on. Dey had 'em in my kitchen, heaps o' times, 'ca'se it was so big. Mine you, I was *down* on sich doin's; beca'se my place was wid de officers, an' it rasp' me to have dem common sojers cavortin' roun' my kitchen like dat. But I alway' stood aroun' an' kep' things straight, I did; an' sometimes dey'd git my dander up, an' den I'd make 'em clar dat kitchen, mine I *tell* you!

"Well, one night—it was a Friday night—dey comes a whole plattoon f'm a *nigger* ridgment dat was on guard at de house,—de house was head-quarters, you know,—an' den I was jist a-*bilin'*! Mad? I was jist a-*boomin'*! I swelled aroun', an' swelled aroun'; I jist was a-itchin' for 'em to do somefin for to start me. *An'* dey was a-waltzin' an a-dancin'! *my!* but dey was havin' a time! an' I jist a-swellin' an' a-swellin' up! Pooty soon, 'long comes *sich* a spruce young nigger a-sailin' down de room wid a yeller wench roun' de wais'; an' roun' an' roun' an' roun' dey went, enough to make a body drunk to look at 'em; an' when dey got abreas' o' me, dey went to kin' o' balancin' aroun', fust on one leg an' den on t'other, an' smilin' at my big red turban, an' makin' fun, an' I ups an' says, '*Git* along wid you!—rubbage!' De young man's face kin' o' changed, all of a sudden, for 'bout a second, but den he went to smilin' ag'in, same as he was befo'. Well, 'bout dis time, in comes some niggers dat played music an' b'long' to de ban', an' dey *never* could git along widout puttin' on airs. An' de very fust air dey put on dat night, I lit into 'em! Dey laughed, an' dat made me wuss. De res' o' de niggers got to laughin', an' den my soul *alive* but I was hot! My eye was jist ablazin'! I jist straightened myself up, so,—jist as I is now, plum to de ceilin', mos',—an' I digs my fists into my hips, an' I says, 'Look-a-heah!' I says, 'I want you niggers to understan' dat I wa'n't bawn in de mash to be fool' by trash! I's one o' de ole Blue Hen's Chickens, *I* is!' an' den I see dat young man stan' astarin' an' stiff, lookin' kin' o' up at de ceilin' like he fo'got somefin, an' couldn't 'member it no mo'. Well, I jist march' on dem niggers,—so, lookin' like a gen'l,—an' dey jist cave' away befo' me an' out at de do'. An' as dis young man was a-goin' out, I heah him say to another nigger, 'Jim,' he says, 'you go 'long an' tell de cap'n I be on han' 'bout eight o'clock in de mawnin'; dey's somefin on my mine,' he says; 'I don't sleep no mo' dis night. You go 'long,' he says, 'an' leave me by my own se'f.'

"Dis was 'bout one o'clock in de mawnin'. Well, 'bout seven, I was up an' on han', gittin' de officers' breakfast. I was a-stoopin' down by de stove,—jist so, same as if yo' foot was de stove,—an' I'd opened de stove do' wid my right han',—so, pushin' it back, jist as I pushes yo' foot,—an' I'd jist got de pan o' hot biscuits in my han' an' was 'bout to raise up, when I see a black face come aroun' under mine, an' de eyes a-lookin' up into mine, jist as I's a-lookin' up clost under yo' face now; an' I jist stopped *right dah*, an' never budged! jist gazed, an' gazed, so; an' de pan begin to tremble, an' all of a sudden I *knowed!* De pan drop' on de flo' an' I grab his lef' han' an' shove back his sleeve,—jist so, as I's doin' to you,—an' den I goes for his forehead an' push de hair back, so, an' 'Boy!' I says, 'if you an't my Henry, what is you doin' wid dis welt on yo' wris' an' dat sk-yar on yo' forehead? De Lord God ob heaven be praise', I got my own ag'in!'

"Oh, no, Misto C—, I hadn't had no trouble. An' no *joy!*"

MARK TWAIN

Sociable Jimmy†

[I sent the following home in a private letter, some time ago, from a certain little village. It was in the days when I was a public lecturer. I did it because I wished to preserve the memory of the most artless, sociable, and exhaustless talker I ever came across. He did not tell me a single remarkable thing, or one that was worth remembering; and yet he was himself so interested in his small marvels, and they flowed so naturally and comfortably from his lips that his talk got the upper hand of my interest, too, and I listened as one who receives a revelation. I took down what he had to say, just as he said it—without altering a word or adding one.]

I had my supper in my room this evening, (as usual,) and they sent up a bright, simple, guileless little darkey boy to wait on me—ten years old—a wide-eyed, observant little chap. I said:

"What is your name, my boy?"

"Dey calls me Jimmy, Sah, but my right name's James, Sah."

I said, "Sit down there, Jimmy—I'll not want you just yet."

He sat down in a big arm-chair, hung both his legs over one of the arms, and looked comfortable and conversational. I said:

"Did you have a pleasant Christmas, Jimmy?"

"No, sah—not zackly. I was kind o' sick den. But de res' o' de people *dey* had a good time—mos' all uv 'em had a good time. Dey all got drunk. Dey all gits drunk heah, every Christmas, and carries on and has awful good times."

"So you were sick, and lost it all. But unless you were *very* sick I should think that if you had asked the doctor he might have let you get—get—a *little* drunk—and—"

"Oh, no, Sah—I don' never git drunk—it's de *white* folks—dem's de ones I means. Pa used to git drunk, but dat was befo' I was big—but he's done quit. He don' git drunk no mo' now. Jis' takes one nip in de mawnin', now, cuz his stomach riles up, he sleeps so soun'. Jis' one nip—over to de s'loon—every mawnin'. He's powerful sickly—powerful—sometimes he can't hardly git aroun', he can't. He goes to de doctor every week—over to Ragtown. An' one time he tuck some stuff, you know, an' it mighty near *fetched* him. Ain't it dish-yer blue-vittles dat's pison?—ain't dat it?—truck what you pisons cats wid?"

"Yes blue vittles [vitriol] is a very convincing article with a cat."

"Well, den, dat was it. De ole man, he tuck de bottle and shuck it, and shuck it—he seed it was blue, and he didn't know but it was blue mass, which he tuck mos' always—blue mass pills—but den he 'spected maybe dish-yer truck might be some other kin' o' blue stuff, and so he sot de bottle down, and drat if it wa'n't blue vittles, sho' nuff, when de

---

† First published in the *New York Times* (29 November 1874), p. 20, this long-ignored early sketch is the foundation of Shelley Fisher Fishkin's argument that *Adventures of Huckleberry Finn* is narrated in an African American "voice." (See "Jimmy," p. 375.)

doctor come. An' de doctor he say if he'd a tuck dat blue vittles it would a highsted him, *sho'*. People can't be too particlar 'bout sich things. Yes, in*deedy*!

"We ain't got no cats heah, 'bout dis hotel. Bill he don't like 'em. He can't stan' a cat no way. Ef he was to ketch one he'd slam it outen de winder in a minute. Yes he would. Bill's down on cats. So is de gals— waiter gals. When dey ketches a cat bummin' aroun' heah, dey jis' *scoops* him—'deed dey do. Dey snake him into de cistern—dey's been cats drownded in dat water dat's in yo' pitcher. I seed a cat in dare yis- tiddy—all swelled up like a pudd'n. I bet you dem gals done dat. Ma says if dey was to drownd a cat for *her*, de fust one of 'em she ketched she'd jam her into de cistern 'long wid de cat. Ma wouldn't *do* dat, I don't reckon, but 'deed an' double, she *said* she would. I can't kill a chicken—well, I kin wring its neck off, cuz dat don't make 'em no suf- ferin scacely; but I can't take and chop dey heads off, like some peo- ple kin. It makes me feel so—so—well, I kin see dat chicken nights so's I can't sleep. Mr. Dunlap, he's de richest man in dis town. Some people says dey's fo' thousan' people in dis town—dis city. But Bill he says dey aint but 'bout thirty-three hund'd. And Bill he knows, cuz he's lived heah all his life, do' dey *do* say he won't never set de river on fire. I don't know how dey fin' out—*I* wouldn't like to count all dem peo- ple. Some folks says dis town would be considerable bigger if it wa'n't on accounts of so much lan' all roun' it dat ain't got no houses on it." [This in perfect seriousness—dense simplicity—no idea of a joke.] "I reckon you seed dat church as you come along up street. Dat's an awful big church—awful high steeple. An' it's all solid stone, excep' jes' de top part—de steeple, I means—dat's wood. It falls off when de win' blows pooty hard, an' one time it stuck in a cow's back and busted de cow all to de mischief. It's gwine to kill some body yit, dat steeple is. A man—big man, he was—bigger'n what Bill is—he tuck it up dare and fixed it again—an' he didn't look no bigger'n a boy, he was so high up. Dat steeple's awful high. If you look out de winder you kin see it." [I looked out, and was speechless with awe and admiration—which gratified Jimmy beyond expression. The wonderful steeple was some sixty or seventy feet high, and had a clock-face on it.] "You see dat arrer on top o' dat steeple? Well, Sah, dat arrer is pooty nigh as big as dis do' [door.] I seed it when dey pulled it outen de cow. It mus' be awful to stan' in dat steeple when de clock is strikin'—dey say it is. Booms and jars so's you think the world's a comin' to an end. *I* would- n't like to be up dare when de clock's a strikin'. Dat clock ain't jest a *striker*, like dese common clocks. It's a *bell*—jist a reglar *bell*—and it's a buster. You kin hear dat bell all over dis city. You ought to hear it boom, boom, boom, when dey's a fire. My sakes! Dey ain't got no bell like dat in Ragtown. *I* ben to Ragtown, an' I ben mos' halfway to Dock- ery [thirty miles.] De bell in Ragtown's got so ole now she don't make no soun', scasely."

[Enter the landlord—a kindly man, verging toward fifty. My small friend, without changing position, says:]

"Bill, didn't you say dat dey was only thirty-three hund'd people in dis city?"

"Yes, about thirty-three hundred is the population now."

"Well, some folks says dey's fo' thousan'."

"Yes, I know they do; but it isn't correct."

"Bill, I don't think dis gen'lman kin eat a whole prairie-chicken, but dey *tole* me to fetch it all up."

"Yes, that's all right—he ordered it."

[Exit "Bill," leaving me comfortable; for I had been perishing to know who "Bill" was.]

"Bill he's de oldest. An' he's de bes', too. Dey's fo'teen in dis fam'ly— all boys an' gals. Bill he suppo'ts 'em all—an' he don' never complain— he's *real* good, Bill is. All dem brothers an' sisters o' his'n ain't no 'count—all ceptin' dat little teeny one dat fetched in dat milk. Dat's Kit, Sah. She ain't only nine year ole. But she's de mos' lady-like one in de whole bilin'. You don't never see Kit a-rairin' an' a-chargin' aroun' an' kickin' up her heels like de res' o' de gals in dis fam'ly does gen'ally. Dat was Nan dat you hearn a-cuttin' dem shines on de pi-anah while ago. An' sometimes ef she don't rastle dat pianah when she gits started! *Tab* can't hole a candle to *her*, but Tab kin *sing* like de very nation. She's de only one in dis family dat kin sing. You don't never hear a yelp outen Nan. Nan can't sing for shucks. I'd jes' lieves hear a tom-cat dat's got scalded. Dey's fo'-teen in dis fam'ly 'sides de ole man an' de ole 'ooman—all brothers an' sisters. But some of 'em don't live heah—do' Bill he suppo'ts 'em—lends 'em money, an' pays dey debts an' he'ps 'em along. I tell you Bill he's *real* good. Dey all gits drunk—all 'cep Bill. De ole man he gits drunk, too, same as de res' uv 'em. Bob, he don't git drunk much—jes' sloshes roun' de s'loons some, an' takes a dram sometimes. Bob he's next to Bill—'bout forty year old. Dey's all married—all de fam'ly's married—cep' some of de gals. Dare's fo'teen. It's de biggest family in dese parts, dey say. Dare's Bill—Bill Nubbles—Nubbles is de name; Bill an' Griz, an' Duke, an' Bob, an' Nan, an' Tab, an' Kit, an' Sol, an' Si, an' Phil, an' Puss, an' Jake, an' Sal—Sal she's married an' got chil'en as big as I is—an' Hoss Nubbles, he's de las'. Hoss is what dey mos' always calls him, but he's got another name dat I somehow disremember, it's so kind o' hard to git de hang of it." [Then observing that I had been taking down this extraordinary list of nicknames for adults, he said:] "But in de mawnin' I can ask Bill what's Hoss's other name, an' den I'll come up an' tell you when I fetches yo' breakfast. An' may be I done got some o' dem names mixed up, but Bill, he kin tell me. Dey's fo'teen."

By this time he was starting off with the waiter, (and a pecuniary consideration for his sociability,) and, as he went out, he paused a moment and said:

"Dad-fetch it, somehow dat other name don't come. But, anyways, you jes' read dem names over an' see if dey's fo'teen." [I read the list from the fly-leaf of Longfellow's *New-England Tragedies*.] "Dat's right, Sah. Dey's all down, I'll fetch up Hoss's other name in de mawnin', Sah. Don't you be oneasy."

[Exit, whistling "Listen to the Mockingbird."]

CRITICISM

Early Responses

[WILLIAM ERNEST HENLEY]

[Review] *The Adventures of Huckleberry Finn*†

For some time past Mr. Clemens has been carried away by the ambition of seriousness and fine writing. In *Huckleberry Finn* he returns to his right mind, and is again the Mark Twain of old time. It is such a book as he, and he only, could have written. It is meant for boys; but there are few men (we should hope) who, once they take it up, will not delight in it. It forms a companion or sequel, to *Tom Sawyer*. Huckleberry Finn, as everybody knows, is one of Tom's closest friends; and the present volume is a record of the adventures which befell him soon after the event which made him a person of property and brought Tom Sawyer's story to a becoming conclusion. They are of the most surprising and delightful kind imaginable, and in the course of them we fall in with a number of types of character of singular freshness and novelty, besides being schooled in half a dozen extraordinary dialects—the Pike County dialect in all its forms, the dialect of the Missouri negro, and 'the extremest form of the backwoods South-Western dialect,' to wit. Huckleberry, it may be noted, is stolen by his disreputable father, to escape from whom he contrives an appearance of robbery and murder in the paternal hut, goes off in a canoe, watches from afar the townsfolk hunting for his dead body, and encounters a runaway negro—Miss Watson's Jim—an old particular friend of Tom Sawyer and himself. With Jim he goes south down the river, and is the hero of such scrapes and experiences as make your mouth water (if you have ever been a boy) to read of them. We do not purpose to tell a single one; it would be unfair to author and reader alike. We shall content ourselves with repeating that the book is Mark Twain at his best, and remarking that Jim and Huckleberry are real creations, and the worthy peers of the illustrious Tom Sawyer.

† From the *Athenaeum* (27 December 1884): 855. Attributed to the poet William Ernest Henley, this unsigned review is the earliest significant critical response to *Huck Finn*, and in referring to the "extraordinary dialects" of the book it struck a keynote that still rings loud and clear in discussions of Mark Twain's contribution to American literature.

BRANDER MATTHEWS

[Review: *Adventures of Huckleberry Finn*]†

The boy of to-day is fortunate indeed, and, of a truth, he is to be con-
gratulated. While the boy of yesterday had to stay his stomach with the
unconscious humour of *Sandford and Merton*, the boy of to-day may get
his fill of fun and of romance and of adventure in *Treasure Island* and in
Tom Brown and in *Tom Sawyer*, and now in a sequel to *Tom Sawyer*,
wherein Tom himself appears in the very nick of time, like a young god
from the machine. Sequels of stories which have been widely popular are
not a little risky. *Huckleberry Finn* is a sharp exception to this general
rule. Although it is a sequel, it is quite as worthy of wide popularity as
Tom Sawyer. An American critic once neatly declared that the late G. P.
R. James hit the bull's-eye of success with his first shot, and that for ever
thereafter he went on firing through the same hole. Now this is just what
Mark Twain has not done. *Huckleberry Finn* is not an attempt to do *Tom
Sawyer* over again. It is a story quite as unlike its predecessor as it is like.
Although Huck Finn appeared first in the earlier book, and although
Tom Sawyer reappears in the later, the scenes and the characters are otherwise wholly different. Above all, the atmosphere of the story is different. *Tom Sawyer* was a tale of boyish adventure in a village in Missouri,
on the Mississippi river, and it was told by the author. *Huckleberry Finn*
is autobiographic; it is a tale of boyish adventure along the Mississippi
river told as it appeared to Huck Finn. There is not in *Huckleberry Finn*
any one scene quite as funny as those in which Tom Sawyer gets his
friends to whitewash the fence for him, and then uses the spoils thereby
acquired to attain the highest situation of the Sunday school the next
morning. Nor is there any distinction quite as thrilling as that awful
moment in the cave when the boy and the girl are lost in the darkness,
and when Tom Sawyer suddenly sees a human hand bearing a light, and
then finds that the hand is the hand of Indian Joe, his one mortal enemy;
we have always thought that the vision of the hand in the cave in *Tom
Sawyer* is one of the very finest things in the literature of adventure since
Robinson Crusoe first saw a single footprint in the sand of the seashore.
But though *Huckleberry Finn* may not quite reach these two highest
points of *Tom Sawyer*, we incline to the opinion that the general level of
the later story is perhaps higher than that of the earlier. For one thing,
the skill with which the character of Huck Finn is maintained is marvel-
lous. We see everything through his eyes—and they are his eyes and not
a pair of Mark Twain's spectacles. And the comments on what he sees are
his comments—the comments of an ignorant, superstitious, sharp,
healthy boy, brought up as Huck Finn had been brought up; they are not
speeches put into his mouth by the author. One of the most artistic
things in the book—and that Mark Twain is a literary artist of a very high

---

† Published in the *Saturday Review* (London) (31 January 1885): 153. Brander Matthews, an
American, then thirty-three and author of two plays and several books on the theater, was con-
tributing to both British and American periodicals and later became a professor at Columbia
University.

order all who have considered his later writings critically cannot but confess—one of the most artistic things in *Huckleberry Finn* is the sober self-
restraint with which Mr. Clemens lets Huck Finn set down, without any
comment at all, scenes which would have afforded the ordinary writer
matter for endless moral and political and sociological disquisition. We
refer particularly to the account of the Grangerford-Shepherdson feud,
and of the shooting of Boggs by Colonel Sherburn. Here are two incidents of the rough old life of the South-Western States, and of the Mississippi Valley forty or fifty years ago, of the old life which is now rapidly
passing away under the influence of advancing civilization and increasing
commercial prosperity, but which has not wholly disappeared even yet,
although a slow revolution in public sentiment is taking place. The
Grangerford-Shepherdson feud is a vendetta as deadly as any Corsican
could wish, yet the parties to it were honest, brave, sincere, good Christian people, probably people of deep religious sentiment. Not the less we
see them taking their guns to church, and, when occasion serves, joining
in what is little better than a general massacre. The killing of Boggs by
Colonel Sherburn is told with equal sobriety and truth; and the later
scene in which Colonel Sherburn cows and lashes the mob which has set
out to lynch him is one of the most vigorous bits of writing Mark Twain
has done.

   In *Tom Sawyer* we saw Huckleberry Finn from the outside; in the present volume we see him from the inside. He is almost as much a delight
to any one who has been a boy as was Tom Sawyer. But only he or she
who has been a boy can truly enjoy this record of his adventures, and of
his sentiments and of his sayings. Old maids of either sex will wholly fail
to understand him or to like him, or to see his significance and his
value. Like Tom Sawyer, Huck Finn is a genuine boy; he is neither a girl
in boy's clothes like many of the modern heroes of juvenile fiction, nor
is he a "little man," a full-grown man cut down; he is a boy, just a boy,
only a boy. And his ways and modes of thought are boyish. As Mr. F.
Anstey understands the English boy, and especially the English boy of
the middle classes, so Mark Twain understands the American boy, and
especially the American boy of the Mississippi Valley of forty or fifty
years ago. The contrast between Tom Sawyer, who is the child of
respectable parents, decently brought up, and Huckleberry Finn, who is
the child of the town drunkard, not brought up at all, is made distinct
by a hundred artistic touches, not the least natural of which is Huck's
constant reference to Tom as his ideal of what a boy should be. When
Huck escapes from the cabin where his drunken and worthless father
had confined him, carefully manufacturing a mass of very circumstan-
tial evidence to prove his own murder by robbers, he cannot help saying, "I did wish Tom Sawyer was there, I knowed he would take an
interest in this kind of business, and throw in the fancy touches.
Nobody could spread himself like Tom Sawyer in such a thing as that."
Both boys have their full share of boyish imagination; and Tom Sawyer,
being given to books, lets his imagination run on robbers and pirates
and genies, with a perfect understanding with himself that, if you want
to get fun out of this life, you must never hesitate to make believe very
hard; and, with Tom's youth and health, he never finds it hard to make

believe and to be a pirate at will, or to summon an attendant spirit, or to rescue a prisoner from the deepest dungeon 'neath the castle moat. But in Huck this imagination has turned to superstition; he is a walking repository of the juvenile folklore of the Mississippi Valley—a folklore partly traditional among the white settlers, but largely influenced by intimate association with the negroes. When Huck was in his room at night all by himself waiting for the signal Tom Sawyer was to give him at midnight, he felt so lonesome he wished he was dead:—

> The stars was shining and the leaves rustled in the woods ever so mournful; and I heard an owl, away off, who-whooing about somebody that was dead, and a whippowill and a dog crying about somebody that was going to die; and the wind was trying to whisper something to me, and I couldn't make out what it was, and so it made the cold shivers run over me. Then away out in the woods I heard that kind of a sound that a ghost makes when it wants to tell about something that's on its mind and can't make itself understood, and so can't rest easy in its grave, and has to go about that way every night grieving. I got so downhearted and scared I did wish I had some company. Pretty soon a spider went crawling up my shoulders, and I flipped it off and it lit in the candle; and before I could budge it was all shrivelled up. I didn't need anybody to tell me that that was an awful bad sign and would fetch me some bad luck, so I was scared and most shook the clothes off me. I got up and turned around in my tracks three times and crossed my breast every time: and then I tied up a little lock of my hair with a thread to keep witches away. But I hadn't no confidence. You do that when you've lost a horse-shoe that you've found, instead of nailing it up over the door, but I hadn't ever heard anybody say it was any way to keep off bad luck when you'd killed a spider.

And, again, later in the story, not at night this time, but in broad daylight, Huck walks along a road:—

> When I got there it was all still and Sunday-like, and hot and sunshiny—the hands was gone to the fields; and there was them kind of faint dronings of bugs and flies in the air that makes it seem so lonesome and like everybody's dead and gone; and if a breeze fans along and quivers the leaves, it makes you feel mournful, because you feel like it's spirits whispering—spirits that's been dead ever so many years—and you always think they're talking about *you*. As a general thing it makes a body wish *he* was dead, too, and done with it all.

Now, none of these sentiments are appropriate to Tom Sawyer, who had none of the feeling for nature which Huck Finn had caught during his numberless days and nights in the open air. Nor could Tom Sawyer either have seen or set down this instantaneous photograph of a summer storm:—

> It would get so dark that it looked all blue-black outside, and lovely; and the rain would thrash along by so thick that the trees off a little ways looked dim and spider-webby; and here would come a

blast of wind that would bend the trees down and turn up the pale underside of the leaves; and then a perfect ripper of a gust would follow along and set the branches to tossing their arms as if they was just wild; and next, when it was just about the bluest and blackest—fst! it was as bright as glory, and you'd have a little glimpse of tree-tops a-plunging about, away off yonder in the storm, hundreds of yards further than you could see before; dark as sin again in a second, and now you'd hear the thunder let go with an awful crash, and then go rumbling, grumbling, tumbling down the sky towards the under side of the world, like rolling empty barrels down stairs, where it's long stairs and they bounce a good deal, you know.

The romantic side of Tom Sawyer is shown in most delightfully humorous fashion in the account of his difficult devices to aid in the easy escape of Jim, a runaway negro. Jim is an admirably drawn character. There have been not a few fine and firm portraits of negroes in recent American fiction, of which Mr. Cable's Bras-Coupé in the *Grandissimes* is perhaps the most vigorous, and Mr. Harris's Mingo and Uncle Remus and Blue Dave are the most gentle. Jim is worthy to rank with these; and the essential simplicity and kindliness and generosity of the Southern negro have never been better shown than here by Mark Twain. Nor are Tom Sawyer and Huck Finn and Jim the only fresh and original figures in Mr. Clemens's new book; on the contrary, there is scarcely a character of the many introduced who does not impress the reader at once as true to life—and therefore as new, for life is so varied that a portrait from life is sure to be as good as new. That Mr. Clemens draws from life, and yet lifts his work from the domain of the photograph to the region of art, is evident to any one who will give his work the honest attention which it deserves. Mr. John T. Raymond, the American comedian, who performs the character of Colonel Sellers to perfection, is wont to say that there is scarcely a town in the West and South-West where some man did not claim to be the original of the character. And as Mark Twain made Colonel Sellers, so has he made the chief players in the present drama of boyish adventure; they are taken from life, no doubt, but they are so aptly chosen and so broadly drawn that they are quite as typical as they are actual. They have one great charm, all of them—they are not written about and about; they are not described and dissected and analysed; they appear and play their parts and disappear; and yet they leave a sharp impression of indubitable vitality and individuality. No one, we venture to say, who reads this book will readily forget the Duke and the King, a pair of as pleasant "confidence operators" as one may meet in a day's journey, who leave the story in the most appropriate fashion, being clothed in tar and feathers and ridden on a rail. Of the more broadly humorous passages—and they abound—we have not left ourselves space to speak; they are to the full as funny as in any of Mark Twain's other books; and, perhaps, in no other book has the humourist shown so much artistic restraint, for there is in *Huckleberry Finn* no mere "comic copy," no straining after effect; one might almost say that there is no waste word in it. . . .

* * *

[ROBERT BRIDGES]

Mark Twain's Blood-Curdling Humor†

Mark Twain is a humorist or nothing. He is well aware of this fact himself, for he prefaces the *Adventures of Huckleberry Finn* with a brief notice, warning persons in search of a moral, motive or plot that they are liable to be prosecuted, banished or shot. This is a nice little artifice to scare off the critics—a kind of 'trespassers on these grounds will be dealt with according to law.'

However, as there is no penalty attached, we organized a search expedition for the humorous qualities of this book with the following hilarious results:

A very refined and delicate piece of narration by Huck Finn, describing his venerable and dilapidated 'pap' as afflicted with delirium tremens, rolling over and over, 'kicking things every which way,' and 'saying there was devils ahold of him.' This chapter is especially suited to amuse the children on long, rainy afternoons.

An elevating and laughable description of how Huck killed a pig, smeared its blood on an axe and mixed in a little of his own hair, and then ran off, setting up a job on the old man and the community, and leading them to believe him murdered. This little joke can be repeated by any smart boy for the amusement of his fond parents.

A graphic and romantic tale of a Southern family feud, which resulted in an elopement and from six to eight choice corpses.

A polite version of the 'Giascutus' story, in which a nude man, striped with the colors of the rainbow, is exhibited as 'The King's Camelopard; or, The Royal Nonesuch.' This is a good chapter for lenten parlor entertainments and church festivals.

A side-splitting account of a funeral, enlivened by a 'sick melodeum,' a 'long-legged undertaker,' and a rat episode in the cellar.

THOMAS SERGEANT PERRY

[The First Major American Review]††

Mark Twain's "Tom Sawyer" is an interesting record of boyish adventure; but, amusing as it is, it may yet be fair to ask whether its most marked fault is not too strong adherence to conventional literary models? A glance at the book certainly does not confirm this opinion, but those who recall the precocious affection of Tom Sawyer, at the age

† Unsigned review from *Life* (26 February 1885): 119. Probably written by the comic weekly's literary critic, Robert Bridges, this brief notice has the distinction of being the first negative review of *Huckleberry Finn*.

††From *Century* XXX.1 (May 1885): 171–72. The first review of any significance published in America and the first to question the ending of the novel. Versed in European languages and literature, Perry wrote regularly for the *Nation* and the *Atlantic*. His works include a history of Greek literature and a biography of John Fiske.

when he is losing his first teeth, for a little girl whom he has seen once or twice, will confess that the modern novel exercises a very great influence. What is best in the book, what one remembers, is the light we get into the boy's heart. The romantic devotion to the little girl, the terrible adventures with murderers and in huge caves, have the air of concessions to jaded readers. But when Tom gives the cat Pain-Killer, is restless in church, and is recklessly and eternally deceiving his aunt, we are on firm ground—the author is doing sincere work.

This later book, "Huckleberry Finn," has the great advantage of being written in autobiographical form. This secures a unity in the narration that is most valuable; every scene is given, not described; and the result is a vivid picture of Western life forty or fifty years ago. While "Tom Sawyer" is scarcely more than an apparently fortuitous collection of incidents, and its thread is one that has to do with murders, this story has a more intelligible plot. Huckleberry, its immortal hero, runs away from his worthless father, and floats down the Mississippi on a raft, in company with Jim, a runaway negro. This plot gives great opportunity for varying incidents. The travelers spend some time on an island; they outwit every one they meet; they acquire full knowledge of the hideous fringe of civilization that then adorned that valley; and the book is a most valuable record of an important part of our motley American civilization.

What makes it valuable is the evident truthfulness of the narrative, and where this is lacking and its place is taken by ingenious invention, the book suffers. What is inimitable, however, is the reflection of the whole varied series of adventures in the mind of the young scapegrace of a hero. His undying fertility of invention, his courage, his manliness in every trial, are an incarnation of the better side of the ruffianism that is one result of the independence of Americans, just as hypocrisy is one result of the English respect for civilization. The total absence of morbidness in the book—for the *mal du siècle* has not yet reached Arkansas—gives it a genuine charm; and it is interesting to notice the art with which this is brought out. The best instance is perhaps to be found in the account of the feud between the Shepherdsons and the Grangerfords, which is described only as it would appear to a semi-civilized boy of fourteen, without the slightest condemnation or surprise,—either of which would be bad art,—and yet nothing more vivid can be imagined. That is the way that a story is best told, by telling it, and letting it go to the reader unaccompanied by sign-posts or directions how he shall understand it and profit by it. Life teaches its lessons by implication, not by didactic preaching; and literature is at its best when it is an imitation of life and not an excuse for instruction.

As to the humor of Mark Twain, it is scarcely necessary to speak. It lends vividness to every page. The little touch in "Tom Sawyer," where, after the murder of which Tom was an eye-witness, it seemed "that his school-mates would never get done holding inquests on dead cats and thus keeping the trouble present to his mind," and that in the account of the spidery six-armed girl of Emmeline's picture in "Huckleberry Finn," are in the author's happiest vein. Another admirable instance is to be seen in Huckleberry Finn's mixed feelings about rescuing Jim, the negro, from slavery. His perverted views regarding the unholiness of his actions are most instructive and amusing. It is possible to feel, however, that the fun in the long account of Tom Sawyer's artificial imitation of escapes from prison is somewhat forced; everywhere simplicity is a good rule, and while the account of the Southern *vendetta* is a masterpiece, the caricature of books of adventure leaves us cold. In one we have a bit of life; in the other Mark Twain is demolishing something that has no place in the book.

Yet the story is capital reading, and the reason of its great superiority to "Tom Sawyer" is that it is, for the most part, a consistent whole. If Mark Twain would follow his hero through manhood, he would condense a side of American life that, in a few years, will have to be delved out of newspapers, government reports, county histories, and misleading traditions by unsympathetic sociologists.

Modern Views

VICTOR A. DOYNO

From Writing *Huck Finn*: Mark Twain's Creative Process†

Taking Our Bearings

Let us imagine that while we were strolling on a hillside high above Elmira, New York, on a windy summer day in 1883, Mark Twain invited us into his octagonal study to look over his shoulder as he composed a part of his novel. The passage we observe involves an emotional farewell scene, including Huck's opinion of an admirable young girl, Miss Mary Jane Wilks, the girl who almost loses her inheritance to the swindling king and duke. She has just offered to pray for Huck. Twain composes Huck's reaction, and the first manuscript version reads:

> Pray for me—good land! I reckoned if she'd a knowed me she'd tackle a job that was nearer her size. But I bet you she done it, just the same—she was just that kind. She had the grit to pray for Judas Iscarott if she took the notion—there wasn't no back-down *to* her, if *I* know a girl by the rake of her stern; and I think I do. You may say what you please, but in my opinion that girl had more sand in her than any girl I ever see; in my opinion she was just *full* of sand. And when it comes to beauty—*and* goodness—she lay over them all. I hain't ever seen her since that time that I see her go out at that door, and turn at the stairs and kinder throw a kiss back at me; no, I hain't ever seen her since; but I reckon I've thought of her a many and a many a million times, and of her saying she would pray for me; and if ever I'd a thought it would do any good for me to pray for *her*, I'm dum'd if I wouldn't a done it or bust. (MS, 351–52)[1]

Among the many intriguing features of the passage, Huck's voice commands attention; he confides his attitudes easily, charmingly, and his

† From *Writing "Huck Finn": Mark Twain's Creative Process* by Victor A. Doyno. Copyright © 1991 by the University of Pennsylvania Press. Reprinted by permission of the publisher.

1. "MS" always indicates the original manuscript portion already available in the Buffalo and Erie County Library. The recently discovered portion will be cited as "MS. A." In all quotations from the manuscript, contractions are silently expanded. Similarly, signs such as "+" for "and" are given in verbal form. Line endings are not preserved in my transcriptions.

   Readers who cannot visit the Buffalo manuscript can consult Lou Budd's two-volume edition, *Adventures of Huckleberry Finn (Tom Sawyer's Comrade): A Facsimile of the Manuscript.* In addition, the appendices of the new Mark Twain Project *Works and Papers of Mark Twain, Adventures of Huckleberry Finn* (Berkeley, CA, 1988), edited by Walter Blair and Victor Fischer, assist the reader in reconstructing the manuscript version. This new California edition of *Huck* (cited hereafter as *Huck*, 1988) provides a wealth of relevant information and sets the new standard. A facsimile of the first edition is readily available in Hamlin Hill and Walter Blair's edition, *The Art of Huckleberry Finn.*

openness and expectation of easy acceptance engages our sympathy as readers.

But Twain revised the passage significantly. Mary Jane's gesture of a *femme fatale*, throwing a kiss from the stair, receives a wavy line of cancellation and a circling line of exclusion. If Twain had allowed this gesture to stand, the novel would have included this explicit hint of sexuality, a topic the book significantly avoids. Part of Huck's innocence depends on his presexual condition. Although the gesture may have been appropriate for the slightly older Mary Jane, its inclusion would complicate the characterization of Huck; he would have to ignore the gesture or respond to it, and either choice would affect both the characterization and the novel. Instead, Twain squeezed in a line above the cancellation so the revised section reads, "I hain't ever seen her since that time that I see her go out at that door, *like light and comfort agoing out of a body's life.*" This simile, combining favorable abstract words and tactile sensation, pays attention only to the deathly emotional impact of separation, and the reader can understand Huck's sorrow. But Twain later decided to drop the addition before the final publication.

Twain also tinkers in the manuscript with a few minor details. The acceptable sentence, "I reckoned if she'd a knowed me she'd tackle a job that was nearer her size," he modified in two ways. Twain changed the folkish "she'd a" to a simple "she." The author gave vitality to Huck's voice by inserting a life-like wordiness in "a job that was *more* nearer her size." Similarly, Twain revised, "she lay over them all" to "lays." These minor changes suggest that Twain gave a respectable amount of meticulous care to his work.

Huck seems to know that it is unusual to praise a girl so much for "grit" or "sand," because abrasiveness is not usually valued in females although determination is. But Huck can praise her independence and strength only from within a young male's verbal system. Twain added, after "*full* of sand," a sentence declaring that *"It sounds like flattery, but it ain't no flattery."* Accordingly, Huck's character as narrator attempts to consider everyone's needs, even the reader's need to know how to regard a description.

Similar considerations about sexuality—and about tone and characterization—clearly influenced Twain's revisions for print. Now we have to imagine a later visit—perhaps in 1884—to observe Twain thoroughly revising his typescript of the same passage for print, making many changes. He modified the opening phrase, "Pray for me—good land!" by dropping "good land." Perhaps this very mild oath would give Huck too polite, too coy, a tone of voice. Huck's voice had first used a slang phrase, "backdown," and then, perhaps, the author's mind shifted to the girl's figure. Huck's voice had momentarily hit an inappropriate tone, a complex adult tone more suitable to an experienced Mississippi riverboat pilot evaluating the physical form of a female's rear angles than to Huck's pre-sexual naturalness: "there warn't no back-down *to* her, if *I* know a girl by the rake of her stern; and I think I do." But this masculine evaluative boasting was dropped, and Twain restores Huck's innocent voice, as he simply praises, "there warn't no back-down to her, I judge." The boy's earlier extreme enthusiasm becomes somewhat tempered by the moderate tone of "I judge"; several other emotional matters are toned down. Most revisions create several overlapping, interactive effects, affecting, for example, tone, characterization, and description.

Huck's innocence is also preserved by a suppression of some intricate satire on religion. The passage opens with Mary Jane's offer to pray for Huck, and he concludes, in the manuscript version, by saying, "if ever I'd a thought it would do any good for me to pray for *her*, I'm dum'd if I wouldn't a done it or bust." This slang phrasing for, "I'm damned if I wouldn't have prayed for her" carries a witty involution that disappeared when Twain shifted the word choice for print to "blamed." Once more Huck seems younger, and the adult author's potential for satiric sharpness remains concealed.

Later in 1884, Twain read the proofs of his novel, and he must have approved this final version of the passage:

> Pray for me! I reckoned if she knowed me she'd take a job that was more nearer her size. But I bet she done it, just the same—she was just that kind. She had the grit to pray for Judus if she took the notion—there warn't no backdown to her, I judge. You may say what you want to, but in my opinion she had more sand in her than any girl I ever see; in my opinion she was just full of sand. It sounds like flattery, but it ain't no flattery. And when it comes to beauty—and goodness too—she lays over them all. I hain't ever seen her since that time that I see her go out of that door; no, I hain't ever seen her since, but I reckon I've thought of her a many and a many a million times, and of her saying she would pray for me; and if ever I'd a thought it would do any good for me to pray for *her*, blamed if I wouldn't a done it or bust.

Purchasers of the first edition, and of all subsequent editions, can read a final, smooth version, enjoying Huck's relatively consistent, somewhat laconic tone.

This brief consideration of the growth and development of one passage can serve as an introductory indication of what can be perceived by the use of genetic criticism, by, in effect, going back in time to look over Twain's shoulder as the novel grew. Although we shall never again have to be quite this concerned with minute matters, one can observe the values of focused textual interpretation, the labor and value of specific understanding, and the dynamic, interacting, compounding effects of revisions. Themes, motifs, meanings can emerge, and emphasis can shift. Moreover, the passages that are not changed can be understood as being, at first, provisional, tentative, conditional, subject to revision, but gradually confirmed, affirmed, as they survive through at least four authorial re-readings. The unchanged passages are never really final until turned over to the printer. And Twain also made some changes even after the printer had the novel.

*   *   *

Inside Mark Twain's Mind: 1875–1884

In order to build a factual foundation for this reassessment of *Huck*, it is necessary to re-examine some documents from the 1875–1884 period. These materials reveal four areas of Twain's early interests: the accurate rendition of children's voices and points of view, children's misunderstandings of literature, the stages of a child's development, and the topic—of crucial importance to an author—of national and international copyright protection.

The beginnings of the long project that would become *Adventures of Huckleberry Finn* combined technical and personal concerns. When Twain completed *The Adventures of Tom Sawyer*, his attention was drawn, almost irresistibly, to the character Huck. This unschooled lad, a person outside normal social definition, fascinated Twain. Huck had begun to live and, in fact, almost takes over the ending of Tom's novel—because his personality possesses more vitality than Tom's.

Two letters which surround, oddly enough, July 4, 1875, indicate *Huck's* conception at the completion of *Tom*. In the first letter, William Dean Howells, writing as an *Atlantic* editor in pursuit of a publication, explores with Twain possibilities, both aesthetic and financial, for the book we know as *Tom*. Howells probably urged that the story continue into Tom's adulthood:

> You must be thinking well of the notion of giving us that story. I really feel very much interested in your making that your chief work; you wont have such another chance; don't waste it on a *boy*, and don't hurry the writing for the sake of making a book. Take your time, and deliberately advertise it by Atlantic publication. Mr Houghton has his back up, and says he would like to catch any newspaper copying it. (July 3, 1875, *Twain-Howells Letters*, Vol. 1, 90–91)

Indeed, Twain would take a great deal of time to create his chiefwork, but it was too late for the well-intentioned advice to apply to *Tom*. Significantly, the problem of piratical publication appears early.

Twain's reply reveals his great concern with the technical matter of point of view and with the literary model for a rogue biographical picaresque fiction:

My Dear Howells:

I have finished the story & didn't take the chap beyond boyhood. I believe it would be fatal to do it in any shape but autobiographically—like Gil Blas. I perhaps made a mistake in not writing it in the first person. If I went on, now, & took him into manhood, he would just be like all the one-horse men in literature & the reader would conceive a hearty contempt for him. It is *not* a boy's book, at all. It will only be read by adults. It is only written for adults.

Moreover, the book is plenty long enough, as it stands. It is about 900 pages of MS., & may be 1000 when I shall have finished "working up" vague places; so it would make from 130 to 150 pages of the Atlantic—about what the Foregone Conclusion made, isn't it?

I would dearly like to see it in the Atlantic, but I doubt if it would pay the publishers to buy the privilege, or me to sell it. Bret Harte has sold his novel (same size as mine, I should say) to Scribner's Monthly for $6,500 (publication to begin in September, I think,) & he gets a royalty of 7 1/2 percent from Bliss in book form afterward. He gets a royalty of ten percent on it in England (issued in serial numbers) & the same royalty on it in book form afterward, & is to receive an advance payment of five hundred pounds the day the first No. of the serial appears. If I could do as well, here & there, with mine, it might possibly pay me, but I seriously doubt it— though it is likely I could do better in England than Bret, who is not widely known there.

You see I take a vile, mercenary view of things—but then my household expenses are something almost ghastly.

By & by I shall take a boy of twelve & run him on through life (in the first person) but not Tom Sawyer—he would not be a good character for it.

I wish you would promise to read the MS of Tom Sawyer some time, & see if you don't really decide that I am right in closing with him as a boy—& point out the most glaring defects for me. It is a tremendous favor to ask, & I expect you to refuse, & would be ashamed to expect you to do otherwise. But the thing has been so many months in my mind that it seems a relief to snake it out. I don't know any other person whose judgment I could venture to take fully & entirely. Don't hesitate about saying no, for I know how your time is taxed, & I would have honest need to blush if you said yes.

Osgood & I are "going for" the puppy Gill on infringement of trademark. To win one or two suits of this kind will set literary folks on a firmer bottom. The New York Tribune doesn't own the world— I wish Osgood would sue it for stealing Holmes's poem. Wouldn't it be gorgeous to sue Whitlaw Read for *petty larceny*? I will promise to go into court & swear I think him capable of stealing pea-nuts from a blind-pedlar. (July 5, 1875, *Twain-Howells Letters*, Vol. 1, 91–92)

This well-known letter indicates an extraordinary amount about the craftsman behind the pose. Twain's evaluative thinking about problems of point of view and narrative voice while completing *Tom* would shape *Huck*. He realized the crucial importance of the narrator, explicitly rejecting Tom as unsuitable. Twain's mind typically repeats the appeal of the first-person narrator. His citation of a literary model, Le Sage's *The Adventures of Gil Blas*, places the conception within a recognized genre. But Twain's attitude toward *Gil Blas* changed through several clearly documented positions. Earlier, on December 27, 1869, Clemens had written Olivia that he was not marking the book for her, saying that she need not read it because, "It would sadly offend your delicacy." But later in his career, after completing *Huck*, when Brander Matthews commented about the similarity between *Gil Blas* and *Huck*, Twain assured Matthews that he had not read *Gil Blas*. Matthews's comment, "I knew he was not a bookish man," is utterly mistaken.

Again, the issue of piratical publication, infringement of trademark, and, by implication, lack of authorial protection appears as a recurrent concern. Any reader who believes Clemens's persona of Mark Twain may be surprised that an unsophisticated bumpkin could be so precise about point of view and about finances, or could be so engaging as he requests technical, editorial help. As the editors of the *Mark Twain-Howells Letters* point out, the letter contains "the germ of *Huckleberry*

Finn. It is significant that the technical problem of point-of-view was present to Twain from the first" (Vol. 1, 93).

Then on July 6, 1875, Howells replied encouragingly, "Perhaps you'll do Boy No. 2 for us." In another letter (September 11, 1875), Howells mentions a series of letters on the problem of international copyright by Charles Reade republished in Whitelaw Reid's New York *Tribune* in June–September. Thus Twain's mind could connect literary theft, international copyright, Whitelaw Reid (a name Twain misspells as "Read") and Charles Reade. Because Twain was repeatedly victimized—robbed really—by pirated editions, these related issues crop up frequently. Twain and Howells were planning a campaign to improve the situation for authors, e.g., letters of September 14 and 18, 1875. Twain did not yet know that pirated editions of *Tom* printed in Canada would rob him of about $5,000 before and while the first American edition went on sale. Thereafter the Canadian editions continued to sell in the U.S. at substantially lower prices than the authorized edition.

After the Clemens family visited the Howells, Twain learned what the Howells' seven-year-old son John, nicknamed Bua or Booah, thought about Homer. Twain seemed interested in what must have been the boy's unsophisticated, naive, probably literalist, almost certainly honest bit of literary criticism because he wrote Howells:

> Booah's idea of the wasteful magnificence of the Greeks is delicious! Pity but you could ingeniously draw him out, on the whole subject, & thus build an article upon A Boy's Comments Upon Homer.
>
> I've got another rattling good character for my novel! That great work is mulling itself into shape gradually. (October 4, 1875, *Twain-Howells Letters*, Vol. 1, 105)

Although the dominant scholarly opinion is that Twain did not begin *Huck* until 1876, it is possible that Twain's mind was busy in a pre-composition stage ("writing it in the first person" and "Boy No. 2"). An extensive cancel in this same letter probably refers to some novel in human terms, and it could refer to a boy's development. It is significant that Twain apparently knew and was thinking about stages of progressive development. The cancelled portion includes:

> Those [?] graded foetuses one sees in bottles of alcohol in anatomical [?] museums. . . . I can look back over my row of bottles, now, & discover that it has already developed from a rather inferior frog into a perceptible though libelous suggestion of a child. I hope to add a bottle a day, now, right along. (October 4, 1875, *Twain-Howells Letters*, Vol. 1, 105)

While the identity of the novel cannot be made incontrovertibly, it is significant that it deals with matters that occur in *Huck*. If the cancel refers to some early form resembling *Huck*, the phrase "libelous suggestion of a child" would make some sense; moreover, the portion after the cancel, which informs Howells that "(All of the above ruthlessly condemned by the Head Chief of the Clemens tribe)," could be interpreted to mean that the new character might be a Finn-type boy, probably not Olivia Clemens's kind of character. Or perhaps Olivia objected to the whole cancel, with the graphic description of foetuses. But aside from these speculations, it is of great consequence that a child's view of literature and Twain's familiarity with stages of child development appear in close proximity.

Apparently Howells kept a journal of comments made by his child because Twain wrote, on August 9, 1876, from Quarry Farm, that:

> I am infringing on your patent—I started a record of our children's sayings, last night. (*Twain-Howells Letters*, Vol. 1, 143)

His handwritten journal survives but is unpublished. "A Record of Small Foolishnesses," contains over eighty separate incidents, spanning the period from August 8, 1876 to 1885, presenting both Clemens's analysis of his children's personalities, his reflections on child rearing, and many precious anecdotes indicative of childish combinations of honesty, naivete, and inexperience. Sensitive parents can easily recognize the bittersweet quality of a child's remarks; the child's understanding of the world may be consistent and intelligent, but utterly innocent, causing gross misperceptions which, by their naive nature, are memorable to the adult's ear. But these misperceptions may convey an implicit criticism of the deceptions or skewed values in the adults' shared world, a world that adults seldom question because they have become familiarized or habituated to the society. Close study of this "Record" reveals that these attitudes, situations, and phrases influenced *Adventures of Huckleberry Finn* and other writings.

In the same letter, Twain told Howells about his creative involvements:

> The double-barreled novel lies torpid. I found I could not go on with it. The chapters I had written were still too new & familiar to me. I may take it up next winter, but cannot tell yet. I waited & waited, to see if my interest in it would not revive, but gave it up a month ago & began another boy's book—more to be at work than anything else. I have written 400 pages on it—therefore it is very nearly half done. It is Huck Finn's Autobiography. I like it only tolerably well, as far as I have got, & may possibly pigeonhole or burn the manuscript when it is done. (Aug. 9, 1876, *Twain-Howells Letters*, Vol. 1, 144)

Both the unwarranted optimism about completion and the ambivalence about the manuscript's fate seem characteristic, but the letter clearly announces the choice of the first-person point of view and Huck's identity as narrator. Although the information in the rediscovered manuscript portion may reveal a new sequence of interpretations, scholarly opinion currently believes that Twain continued the work at two separate periods, 1879 or 1880, and 1883–1884. His famous comparison of the well of inspiration which needed time to fill up aptly represents the temporal dimension. By the end of 1876 he had probably completed what would become Chapters I through XVI (including the famous Raftsman passage) but excluding the adventure on the *Walter Scott* and the following debate on King Sollermun and the French language (half of XII, XIII, and XIV). Probably at that point Huck had apologized to Jim, changing the possibilities for the novel, and the raft was run over by the steamer.

In 1880 he probably resumed the story, creating the story of the Grangerford-Shepherdson feud (Chapters XVII–XVIII). Then sometime between 1880 and 1883, possibly in 1882, he created the king and duke, the two unprincipled adult con-men (at least part of XIX, XX, and XXI).[2]

Accordingly, in May of 1883 he had a manuscript of about 50,000 words. Twain would complete about 70,000 words and revise the novel extensively in a period of high energy and in an atmosphere of artistic exhilaration. On July 20, 1883, Twain wrote to Howells, probably primarily about what we would call the discovery or exploratory draft stage of composition:

> I haven't piled up MS so in years as I have done since we came here to the farm three weeks & a half ago. Why, it's like old times, to step straight into the study, damp from the breakfast table, & sail right in & sail right on, the whole day long, without thought of running short of stuff or words. I wrote 4000 words to-day & I touch 3000 & upwards pretty often, & don't fall below 2600 on any working day. And when I get fagged out, I lie abed a couple of days & read and smoke, & then go it again for 6 or 7 days. I have finished one small book, & am away along in a big one that I half-finished two or three years ago. I expect to complete it in a month or six weeks or two months more. And *I* shall *like* it, whether anybody else does or not. It's a kind of companion to Tom Sawyer. There's a raft episode from it in second or third chapter of Life on the Mississippi. (*Twain-Howells Letters*, Vol. 1, 435)

Although the optimism about finishing is both vague and unrealistic, the tone is exuberant and infectious!

The book was created in a supportive, loving familial context. Although no critic has yet made a case for communal authorship of *Adventures of Huckleberry Finn*, a large number of people could have influenced the text in a variety of ways. We know that Clemens's wife, Olivia, his children, his good friend William Dean Howells, his nephew-in-law and business agent Charles Webster, the Elmira typist Harry M. Clarke, and two compositors had the opportunity to affect the text.

The standard view of family participation in the process is captured by Susy Clemens's word, "expergation." Her biography of her father has the following explanation:

> Ever since papa and mamma were married papa has written his books and then taken them to mamma in manuscript and she has expergated them. Papa read "Huckleberry Finn" to us in manuscript just before it came out, and then he would leave parts of it with mamma to expergate, while he went off up to the study to

2. Although Walter Blair's detailed explanation of the composition, as given above, seems convincing and is widely accepted, it should be noted that Sherwood Cummings argued intriguingly in 1989 in *Mark Twain and Science* that the Mississippi trip influenced this portion. The recent rediscovery of the first 665 pages of manuscript may cast a new light on this entire topic.

work, and sometimes Clara and I would be sitting with mamma while she was looking the manuscript over and I remember so well, with what pangs of regret we used to see her turn down the leaves of the pages which meant, that some delightfully dreadful part must be scratched out. And I remember one part pertickularly which was perfectly fascinating it was dreadful, that Clara and I used to delight in, and oh with what despare we saw mamma turn down the leaf on which it was written, we thought the book would be almost spoiled without it. But after it was published we changed our minds. We gradually came to feel as mamma did. (*Papa*, 188–89)

The possibility arises, and Walter Blair agrees, that Susy confused the manuscript and the proofs ("just before it came out"). But there is, characteristically, a more complex explanation in Twain's memory. Perhaps Twain was, in his later comments, fabricating to maintain his dignity and independence. But his explanations present the kind of trickery Clemens enjoyed:

I remember the special case mentioned by Susy, and can see the group yet—two-thirds of it pleading for the life of the culprit sentence that was so fascinatingly dreadful, and the other third of it patiently explaining why the court could not grant the prayer of the pleaders; but I do not remember what the condemned phrase was. It had much company, and they all went to the gallows; but it is possible that that especially dreadful one which gave those little people so much delight was cunningly devised and put into the book for just that function, and not with any hope or expectation that it would get by the expergator alive. It is possible, for I had that custom, and have it yet. (*Papa*, 189–90)

Although the comment concedes that a good many passages went "to the gallows" it appears that the teasing and the ultimate result was within the author's control. In the *Autobiography*, Twain's explanation seems similar:

The children always helped their mother to edit my books in manuscript. She would sit on the porch at the farm and read aloud, with her pencil in her hand, and the children would keep an alert and suspicious eye upon her right along, for the belief was well grounded in them that whenever she came across a particularly satisfactory passage she would strike it out. Their suspicions were well founded. The passages which were so satisfactory to them always had an element of strength in them which sorely needed modification or expurgation, and was always sure to get it at their mother's hand. For my own entertainment, and to enjoy the protests of the children, I often abused my editor's innocent confidence. I often interlarded remarks of a studied and felicitously atrocious character purposely to achieve the children's delight and see the pencil do its fatal work. I often joined my supplications to the children's for mercy, and strung the argument out and pretended to be in earnest. They were deceived, and so was their mother. It was three against one, and most unfair. But it was very delightful, and I could not resist the temptation. Now and then we gained the victory and there was much rejoicing. Then I privately struck the passage out myself. It had served its purpose. It had furnished three of us with good entertainment, and in being removed from the book by me it was only suffering the fate originally intended for it. (*Autobiography*, Vol. 1, 89–90)

Yet we know that Twain did bend the truth in his *Autobiography*. Although the psychological interaction is beyond exact reconstruction, there is only minimal evidence in the manuscript of familial censorship. Neither Victor Fischer nor I have found evidence of Livy's handwriting in the later portion of the manuscript.

On August 22, 1883, Twain was still quite enthusiastic:

My Dear Howells—

How odd it seems, to sit down to write a letter with the feeling that you've got *time* to do it. But I'm done work, for this season, & so have got time. I've done two seasons' work in one, & haven't anything left to do, now, but revise. I've written eight or nine hundred MS pages in such a brief space of time that I mustn't name the number of days; *I* shouldn't believe it myself, & (therefore) of course couldn't expect you to. I used to restrict myself to 4 & 5 hours a day & 5 days in the week; but this time I've wrought from breakfast till 5.15 p.m. six days in the week; & once or twice I smouched a Sunday when the boss wasn't looking. Nothing is half so good as literature hooked on Sunday on the sly. (*Twain-Howells Letters*, Vol. 1, 438)

Livy also commented on this unusually good attitude:

We are having a delightful time here. Mr. Clemens is at work— and I never saw him in better working condition, or with more enthusiasm for his work. (Salsbury, ed., *Susy and Mark Twain*, 168)

The influence of William Dean Howells was considerable. I believe that Howells queried passages and offered helpful suggestions; we know that that Howells had the manuscript typed and edited it and, as well, assisted with proofreading. Letters document that Twain relied on his friend's judgment, taste, and proofreading ability (see, for examples *Twain-Howells Letters*, 122, 124, 129, 493–500). Twain gave Howells *carte blanche* in making corrections on *Huck* and expressed great gratitude for the help. Yet Twain apparently exercised professional care— albeit exasperated or accompanied by cursing—while handling his proofs. He wrote to Howells on June 28, 1884:

My days are given up to cursings—both loud & deep—for I am reading the H. Finn proofs. They don't make a very great many mistakes; but those that do occur are of a nature to make a man curse his teeth loose. (*Twain-Howells Letters*, Vol. 2, 493)

Walter Blair writes that "despite the groaning, the author depended upon Howells to read only a small portion of the page proofs and read the rest himself, finishing up by the end of August [1884]" (*Mark Twain and Huck Finn*, 360).[3]

Two brief letters, from the end of that summer, to Charles Webster reveal both Twain's care and temper:

Aug 11 [1884]

Dear Charley—
Most of the proof was clean & beautiful, & a pleasure to read; but the rest of it was read by that blind idiot whom I have cursed so much, & is a disgraceful mess.
Send me slips from where the frauds arrive & *sit down to supper* in Miss Mary's house, up to slip No. 73.
Send me also slips from No. 75 up to 81.
And insist that the rest of the proofs be *better read*.

Yrs.
S L C
(Webster, ed., *Mark Twain Business Man*, 272)

Twain's casual but angry charge that the proofreading had been done by "that blind idiot," with the implication that Webster also hired sighted idiots, must have irritated Webster. But Twain certainly seems quite careful. Just three days later he wrote:

Dear Charley—
The missing galleys are the ones I sent to Howells, no doubt. In that case I don't need to re-read them.
If all the proofs had been as well read as the first 2 or 3 chapters were, I should not have needed to see the revises at all. On the contrary it was the worst & silliest proof-reading I have ever seen. It was never read by copy at all—not a single galley of it. . . .

Yrs
S L C
(Webster, ed., *Mark Twain Business Man*, 272)

Apparently his workman-like attitude toward his texts remained at least through August 14, 1884.[4]

I have concluded that Twain approved the changes, either idly or with full concentration. I consider Twain responsible for the text, although probably not responsible for the titles of the illustrations or the running titles. For the sake of alertness, I suggest that modern readers continuously judge whether the changes within the manuscript are similar to or different from those which occur between the revised manuscript and the printed text. I have concluded, as stated, that the artistic and thematic achievements of the finished novel belong to Mark Twain.

*   *   *

3. Further detailed information about this period of proofreading and book making can be found in Blair's Mark Twain and Huck Finn, Chapter 25, and essay and in the new California edition's Textual Introduction.
4. More information about the text appears in essays by Allison Ensor in *American Literature* and by John C. Gerber in *Proof*. Victor Fischer's Textual Introduction in the California *Huck*, 1988 (432–514), is a model of concise, detailed information.

Works Cited

Blair, Walter. *Mark Twain and "Huck Finn."* Berkeley: University of California Press, 1962.

Clemens, Susy. *Papa: An Intimate Biography of Mark Twain.* Charles Neider, ed. Garden City, NY: Doubleday, 1985.

Twain, Mark. *Mark Twain's Autobiography.* 2 vols. Edited by Albert Bigelow Paine. New York: Harper and Brothers, 1924.

Salsbury, Edith Colgate, ed. *Susy and Mark Twain: Family Dialogue.* New York: Harper, 1965.

Smith, Henry Nash, and William M. Gibson, eds. *Mark Twain–Howells Letters: The Correspondence of Samuel L. Clemens and William D. Howells, 1872–1910.* 2 vols. Cambridge: Harvard University Press, 1960.

T. S. ELIOT

[Introduction to *Adventures of Huckleberry Finn*]†

The Adventures of Huckleberry Finn is the only one of Mark Twain's various books which can be called a masterpiece. I do not suggest that it is his only book of permanent interest; but it is the only one in which his genius is completely realized, and the only one which creates its own category. There are pages in *Tom Sawyer* and in *Life on the Mississippi* which are, within their limits, as good as anything with which one can compare them in *Huckleberry Finn*; and in other books there are drolleries just as good of their kind. But when we find one book by a prolific author which is very much superior to all the rest, we look for the peculiar accident or concourse of accidents which made that book possible. In the writing of *Huckleberry Finn* Mark Twain had two elements which, when treated with his sensibility and his experience, formed a great book: these two are the Boy and the River.

Huckleberry Finn is, no doubt, a book which boys enjoy. I cannot speak from memory: I suspect that a fear on the part of my parents lest I should acquire a premature taste for tobacco, and perhaps other habits of the hero of the story, kept the book out of my way. But *Huckleberry Finn* does not fall into the category of juvenile fiction. The opinion of my parents that it was a book unsuitable for boys left me, for most of my life, under the impression that it was a book suitable only for boys. Therefore it was only a few years ago that I read for the first time, and in that order, *Tom Sawyer* and *Huckleberry Finn*.

Tom Sawyer did not prepare me for what I was to find its sequel to be. *Tom Sawyer* seems to me to be a boys' book, and a very good one. The River and *the* Boy make their appearance in it; the narrative is good; and there is also a very good picture of society in a small mid-Western river town (for St. Petersburg is more Western than Southern) a hun-

† From T. S. Eliot's Introduction to *The Adventures of Huckleberry Finn*, The Cresset Press, London, 1950, pp. vii–xvi. Published in the U.S. by Chanticleer Press, New York, 1950. Reprinted by permission of the estate of T. S. Eliot. Bracketed page references are to this Norton Critical Edition.

dred years ago. But the point of view of the narrator is that of an adult observing a boy. And Tom is the ordinary boy, though of quicker wits, and livelier imagination, than most. Tom is, I suppose, very much the boy that Mark Twain had been: he is remembered and described as he seemed to his elders, rather than created. Huck Finn, on the other hand, is the boy that Mark Twain still was, at the time of writing his adventures. We look at Tom as the smiling adult does: Huck we do not look at—we see the world through his eyes. The two boys are not merely different types; they were brought into existence by different processes. Hence in the second book their roles are altered. In the first book Huck is merely the humble friend—almost a variant of the traditional valet of comedy; and we see him as he is seen by the conventional respectable society to which Tom belongs, and of which, we feel sure, Tom will one day become an eminently respectable and conventional member. In the second book their nominal relationship remains the same; but here it is Tom who has the secondary role. The author was probably not conscious of this, when he wrote the first two chapters: *Huckleberry Finn* is not the kind of story in which the author knows, from the beginning, what is going to happen. Tom then disappears from our view; and when he returns, he has only two functions. The first is to provide a foil for Huck. Huck's persisting admiration for Tom only exhibits more clearly to our eyes the unique qualities of the former and the commonplaceness of the latter. Tom has the imagination of a lively boy who has read a good deal of romantic fiction: he might, of course, become a writer— he might become Mark Twain. Or rather, he might become the more commonplace aspect of Mark Twain. Huck has not imagination, in the sense in which Tom has it: he has, instead, vision. He sees the real world; and he does not judge it—he allows it to judge itself.

Tom Sawyer is an orphan. But he has his aunt; he has, as we learn later, other relatives; and he has the environment into which he fits. He is wholly a social being. When there is a secret band to be formed, it is Tom who organizes it and prescribes the rules. Huck Finn is alone: there is no more solitary character in fiction. The fact that he has a father only emphasizes his loneliness; and he views his father with a terrifying detachment. So we come to see Huck himself in the end as one of the permanent symbolic figures of fiction; not unworthy to take a place with Ulysses, Faust, Don Quixote, Don Juan, Hamlet and other great discoveries that man has made about himself.

It would seem that Mark Twain was a man who—perhaps like most of us—never became in all respects mature. We might even say that the adult side of him was boyish, and that only the boy in him, that was Huck Finn, was adult. As Tom Sawyer grown up, he wanted success and applause (Tom himself always needs an audience). He wanted prosperity, a happy domestic life of a conventional kind, universal approval, and fame. All of these things he obtained. As Huck Finn he was indifferent to all these things; and being composite of the two, Mark Twain both strove for them, and resented their violation of his integrity. Hence he became the humorist and even clown: with his gifts, a certain way to success, for everyone could enjoy his writings without the slightest feeling of discomfort, self-consciousness or self-criticism. And hence, on the other hand, his pessimism and misanthropy. To be a misanthrope is to be in some way divided; or it is a sign of an uneasy conscience. The pessimism which Mark Twain discharged into *The Man That Corrupted Hadleyburg* and *What is Man?* springs less from observation of society, than from his hatred of himself for allowing society to tempt and corrupt him and give him what he wanted. There is no wisdom in it. But all this personal problem has been diligently examined by Mr. Van Wyck Brooks; and it is not Mark Twain, but *Huckleberry Finn*, that is the subject of this introduction.

You cannot say that Huck himself is either a humorist or a misanthrope. He is the impassive observer: he does not interfere, and, as I have said, he does not judge. Many of the episodes that occur on the voyage down the river, after he is joined by the Duke and the King (whose fancies about themselves are akin to the kind of fancy that Tom Sawyer enjoys) are in themselves farcical; and if it were not for the presence of Huck as the reporter of them, they would be no more than farce. But, seen through the eyes of Huck, there is a deep human pathos in these scoundrels. On the other hand, the story of the feud between the Grangerfords and the Shepherdsons is a masterpiece in itself: yet Mark Twain could not have written it so, with that economy and restraint, with just the right details and no more, and leaving to the reader to make his own moral reflections, unless he had been writing in the person of Huck. And the *style* of the book, which is the style of Huck, is what makes it a far more convincing indictment of slavery than the sensationalist propaganda of *Uncle Tom's Cabin*. Huck is passive and impassive, apparently always the victim of events; and yet, in his acceptance of his world and of what it does to him and others, he is more powerful than his world, because he is more *aware* than any other person in it.

Repeated readings of the book only confirm and deepen one's admiration of the consistency and perfect adaptation of the writing. This is a style which at the period, whether in America or in England, was an innovation, a new discovery in the English language. Other authors had achieved natural speech in relation to particular characters—Scott with characters talking Lowland Scots, Dickens with cockneys: but no one else had kept it up through the whole of a book. Thackeray's Yellowplush, impressive as he is, is an obvious artifice in comparison. In *Huckleberry Finn* there is no exaggeration of grammar or spelling or speech, there is no sentence or phrase to destroy the illusion that these are Huck's own words. It is not only in the way in which he tells his story, but in the details he remembers, that Huck is true to himself. There is, for instance, the description of the Grangerford interior as Huck sees it on his arrival; there is the list of the objects which Huck and Jim salvaged from the derelict house:

> We got an old tin lantern, and a butcher-knife without any handle, and a bran-new Barlow knife worth two bits in any store, and a lot of tallow candles, and a tin candlestick, and a gourd, and a tin cup, and a ratty old bedquilt off the bed, and a reticule with needles and pins and beeswax and buttons and thread and all such truck in it, and a hatchet and some nails, and a fish-line as thick as my little finger, with some monstrous hooks on it, and a roll of buckskin,

and a leather dog-collar, and a horseshoe, and some vials of medicine that didn't have no label on them; and just as we was leaving I found a tolerable good curry-comb, and Jim he found a ratty old fiddle-bow, and a wooden leg. The straps was broke off of it, but barring that, it was a good enough leg, though it was too long for me and not long enough for Jim, and we couldn't find the other one, though we hunted all round.

And so, take it all round, we made a good haul. [62]

This is the sort of list that a boy reader should pore over with delight; but the paragraph performs other functions of which the boy reader would be unaware. It provides the right counterpoise to the horror of the wrecked house and the corpse; it has a grim precision which tells the reader all he needs to know about the way of life of the human derelicts who had used the house; and (especially the wooden leg, and the fruitless search for its mate) reminds us at the right moment of the kinship of mind and the sympathy between the boy outcast from society and the negro fugitive from the injustice of society.

Huck in fact would be incomplete without Jim, who is almost as notable a creation as Huck himself. Huck is the passive observer of men and events, Jim the submissive sufferer from them; and they are equal in dignity. There is no passage in which their relationship is brought out more clearly than the conclusion of the chapter in which, after the two have become separated in the fog, Huck in the canoe and Jim on the raft, Huck, in his impulse of boyish mischief, persuades Jim for a time that the latter had dreamt the whole episode.

"... my heart wuz mos' broke bekase you wuz los', en I didn' k'yer no mo' what become er me en de raf'. En when I wake up en fine you back agin', all safe en soun', de tears come en I could a got down on my knees en kiss' yo' foot, I's so thankful. En all you wuz thinkin' 'bout wuz how you could make a fool uv ole Jim wid a lie. Dat truck dah is *trash*; en trash is what people is dat puts dirt on de head er dey fren's en makes 'em ashamed.' ..."

It was fifteen minutes before I could work myself up to go and humble myself to a nigger—but I done it, and I warn't ever sorry for it afterwards, neither. [95]

This passage has been quoted before; and if I quote it again, it is because I wish to elicit from it one meaning that is, I think, usually overlooked. What is obvious in it is the pathos and dignity of Jim, and this is moving enough; but what I find still more disturbing, and still more unusual in literature, is the pathos and dignity of the boy, when reminded so humbly and humiliatingly, that his position in the world is not that of other boys, entitled from time to time to a practical joke; but that he must bear, and bear alone, the responsibility of a man.

It is Huck who gives the book style. The River gives the book its form. But for the River, the book might be only a sequence of adventures with a happy ending. A river, a very big and powerful river, is the only natural force that can wholly determine the course of human peregrination. At sea, the wanderer may sail or be carried by winds and currents in one direction or another; a change of wind or tide may determine fortune. In the prairie, the direction of movement is more or less at the choice of the caravan; among mountains there will often be an alternative, a guess at the most likely pass. But the river with its strong, swift current is the dictator to the raft or to the steamboat. It is a treacherous and capricious dictator. At one season, it may move sluggishly in a channel so narrow that, encountering it for the first time at that point, one can hardly believe that it has travelled already for hundreds of miles, and has yet many hundreds of miles to go; at another season, it may obliterate the low Illinois shore to a horizon of water, while in its bed it runs with a speed such that no man or beast can survive in it. At such times, it carries down human bodies, cattle and houses. At least twice, at St. Louis, the western and the eastern shores have been separated by the fall of bridges, until the designer of the great Eads Bridge devised a structure which could resist the floods. In my own childhood, it was not unusual for the spring freshet to interrupt railway travel; and then the traveller to the East had to take steamboat from the levee up to Alton, at a higher level on the Illinois shore, before he could begin his rail journey. The river is never wholly chartable; it changes its pace, it shifts its channel, unaccountably; it may suddenly efface a sandbar, and throw up another bar where before was navigable water.

It is the River that controls the voyage of Huck and Jim; that will not let them land at Cairo, where Jim could have reached freedom; it is the River that separates them and deposits Huck for a time in the Grangerford household; the River that re-unites them, and then compels upon them the unwelcome company of the King and the Duke. Recurrently we are reminded of its presence and its power.

> When I woke up, I didn't know where I was for a minute. I set up and looked around, a little scared. Then I remembered. The river looked miles and miles across. The moon was so bright I could a counted the drift-logs that went a-slipping along, black and still, hundreds of yards out from shore. Everything was dead quiet, and it looked late, and *smelt* late. You know what I mean—I don't know the words to put it in.
>
> It was kind of solemn, drifting down the big still river, laying on our backs looking up at the stars, and we didn't ever feel like talking loud, and it warn't often that we laughed, only a little kind of a low chuckle. We had mighty good weather as a general thing, and nothing ever happened to us at all, that night, nor the next, nor the next.
>
> Every night we passed towns, some of them away up on black hillsides, nothing but just a shiny bed of lights, not a house could you see. The fifth night we passed St. Louis, and it was like the whole world lit up. In St. Petersburg they used to say there was twenty or thirty thousand people in St. Louis, but I never believed it till I see that wonderful spread of lights at two o'clock that still night. There warn't a sound there; everybody was asleep. [75]

We come to understand the River by seeing it through the eyes of the Boy; but the Boy is also the spirit of the River. *Huckleberry Finn*, like other great works of imagination, can give to every reader whatever he is capable of taking from it. On the most superficial level of observation, Huck is convincing as a boy. On the same level, the picture of social life on the shores of the Mississippi a hundred years ago is, I feel sure, accurate. On any level, Mark Twain makes you see the River, as it is and was and always will be, more clearly than the author of any other description of a river known to me. But you do not merely see the River, you do not merely become acquainted with it through the sense: you experience the River. Mark Twain, in his later years of success and fame, referred to his early life as a steamboat pilot as the happiest he had known. With all allowance for the illusions of age, we can agree that those years were the years in which he was most fully alive. Certainly, but for his having practised that calling, earned his living by that profession, he would never have gained the understanding which his genius for expression communicates in this book. In the pilot's daily struggle with the River, in the satisfaction of activity, in the constant attention to the River's unpredictable vagaries, his consciousness was fully occupied, and he absorbed knowledge of which, as an artist, he later made use. There are, perhaps, only two ways in which a writer can acquire the understanding of environment which he can later turn to account: by having spent his childhood in that environment—that is, living in it at a period of life in which one experiences much more than one is aware of; and by having had to struggle for a livelihood in that environment—a livelihood bearing no direct relation to any intention of writing about it, of *using* it as literary material. Most of Joseph Conrad's understanding came to him in the latter way. Mark Twain knew the Mississippi in both ways: he had spent his childhood on its banks, and he had earned his living matching his wits against its currents.

Thus the River makes the book a great book. As with Conrad, we are continually reminded of the power and terror of Nature, and the isolation and feebleness of Man. Conrad remains always the European observer of the tropics, the white man's eye contemplating the Congo and its black gods. But Mark Twain is a native, and the River God is his God. It is as a native that he accepts the River God, and it is the subjection of Man that gives to Man his dignity. For without some kind of God, Man is not even very interesting.

Readers sometimes deplore the fact that the story descends to the level of *Tom Sawyer* from the moment that Tom himself re-appears. Such readers protest that the escapades invented by Tom, in the attempted "rescue" of Jim, are only a tedious development of themes with which we were already too familiar—even while admitting that the escapades themselves are very amusing, and some of the incidental observations memorable.[1] But it is right that the mood of the end of the book should bring us back to that of the beginning. Or, if this was not the right ending for the book, what ending would have been right?

In *Huckleberry Finn* Mark Twain wrote a much greater book than he could have known he was writing. Perhaps all great works of art mean much more than the author could have been aware of meaning: certainly, *Huckleberry Finn* is the one book of Mark Twain's which, as a whole, has this unconsciousness. So what seems to be the rightness, of reverting at

---

1. *e.g.*, "*Jim* don't know anybody in China."

the end of the book to the mood of *Tom Sawyer*, was perhaps unconscious art. For Huckleberry Finn, neither a tragic nor a happy ending
would be suitable. No worldly success or social satisfaction, no domestic
consummation would be worthy of him; a tragic end also would reduce
him to the level of those whom we pity. Huck Finn must come from
nowhere and be bound for nowhere. His is not the independence of the
typical or symbolic American Pioneer, but the independence of the
vagabond. His existence questions the values of America as much as the
values of Europe; he is as much an affront to the "pioneer spirit" as he is
to "business enterprise"; he is in a state of nature as detached as the state
of the saint. In a busy world, he represents the loafer; in an acquisitive
and competitive world, he insists on living from hand to mouth. He could
not be exhibited in any amorous encounters or engagements, in any of
the juvenile affections which are appropriate to Tom Sawyer. He belongs
neither to the Sunday School nor to the Reformatory. He has no beginning and no end. Hence, he can only disappear; and his disappearance
can only be accomplished by bringing forward another performer to
obscure the disappearance in a cloud of whimsicalities.

Like Huckleberry Finn, the River itself has no beginning or end. In its
beginning, it is not yet the River; in its end, it is no longer the River. What
we call its headwaters is only a selection from among the innumerable
sources which flow together to compose it. At what point in its course
does the Mississippi become what the Mississippi *means*? It is both one
and many; it is the Mississippi of this book only after its union with the
Big Muddy—the Missouri; it derives some of its character from the Ohio,
the Tennessee and other confluents. And at the end it merely disappears
among its deltas: it is no longer there, but it is still where it was, hundreds
of miles to the North. The River cannot tolerate any design, to a story
which is its story, that might interfere with its dominance. Things must
merely happen, here and there, to the people who live along its shores or
who commit themselves to its current. And it is as impossible for Huck as
for the River to have a beginning or end—a *career*. So the book has the
right, the only possible concluding sentence. I do not think that any book
ever written ends more certainly with the right words:

> But I reckon I got to light out for the Territory ahead of the rest,
> because aunt Sally she's going to adopt me and civilize me, and I
> can't stand it. I been there before.

JANE SMILEY

Say It Ain't So, Huck: Second Thoughts on Mark Twain's "Masterpiece"†

So I broke my leg. Doesn't matter how—since the accident I've heard
plenty of broken-leg tales, and, I'm telling you, I didn't realize that walking down the stairs, walking down hills, dancing in high heels, or

stamping your foot on the brake pedal could be so dangerous. At any rate, like numerous broken-legged intellectuals before me, I found the prospect of three months in bed in the dining room rather seductive from a book-reading point of view, and I eagerly got started. Great novels piled up on my table, and right at the top was *The Adventures of Huckleberry Finn*, which, I'm embarrassed to admit, I hadn't read since junior high school. The novel took me a couple of days (it was longer than I had remembered), and I closed the cover stunned. Yes, stunned. Not, by any means, by the artistry of the book but by the notion that this is the novel all American literature grows out of, that this is a great novel, that this is even a serious novel.

Although Huck had his fans at publication, his real elevation into the pantheon was worked out early in the Propaganda Era, between 1948 and 1955, by Lionel Trilling, Leslie Fiedler, T. S. Eliot, Joseph Wood Krutch, and some lesser lights, in the introductions to American and British editions of the novel and in such journals as *Partisan Review* and *The New York Times Book Review*. The requirements of Huck's installation rapidly revealed themselves: the failure of the last twelve chapters (in which Huck finds Jim imprisoned on the Phelps plantation and Tom Sawyer is reintroduced and elaborates a cruel and unnecessary scheme for Jim's liberation) had to be diminished, accounted for, or forgiven; after that, the novel's special qualities had to be placed in the context first of other American novels (to their detriment) and then of world literature. The best bets here seemed to be Twain's style and the river setting, and the critics invested accordingly: Eliot, who had never read the novel as a boy, traded on his own childhood beside the big river, elevating Huck to the Boy, and the Mississippi to the River God, therein finding the sort of mythic resonance that he admired. Trilling liked the river god idea, too, though he didn't bother to capitalize it. He also thought that Twain, through Huck's lying, told truths, one of them being (I kid you not) that "something ... had gone out of American life after the [Civil War], some simplicity, some innocence, some peace." What Twain himself was proudest of in the novel—his style—Trilling was glad to dub "not less than definitive in American literature. The prose of *Huckleberry Finn* established for written prose the virtues of American colloquial speech. . . . He is the master of the style that escapes the fixity of the printed page, that sounds in our ears with the immediacy of the heard voice, the very voice of unpretentious truth." The last requirement was some quality that would link Huck to other, though "lesser," American novels such as Herman Melville's *Moby-Dick*, that would possess some profound insight into the American character. Leslie Fiedler obligingly provided it when he read homoerotic attraction into the relationship between Huck and Jim, pointing out the similarity of this to such other white man–dark man friendships as those between Ishmael and Queequeg in *Moby-Dick* and Natty Bumppo and Chingachgook in James Fenimore Cooper's *Last of the Mohicans*.

The canonization proceeded apace: great novel (Trilling, 1950), greatest novel (Eliot, 1950), world-class novel (Lauriat Lane Jr., 1955). Sensible naysayers, such as Leo Marx, were lost in the shuffle of propaganda. But, in fact, *The Adventures of Huckleberry Finn* has little to offer in the way of greatness. There is more to be learned about the

American character *from* its canonization than *through* its canonization.

Let me hasten to point out that, like most others, I don't hold any grudges against Huck himself. He's just a boy trying to survive. The villain here is Mark Twain, who knew how to give Huck a voice but didn't know how to give him a novel. Twain was clearly aware of the story's difficulties. Not finished with having revisited his boyhood in *Tom Sawyer*, Twain conceived of a sequel and began composition while still working on *Tom Sawyer*'s page proofs. Four hundred pages into it, having just passed Cairo and exhausted most of his memories of Hannibal and the upper Mississippi, Twain put the manuscript aside for three years. He was facing a problem every novelist is familiar with: his original conception was beginning to conflict with the implications of the actual story. It is at this point in the story that Huck and Jim realize two things: they have become close friends, and they have missed the Ohio River and drifted into what for Jim must be the most frightening territory of all—down the river, the very place Miss Watson was going to sell him to begin with. Jim's putative savior, Huck, has led him as far astray as a slave can go, and the farther they go, the worse it is going to be for him. Because the Ohio was not Twain's territory, the fulfillment of Jim's wish would necessarily lead the novel away from the artistic integrity that Twain certainly sensed his first four hundred pages possessed. He found himself writing not a boy's novel, like *Tom Sawyer*, but a man's novel, about real moral dilemmas and growth. The patina of nostalgia for a time and place, Missouri in the 1840s (not unlike former President Ronald Reagan's nostalgia for his own boyhood, when "Americans got along"), had been transformed into actual longing for a timeless place of friendship and freedom, safe and hidden, on the big river. But the raft had floated Huck and Jim, and their author with them, into the truly dark heart of the American soul and of American history: slave country.

Twain came back to the novel and worked on it twice again, once to rewrite the chapters containing the feud between the Grangerfords and the Shepherdsons, and later to introduce the Duke and the Dauphin. It is with the feud that the novel begins to fail, because from here on the episodes are mere distractions from the true subject of the work: Huck's affection for and responsibility to Jim. The signs of this failure are everywhere, as Jim is pushed to the side of the narrative, hiding on the raft and confined to it, while Huck follows the Duke and the Dauphin onshore to the scenes of much simpler and much less philosophically taxing moral dilemmas, such as fraud. Twain was by nature an improviser, and he was pleased enough with these improvisations to continue. When the Duke and the Dauphin finally betray Jim by selling him for forty dollars, Huck is shocked, but the fact is neither he nor Twain has come up with a plan that would have saved Jim in the end. Tom Sawyer does that.

Considerable critical ink has flowed over the years in an attempt to integrate the Tom Sawyer chapters with the rest of the book, but it has flowed in vain. As Leo Marx points out, and as most readers sense intuitively, once Tom reappears, "[m]ost of those traits which made [Huck] so appealing a hero now disappear. . . . It should be added at once that Jim doesn't mind too much. The fact is that he has undergone a similar trans-formation. On the raft he was an individual, man enough to denounce Huck when Huck made him the victim of a practical joke. In the closing episode, however, we lose sight of Jim in the maze of farcical invention." And the last twelve chapters are boring, a sure sign that an author has lost the battle between plot and theme and is just filling in the blanks.

As with all bad endings, the problem really lies at the beginning, and at the beginning of *The Adventures of Huckleberry Finn* neither Huck nor Twain takes Jim's desire for freedom at all seriously; that is, they do not accord it the respect that a man's passion deserves. The sign of this is that not only do the two never cross the Mississippi to Illinois, a free state, but they hardly even consider it. In both *Tom Sawyer* and *Huck-leberry Finn*, the Jackson's Island scenes show that such a crossing, even in secret, is both possible and routine, and even though it would present legal difficulties for an escaped slave, these would certainly pose no more hardship than locating the mouth of the Ohio and then finding passage up it. It is true that there could have been slave catch-ers in pursuit (though the novel ostensibly takes place in the 1840s and the Fugitive Slave Act was not passed until 1850), but Twain's moral failure, once Huck and Jim link up, is never even to account for their choice to go down the river rather than across it. What this reveals is that for all his lip service to real attachment between white boy and black man, Twain really saw Jim as no more than Huck's sidekick, homoerotic or otherwise. All the claims that are routinely made for the book's humanitarian power are, in the end, simply absurd. Jim is never autonomous, never has a vote, always finds his purposes subordinate to Huck's, and, like every good sidekick, he never minds. He grows ever more passive and also more affectionate as Huck and the Duke and the Dauphin and Tom (and Twain) make ever more use of him for their own purposes. But this use they make of him is not supplementary; it is inte-gral to Twain's whole conception of the novel. Twain thinks that Huck's affection is a good enough reward for Jim.

The sort of meretricious critical reasoning that has raised Huck's pal-try good intentions to a "strategy of subversion" (David L. Smith) and a "convincing indictment of slavery" (Eliot) precisely mirrors the same sort of meretricious reasoning that white people use to convince them-selves that they are not "racist." If Huck *feels* positive toward Jim, and *loves* him, and *thinks* of him as a man, then that's enough. He doesn't actually have to act in accordance with his feelings. White Americans always think racism is a feeling, and they reject it or they embrace it. To most Americans, it seems more honorable and nicer to reject it, so they do, but they almost invariably fail to understand that how they *feel* means very little to black Americans, who understand racism as a way of structuring American culture, American politics, and the American economy. To invest *The Adventures of Huckleberry Finn* with "great-ness" is to underwrite a very simplistic and evasive theory of what racism is and to promulgate it, philosophically, in schools and the media as well as in academic journals. Surely the discomfort of many readers, black and white, and the censorship battles that have dogged *Huck Finn* in the last twenty years are understandable in this context. No matter how often the critics "place in context" Huck's use of the word "nigger," they can never excuse or fully hide the deeper racism of the novel—the way Twain and Huck use Jim because they really don't care enough about his desire for freedom to let that desire change their plans. And to give credit to Huck suggests that the only racial insight Americans of the nineteenth or twentieth century are capable of is a recognition of the obvious—that blacks, slave and free, are human.

Ernest Hemingway, thinking of himself, as always, once said that all American literature grew out of *Huck Finn*. It undoubtedly would have been better for American literature, and American culture, if our literature had grown out of one of the best-selling novels of all time, another American work of the nineteenth century, *Uncle Tom's Cabin*, which for its portrayal of an array of thoughtful, autonomous, and passionate black characters leaves *Huck Finn* far behind. *Uncle Tom's Cabin* was published in 1852, when Twain was seventeen, still living in Hannibal and contributing to his brother's newspapers, still sympathizing with the South, nine years before his abortive career in the Confederate Army. *Uncle Tom's Cabin* was the most popular novel of its era, universally controversial. In 1863, when Harriet Beecher Stowe visited the White House, Abraham Lincoln condescended to remark to her, "So this is the little lady who made this great war."

The story, familiar to most nineteenth-century Americans, either through the novel or through the many stage adaptations that sentimentalized Stowe's work, may be sketched briefly: A Kentucky slave, Tom, is sold to pay off a debt to a slave trader, who takes him to New Orleans. On the boat trip downriver, Tom is purchased by the wealthy Augustine St. Clare at the behest of his daughter, Eva. After Eva's death, and then St. Clare's, Tom is sold again, this time to Simon Legree, whose remote plantation is the site of every form of cruelty and degradation. The novel was immediately read and acclaimed by any number of excellent judges: Charles Dickens, George Eliot, Leo Tolstoy, George Sand—the whole roster of nineteenth-century liberals whose work we read today and try to persuade ourselves that *Huck Finn* is equal to. English novelist and critic Charles Kingsley thought *Uncle Tom's Cabin* the best novel ever written. These writers honored Stowe's book for all its myriad virtues. One of these was her adept characterization of a whole world of whites and blacks who find themselves gripped by slavery, many of whose names have entered the American language as expressions—not only Uncle Tom himself but Simon Legree and, to a lesser extent, little Eva and the black child Topsy. The characters appear, one after another, vivified by their attitudes, desires, and opinions as much as by their histories and their fates. Surely Augustine St. Clare, Tom's owner in New Orleans, is an exquisite portrayal of a humane but indecisive man, who knows what he is doing but not how to stop it. Surely Cassy, a fellow slave whom Tom meets on the Legree plantation, is one of the great angry women in all of literature—not only bitter, murderous, and nihilistic but also intelligent and enterprising. Surely the midlife spiritual journey of Ophelia St. Clare, Augustine's Yankee cousin, from self-confident ignorance to affectionate understanding is most convincing, as is Topsy's parallel journey from ignorance and self-hatred to humanity. The ineffectual Mr. Shelby and his submissive, and subversive, wife; the slave trader Haley; Tom's wife, Chloe; Augustine's wife, Marie; Legree's overseers, Sambo and Quimbo—good or evil, they all live.

As for Tom himself, we all know what an "Uncle Tom" is, except we don't. The popular Uncle Tom sucks up to the master and exhibits bovine patience. The real Uncle Tom is both a realist and a man of deep principle. When he is sold by Mr. Shelby in Kentucky, he knows enough of Shelby's affairs to know that what his master asserts is true: it's Tom who must go or the whole estate will be sold off for debt, including Tom's wife and three children. Later, on the Legree estate, his religious faith tells him that the greatest danger he finds there is not to his life but to his soul. His logic is impeccable. He holds fast to his soul, in the face of suffering, in a way that even nonbelievers like myself must respect. In fact, Tom's story eerily prefigures stories of spiritual solace through deep religious belief that have come out of both the Soviet Gulag and the Nazi concentration camp in the same way that the structure of power on Legree's plantation, and the suffering endured there, forecasts and duplicates many stories of recent genocides.

The power of *Uncle Tom's Cabin* is the power of brilliant analysis married to great wisdom of feeling. Stowe never forgets the logical end of any relationship in which one person is the subject and the other is the object. No matter how the two people feel, or what their intentions are, the logic of the relationship is inherently tragic and traps both parties until the false subject/object relationship is ended. Stowe's most oft-repeated and potent representation of this inexorable logic is the forcible separation of family members, especially of mothers from children. Eliza, faced with the sale of her child, Harry, escapes across the breaking ice of the Ohio River. Lucy, whose ten-month-old is sold behind her back, kills herself. Prue, who has been used for breeding, must listen to her last child cry itself to death because her mistress won't let her save it; she falls into alcoholism and thievery and is finally whipped to death. Cassy, prefiguring a choice made by one of the characters in Toni Morrison's *Beloved*, kills her last child so that it won't grow up in slavery. All of these women have been promised something by their owners—love, education, the privilege and joy of raising their children—but, owing to slavery, all of these promises have been broken. The grief and despair these women display is no doubt what T. S. Eliot was thinking of when he superciliously labeled *Uncle Tom's Cabin* "sensationalist propaganda," but, in fact, few critics in the nineteenth century ever accused Stowe of making up or even exaggerating such stories. One group of former slaves who were asked to comment on Stowe's depiction of slave life said that she had failed to portray the very worst, and Stowe herself was afraid that if she told some of what she had heard from escaped slaves and other informants during her eighteen years in Cincinnati, the book would be too dark to find any readership at all.

Stowe's analysis does not stop with the slave owners and traders, or with the slaves themselves. She understands perfectly that slavery is an economic system embedded in America as a whole, and she comments ironically on Christian bankers in New York whose financial dealings result in the sale of slaves, on Northern politicians who promote the capture of escaped slaves for the sake of the public good, on ministers of churches who give the system a Christian stamp of approval. One of Stowe's most skillful techniques is her method of weaving a discussion of slavery into the dialogue of her characters. Especially interesting is a conversation Mark Twain could have paid attention to. Augustine St. Clare and his abolitionist cousin, Ophelia, are discussing his failure to act in accordance with his feelings of revulsion against slavery. After entertaining Ophelia's criticisms for a period, Augustine points out that Ophelia herself is personally disgusted by black people and doesn't like to come into contact with them. He says, "You would think no harm in a child's caressing a large dog, even if he was black . . . custom with us does what Christianity ought to do,—obliterates the feeling of personal prejudice." When Ophelia takes over the education of Topsy, a child who has suffered a most brutal previous upbringing, she discovers that she can do nothing with her until she takes her, literally, to her bosom. But personal relationships do not mitigate the evils of slavery; Ophelia makes sure to give Topsy her freedom.

Stowe also understands that the real root of slavery is that it is profitable as well as customary. Augustine and his brother live with slavery because it is the system they know and because they haven't the imagination to live without it. Simon Legree embraces slavery because he can make money from it and because it gives him even more absolute power over his workers than he could find in the North or in England.

The very heart of nineteenth-century American experience and literature, the nature and meaning of slavery, is finally what Twain cannot face in *The Adventures of Huckleberry Finn*. As Jim and Huck drift down Twain's beloved river, the author finds himself nearing what must have been a crucial personal nexus: how to reconcile the felt memory of boyhood with the cruel implications of the social system within which that boyhood was lived. He had avoided this problem for the most part in *Tom Sawyer*: slaves hardly impinge on the lives of Tom and the other boys. But once Twain allows Jim a voice, this voice must speak in counterpoint to Huck's voice and must raise issues that cannot easily be resolved, either personally or culturally. Harriet Beecher Stowe, New Englander, daughter of Puritans and thinkers, active in the abolitionist movement and in the effort to aid and educate escaped slaves, had no such personal conflict when she sat down to write *Uncle Tom's Cabin*. Nothing about slavery was attractive to her either as a New Englander or as a resident of Cincinnati for almost twenty years. Her lack of conflict is apparent in the clarity of both the style and substance of the novel.

Why, then, we may ask, did *Uncle Tom's Cabin*, for all its power and popularity, fail to spawn American literature? Fail, even, to work as a model for how to draw passionate, autonomous, and interesting black literary characters? Fail to keep the focus of the American literary imagination on the central dilemma of the American experience: race? Part of the reason is certainly that the public conversation about race and slavery that had been a feature of antebellum American life fell silent after the Civil War. Perhaps the answer is to be found in *The Adventures of Huckleberry Finn*: everyone opted for the ultimate distraction, lighting out for the territory. And the reason is to be found in *Uncle Tom's Cabin*: that's where the money was.

But so what? These are only authors, after all, and once a book is published the author can't be held accountable for its role in the culture. For that we have to blame the citizens themselves, or their teachers, or *their* teachers, the arbiters of critical taste. In "Melodramas of Beset Manhood: How Theories of American Fiction Exclude Women Authors," the scholar Nina Baym has already detailed how the canonization of a very narrow range of white, Protestant, middle-class male authors (Twain, Hawthorne, Melville, Emerson, etc.) has misrepresented our literary life—first by defining the only worthy American literary subject as "the struggle of the individual against society [in which] the essential quality of America comes to reside in its unsettled wilderness and the opportunities that such a wilderness offers to the individual as the medium on which he may inscribe, unhindered, his own destiny and his own nature," and then by casting women, and especially women writers (specialists in the "flagrantly bad best-seller," according to Leslie Fiedler), as the enemy. In such critical readings, all other themes and modes of literary expression fall out of consideration as "un-American." There goes *Uncle Tom's Cabin*, there goes Edith Wharton, there goes domestic life as a subject, there go almost all the best-selling novelists of the nineteenth century and their readers, who were mostly women. The real loss, though, is not to our literature but to our culture and ourselves, because we have lost the subject of how the various social groups who may not escape to the wilderness are to get along in society; and, in the case of *Uncle Tom's Cabin*, the hard-nosed, unsentimental dialogue about race that we should have been having since before the Civil War. Obviously, *Uncle Tom's Cabin* is no more the last word on race relations than *The Brothers Karamazov* or *David Copperfield* is on any number of characteristically Russian or English themes and social questions. Some of Stowe's ideas about inherent racial characteristics (whites: cold, heartless; blacks: naturally religious and warm) are bad and have been exploded. One of her solutions to the American racial conflicts that she foresaw, a colony in Africa, she later repudiated. Nevertheless, her views about many issues were brilliant, and her heart was wise. She gained the respect and friendship of many men and women of goodwill, black and white, such as Frederick Douglass, the civil-rights activist Mary Church Terrill, the writer and social activist James Weldon Johnson, and W. E. B. Du Bois. What she did was find a way to talk about slavery and family, power and law, life and death, good and evil, North and South. She truly believed that all Americans together had to find a solution to the problem of slavery in which all were implicated. When her voice, a courageously public voice—as demonstrated by the public arguments about slavery that rage throughout *Uncle Tom's Cabin*—fell silent in our culture and was replaced by the secretive voice of Huck Finn, who acknowledges Jim only when they are alone on the raft together out in the middle of the big river, racism fell out of the public world and into the private one, where whites think it really is but blacks know it really isn't.

Should *Huckleberry Finn* be taught in the schools? The critics of the Propaganda Era laid the groundwork for the universal inclusion of the book in school curriculums by declaring it great. Although they pre-dated the current generation of politicized English professors, this was clearly a political act, because the entry of *Huck Finn* into classrooms sets the terms of the discussion of racism and American history, and sets them very low: all you have to do to be a hero is acknowledge that your poor sidekick is human; you don't actually have to act in the inter-ests of his humanity. Arguments about censorship have been regularly turned into nonsense by appeals to Huck's "greatness." Moreover, so much critical thinking has gone into defending Huck so that he *can* be great, so that American literature can be found different from and maybe better than Russian or English or French literature, that the very integrity of the critical enterprise has been called into question. That most readers intuitively reject the last twelve chapters of the novel on the grounds of tedium or triviality is clear from the fact that so many critics have turned themselves inside out to defend them. Is it so mys-terious that criticism has failed in our time after being so robust only a generation ago? Those who cannot be persuaded that *The Adventures of Huckleberry Finn* is a great novel have to draw *some* conclusion.

I would rather my children read *Uncle Tom's Cabin*, even though it is far more vivid in its depiction of cruelty than *Huck Finn*, and this is because Stowe's novel is clearly and unmistakably a tragedy. No white-wash, no secrets, but evil, suffering, imagination, endurance, and redemption—just like life. Like little Eva, who eagerly but fearfully lis-tens to the stories of the slaves that her family tries to keep from her, our children want to know what is going on, what has gone on, and what we intend to do about it. If "great" literature has any purpose, it is to help us face up to our responsibilities instead of enabling us to avoid them once again by lighting out for the territory.

DAVID L. SMITH

Huck, Jim, and American Racial Discourse†

> They [blacks] are at least as brave, and more adventuresome [compared with whites]. But this may perhaps proceed from a want of forethought, which prevents their seeing a danger till it be present. . . . They are more ardent after their female: but love seems with them to be more an eager desire, than a tender delicate mixture of sentiment and sensation. Their griefs are transient. Those numberless afflictions, which render it doubtful whether heaven has given life to us in mercy or in wrath, are less felt, and sooner forgotten with them. In general, their existence appears to participate more of sensation than reflection. To this must be ascribed their disposition to sleep when abstracted from their diversions, and unemployed in labor.
> —Thomas Jefferson, *Notes on the State of Virginia*[1]

† From *Satire or Evasion? Black Perspectives on "Huckleberry Finn,"* ed. James S. Leonard, Thomas A. Tenney, and Thadious M. Davis (Durham: Duke University Press, 1992) 103–20. Reprinted with permission.
1. *The Portable Thomas Jefferson,* ed. Merrill D. Peterson (New York: Viking, 1975) 187–88.

Almost any Euro-American intellectual of the nineteenth century could have written the preceding words. The notion of Negro inferiority was so deeply pervasive among those heirs of "The Enlightenment" that the categories and even the vocabulary of Negro inferiority were formalized into a tedious, unmodulated litany. This uniformity increased rather than diminished during the course of the century. As Leon Litwack and others have shown, even the abolitionists, who actively opposed slavery, frequently regarded blacks as inherently inferior. This helps to explain the widespread popularity of colonization schemes among abolitionists and other liberals.[2] As for Jefferson, it is not surprising that he held such ideas, but it is impressive that he formulated so clearly at the end of the eighteenth century what would become the dominant view of the Negro in the nineteenth-century. In many ways this father of American democracy—and quite possibly of five mulatto children—was a man of his time and ahead of his time.[3]

In July 1876, exactly one century after the American Declaration of Independence, Mark Twain began writing *Adventures of Huckleberry Finn*, a novel that illustrates trenchantly the social limitations that American "civilization" imposes on individual freedom.[4] The book takes special note of ways in which racism impinges upon the lives of Afro-Americans, even when they are legally "free." It is therefore ironic that *Huckleberry Finn* has often been attacked and even censored as a racist work. I would argue, on the contrary, that except for Melville's work, *Huckleberry Finn* is without peer among major Euro-American novels for its explicitly antiracist stance.[5] Those who brand the book racist generally do so with-

2. The literature on the abolition movement and on antebellum debates regarding the Negro is, of course, voluminous. George M. Fredrickson's excellent *The Black Image in the White Mind* (New York: Harper Torchbooks, 1971) is perhaps the best general work of its kind. Fredrickson's *The Inner Civil War* (New York: Harper Torchbooks, 1971) is also valuable, especially pp. 53–64. Leon Litwack, in *North of Slavery* (Chicago: U of Chicago P, 1961) 214–46, closely examines the ambivalence of abolitionists regarding racial intermingling. Benjamin Quarles presents the most detailed examination of black abolitionists in *Black Abolitionists* (New York: Oxford UP, 1969), although Vincent Harding offers a more vivid (and overtly polemical) account of their relationships to white abolitionists; see *There Is a River* (New York: Harcourt, Brace, Jovanovich, 1981).

3. The debate over Jefferson's relationship to Sally Hemings has raged for two centuries. The most thorough scholarly accounts are by Fawn Brodie, who suggests that Jefferson did have a prolonged involvement with Hemings (*Thomas Jefferson, an Intimate History* [New York: Norton, 1974]), and by Virginius Dabney, who endeavors to exonerate Jefferson of such charges (*The Jefferson Scandals* [New York: Dodd, Mead, 1981]). Barbara Chase-Riboud presents a fictionalized version of this relationship in *Sally Hemings* (New York: Viking, 1979). The first Afro-American novel, *Clotel; or, The President's Daughter* (1853; New York: Arno, 1969), by William Wells Brown, was also based on this alleged affair.

4. For dates of composition, see Walter Blair, "When Was *Huckleberry Finn* Written?" *American Literature* 30 (Mar. 1958): 1–25.

5. For a discussion of Melville's treatment of race, Carolyn Karcher's *Shadow over the Promised Land* (Baton Rouge: Louisiana State UP, 1980) is especially valuable. Also noteworthy are two articles on "Benito Cereno": Joyce Adler, "Melville's *Benito Cereno*: Slavery and Violence in the Americas," *Science and Society* 38 (1974): 19–48; and Jean Fagan Yellin, "Black Masks: Melville's *Benito Cereno*," *American Quarterly* 22 (Fall 1970): 678–89. Rayford Logan, *The Negro in American Life and Thought: The Nadir, 1877–1901* (New York: Dial, 1954), and Lawrence J. Friedman, *The White Savage: Racial Fantasies in the Postbellum South* (Englewood Cliffs, N.J.: Prentice-Hall, 1970), provide detailed accounts of the racist climate in post-Reconstruction America, emphasizing the literary manifestations of such attitudes. Friedman's discussion of George Washington Cable, the outspoken southern liberal (99–118), is very informative. For a general historical overview of the period, C. Vann Woodward's *Origins of the New South* (Baton Rouge: Louisiana State UP, 1971) and *The Strange Career of Jim Crow*, 3rd ed. (New York: Oxford UP, 1974) remain unsurpassed. John W. Cell, in *The Highest Stage of White Supremacy* (New York: Cambridge UP, 1982), offers a provocative reconsideration of Woodward's arguments. Finally, Joel Williamson's *The Crucible of Race* (New York: Oxford UP, 1984) documents the excessively violent tendencies of southern racism at the end of the century.

out having considered the specific form of racial discourse to which the novel responds. Furthermore, *Huckleberry Finn* offers much more than the typical liberal defenses of "human dignity" and protests against cruelty. Though it contains some such elements, it is more fundamentally a critique of those socially constituted fictions—most notably romanticism, religion, and the concept of "the Negro"—which serve to justify and disguise selfish, cruel, and exploitative behavior.

When I speak of "racial discourse," I mean more than simply attitudes about race or conventions of talking about race. Most importantly, I mean that race itself is a discursive formation which delimits social relations on the basis of alleged physical differences.[6] "Race" is a strategy for relegating a segment of the population to a permanent inferior status. It functions by insisting that each "race" has specific, definitive, inherent behavioral tendencies and capacities which distinguish it from other races. Though scientifically specious, race has been powerfully effective as an ideology and as a form of social definition that serves the interests of Euro-American hegemony. In America, race has been deployed against numerous groups, including Native Americans, Jews, Asians, and even—for brief periods—an assortment of European immigrants.

For obvious reasons, however, the primary emphasis historically has been on defining "the Negro" as a deviant from Euro-American norms. "Race" in America means white supremacy and black inferiority,[7] and "the Negro," a socially constituted fiction, is a generalized, one-dimensional surrogate for the historical reality of Afro-American people. It is this reified fiction that Twain attacks in *Huckleberry Finn*.

Twain adopts a strategy of subversion in his attack on race. That is, he focuses on a number of commonplaces associated with "the Negro" and then systematically dramatizes their inadequacy. He uses the term "nigger," and he shows Jim engaging in superstitious behavior. Yet he portrays Jim as a compassionate, shrewd, thoughtful, self-sacrificing, and even wise man. Indeed, his portrayal of Jim contradicts every claim presented in Jefferson's description of "the Negro." Jim is cautious, he gives excellent advice, he suffers persistent anguish over separation

6. My use of "racial discourse" has some affinities to Foucault's conception of "discourse." This is not, however, a strictly Foucaultian reading. While Foucault's definition of discursive practices provides one of the most sophisticated tools presently available for cultural analysis, his conception of power seems to me problematic. I prefer an account of power which allows for a consideration of interest and hegemony. Theorists such as Marshall Berman, *All That Is Solid Melts into Air* (New York: Simon & Schuster, 1982) 34–35, and Catherine A. MacKinnon, "Feminism, Marxism, Method, and the State: An Agenda for Theory," *Signs* 7.3 (1982): 526, have indicated similar reservations. However, Frank Lentricchia ("Reading Foucault [Punishment, Labor, Resistance]," *Raritan* 1.4 [1981]: 5–32; 2.1 [1982]: 41–70) has made a provocative effort to modify Foucaultian analysis, drawing upon Antonio Gramsci's analysis of hegemony in *Selections from the Prison Notebooks* (New York: International Publishers, 1971). See Foucault, *The Archaeology of Knowledge, Power/Knowledge*, ed. Colin Gordon (New York: Pantheon, 1980) esp. 92–108; and *The History of Sexuality*, vol. 1 (New York: Vintage, 1980) esp. 92–102.

7. This is not to discount the sufferings of other groups. But historically, the philosophical basis of Western racial discourse—which existed even before the European "discovery" of America—has been the equation of "good" and "evil" with light and darkness (or white and black). See Jacques Derrida, "White Mythology," *New Literary History* 6 (1974): 5–74; Winthrop Jordan, *White over Black* (New York: Norton, 1968) 1–40; and Cornel West, *Prophesy Deliverance* (Philadelphia: Westminster P, 1982) 47–65. Economically, the slave trade, chattel slavery, agricultural peonage, and color-coded wage differentials have made the exploitation of African Americans the most profitable form of racism. Finally, Afro-Americans have long been the largest American "minority" group. Consequently, the primacy of "the Negro" in American racial discourse is "overdetermined," to use Louis Althusser's term (*For Marx* [London: Verso, 1979] 87–126). The acknowledgment of primary status, however, is hardly a claim of privilege.

from his wife and children, and he even sacrifices his own sleep so that Huck may rest. Jim, in short, exhibits all the qualities that "the Negro" supposedly lacks. Twain's conclusions do more than merely subvert the justifications of slavery, which was already long since abolished. Twain began his book during the final disintegration of Reconstruction, and his satire on antebellum southern bigotry is also an implicit response to the Negrophobic climate of the post-Reconstruction era.[8] It is troubling, therefore, that so many readers have completely misunderstood Twain's subtle attack on racism.

Twain's use of the term "nigger" has provoked some readers to reject the novel.[9] As one of the most offensive words in our vocabulary, "nigger" remains heavily shrouded in taboo. A careful assessment of this term within the context of American racial discourse, however, will allow us to understand the particular way in which the author uses it. If we attend closely to Twain's use of the word, we may find in it not just a trigger to outrage but, more important, a means of understanding the precise nature of American racism and Mark Twain's attack on it.

Most obviously, Twain uses "nigger" throughout the book as a synonym for "slave." There is ample evidence from other sources that this corresponds to one usage common during the antebellum period. We first encounter it in reference to "Miss Watson's big nigger, named Jim" (chap. 2). This usage, like the term "nigger stealer," clearly designates the "nigger" as an item of property: a commodity, a slave. This passage also provides the only apparent textual justification for the common critical practice of labeling Jim "Nigger Jim," as if "nigger" were a part of his proper name. This loathsome habit goes back at least as far as Albert Bigelow Paine's biography of Twain (1912).[1] In any case, "nigger" in this sense connotes an inferior, even subhuman, creature who is properly owned by and subservient to Euro-Americans.

Both Huck and Jim use the word in this sense. For example, when Huck fabricates his tale about the riverboat accident, the following exchange occurs between him and Aunt Sally:

> "Good gracious! anybody hurt?"
> "No'm. Killed a nigger."
> "Well, it's lucky; because sometimes people do get hurt."
> (Chap. 32)

Huck has never met Aunt Sally prior to this scene, and in spinning a lie which this stranger will find unobjectionable, he correctly assumes that the common notion of Negro subhumanity will be appropriate. Huck's offhand remark is intended to exploit Aunt Sally's attitudes, not to express Huck's own. A nigger, Aunt Sally confirms, is not a person. Yet

8. See Lawrence I. Berkove, "The Free Man of Color in *The Grandissimes* and Works by Harris and Mark Twain," *Southern Quarterly* 18.4 (1981): 60–73; Richard Gollin and Rita Gollin, "*Huckleberry Finn* and the Time of the Evasion," *Modern Language Studies* 9 (Spring 1979): 5–15; Michael Egan, *Mark Twain's Huckleberry Finn: Race, Class and Society* (Atlantic Highlands, N.J.: Humanities P, 1977) esp. 66–102.
9. See Nat Hentoff's series of four columns in the *Village Voice* 27 (1982): "Huck Finn Better Get out of Town by Sundown" (May 4); "Is Any Book Worth the Humiliation of Our Kids?" (May 11); "Huck Finn and the Shortchanging of Black Kids" (May 18); and "These Are Little Battles Fought in Remote Places" (May 25).
1. *Mark Twain: A Biography* (New York: Harper, 1912).

this exchange is hilarious precisely because we know that Huck is playing on her glib and conventional bigotry. We know that Huck's relationship to Jim has already invalidated for him such obtuse racial notions.
The conception of the "nigger" is a socially constituted and sanctioned
fiction, and it is just as false and absurd as Huck's explicit fabrication,
which Aunt Sally also swallows whole.

In fact, the exchange between Huck and Aunt Sally reveals a great
deal about how racial discourse operates. Its function is to promulgate
a conception of "the Negro" as a subhuman and expendable creature
who is by definition feeble-minded, immoral, lazy, and superstitious.
One crucial purpose of this social fiction is to justify the abuse and
exploitation of Afro-American people by substituting the essentialist fiction of "Negroism" for the actual character of individual Afro-Americans. Hence, in racial discourse every Afro-American becomes just
another instance of "the Negro"—just another "nigger." Twain recognizes this invidious tendency of race thinking, however, and he takes
every opportunity to expose the mismatch between racial abstractions
and real human beings.

For example, when Pap drunkenly inveighs against the free mulatto
from Ohio, he is outraged by what appears to him to be a crime against
natural laws (chap. 6). In the first place, a "free nigger" is, for Pap, a
contradiction in terms. Indeed, the man's clothes, his demeanor, his
education, his profession, and even his silver-headed cane bespeak a
social status normally achieved by only a small elite of white men. He
is, in other words, a "nigger" who refuses to behave like one. Pap's ludicrous protestations discredit both himself and other believers in "the
Negro," as many critics have noted. But it has not been sufficiently
stressed that Pap's racial views correspond very closely to those of most
of his white southern contemporaries, in substance if not in manner of
expression. Such views were held not only by poor whites but by all
"right-thinking" southerners, regardless of their social class. Indeed,
not even the traumas of the Civil War could cure southerners of this
folly. Furthermore, Pap's indignation at the Negro's right to vote is precisely analogous to the southern backlash against the enfranchisement
of Afro-Americans during Reconstruction. Finally, Pap's comments are
rather mild compared with the anti-Negro diatribes that were beginning
to emerge among politicians even as Twain was writing *Huckleberry
Finn.* He began writing this novel during the final days of Reconstruction, and it seems more than reasonable to assume that the shameful
white supremacist bluster of that epoch—exemplified by Pap's tirade—
informed Twain's critique of racism in *Huckleberry Finn.*[2]

Pap's final description of this Ohio gentleman as "a prowling, thieving, infernal, white-shirted free nigger" (chap. 6) almost totally contradicts his previous description of the man as a proud, elegant, dignified
figure. Yet this contradiction is perfectly consistent with Pap's need to
reassert "the Negro" in lieu of social reality. Despite the vulgarity of
Pap's personal character, his thinking about race is highly conventional,
and therefore respectable. But most of us cannot respect Pap's views,

2. See Arthur G. Pettit, *Mark Twain and the South* (Lexington: U of Kentucky P, 1974).

and when we reject them, we reject the standard racial discourse of both 1840 and 1880.

A reader who objects to the word "nigger" might still insist that Twain could have avoided using it. But it is difficult to imagine how Twain could have debunked a discourse without using the specific terms of that discourse. Even when Twain was writing his book, "nigger" was universally recognized as an insulting, demeaning word. According to Stuart Berg Flexner, "Negro" was generally pronounced "nigger" until about 1825, at which time abolitionists began objecting to that term.[3] They preferred "colored person" or "person of color." Hence, W. E. B. Du Bois reports that some black abolitionists of the early 1830s declared themselves united "as men, . . . not as slaves; as 'people of color,' not as 'Negroes.' "[4] Writing a generation later in *Army Life in a Black Regiment* (1869), Thomas Wentworth Higginson deplored the common use of "nigger" among freedmen, which he regarded as evidence of low self-esteem.[5] The objections to "nigger," then, are not a consequence of the modern sensibility but had been common for a half century before *Huckleberry Finn* was published. The specific function of this term in the book, however, is neither to offend nor merely to provide linguistic authenticity. Much more importantly, it establishes a context against which Jim's specific virtues may emerge as explicit refutations of racist presuppositions.

Of course, the concept of "nigger" entails far more than just the deployment of certain vocabulary. Most of the attacks on the book focus on its alleged perpetuation of racial stereotypes. Twain does indeed use racial stereotypes here. That practice could be excused as characteristic of the genre of humor within which Twain works. Frontier humor relies upon the use of stock types, and consequently racial stereotypes are just one of many types present in *Huckleberry Finn*. Yet while valid, such an appeal to generic convention would be unsatisfactory because it would deny Twain the credit he deserves for the sophistication of his perceptions.[6]

As a serious critic of American society, Twain recognized that racial discourse depends upon the deployment of a system of stereotypes which constitute "the Negro" as fundamentally different from and inferior to Euro-Americans. As with his handling of "nigger," Twain's strategy with racial stereotypes is to elaborate them in order to undermine them. To be sure, those critics are correct who have argued that Twain uses this narrative to reveal Jim's humanity. Jim, however, is just one individual. Twain uses the narrative to expose the cruelty and hollowness of that racial discourse which exists only to obscure the humanity of *all* Afro-American people.

One aspect of *Huckleberry Finn* that has elicited copious critical commentary is Twain's use of superstition.[7] In nineteenth-century

---

3. *I Hear America Talking* (New York: Van Nostrand Reinhold, 1976) 57.
4. *The Souls of Black Folk*, in *Three Negro Classics*, ed. John Hope Franklin (New York: Avon, 1965) 245.
5. (Boston: Beacon, 1962) 28.
6. See Ralph Ellison, "Change the Joke and Slip the Yoke," in *Shadow and Act* (New York: Random House, 1964) 45–59; Chadwick Hansen, "The Character of Jim and the Ending of *Huckleberry Finn*," *Massachusetts Review* 5 (Autumn 1963): 45–66; Kenneth S. Lynn, *Mark Twain and Southwestern Humor* (Boston: Little, Brown, 1959).
7. See especially Daniel Hoffman, "Jim's Magic: Black or White?" *American Literature* 32 (Mar. 1960): 47–54.

racial discourse, "the Negro" was always defined as inherently superstitious.[8] Many critics, therefore, have cited Jim's superstitious behavior as an instance of negative stereotyping. One cannot deny that in this respect Jim closely resembles the entire tradition of comic darkies,[9] but in some instances apparent similarities conceal fundamental differences. The issue is: does Twain merely reiterate clichés, or does he use these conventional patterns to make an unconventional point? A close examination will show that, in virtually every instance, Twain uses Jim's superstition to make points that undermine rather than revalidate the dominant racial discourse.

The first incident of this superstitious behavior occurs in chapter 2, as a result of one of Tom Sawyer's pranks. When Jim falls asleep under a tree, Tom hangs Jim's hat on a branch. Subsequently Jim concocts an elaborate tale about having been hexed and ridden by witches. The tale grows more grandiose with each repetition, and eventually Jim becomes a local celebrity, sporting a five-cent piece on a string around his neck as a talisman. "Niggers would come miles to hear Jim tell about it, and he was more looked up to than any nigger in that country," the narrator reports. Jim's celebrity finally reaches the point that "Jim was most ruined, for a servant, because he got so stuck up on account of having seen the devil and been rode by witches." That is, no doubt, amusing. Yet whether Jim believes his own tale or not—and the "superstitious Negro" thesis requires us to assume that he does—the fact remains that Jim clearly benefits from becoming more a celebrity and less a "servant." It is his owner, not Jim, who suffers when Jim reduces the amount of his uncompensated labor.[1]

This incident has often been interpreted as an example of risible Negro gullibility and ignorance as exemplified by blackface minstrelsy. Such a reading has more than a little validity, but it can only partially account for the implications of this scene. If not for the final sentence, such an account might seem wholly satisfactory, but the information that Jim becomes, through his own story telling, unsuited for life as a slave introduces unexpected complications. Is it likely that Jim has been deceived by his own creative prevarications—especially given what we learn about his character subsequently? Or has he cleverly exploited the conventions of "Negro superstition" in order to turn a silly boy's prank to his own advantage?

Regardless of whether we credit Jim with forethought in this matter, it is undeniable that he turns Tom's attempt to humiliate him into a major personal triumph. In other words, Tom gives him an inch, and he takes an ell. It is also obvious that he does so by exercising remarkable skills as a rhetorician. By constructing a fictitious narrative of his own

8. Even the allegedly scientific works on the Negro focused on superstition as a definitive trait. See, for example, W. D. Weatherford, *Negro Life in the South* (New York: Young Men's Christian Association P, 1910); and Jerome Dowd, *Negro Races* (New York: Macmillan, 1907). No one has commented more scathingly on Negro superstitions than William Hannibal Thomas in *The American Negro* (1901; New York: Negro Universities P, 1969); by American definitions he was himself a Negro.

9. See Fredrick Woodard and Donnarae MacCann, "*Huckleberry Finn* and the Traditions of Blackface Minstrelsy," *Interracial Books for Children Bulletin* 15.1–2 (1984): 4–13.

1. Daniel Hoffman, in *Form and Fable in American Fiction* (New York: Oxford UP, 1961), reveals an implicit understanding of Jim's creativity, but he does not pursue the point in detail (331).

experience, Jim elevates himself above his prescribed station in life. By becoming, in effect, an author, Jim writes himself a new destiny. Jim's triumph may appear to be dependent upon the gullibility of other "superstitious" Negroes, but since we have no direct encounter with them, we cannot know whether they are unwitting victims of Jim's ruse or not. A willing audience need not be a totally credulous one. In any case, it is intelligence, not stupidity, that facilitates Jim's triumph. Tom may have had his chuckle, but the last laugh clearly belongs to Jim.

In assessing Jim's character, we should keep in mind that forethought, creativity, and shrewdness are qualities that racial discourse—as in the passage from Thomas Jefferson—denies to "the Negro." In that sense, Jim's darky performance here subverts the fundamental definition of "darky." For "the Negro" is defined to be an object, not a subject. But does an object construct its own narrative? Viewed in this way, the fact of superstition, which traditionally connotes ignorance and unsophistication, becomes far less important than the ends to which superstition is put. This inference exposes, once again, the inadequacy of a positivist epistemology, which holds, for example, that "a rose is a rose is a rose." No one will deny the self-evidence of a tautology; but a rose derives whatever meaning it has from the context within which it is placed (including the context of traditional symbolism). It is the contextualizing activity, not *das Ding-an-sich*, which generates meaning. Again and again Twain attacks racial essentialism by directing our attention instead to the particularity of individual action. We find that Jim is not "the Negro." Jim is Jim, and we, like Huck, come to understand what Jim is by attending to what he does in specific situations.

In another instance of explicitly superstitious behavior, Jim uses a hair ball to tell Huck's fortune. One may regard this scene as a comical example of Negro ignorance and credulity, acting in concert with the ignorance and credulity of a fourteen-year-old white boy. That reading would allow one an unambiguous laugh at Jim's expense. If one examines the scene carefully, however, the inadequacy of such a reductive reading becomes apparent. Even if Jim does believe in the supernatural powers of this hair ball, the fact remains that most of the transaction depends upon Jim's quick wits. The soothsaying aside, much of the exchange between Huck and Jim is an exercise in wily and understated economic bartering. In essence, Jim wants to be paid for his services, while Huck wants free advice. Jim insists that the hair ball will not speak without being paid. Huck, who has a dollar, will only admit to having a counterfeit quarter. Jim responds by pretending to be in collusion with Huck. He explains how to doctor the quarter so that "anybody in town would take it in a minute, let alone a hair-ball" (chap. 4). But obviously it is not the hair ball that will benefit from acquiring and spending this counterfeit coin.[2]

In this transaction, Jim serves his own interest while appearing to serve Huck's interest. He takes a slug which is worthless to Huck, and through the alchemy of his own cleverness contrives to make it worth

---

2. See Thomas Weaver and Merline Williams, "Mark Twain's Jim: Identity as an Index to Cultural Attitudes," *American Literary Realism* 13 (Spring 1980): 19–30.

twenty-five cents to himself. That, in antebellum America, is not a bad price for telling a fortune. But more important, Twain shows Jim self-consciously subverting the prescribed definition of "the Negro," even as he performs within the limitations of that role. He remains the conventional "Negro" by giving the white boy what he wants, at no real cost, and by consistently appearing to be passive and subservient to the desires of Huck and the hair ball. But in fact, he serves his own interests all along. Such resourcefulness is hardly consistent with the familiar one-dimensional concept of "the superstitious Negro."

And while Jim's reading is formulaic, it is hardly simpleminded. He sees the world as a kind of Manichean universe, in which forces of light and darkness—white and black—vie for dominance. Pap, he says, is uncertain what to do, torn between his white and black angels. Jim's advice, "to res' easy en let de ole man take his own way" (chap. 4), turns out to be good advice, because Huck enjoys life in the cabin, despite Pap's fits of drunken excess. This mixture of pleasure and pain is precisely what Jim predicts. Admittedly, Jim's conceptual framework is not original. Nonetheless, his reading carries considerable force because it corresponds so neatly to the dominant thematic patterns in this book, and, more broadly, to the sort of dualistic thinking that informs much of Twain's work. (To take an obvious example, consider the role reversals and character contrasts in *Pudd'nhead Wilson* or *The Prince and the Pauper*.) And most immediately, Jim's comments here reflect tellingly upon his situation as a black slave in racist America. The slave's fate is always torn between his master's will and his own.

In this reading and other incidents, Jim emerges as an astute and sensitive observer of human behavior, both in his comments regarding Pap and in his subtle remarks to Huck. Jim clearly possesses a subtlety and intelligence which "the Negro" allegedly lacks. Twain makes this point more clearly in the debate scene in chapter 14. True enough, most of this debate is, as several critics have noted, conventional minstrel-show banter. Nevertheless, Jim demonstrates impressive reasoning abilities, despite his factual ignorance. For instance, in their argument over "Poly-voo-franzy," Huck makes a category error by implying that the difference between languages is analogous to the difference between human language and cat language. While Jim's response—that a man should talk like a man—betrays his ignorance of cultural diversity, his argument is otherwise perceptive and structurally sound. The humor in Huck's conclusion, "you can't learn a nigger to argue," arises precisely from our recognition that Jim's argument is better than Huck's.

Throughout the novel Twain presents Jim in ways which render ludicrous the conventional wisdom about "Negro character." As an intelligent, sensitive, wily, and considerate individual, Jim demonstrates that race provides no useful index of character. While that point may seem obvious to contemporary readers, it is a point rarely made by nineteenth-century Euro-American novelists. Indeed, except for Melville, J. W. DeForest, Albion Tourgée, and George Washington Cable, white novelists virtually always portrayed Afro-American characters as exemplifications of "Negroness." In this regard the twentieth century has been little better. By presenting us with a series of glimpses which penetrate the "Negro" exterior and reveal the person beneath it, Twain debunks American racial discourse. For racial discourse maintains that the "Negro" exterior is all that a Negro really has.

This insight in itself is a notable accomplishment. Twain, however, did not view racism as an isolated phenomenon, and his effort to place racism within the context of other cultural traditions produced the most problematic aspect of his novel. For it is in the final chapters—the Tom Sawyer section—which most critics consider the weakest part of the book, that Twain links his criticisms of slavery and southern romanticism, condemning the cruelties that both of these traditions entail.[3] Critics have objected to these chapters on various grounds. Some of the most common are that Jim becomes reduced to a comic darky,[4] that Tom's antics undermine the seriousness of the novel, and that these burlesque narrative developments destroy the structural integrity of the novel. Most critics see this conclusion as an evasion of the difficult issues the novel has raised. There is no space here for a discussion of the structural issues, but it seems to me that as a critique of American racial discourse, these concluding chapters offer a harsh, coherent, and uncompromising indictment.

Tom Sawyer's absurd scheme to "rescue" Jim offends because the section has begun with Huck's justly celebrated crisis of conscience culminating in his resolve to free Jim, even if doing so condemns him to hell. The passage that leads to Huck's decision, familiar as it is, merits reexamination:

> I'd see him standing my watch on top of his'n, stead of calling me—so I could go on sleeping; and see him how glad he was when I come back out of the fog; and when I come to him again in the swamp, up there where the feud was; and such-like times; and would always call me honey, and pet me, and do everything he could think of for me, and how good he always was; and at last I struck the time I saved him by telling the men we had small-pox aboard, and he was so grateful, and said I was the best friend old Jim ever had in the world, and the *only* one he's got now; and then I happened to look around, and see that paper. . . . I studied a minute, sort of holding my breath, and then says to myself: "All right, then, I'll *go* to hell"—and tore it up. (Chap. 31)

The issue here is not just whether or not Huck should return a fugitive slave to its lawful owner. More fundamentally, Huck must decide whether to accept the conventional wisdom, which defines "Negroes" as subhuman commodities, or the evidence of his own experience, which has shown Jim to be a good and kind man and a true friend.

Huck makes what is obviously the morally correct decision, but his doing so represents more than simply a liberal choice of conscience over social convention. Twain explicitly makes Huck's choice a sharp attack on the southern church. Huck scolds himself: "There was the Sunday

---

3. See Lynn Altenbernd, "Huck Finn, Emancipator," *Criticism* 1 (1959): 298–307.
4. See, for example, Leo Marx, "Mr. Eliot, Mr. Trilling, and *Huckleberry Finn*," *American Scholar* 22 (Autumn 1953): 423–40; and Neil Schmitz, "Twain, *Huckleberry Finn*, and the Reconstruction," *American Studies* 12 (Spring 1971): 59–67.

school, you could a gone to it; and if you'd a done it they'd a learnt you, there, that people that acts as I'd been acting about that nigger goes to everlasting fire" (chap. 31). Yet despite Huck's anxiety, he transcends the moral limitations of his time and place. By the time Twain wrote these words, more than twenty years of national strife, including the Civil War and Reconstruction, had established Huck's conclusion regarding slavery as a dominant national consensus; not even reactionary southerners advocated a reinstitution of slavery. But since the pre–Civil War southern church taught that slavery was God's will, Huck's decision flatly repudiates the church's teachings regarding slavery. And implicitly, it also repudiates the church as an institution by suggesting that the church functions to undermine, not to encourage, a reliance on one's conscience. To define "Negroes" as subhuman removes them from moral consideration and therefore justifies their callous exploitation. This view of religion is consistent with the cynical iconoclasm that Twain expressed in *Letters from the Earth* and other "dark" works.[5]

In this context, Tom Sawyer appears to us as a superficially charming but fundamentally distasteful interloper. His actions are governed not by conscience but rather by romantic conventions and literary "authorities." Indeed, while Tom may appear to be a kind of renegade, he is in essence thoroughly conventional in his values and proclivities. Despite all his boyish pranks, Tom represents a kind of solid respectability—a younger version of the southern gentleman as exemplified by the Grangerfords and Shepherdsons.[6] Hence, when Tom proposes to help Huck steal Jim, Huck laments that "Tom Sawyer fell, considerable, in my estimation. Only I couldn't believe it. Tom Sawyer a *nigger stealer!*" (chap. 33). Such liberating activity is proper for Huck, who is not respectable, but not for Tom, who is. As with the previous example, however, this one implies a deep criticism of the status quo. Huck's act of conscience, which most of us now (and in Twain's own time) would endorse, is possible only for an outsider. This hardly speaks well for the moral integrity of southern (or American) "civilization."

To examine Tom's role in the novel, let us begin at the end. Upon learning of the failed escape attempt and Jim's recapture, Tom cries out, selfrighteously: "Turn him loose! he ain't no slave; he's as free as any cretur that walks this earth!" (chap. 42). Tom has known all along that his cruel and ludicrous scheme to rescue the captured "prisoner" was being enacted upon a free man; and indeed, only his silence regarding Jim's status allowed the scheme to proceed with Jim's cooperation. Certainly, neither Huck nor Jim would otherwise have indulged Tom's foolishness. Tom's gratuitous cruelty here in the pursuit of his own amusement corresponds to his less vicious prank against Jim in chapter 2. And just as before, Twain converts Tom's callous mischief into a personal triumph for Jim.

Not only has Jim suffered patiently, which would, in truth, represent a doubtful virtue (Jim is not Uncle Tom); he demonstrates his moral

---

5. A number of critical works comment on Twain's religious views and the relation between his critiques of religion and racism. See Allison Ensor, *Mark Twain and the Bible* (Lexington: U of Kentucky P, 1969); Arthur G. Pettit, "Mark Twain and the Negro, 1867–1869," *Journal of Negro History* 56 (Apr. 1971): 88–96; and Gollin and Gollin 5–15.
6. See Hoffman, *Form and Fable* 327–28.

superiority by surrendering himself in order to assist the doctor in treating his wounded tormentor. This is hardly the behavior one would expect from a commodity, and it is *precisely* Jim's status—man or chattel—that has been fundamentally at issue throughout the novel. It may be true that the lengthy account of Tom's juvenile antics subverts the tone of the novel, but they also provide the necessary backdrop for Jim's noble act. Up to this point we have been able to admire Jim's good sense and to respond sentimentally to his good character. This, however, is the first time that we see him making a significant (and wholly admirable) moral decision. His act sets him apart from everyone else in the novel except Huck. And modestly (if not disingenuously), he claims to be behaving just as Tom Sawyer would. Always conscious of his role as a "Negro," Jim knows better than to claim personal credit for his good deed. Yet the contrast between Jim's behavior and Tom's is unmistakable. Huck declares that Jim is "white inside" (chap. 40). He apparently intends this as a compliment, but Tom is fortunate that Jim does not behave like most of the whites in the novel.

Twain also contrasts Jim's self-sacrificing compassion with the cruel and mean-spirited behavior of his captors, emphasizing that white skin does not justify claims of superior virtue. They abuse Jim, verbally and physically, and some want to lynch him as an example to other slaves. The moderates among them resist, however, pointing out that they could be made to pay for the destruction of private property. As Huck observes, "the people that's always the most anxious for to hang a nigger that hain't done just right, is always the very ones that ain't the most anxious to pay for him when they've got their satisfaction out of him" (chap. 42). As if these enforcers of white supremacy did not appear contemptible enough already, Twain then has the doctor describe Jim as the best and most faithful nurse he has ever seen, despite Jim's "resking his freedom" and his obvious fatigue. These vigilantes do admit that Jim deserves to be rewarded, but their idea of a reward is to cease punching and cursing him. They are not even generous enough to remove Jim's heavy shackles.

Ultimately, *Huckleberry Finn* renders a harsh judgment on American society. Freedom from slavery, the novel implies, is not freedom from gratuitous cruelty; and racism, like romanticism, is finally just an elaborate justification which the adult counterparts of Tom Sawyer use to facilitate their exploitation and abuse of other human beings. Tom feels guilty, with good reason, for having exploited Jim, but his final gesture of paying Jim off is less an insult to Jim than it is Twain's commentary on Tom himself. Just as slaveholders believe that economic relations (ownership) can justify their privilege of mistreating other human beings, Tom apparently believes that an economic exchange can suffice as atonement for his misdeeds. Perhaps he finds a forty-dollar token more affordable than an apology. But then, just as Tom could only "set a free nigger free," considering, as Huck says, "his bringing-up" (chap. 42), he similarly could hardly be expected to apologize for his pranks. Huck, by contrast, is equally rich, but he *has* apologized to Jim earlier in the novel. And this is the point of Huck's final remark rejecting the prospect of civilization. To become civilized is not just to become like Aunt Sally. More immediately, it is to become like Tom Sawyer.

Jim is indeed "as free as any cretur that walks this earth." In other words, he is a man, like all men, at the mercy of other men's arbitrary cruelties. In a sense, given Twain's view of freedom, to allow Jim to escape to the North or to have Tom announce Jim's manumission earlier would have been an evasion of the novel's ethical insights. While one may escape from legal bondage, there is no escape from the cruelties of this "civilization." There is no promised land where one may enjoy absolute personal freedom. An individual's freedom is always constrained by social relations to other people. Being legally free does not spare Jim from gratuitous humiliation and physical suffering in the final chapters, precisely because Jim is still regarded as a "nigger." Even if he were as accomplished as the mulatto from Ohio, he would not be exempt from mistreatment. Furthermore, since Tom represents the hegemonic values of his society, Jim's "freedom" amounts to little more than an obligation to live by his wits and make the best of a bad situation, just as he has always done.

Slavery and racism, then, are social evils that take their places alongside various others which the novel documents, such as the insane romanticism that inspires the Grangerfords and Shepherdsons blithely to murder each other, generation after generation. Twain rejects entirely the mystification of race and demonstrates that Jim is in most ways a better man than the men who regard him as their inferior. But he also shows how little correlation there may be between the treatment one deserves and the treatment one receives.

If this conclusion sounds uncontroversial from the perspective of the 1980s, we would do well to remember that it contradicts entirely the overwhelming and optimistic consensus of the 1880s No other nineteenth-century novel so effectively locates racial discourse within the context of a general critique of American institutions and traditions. Indeed, the novel suggests that real individual freedom, in this land of the free, cannot be found. "American civilization" enslaves and exploits rather than liberating. It is hardly an appealing message.

Given the subtlety of Mark Twain's approach, it is not surprising that most of his contemporaries misunderstood or simply ignored the novel's demystification of race. Despite their patriotic rhetoric, they, like Pap, were unprepared to take seriously the implications of "freedom, justice, and equality." They, after all, espoused an ideology and an explicit language of race that was virtually identical to Thomas Jefferson's. Yet racial discourse flatly contradicts and ultimately renders hypocritical the egalitarian claims of liberal democracy. The heart of Twain's message to us is that an honest person must reject one or the other. But hypocrisy, not honesty, is our norm. Many of us continue to assert both racial distinction and liberal values simultaneously. If we, a century later, continue to be confused about *Adventures of Huckleberry Finn*, perhaps it is because we remain more deeply committed to both racial discourse and a self-deluding optimism than we care to admit.[7]

---

7. I would like to thank my colleagues, David Langston and Michael Bell, for the helpful suggestions they offered me regarding this essay.

SHELLEY FISHER FISHKIN

Jimmy [from *Was Huck Black?*]†

Twentieth-century American criticism abounds in pronouncements about how Twain's choice of a vernacular narrator in *Huckleberry Finn* transformed modern American literature. Lionel Trilling, for example, felt that

> The prose of *Huckleberry Finn* established for written prose the virtues of American colloquial speech. . . . It has something to do with ease and freedom in the use of language. Most of all it has to do with the structure of the sentence, which is simple, direct, and fluent, maintaining the rhythm of the word-groups of speech and the intonations of the speaking voice. . . . [Twain] is the master of the style that escapes the fixity of the printed page, that sounds in our ears with the immediacy of the heard voice. . . .[1]

"As for the style of the book," Trilling concluded, "it is not less than definitive in American literature."[2] As Louis Budd noted in 1985, "today it is standard academic wisdom that Twain's central, precedent-setting achievement is Huck's language."[3]

Before Twain wrote *Huckleberry Finn*, no American author had entrusted his narrative to the voice of a simple, untutored vernacular speaker—or, for that matter, to a child. Albert Stone has noted that "the vernacular language . . . in *Huckleberry Finn* strikes the ear with the freshness of a real boy talking out loud."[4] Could the voice of an *actual* "real boy talking out loud" have helped Twain recognize the potential of such a voice to hold an audience's attention and to win its trust?

Twain himself noted in his autobiography that he based Huck Finn on Tom Blankenship, the poor-white son of the local drunkard whose pariah status (and exemption from school, church, etc.) made him the envy of every "respectable" boy in Hannibal. Twain wrote,

> In *Huckleberry Finn* I have drawn Tom Blankenship exactly as he was. He was ignorant, unwashed, insufficiently fed; but he had as good a heart as any boy had. His liberties were totally unrestricted. He was the only really independent person—boy or man—in the community, and by consequence he was tranquilly and continuously happy, and was envied by all the rest of us. We liked him, we enjoyed his society. And as his society was forbidden us by our parents, the prohibition trebled and quadrupled its value, and therefore we sought and got more of his society than of any other boy's.[5]

---

† From *Was Huck Black? Mark Twain and African-American Voices* (New York: Oxford University Press, 1993). Copyright © 1993 by Shelley Fisher Fishkin. Used by permission of Oxford University Press, Inc. The author's notes have been edited. Fishkin's citations from *Adventures of Huckleberry Finn* are to the version edited by Walter Blair and Victor Fischer in *The Works of Mark Twain* (Berkeley: University of California Press, 1988). Bracketed page references are to this Norton Critical Edition.

1. Lionel Trilling, "The Greatness of *Huckleberry Finn*," 91–92.
2. Trilling, "The Greatness of *Huckleberry Finn*," 90–91.
3. Louis J. Budd, "Introduction," *New Essays on "Huckleberry Finn*," 15.
4. Albert Stone, *The Innocent Eye: Childhood in Mark Twain's Imagination*, 151–52.
5. *Mark Twain's Autobiography*, ed. Paine, 2: 174–75.

What demands our notice is that although Tom Blankenship may have been the model for Huck's place in society, Twain never suggested that there was anything memorable about the nature of his "talk." Huck's talk, on the other hand, as many critics have noted, is the most memorable thing about him.[6] I suggest that there was another "real boy talking out loud" whose role in the genesis of *Huckleberry Finn* has never been acknowledged.

On 29 November 1874, two years before he published *Tom Sawyer* or began *Adventures of Huckleberry Finn*, Mark Twain published an article called "Sociable Jimmy" in the *New York Times*.[7] *"Sociable Jimmy" takes the place of honor as the first piece Twain published that is dominated by the voice of a child.* This fact alone would seem to mark it as deserving of scholars' attention. Strangely enough, however, it has been almost totally ignored.

In this article, Twain says he originally sent the sketch of "Jimmy" home in a letter in the days when he was a public lecturer. Although this initial letter has disappeared, subsequent letters Twain wrote home to his wife allow us to determine that the encounter he relates happened in December 1871 or January 1872, in a small town in the Midwest, probably Paris, Illinois, and that the child in question definitely existed. Twain reports that he had supper in his room, as was his habit, and that a "bright, simple, guileless little darkey boy . . . ten years old—a wide-eyed, observant little chap" was sent to wait on him. The intensity of Twain's response to the child is striking. He notes that he wrote down what the child said, and sent the record home because he

> . . . wished to preserve the memory of *the most artless, sociable, and exhaustless talker I ever came across.* He did not tell me a single remarkable thing, or one that was worth remembering; and yet he was himself so interested in his small marvels, and they flowed so naturally and comfortably from his lips, that his talk got the upper hand of my interest, too, and *I listened as one who receives a revelation.* I took down what he had to say, just as he said it—without altering a word or adding one.[8]

Twain's "revelation" involved his recognition of the potential of a "bright, simple, guileless . . . wide-eyed, observant" child as narrator. I suggest that the voice of Jimmy, the "most artless, sociable, and exhaustless talker" Twain had ever come across, became a model for the voice with which Twain would change the shape of American literature.

It was a voice that Twain contained within himself, a language and set of cadences and rhythms he could generate fluently on his own, having been exposed to many such voices in his youth. Jimmy triggered his recollection of those voices, and sparked his apprehension of the creative possibilities they entailed. We can view the remarkable impression

6. Tony Tanner, for example, observed in 1965 in *Reign of Wonder* that "Huck remains a voice. . . ." (181); and Keith Opdahl noted in 1990 in " 'The Rest Is Just Cheating,' " "Huck comes to life for us not as a physical being, since his appearance is barely described in the book (we know only that he dresses in 'rags' and fidgets at the dinner table) but as a voice . . ." (277).

7. "Sociable Jimmy" ran on page 7 of the *New York Times*, 29 November 1874, over Mark Twain's by-line. All my quotations from the piece are taken from the original publication. Twain had begun to write *Tom Sawyer* the preceding summer.

8. Mark Twain, "Sociable Jimmy." Emphasis added.

Jimmy made upon Twain, then, as connected to Twain's awareness of the ease with which he could speak in that voice himself. As he put it in a letter to Livy written shortly after he met Jimmy, "*I think I could swing my legs over the arms of a chair & that boy's spirit would descend upon me & enter into me.*"[9] It was a crucial step on the road to creating Huck.

"Sociable Jimmy" consists mainly of what Twain presents as a transcription of Jimmy's engaging conversation. Twain had been intrigued for several years by the possibilities of a child as narrator, but this was the first time that he developed this perspective at any length in print.[1] Along with "A True Story," which ran in the *Atlantic Monthly* the same month "Sociable Jimmy" ran in the *Times*, it also represented one of Twain's first extended efforts to translate African-American speech into print. Indeed, to the extent that critics took notice of the piece at all, it was as an experiment in African-American dialect. Jimmy's defining characteristic for critics seemed to be the fact that he was black. For Twain, however, Jimmy was mainly a charming and delightful *child* who captured his heart and captivated his imagination.

In the "Explanatory" with which *Huckleberry Finn* begins, Twain enumerates seven dialects used in the book, one of which is "Missouri negro dialect." Critics have debated whether Twain did, in fact, use seven dialects, or more, or fewer; but they have generally assumed that the only "negro dialect" in the book is that spoken by African-American characters. On a phonological level, that assumption is correct: only African-American characters, for example, say "dat," as opposed to "that." But phonology alone does not describe a *voice*, as the voluminous criticism about what makes Huck's voice distinctive clearly shows. Voice involves syntax and diction, the cadences and rhythms of a speaker's sentences, the flow of the prose, the structures of the mental processes, the rapport with the audience, the characteristic stance as regards the material related.

The cadences and rhythms of Jimmy's speech, his syntax and diction, his topics of conversation, attitudes, limitations, and his ability to hold our interest and our trust bear a striking resemblance to those qualities of speech and character that we have come to identify indelibly with Huck. Both boys are naive and open, engaging and bright. They are unpretentious, uninhibited, easily impressed, and unusually loquacious. They free-associate with remarkable energy and verve. And they are supremely self-confident: neither doubts for a minute that Twain (in Jimmy's case) or the reader (in Huck's) is completely absorbed by everything he has to say. I am not suggesting that Twain was being intentionally misleading either in his "Explanatory" or in his comments about the roots of Huck in Tom Blackenship: rather, I put forth the far from controversial notion that artists are notoriously unreliable critics of their own work. As I point out later on, Twain's blending of black voices with white to create the voice we know as Huck's may well have been unconscious.

9. SLC to Olivia Langdon Clemens, 10–11 January 1872, Mark Twain Papers. Quoted with permission. Emphasis added. I am grateful to Victor Fischer and Louis J. Budd for having brought this letter to my attention.
1. A child's perspective surfaces briefly in his presentation of the letter he allegedly received from his niece Annie in "An Open Letter to the American People" (1866). Twain also experimented with a child narrator in his unpublished fragment, "Boy's Manuscript" (1868).

* * *

Clearly, Twain is experimenting with African-American dialect in "Sociable Jimmy," just as he was in "A True Story, Repeated Word for Word as I Heard It," which appeared in the *Atlantic Monthly* the same month that "Sociable Jimmy" appeared in the *New York Times*. But although on the phonological level Jimmy's dialect bears some obvious resemblances to the speech of black characters in the novel, particularly Jim's, in a number of other ways his speech is closer to that of Huck. It is not just linguistically, however, that Jimmy and Huck have much in common. Even more striking than the similarities between Jimmy and Huck on the level of cadence, syntax, and diction, are the similarities between the two boys' character traits and topics of conversation.

The adult world remains rather confusing and cryptic to both Jimmy and Huck, who are blissfully oblivious to the gaps in their understanding. Part of the humor in both "Sociable Jimmy" and *Huckleberry Finn* stems from the reader's awareness that sometimes neither Jimmy nor Huck understands that a joke is being perpetrated. Twain finds Jimmy's "dense simplicity" so engaging that he devotes a bracketed aside in the piece to explicating it:

> Some folks say dis town would be considerable bigger if it wa'n't on accounts of so much lan' all roun' it dat ain't got no houses on it. [This in perfect seriousness—dense simplicity—no idea of a joke.]

Huck, too, sometimes fails to "get" a joke. At the circus, for example, the "drunk" who had argued with the ringmaster until he gave him a chance to ride jumps on a charging horse, pulls off his outer clothes, and turns out to be one of the regular circus performers in disguise. Huck says,

> . . . then the ring-master he see how he had been fooled, and he *was* the sickest ring-master you ever see, I reckon. Why, it was one of his own men! He had got up that joke all out of his own head, and never let on to nobody. Well, I felt sheepish enough, to be took in so, but I wouldn't a been in that ring-master's place, not for a thousand dollars. [164–65]

Huck has been taken in even more than he realizes, of course, since he is oblivious to the fact that the ringmaster's "embarrassment" is part of the circus routine as well. His typical stance is dead earnestness, particularly in the face of circumstances that would strike most readers as funny. As Walter Blair put it, "since he was almost completely humorless, he was bound to be incongruously naive and somber on many laugh-provoking occasions."[2] (It is interesting that in "Sociable Jimmy," written early in his career, Twain felt the need to flag the gaps in the child's understanding for the reader; by *Huckleberry Finn*, he would allow that character trait to emerge without authorial comment.) A year or so before Twain met Jimmy, in "Disgraceful Persecution of a Boy" (1870), Twain had experimented with creating a narrator too bigoted to understand the full import of what he related. In "Sociable Jimmy," Twain gave

2. Walter Blair, *Mark Twain and "Huck Finn,"* 75.

his reader an early glimpse of a narrator too *innocent* to understand the meaning of all he said. By the time he wrote *Huckleberry Finn*, of course, Twain had figured out how to use a narrator's naive responses to the world around him to unmask the hypocrisy and pretensions of that world, a strategy with which he had begun to experiment in 1870 and 1871 in "Goldsmith's Friend Abroad Again." Although Jimmy's naiveté, as conveyed by Twain, serves no satirical purpose, it *is* completely convincing. That totally believable, authentic innocence would be a crucial component of what readers would find compelling about Huck.

Both Jimmy and Huck casually pepper their conversation with accidents that are simultaneously bizarre, grisly, and preposterous. In Jimmy's case, it is the cow that got skewered by the church steeple:

> I reckon you seed dat church as you come along up street. . . . [I]t's all solid stone, excep' jes de top part—de steeple, I means—dat's wood. It falls off when de win' blows pooty hard, an' one time it stuck in a cow's back and busted de cow all to de mischief. . . . You see dat arrer on top o' dat steeple? Well, Sah, dat arrer is pooty nigh as big as dis do' [door]. I seed it when dey pulled it outen de cow.

For Huck, it is the flattening of Hank Bunker:

> . . . I've always reckoned that looking at the new moon over your left shoulder is one of the carelessest and foolishest things a body can do. Old Hank Bunker done it once, and bragged about it; and in less than two years he got drunk and fell off of the shot tower and spread himself out so that he was just a kind of a layer, as you may say; and they slid him edgeways between two barn doors for a coffin, and buried him so, so they say, but I didn't see it. Pap told me. But anyway, it all come of looking at the moon that way, like a fool. [65]

As David Sloane notes, "Effortlessly blended into Huck's comments on omens of bad luck, this anecdote disappears in the run of his talk."[3] Jimmy's anecdote slips unobtrusively into his talk, as well. Both boys apparently wish to be scrupulously accurate about whether their reports are first- or secondhand, reinforcing, in the process, the reader's trust in the candor of their narratives.

Another element Jimmy and Huck have in common is an aversion to violence and cruelty. Both boys have bad dreams about cruel and violent acts they've witnessed, and have difficulty talking about the subject. Jimmy tells us,

> I can't kill a chicken—well, I kin wring its neck off, cuz dat don't make 'em no sufferin scacely; but I can't take and chop dey heads off, like some people kin. It makes me feel so—so—well, I kin see dat chicken nights so's I can't sleep.

After the mindless killings during the feud, Huck comments:

> It made me so sick I most feel out of the tree. I ain't agoing to tell *all* that happened—it would make me sick again if I was to do that. I wish I hadn't ever come ashore that night, to see such things. I

---

3. Sloane, *Mark Twain as a Literary Comedian*, 132.

ain't ever going to get shut of them—lots of times I dream about them. [133–34]

While Jimmy's comments involve chickens and Huck's involve human beings, the visceral rejection of violence and cruelty in each case is similar, as is each child's reluctance to talk about it, and the expression of personal anguish with the barely understood sleep disturbance of a child.

When either Jimmy or Huck is truly determined to fascinate his listener he launches into a long, name-filled family narrative. In neither case is the family his own. Jimmy talks about the family that runs the inn in which he works, and Huck about an invented family designed to make convincing whatever identity he has chosen (for pragmatic reasons) at that moment. "Dey's fo'teen in dis fam'ly," Jimmy notes,

> —all boys an' gals. Bill he suppo'ts 'em all—an he don' never complain—he's *real* good, Bill is. . . . Dat was Nan dat you hearn a cuttin' dem shines on de pi-anah while ago. . . . *Tab* can't hole a candle to *her*, but Tab kin *sing* like de very nation. She's de only one in dis family dat kin sing. You don't never hear a yelp outen Nan. Nan can't sing for shucks. I'd jes lieves hear a tom-cat dat's got scalded. Dey's fo'teen in dis fam'ly 'sides de ole man and de ole 'ooman—all brothers an' sisters. . . . Dey all gits drunk—all 'cep Bill. . . . Dey's all married—all de fam'ly's married—cep' some of de gals. Dare's fo'teen. It's de biggest family in dese parts, dey say. Dare's Bill—Bill Nubbles—Nubbles is de name; Bill, an' Griz, an' Duke, an' Bob, an' Nan, an' Tab, an' Kit, an' Sol, an' Si, an' Phil, an' Puss, an' Jake, an' Sal—Sal she's married an' got chil'en as big as I is—an' Hoss Hubbles, he's de las'. Hoss is what dey mos' always calls him, but he's got another name dat I somehow disremember, it's so kind o' hard to git the hang of it.

Jimmy is convinced that all of these details will intrigue his listener—and, as it turns out, they do. Twain interjects,

> [Then, observing that I had been taking down the extraordinary list of nicknames for adults, he said]: "But in de mawnin' I can ask Bill what's Hoss's other name, an' den I'll come up an' tell you when I fetches yo' breakfast. An' may be I done got some o' dem names mixed up, but Bill, he kin tell me. Dey's fo'teen." . . . By this time he was starting off with the waiter, (and a pecuniary consideration for his sociability), and, as he went out he paused a moment and said: "Dad-fetch it, somehow dat other name don't come. But, anyways, you jes' read dem names over an' see if dey's fo'teen." [I read the list from the flyleaf of Longfellow's *New-England Tragedies*.] "Dat's right, sah. Dey's all down. I'll fetch up Hoss's other name in de mawnin', sah. Don't you be oneasy."
> [Exit, whistling "Listen to the Mocking Bird."]

Jimmy's concern that Twain might lose sleep over the fact that Jimmy hadn't been able to recall all the names reveals a blithe self-assurance that Twain found utterly charming and delightful.

Similarly, when the Grangerfords quiz Huck on who he is, he tells them a tale about "pap and me . . . and Mary Ann . . . and Bill . . . and Tom and Mort." Huck offers the fugitive-slave-hunters a family narrative about "pap, and mam, and sis, and Miss Hooker," and regales the king and the duke with a tale about "Pa and my brother Ike . . . [and] uncle Ben [and] our nigger, Jim." The language Huck uses in one such tale echoes Jimmy's precise phrasing. Huck says, "All of us was saved but Bill Whipple—and oh, he *was* the best cretur!" As Jimmy had put it years earlier, "Bill, he's de oldest. An he's de bes', too."

The only "real" family that each boy has is "Pa" or "Pap" and in both cases the father has a history of alcohol problems that both children describe with unembarrassed frankness. In both cases (despite Jimmy's assertion that Pa's drinking days are over), the problem is ongoing.

Jimmy and Huck also share some matters of taste: each boy is especially awed by a particular clock, and both set themselves up as judges of refinement.[4] Jimmy and Huck are both easily impressed by other things as well—Jimmy by the size of the church steeple and the weather vane at its top, Huck by the Grangerfords' fake plaster fruits and Emmeline's dreadful poetry.

Finally, Jimmy and Huck are both at home with dead animals—dead cats, dead fish. These are simply a part of their world and they wouldn't dream of omitting them from their chatty conversation. They bring them in casually and comfortably, unaware that details about the dead animal might disrupt their listener's equilibrium or digestion. Jimmy entertains Twain at dinner, apropos of nothing in particular, with an anecdote about the dead cat in the well that supplied Twain's drinking water:

> Bill's down on cats. So is de gals—waiter gals. When dey ketches a cat bummin' aroun' heah, dey jis' *scoops* him—'deed dey do. Dey snake him into de cistern—dey's been cats drownded in dat water dat's in yo' pitcher. I seed a cat in dare yistiddy—all swelled up like a pudd'n. I bet you dem gals done dat.

With similarly jarring candor, Huck fails to edit out of his lyrical description of dawn on the river a decidedly pungent dead fish:

> then the nice breeze springs up, and comes fanning you from over there, so cool and fresh, and sweet to smell, on account of the woods and the flowers; but sometimes not that way, because they've left dead fish laying around, gars, and such, and they do get pretty rank . . . [135–36]

Perhaps Jimmy's sociable chatter about the dead cats remained in Twain's subconscious, when, a few years after his encounter with

---

4. Jimmy enthusiastically admires the clock on the local church: "Dat clock ain't just a striker, like dese common clocks. It's a *bell*—jist a reglar *bell*—and it's a buster." Huck is just as impressed by the clock he encounters on the Grangerford mantelpiece: "It was beautiful to hear that clock tick; and sometimes when one of these peddlers had been along and scoured her up and got her in good shape, she would start in and strike a hundred and fifty before she got tuckered out. They wouldn't took any money for her" (136) [120]. Both Jimmy and Huck on occasion set themselves up as judges of refinement, unaware of the irony that their taking this role inevitably entails. Thus Jimmy passes judgment on the manners of the women in his house, and Huck on the wall markings left by some rough characters.

Jimmy, he introduced Huck Finn to the world in *Tom Sawyer* carrying a dead cat.

> Tom hailed the romantic outcast:
> "Hello, Huckleberry!"
> "Hello yourself, and see how you like it."
> "What's that you got?"
> "Dead Cat."

Dead cats enter the scene in *Huckleberry Finn* as well, this time *en masse*, when the Bricksville crowd is gunning for the king and the duke at their third performance of "The Royal Nonesuch." Huck says,

> If I know the signs of a dead cat being around, and I bet I do, there was sixty-four of them went in. [167]

Both Jimmy and Huck are proud that they "know the signs of a dead cat being around" and are only too glad to share their knowledge.

Twain had long admired the artful presentation of many of those qualities Jimmy so fully embodied. For example, referring to a story James Whitcomb Riley told, Twain commented,

> The simplicity and innocence and unconsciousness of the old farmer are perfectly simulated, and the result is a performance which is thoroughly charming and delicious. This is art—and fine and beautiful.[5]

If "simplicity and innocence and unconsciousness" are to be desired, who better to embody these traits than a child?

"Sociable Jimmy" was Twain's first published work in which the voice of a child took center stage.[6] In the years that immediately followed its publication, Twain became increasingly aware of the distinctive possibilities of the choice of a child narrator. As he once put it, "Experience has taught me long ago that if ever *I* tell a boy's story . . . it is never worth printing. . . . To be successful and worth printing, the imagined boy would have to tell the story *himself* and let me act merely as his amanuensis."[7] That was, of course, precisely the role in which Twain placed himself as he copied down Jimmy's speech that evening. It is the same role Twain assumed in his imagination when he began writing *Huckleberry Finn*. In the recently discovered manuscript of the beginning of the novel, Huck's opening lines, "You don't know about me . . . " are preceded by the words,

> Huckleberry Finn
> reported by Mark Twain.[8]

* * *

5. Twain, quoted in Walter Blair and Hamlin Hill, *America's Humor*, 322.
6. In a sketch written in 1868, which remained unpublished until Bernard DeVoto included it in *Mark Twain at Work* in 1942, Twain had experimented with telling a story from a boy's point of view. Twain presented the sketch as the diary of a boy named Billy Rogers. The sketch is, in some ways, a preparation for *Tom Sawyer*, and Billy is a precursor of Tom.
7. Twain, quoted in Blair and Hill, *America's Humor*, 327.
8. Doyno, *Writing "Huck Finn,"* 40.

Works Cited

Blair, Walter. *Mark Twain and "Huck Finn."* Berkeley: University of California Press, 1960.

Blair, Walter and Hamlin Hill. *America's Humor.* New York: Oxford University Press, 1978.

Budd, Louis J. "Introduction." In *New Essays on "Adventures of Huckleberry Finn,"* edited by Louis J. Budd, 1–33. Cambridge: Cambridge University Press, 1985.

Doyno, Victor A. *Writing "Huck Finn": Mark Twain's Creative Process.* Philadelphia: University of Pennsylvania Press, 1992.

Sloan, David E. *Mark Twain as Literary Comedian.* Baton Rouge: Louisiana State University Press, 1979.

Stone, Albert. *The Innocent Eye: Childhood in Mark Twain's Imagination.* 1961. Reprint. Hamden, Conn.: Archon Books, 1970.

Tanner, Tony. *Reign of Wonder: Naivete and Reality in American Literature.* Cambridge: Cambridge University Press, 1964.

Trilling, Lionel. "The Greatness of *Huckleberry Finn.*" (From *The Liberal Imagination,* 1950). Reprinted in *"Huck Finn" Among the Critics,* edited by Thomas M. Inge, 81–92. Frederick, Md.: University Publications of America, 1985.

Twain, Mark. *Mark Twain's Autobiography.* 2 vols. Edited by Albert Bigelow Paine. New York: Harper and Brothers, 1924.

JAMES R. KINCAID

Voices on the Mississippi
[Review of *Was Huck Black?*]†

"How will Americans respond to the news that the voice of Huck Finn, the beloved national symbol and cultural icon, was part black?" So opens the last paragraph of *Was Huck Black?* Shelley Fisher Fishkin's book has a way of turning the spotlight on itself, insisting on its well-intentioned revolutionary energies and its national importance, about every second page. Readers may be annoyed by that. Worse, though, is the willingness to extend the carnival-barker swagger so evident in the title into the conduct of the argument itself, muddying distinctions, mixing weak claims with strong, and distracting us from the good archival research and the significant contribution this slim book may make.

Was Huck Black? has within it (somewhere) a sharp and important argument. Such an argument takes shape as a demonstration of how *The Adventures of Huckleberry Finn* drew upon a vernacular formed by black voices as well as white, of how some of Mark Twain's particular experiences with black Americans may have extended his linguistic range, of how his success made available a powerful model both to white writers and to black, and of how it happens that all of this has

---

† From the *New York Times* (23 May 1993), Section 7, p. 12. Reprinted by permission. James R. Kincaid is the author of *Child-Loving: The Erotic Child and Victorian Culture* and *Annoying the Victorians.*

been so little explored by scholars, most of whom have tacitly assumed that there are separate white and black traditions. All this is in the book, but it is available in this moderate form only if one makes use of the excellent and extensive footnotes, which consistently cool down the sizzling prose of the text.

The galvanic text keeps pulling us away from a developing argument to return us to Ms. Fishkin's particular scholarly obsession with real-life original models for literary characters. She has two in particular: Jerry, a young slave Twain mentions as a "gay and impudent and satirical" friend of his teen-age years in the opening paragraphs of an essay, "Corn-Pone Opinions"; and 10-year-old Jimmy, the subject of "Sociable Jimmy," a neglected sketch Twain published in *The New York Times* in November 1874, two years before beginning *Huckleberry Finn*.

Jerry, who may or may not have existed—Ms. Fishkin says either he "or someone very much like him" probably did—is said to have opened to Twain the satirical possibilities of the imitative rhetorical device called signifying. But it is Jimmy that Ms. Fishkin and the jumped-up title of her book are caught by: "Compelling evidence indicates that the model for Huck Finn's voice was a black child instead of a white one." Now, Twain said Huck was drawn from a boy named Tom Blankenship "exactly as he was," but he said nothing about that white boy's voice, and it's Huck's voice, his talk, after all, that matters so much.

Jimmy, described by Twain as "artless" and "sociable," "a bright, simple, guileless darkey boy," is indeed a talker worth hearing: "Bill's down on cats. So is de gals. . . . When dey ketches a cat bummin' aroun' heah, dey jis' scoops him—'deed dey do. Dey snake him into de cistern—dey's been cats drownded in dat water dat's in yo' pitcher. I seed a cat in dare yistiddy—all swelled up like a pudd'n." The evidence presented to link this talk to Huck's seems to me strong insofar as it relates to general features of black American speech, and trivial when it insists that Huck in some way is Jimmy. It is not a good use of our time to read that both Huck and Jimmy are humorless, at home with dead animals, and the like.

Insisting on the direct connections among Jimmy and blackness and Huck prompts us to ask, "What sort of Huck?" "What sort of black?" Are all the possibilities of angry beauty and cultural resistance and edgy affection so marked in Huck to be convincingly attached to black American speech and experience—only to lead to a little cute "darkey," bright but guileless? Leaving aside that Huck hardly seems guileless, such a reductive chain leaves both Huck and blackness diminished, caricatured. Jimmy is a cross between a lawn ornament and a minstrel clown, represented pretty well by the insipid Huck of the latest Disney film but not by anything in black culture, or by Twain's Huck either. Besides, if one registers Huck as black in any literal way, much of the powerful moral and social irony of the story disappears and some central scenes become nonsense.

Now and then, Ms. Fishkin actually makes a different claim: that Twain's experience with Jimmy released memories of childhood experiences with black friends, sounds and sights that made possible the formation of the most important literary voice in our culture. That such a voice is so rich, carrying with it so much that is not simply white and colloquial and boyish and safely charming, is a point that has not before been much discussed.

Ms. Fishkin, a professor of American studies at the University of Texas, has some sharp words for a critical tradition she is not averse to associating with "segregation" and "miscegenation," but she gives little attention to the implications of her own position. She does not much consider this "blending" of black and white in the vernacular, even whether it is really a blending or, as one of her notes puts it, a "warring" between the two voices.

Finally, while she addresses the blunt charge of white literary tradition "appropriating" black experience, she does not consider the possibility that her reassuring book may simply make things comfy again, make Huck into a cute little "darkey" like Jimmy, one who can protect us from such things as Toni Morrison's frightening readings of "the parasitical nature of white freedom" portrayed in the novel, the way in which Huck's growth depends on Jim's "serviceability" and thus is inextricably tied to "the term 'nigger'." Ms. Fishkin's smooth talk about cultural blending and her gush about such things as black spirituals flowing "to the core of [Twain's] being" are all soul-butter and flapdoodle in comparison.

TONI MORRISON

[This Amazing, Troubling Book]†

Fear and alarm are what I remember most about my first encounter with Mark Twain's *Adventures of Huckleberry Finn*. Palpable alarm. Unlike the treasure-island excursion of *Tom Sawyer*, at no point along Huck's journey was a happy ending signaled or guaranteed. Reading *Huckleberry Finn*, chosen randomly without guidance or recommendation, was deeply disturbing. My second reading of it, under the supervision of an English teacher in junior high school, was no less uncomfortable—rather more. It provoked a feeling I can only describe now as muffled rage, as though appreciation of the work required my complicity in and sanction of something shaming. Yet the satisfactions were great: riveting episodes of flight, of cunning; the convincing commentary on adult behavior, watchful and insouciant; the authority of a child's voice in language cut for its renegade tongue and sharp intelligence. Liberating language—not baby talk for the young, nor the doggedly patronizing language of so many books on the "children's shelf." And there were interesting female characters: the clever woman undeceived by Huck's disguise; the young girl whose sorrow at the sale of slaves is grief for a family split rather than conveniences lost.

Nevertheless, for the second time, curling through the pleasure, clouding the narrative reward, was my original alarm, coupled now with a profoundly distasteful complicity.

---

† Introduction to *Adventures of Huckleberry Finn* (New York: Oxford University Press, 1996) xxxi–xli. Reprinted by permission of International Creative Management, Inc. Copyright © 1996 by Toni Morrison. Bracketed page references to this Norton Critical Edition have been added after the original references.

Then, in the mid-fifties, I read it again—or sort of read it. Actually I read it through the lenses of Leslie Fiedler and Lionel Trilling. Exposed to Trilling's reverent intimacy and Fiedler's irreverent familiarity, I concluded that their criticisms served me better than the novel had, not only because they helped me see many things I had been unaware of, but precisely because they ignored or rendered trivial the things that caused my unease.

In the early eighties I read *Huckleberry Finn* again, provoked, I believe, by demands to remove the novel from the libraries and required reading lists of public schools. These efforts were based, it seemed to me, on a narrow notion of how to handle the offense Mark Twain's use of the term "nigger" would occasion for black students and the corrosive effect it would have on white ones. It struck me as a purist yet elementary kind of censorship designed to appease adults rather than educate children. Amputate the problem, band-aid the solution. A serious comprehensive discussion of the term by an intelligent teacher certainly would have benefited my eighth-grade class and would have spared all of us (a few blacks, many whites—mostly second-generation immigrant children) some grief. Name calling is a plague of childhood and a learned activity ripe for discussion as soon as it surfaces. Embarrassing as it had been to hear the dread word spoken, and therefore sanctioned, in class, my experience of Jim's epithet had little to do with my initial nervousness the book had caused. Reading "nigger" hundreds of times embarrassed, bored, annoyed—but did not faze me. In this latest reading I was curious about the source of my alarm—my sense that danger lingered after the story ended. I was powerfully attracted to the combination of delight and fearful agitation lying entwined like crossed fingers in the pages. And it was significant that this novel which had given so much pleasure to young readers was also complicated territory for sophisticated scholars.

Usually the divide is substantial: if a story that pleased us as novice readers does not disintegrate as we grow older, it maintains its value only in its retelling for other novices or to summon uncapturable pleasure as playback. Also, the books that academic critics find consistently rewarding are works only partially available to the minds of young readers. *Adventures of Huckleberry Finn* manages to close that divide, and one of the reasons it requires no leap is that in addition to the reverence the novel stimulates is its ability to transform its contradictions into fruitful complexities and to seem to be deliberately cooperating in the controversy it has excited. The brilliance of *Huckleberry Finn* is that it *is* the argument it raises.

My 1980s reading, therefore, was an effort to track the unease, nail it down, and learn in so doing the nature of my troubled relationship to this classic American work.

Although its language—sardonic, photographic, persuasively aural—and the structural use of the river as control and chaos seem to me quite the major feats of *Huckleberry Finn*, much of the novel's genius lies in its quiescence, the silences that pervade it and give it a porous quality that is by turns brooding and soothing. It lies in the approaches to and exits from action; the byways and inlets seen out of the corner of the eye; the subdued images in which the repetition of a simple word, such as "lonesome," tolls like an evening bell; the moments when nothing is said, when scenes and incidents swell the heart unbearably precisely because unarticulated, and force an act of imagination almost against the will. Some of the stillness, in the beautifully rendered eloquence of a child, is breathtaking. "The sky looks ever so deep when you lay down on your back in the moonshine" (59)[47]. " . . . it was big trees all about, and gloomy in there amongst them. There was freckled places on the ground where the light sifted down through the leaves, and the freckled places swapped about a little" (61)[49]. Other moments, however, are frightening meditations on estrangment and death. Huck records a conversation he overhears among happy men he cannot see but whose voices travel from the landing over the water to him. Although he details what the men say, it is how distant Huck is from them, how separated he is from their laughing male camaraderie, that makes the scene memorable. References to death, looking at it or contemplating it, are numerous. " . . . this drownded man was just his [Pap's] size, . . . but they couldn't make nothing out of the face . . . floating on his back in the water. . . . took him and buried him on the bank. . . . I knowed mighty well that a drownded man don't float on his back, but on his face" (30)[24]. The emotional management of death seeds the novel: Huck yearns for death, runs from its certainty and feigns it. His deepest, uncomic feelings about his status as an outsider, someone "dead" to society, are murmuring interludes of despair, soleness, isolation and unlove. A plaintive note of melancholy and dread surfaces immediately in the first chapter, after Huck sums up the narrative of his life in a prior book.

> Then I set down in a chair by the window and tried to think of something cheerful, but it warn't no use. I felt so lonesome I most wished I was dead. The stars were shining, and the leaves rustled in the woods ever so mournful; and I heard an owl, away off, who-whooing about somebody that was dead, and a whippowill and a dog crying about somebody that was going to die; and the wind was trying to whisper something to me and I couldn't make out what it was, and so it made the cold shivers run over me. Then away out in the woods I heard that kind of a sound that a ghost makes. . . . I got so downhearted and scared I did wish I had some company. (2)[16]

Although Huck complains bitterly of rules and regulations, I see him to be running not from external control but from external chaos. Nothing in society makes sense; all is in peril. Upper-class, churchgoing, elegantly housed families annihilate themselves in a psychotic feud, and Huck has to drag two of their corpses from the water—one of whom is a just-made friend, the boy Buck; he sees the public slaughter of a drunk; he hears the vicious plans of murderers on a wrecked steamboat; he spends a large portion of the book in the company of "[Pap's] kind of people" (166)[142]—the fraudulent, thieving Duke and King who wield brutal power over him, just as his father did. No wonder that when he is alone, whether safe in the Widow's house or hiding from his father, he is so very frightened and frequently suicidal.

If the emotional environment into which Twain places his protagonist is dangerous, then the leading question the novel poses for me is, What does Huck need to live without terror, melancholy and suicidal thoughts? The answer, of course, is Jim. When Huck is among society—whether respectable or deviant, rich or poor—he is alert to and consumed by its deception, its illogic, its scariness. Yet he is depressed by himself and sees nature more often as fearful. But when he and Jim become the only "we," the anxiety is outside, not within. " . . . we would watch the lonesomeness of the river . . . for about an hour . . . just solid lonesomeness" (158)[136]. Unmanageable terror gives way to a pastoral, idyllic, intimate timelessness minus the hierarchy of age, status or adult control. It has never seemed to me that, in contrast to the entrapment and menace of the shore, the river itself provides this solace. The consolation, the healing properties Huck longs for, is made possible by Jim's active, highly vocal affection. It is in Jim's company that the dread of contemplated nature disappears, that even storms are beautiful and sublime, that real talk—comic, pointed, sad—takes place. Talk so free of lies it produces an aura of restfulness and peace unavailable anywhere else in the novel.

Pleasant as this relationship is, suffused as it is by a lightness they both enjoy and a burden of responsibility both assume, it cannot continue. Knowing the relationship is discontinuous, doomed to separation, is (or used to be) typical of the experience of white/black childhood friendships (mine included), and the cry of inevitable rupture is all the more anguished by being mute. Every reader knows that Jim will be dismissed without explanation at some point; that no enduring adult fraternity will emerge. Anticipating this loss may have led Twain to the over-the-top minstrelization of Jim. Predictable and common as the gross stereotyping of blacks was in nineteenth-century literature, here, nevertheless, Jim's portrait seems unaccountably excessive and glaring in its contradictions—like an ill-made clown suit that cannot hide the man within. Twain's black characters were most certainly based on real people. His nonfiction observations of and comments on "actual" blacks are full of references to their guilelessness, intelligence, creativity, wit, caring, etc. None is portrayed as relentlessly idiotic. Yet Jim is unlike, in many ways, the real people he must have been based on. There may be more than one reason for this extravagance. In addition to accommodating a racist readership, writing Jim so complete a buffoon solves the problem of "missing" him that would have been unacceptable at the novel's end, and helps to solve another problem: how effectively to bury the father figure underneath the minstrel paint. The foregone temporariness of the friendship urges the degradation of Jim (to divert Huck's and our inadvertent sorrow at the close), and minstrelizing him necessitates and exposes an enforced silence on the subject of white fatherhood.

The withholdings at critical moments, which I once took to be deliberate evasions, stumbles even, or a writer's impatience with his or her material, I began to see as otherwise: as entrances, crevices, gaps, seductive invitations flashing the possibility of meaning. Unarticulated eddies that encourage diving into the novel's undertow—the real place where writer captures reader. An excellent example of what is available in this undertow is the way Twain comments on the relationship between the antebellum period in which the narrative takes place and the later period in which the novel was composed. The 1880s saw the collapse of civil rights for blacks as well as the publication of *Huckleberry Finn*. This collapse was an effort to bury the combustible issues Twain raised in his novel. The nation, as well as Tom Sawyer, was deferring Jim's freedom in agonizing play. The cyclical attempts to remove the novel from classrooms extend Jim's captivity on into each generation of readers.

Or consider Huck's inability to articulate his true feelings for Jim to anybody other than the reader. When he "humbles himself" in apology to Jim for the painful joke he plays on him, we are not given the words. Even to Tom, the only other friend he has and the only one his own age, he must mask his emotions. Until the hell-or-heaven choice, Huck can speak of the genuine affection and respect for Jim that blossoms throughout the narrative only aslant, or comically to the reader—never directly to any character or to Jim himself. While Jim repeatedly iterates his love, the depth of Huck's feelings for Jim is stressed, underscored and rendered unimpeachable by Twain's calculated use of speechlessness. The accumulated silences build to Huck's ultimate act of love, in which he accepts the endangerment of his soul. These silences do not appear to me of merely historical accuracy—a realistic portrait of how a white child *would* respond to a black slave; they seem to be expert technical solutions to the narrative's complexities and, by the way, highly prophetic descriptions of contemporary negotiations between races.

Consider the void that follows the revelation of Jim as a responsible adult and caring parent in chapter 23. Huck has nothing to say. The chapter does not close; it simply stops. Blanketed by eye dialect, placed auspiciously at chapter's end, held up, framed, as it were, for display by Huck's refusal to comment, it is one of the most moving remembrances in American literature. Then comes the "meanwhile-back-at-the ranch" first line of the next chapter. The hush between these two chapters thunders. And its roar is enhanced by Huck's observation on the preceding page: that although Jim's desperate love for his wife and children "don't seem natural," Huck "reckon[s] it's so" (201) [170]. This comment is fascinating less for its racism than for the danger it deflects from Huck himself. Huck has never seen nor experienced a tender, caring father— yet he steps out of this well of ignorance to judge Jim's role as a father.

What I read into this observation and the hiatus that follows Jim's confirmation of his "naturalness" is that the line of thought Jim's fatherhood might provoke cannot be pursued by the author or his protagonist for fear of derailing the text into another story or destabilizing its center (this is *Huck*'s adventure, not Jim's). It invites serious speculation about fatherhood—its expectations and ramifications—in the novel. First of all, it's hard not to notice that except for Judge Thatcher all of the white men who might function as father figures for Huck are ridiculed for their hypocrisy, corruption, extreme ignorance and/or violence. Thus Huck's "no comment" on Jim's status as a father works either as a comfortable evasion for or as a critique of a white readership, as well as being one of the gags Twain shoves in Huck's mouth to protect him from the line of thought neither he nor Twain can safely pursue.

As an abused and homeless child running from a feral male parent, Huck cannot dwell on Jim's confession and regret about parental negligence without precipitating a crisis from which neither he nor the text could recover. Huck's desire for a father who is adviser and trustworthy companion is universal, but he also needs something more: a father whom, unlike his own, he can control. No white man can serve all three functions. If the runaway Huck discovered on the island had been a white convict with protective paternal instincts, none of this would work, for there could be no guarantee of control and no games-playing nonsense concerning his release at the end. Only a black male slave can deliver all Huck desires. Because Jim can be controlled, it becomes possible for Huck to feel responsible for and to him—but without the onerous burden of lifelong debt that a real father figure would demand. For Huck, Jim is a father-for-free. This delicate, covert and fractious problematic is thus hidden and exposed by litotes and speechlessness, both of which are dramatic ways of begging attention.

Concerning this matter of fatherhood, there are two other instances of silence—one remarkable for its warmth, the other for its glacial coldness. In the first, Jim keeps silent for practically four-fifths of the book about having seen Pap's corpse. There seems no reason for this withholding except his concern for Huck's emotional well-being. Although one could argue that knowing the menace of his father was over might relieve Huck enormously, it could also be argued that dissipating that threat would remove the principal element of the necessity for escape— Huck's escape, that is. In any case, silence on this point persists and we learn its true motive in the penultimate paragraph in the book. And right there is the other speech void—cold and shivery in its unsaying. Jim tells Huck that his money is safe because his father is dead.

"Doan' you 'member de house dat was float'n down de river, en dey wuz a man in dah kivered up, en I went in en unkivered him and didn' let you come in? . . . dat wuz him" (365–66) [295]. Huck says and thinks nothing about it. The following sentence, we are to believe, is Huck's very next thought: "Tom's most well now. . . . "

As a reader I am relieved to know Pap is no longer a menace to his son's well-being, but Huck does not share my relief. Again the father business is erased. What after all could Huck say? That he is as glad as I am? That would not do. Huck's decency prevents him from taking pleasure in anybody's death. That he is sorry? Wishes his father were alive? Hardly. The whole premise of escape while fearing and feigning death would collapse, and the contradiction would be unacceptable. Instead the crevice widens and beckons reflection on what this long-withheld information means. Any comment at this juncture, positive or negative, would lay bare the white father/white son animosity and harm the prevailing though illicit black father/white son bonding that has already taken place.

Such profoundly realized and significant moments, met with startling understatement or shocking absence of any comment at all, constitute the entrances I mentioned earlier—the invitation Twain offers that I could not refuse.

Earlier I posed the question, What does Huck need to live without despair and thoughts of suicide? My answer was, Jim. There is another question the novel poses for me: What would it take for Huck to live happily without Jim? That is the problem that gnarls the dissolution of their relationship. The freeing of Jim is withheld, fructified, top-heavy with pain, because without Jim there is no more book, no more story to tell.

There is a moment when it could have happened, when Jim, put ashore at Cairo, would have gone his way, leaving Huck to experience by himself the other adventures that follow. The reasons they miss Cairo are: there are only saplings to secure the raft; the raft tears away; Huck "couldn't budge" for half a minute; Huck forgets he has tied the canoe, can't "hardly do anything" with his hands and loses time releasing it; they are enveloped in a "solid white fog"; and for a reason even Huck doesn't understand, Jim does not do what is routine in foggy weather—beat a tin pan to signal his location (115–16) [91–92]. During the separation Huck notes the "dismal and lonesome" scene and searches for Jim until he is physically exhausted. Readers are as eager as he is to locate Jim, but when he does, receiving Jim's wild joy, Huck does not express his own. Rather Twain writes in the cruel joke that first sabotages the easily won relief and sympathy we feel for Jim, then leads Huck and us to a heightened restoration of his stature. A series of small accidents prevents Jim's exit from the novel, and Huck is given the gift of an assertive as well as already loving black father. It is to the father, not the nigger, that he "humbles" himself.

So there will be no "adventures" without Jim. The risk is too great. To Huck and to the novel. When the end does come, when Jim is finally, torturously, unnecessarily freed, able now to be a father to his own children, Huck runs. Not back to the town—even if it is safe now—but a further run, for the "territory." And if there are complications out there in the world, Huck, we are to assume, is certainly ready for them. He has had a first-rate education in social and individual responsibility, and it is interesting to note that the lessons of his growing but secret activism begin to be punctuated by speech, not silence, by moves toward truth, rather than quick lies.

When the King and Duke auction Peter Wilks's slaves, Huck is moved by the sorrow of Wilks's nieces—which is caused not by losing the slaves but by the blasting of the family.

> . . . along about noon-time, the girls' joy got the first jolt. A couple of nigger-traders come along, and the king sold them the niggers reasonable, for three-day, drafts as they called it, and away they went, the two sons up the river to Memphis, and their mother down the river to Orleans. I thought them poor girls and them niggers would break their hearts for grief; they cried around each other, and took on so it most made me down sick to see it. The girls said they hadn't ever dreamed of seeing the family separated or sold away from the town. . . .
>
> The thing made a big stir in the town, too, and a good many come out flatfooted and said it was scandalous to separate the mother and the children that way. (234–35) [195].

Later, when Huck sees Mary Jane Wilks with "her face in her hands, crying," he knows what is bothering her even before he asks her to tell him about it. "And it was the niggers—I just expected it." I think it is important to note that he is responding to the separation of parents and children. When Mary Jane sobs, "Oh, dear, dear, to think they ain't *ever* going to see each other any more!" Huck reacts so strongly he blurts out a part of the truth just to console her. "But they *will*—and inside of two weeks—and I *know* it" (240) [198]. Her dismay over the most grotesque consequences of slavery catapults him into one of his most mature and difficult decisions—to abandon silence and chance the truth.

The change from underground activist to vocal one marks Huck's other important relationship—that between himself and Tom Sawyer, to whom Huck has always been subservient. Huck's cooperation in Jim's dehumanization is not total. It is pierced with mumbling disquiet as the degradation becomes more outré. "That warn't the plan"; "there ain't no necessity for it"; "we're going to get into trouble with Aunt Polly"; " . . . if you'll take my advice"; "what's the sense in . . . "; "Confound it, it's foolish, Tom"; "Jim's too old. . . . He won't last"; "How long will it take?"; "it's one of the most jackass ideas I ever struck." But these objections are not enough. Our apprehension as we follow the free fall of the father is only mildly subdued by our satisfaction at the unmanacled exit of the freedman. Tom Sawyer's silence about Jim's legal status is perverse. So perverse that the fact that Huck never speaks of or considers returning to his hometown to carry on with his erstwhile best friend (this time in safety *and* with money of his own) but wants to leave civilization altogether is more than understandable. Huck cannot have an enduring relationship with Jim; he refuses one with Tom.

The source of my unease reading this amazing, troubling book now seems clear: an imperfect coming to terms with three matters Twain addresses—Huck Finn's estrangement, soleness and morbidity as an outcast child; the disproportionate sadness at the center of Jim's and his relationship; and the secrecy in which Huck's engagement with (rather than escape from) a racist society is necessarily conducted. It is also clear that the rewards of my effort to come to terms have been abundant. My alarm, aroused by Twain's precise rendering of childhood's fear of death and abandonment, remains—as it should. It has been extremely worthwhile slogging through Jim's shame and humiliation to recognize the sadness, the tragic implications at the center of his relationship with Huck. My fury at the maze of deceit, the risk of personal harm that a white child is forced to negotiate in a race-inflected society, is dissipated by the exquisite uses to which Twain puts that maze, that risk.

Yet the larger question, the danger that sifts from the novel's last page, is whether Huck, minus Jim, will be able to stay those three monsters as he enters the "territory." Will that undefined space, so falsely imagined as "open," be free of social chaos, personal morbidity, and further moral complications embedded in adulthood and citizenship? Will it be free not only of nightmare fathers but of dream fathers too? Twain did not write Huck there. He imagined instead a reunion—Huck, Jim and Tom, soaring in a balloon over Egypt.

For a hundred years, the argument that this novel *is* has been identified, reidentified, examined, waged and advanced. What it cannot be is dismissed. It is classic literature, which is to say it heaves, manifests and lasts.

Mark Twain: A Chronology

1835	Samuel Langhorne Clemens born November 30 in Florida, Missouri, to Jane Lampton Clemens and John Marshall Clemens.
1835–46	Though financially strapped, John Clemens, a justice of the peace, is a pillar of the community in Florida and nearby Hannibal, to which the family moves in 1839.
1847–52	John Clemens dies. Sam is apprenticed to a Hannibal printer, Joseph P. Ament. Writes early sketch, "A Gallant Fireman," for his brother Orion's newspaper, *The Western Union*.
1853–57	Works as printer and reporter in St. Louis; New York; Philadelphia; Keokuk, Iowa; and Cincinnati. Publishes three "Thomas Jefferson Snodgrass" letters in *Keokuk Post*.
1857–61	Apprenticed to Horace Bixby, senior pilot of the riverboat *Paul Jones*. Earns his pilot's license in April 1859. Forced to give up his new career when Union gunboats close the river to commercial traffic.
1861–64	Tries soldiering for two weeks with a group of Confederate volunteers, the Marion Rangers. Travels by stagecoach with Orion Clemens to the Nevada Territory, where he attempts to stake a timber claim and to prospect for silver. Gives up prospecting and returns to his old trade as a reporter on the *Territorial Enterprise* in Virginia City, Nevada. In February 1863, begins signing his articles "Mark Twain."
1864–66	Moves to San Francisco as a reporter for the *Morning Call*. On November 18, the New York *Saturday Press* publishes "Jim Smiley and His Jumping Frog," a tall tale that is pirated by newspapers across the country, helping to make Mark Twain famous. Spends four months in Hawaii, returning to San Francisco to lecture on the "Sandwich Islands." Sails to New York as a correspondent for the *San Francisco Alta Californian*.
1867–68	Visits Europe and the Holy Land on the ship *Quaker City*; the trip is the inspiration for *The Innocents Abroad* (1869). Lectures on his adventures.
1869–71	Lives in Buffalo and becomes a dues-paying member of the Young Men's Association (Y.M.A.), whose library curator will later receive the manuscript of *Huckleberry Finn*. In February 1870, marries Olivia Langdon, the

daughter of his business partner; their only son, Langdon Clemens, born prematurely in November.

1871–77   Moves with family to Hartford, Connecticut. Susan Olivia (Susy) Clemens born in March 1872; Langdon dies later that year. Clara Clemens born in 1874, and family moves into new house in Nook Farm area of Hartford. July–August 1876, writes chapters 1–11, the first half of 12, and 15–17 (to where Huck asks Buck what a feud is) of *Huck Finn*. Publishes *Roughing It* (1872), *The Gilded Age* (with Charles Dudley Warner, 1873), *Sketches New and Old* (1875), and *The Adventures of Tom Sawyer* (1876).

1878–79   Travels with family in Europe.

1879–84   Writes chapters 17–21 (feud to shooting of Boggs) of *Huck Finn* in October–June. Begins investing in Paige typesetting machine. Daughter Jean Clemens born in July 1880. Writes the second half of chapter 12 (the *Walter Scott* episode) and chapters 21 (from where Colonel Sherburn faces down the mob) to 43 of *Huck Finn* in June–August 1883. Publishes *A Tramp Abroad* (1880), *The Prince and The Pauper* (1882), and *Life on The Mississippi* (1883).

1885   *Adventures of Huckleberry Finn* published in February, the British edition having appeared two months before. Asked for a sample of his writing for the Young Men's Association of Buffalo, the author sends 487 pages of his manuscript to James Fraser Gluck. Gluck has leaves bound.

1886   Mark Twain sends (probably in this year) another 209 leaves of the manuscript of *Huck Finn* to Mr. Gluck.

1887   The author finds the first half of the manuscript he thought he had lost and sends an additional 665 leaves to Gluck in July.

1887–1900   Mark Twain publishes *A Connecticut Yankee in King Arthur's Court* (1889), *The American Claimant* (1892), *Pudd'nhead Wilson* (1894), *Tom Sawyer Abroad* (1894), *Personal Recollections of Joan of Arc* (1896), and *Following the Equator* (1897). The family moves to Europe for most of the 1890s. Investments in the Paige typesetter leave Mark Twain bankrupt in the panic of 1893, and in 1895, at age 60, he embarks on a lecture tour around the world to rebuild his fortune. Susy Clemens dies of meningitis in August 1896. The following year, James Fraser Gluck dies, and the "first half" of the manuscript of *Huck Finn* is packed away and "lost" again.

1900–03   Returns to America and national acclaim; settles in New York City.

1903–08   Returns to Italy for Olivia Clemens's health. Mrs. Clemens dies in June 1904. Mark Twain returns to America. *What Is Man?* appears anonymously in 1906.

1908–09	Mark Twain moves to Stormfield, Redding, Connecticut. Clara marries the pianist and conductor Ossip Gabrilow-itsch. Jean dies.
1910	Mark Twain dies on April 21 and is buried in Elmira, New York.
1958	Walter Blair examines available half of *Huck Finn* man-uscript and publishes "When Was *Huck Finn* Written?" in the journal *American Literature*.
1983	Leaves of second half of *Huck Finn* manuscript bound by Gluck are disbound so that the Buffalo and Erie County Public Library can produce a facsimile, edited by distinguished Mark Twain scholar Louis J. Budd.
1991	Early in the year (or late in 1990) a granddaughter of James Fraser Gluck discovers the missing half of the *Huck Finn* manuscript in an attic in Hollywood.
1992	After 105 years of separation, the two halves of the man-uscript are formally reunited in a ceremony in the Rare Book Room of the Buffalo and Erie County Public Library.

Selected Bibliography

MARK TWAIN: GENERAL

Baetzhold, Howard G. *Mark Twain and John Bull: The British Connection*. Bloomington: Indiana UP, 1970.

Bridgman, Richard. *Travelling in Mark Twain*. Berkeley: U of California P, 1987.

Brooks, Van Wyck. *The Ordeal of Mark Twain*. Rev. Ed. New York: E. P. Dutton, 1933.

Budd, Louis J. *Mark Twain: Social Philosopher*. Bloomington: Indiana UP, 1962.

———. *Our Mark Twain: The Making of His Public Personality*. Philadelphia: U of Pennsylvania P, 1983.

Cardwell, Guy. *The Man Who Was Mark Twain: Images and Ideologies*. New Haven: Yale UP, 1991.

Cox, James M. *Mark Twain: The Fate of Humor*. Princeton: Princeton UP, 1966.

DeVoto, Bernard. *Mark Twain at Work*. Cambridge: Harvard UP, 1942.

Gibson, William M. *The Art of Mark Twain*. New York: Oxford UP, 1976.

Kaplan, Justin. *Mr. Clemens and Mark Twain*. New York: Simon and Schuster, 1966.

Lynn, Kenneth S. *Mark Twain and South Western Humor*. Westport, Conn.: Greenwood Press, 1972.

Paine, Albert Bigelow. *Mark Twain, A Biography*. New York: Harper, 1912.

Robinson, Forrest G. *In Bad Faith: The Dynamics of Deception in Mark Twain's America*. Cambridge: Harvard UP, 1986.

———, ed. *The Cambridge Companion to Mark Twain*. Cambridge: Cambridge UP, 1995.

Sewell, David R. *Mark Twain's Languages: Discourse, Dialogue, and Linguistic Variety*. Berkeley: U of California P, 1987.

Smith, Henry Nash. *Mark Twain: The Development of a Writer*. Cambridge: Belknap Press, 1962.

Wecter, Dixon. *Sam Clemens of Hannibal*. Boston: Houghton Mifflin, 1952.

ADVENTURES OF HUCKLEBERRY FINN

•Bullet indicates those works represented in this Norton Critical Edition.

Beaver, Harold. *Huckleberry Finn*. London: Allen and Unwin, 1987.

Blair, Walter. *Mark Twain and "Huck Finn."* Berkeley: U of California P, 1960.

———. "When Was *Huckleberry Finn* Written?" *American Literature*, XXX (March 1958): 1–25.

•Briden, Earl F. "Kemble's 'Specialty' and the Pictorial Countertext of *Huckleberry Finn*." *Mark Twain Journal* 26.2 (Fall 1988): 2–14.

Budd, Louis J. *New Essays on "Adventures of Huckleberry Finn."* Cambridge: Cambridge UP, 1985.

•Carkeet, David. "The Dialects in *Huckleberry Finn*." *American Literature* 51 (November 1979): 315–32.

Champion, Laurie, ed. *The Critical Response to Mark Twain's "Huckleberry Finn."* Westport, Conn.: Greenwood Press, 1991.

Doyno, Victor A. *Writing "Huck Finn": Mark Twain's Creative Process*. Philadelphia: U of Pennsylvania P, 1991.

———. "The Composition of *Adventures of Huckleberry Finn*." From Afterward to *Adventures of Huckleberry Finn*. New York: Oxford UP, 1996.

•Eliot, T. S. Introduction to *Adventures of Huckleberry Finn*. London: Cresset Press, 1950.

Fiedler, Leslie. "'As Free as Any Cretur . . . '" *The New Republic* 133.7 (August 1955): 17–18; 133.8 (August 1955): 16–18.

•Fishkin, Shelley Fisher. *Was Huck Black? Mark Twain and African-American Voices*. New York: Oxford UP, 1993.

Inge, M. Thomas, ed. *"Huck Finn" Among the Critics: A Centennial Selection*. Frederick, Md.: University Publications of America, 1985.

•Kincaid, James R. "Voices on the Mississippi." *New York Times*, 23 May 1993, Section 7, p. 12.

Leonard, James S. et al., eds. *Satire or Evasion? Black Perspectives on "Huckleberry Finn."* Durham: Duke UP, 1992.

Lynn, Kenneth S. "Huck and Jim." *Yale Review*, 47 (Spring 1958): 421–31.

•Morrison, Toni. Introduction to *Adventures of Huckleberry Finn*. New York: Oxford UP, 1996.

Sattelmeyer, Robert, and J. Donald Crowley. *One Hundred Years of "Huckleberry Finn": The Boy, His Book, and American Culture*. Columbia: U of Missouri P, 1985.

•Smiley, Jane. "Say It Ain't So, Huck: Second Thoughts on Mark Twain's 'Masterpiece.'" *Harper's Magazine*, January 1996, 61–67.

•Smith, David L. "Huck, Jim, and American Racial Discourse." Collected in James S. Leonard et al., eds., *Satire or Evasion? Black Perspectives on "Huckleberry Finn."* Durham: Duke UP, 1992.

Tractenburg, Alan. "The Form of Freedom in *Adventures of Huckleberry Finn.*" *Southern Review* (Autumn 1970): 954–71.

Trilling, Lionel. "The Greatness of *Huckleberry Finn.*" Collected in *The Liberal Imagination*, 1950. Reprinted in Inge, 81–92.

•Wallace, John H. "The Case Against *Huck Finn.*" Collected in James S. Leonard et al., eds., *Satire or Evasion? Black Perspectives on "Huckleberry Finn."* Durham: Duke UP, 1992.